McGRAW-HILL PUBLICATIONS IN PSYCHOLOGY

J. F. DASHIELL, Ph.D., Consulting Editor

RELIGION

Its Functions in
Human Life

McGraw-Hill Publications in Psychology

J. F. DASHIELL

CONSULTING EDITOR

RELIGION

Its Functions in Human Life

A Study of Religion from the Point of
View of Psychology

BY

KNIGHT DUNLAP

*Professor of Psychology, University of California
at Los Angeles*

First Edition

New York   *London*

McGRAW-HILL BOOK COMPANY, Inc.

1946

RELIGION: ITS FUNCTIONS IN HUMAN LIFE

COPYRIGHT, 1946, BY THE

McGRAW-HILL BOOK COMPANY, INC.

PRINTED IN THE UNITED STATES OF AMERICA

THE MAPLE PRESS COMPANY, YORK, PA.

PREFACE

It is the purpose of this book to present religion as a normal product of man's conscious processes: his desires, his fears, and especially his planning for future contingencies. This book, accordingly, might properly have been called *The Psychology of Religion*, but that would lead persons familiar with publications so entitled to expect the volume to be preoccupied with topics such as repentance, fear of punishment, conversion, and similar pathological features of religion, which we propose to keep in proper subordination to the normal aspect. It is no more possible to construct a psychology of normal religion on a foundation gathered from religious pathology than it is to construct a psychology of normal persons from data collected from abnormal persons. Our interest in religious pathology is, and should be, directed only toward elimination of maladjustments, a prophylactic interest.

In order to understand the role a religion may or may not play in the civilization of the future, it is necessary to understand the roles that the religions of the past, from which religions of the present day have developed, have played in the cultures of which they were integral parts. Only through the study of these roles is it possible to discover what religion really is. This historical or genetic method is only one part of the full comparative method that is essential for a complete study of religion. The other part of the comparative method is the comparison of religions that exist contemporaneously and which have little, if any, genetic relation to one another.

Comparison of the religions of civilized groups with the religions of 'unlettered peoples'—the savages whom some writers call 'primitive,' but who are really no more primitive than we are—is difficult because the explorers, missionaries, and ethnologists who have reported the religious concepts of the savages have usually transformed the native concepts into concepts of modern civilization. Frazer, who understood this difficulty better than have most writers, was hampered in the compilation and organization of the twelve volumes of his *Golden Bough* by the inadequacies of the available materials. A few writers give the native terms for the native concepts, which is a help in the interpretation of the concepts, but most of them substitute terms from civilized languages, which at best is equivalent to the substitution of a civilized concept for one or several native concepts and at worst is an utter confusion.

Somewhat the same difficulty is encountered when one attempts to compare civilized religions with those of semicivilized peoples. Translators are notoriously careless in rendering terms from the Arabic, Turki, and Hindu tongues into modern languages. A further difficulty is encountered when one uses secondhand sources in attempting to evaluate the development of one of these religions, since the scholars tend to accept naïvely the traditions of the semicivilized peoples—acceptance which, as we indicate to some extent in this volume, is often improper.

Fortunately, the religions of civilized peoples can be understood by tracing them back to their foundations in religions of ancient cultures from which our civilization developed. This genetic method at least gives a primary understanding of the nature and functions of religion, which suffices for the purpose of this volume; the religions of civilized peoples having borrowed little from either the religions of present-day savages or those of semicivilized peoples, the full comparative method is not essential for our purposes.

For the understanding of the changes that modern religions, such as Islam and Christianity, have suffered when populations have been proselyted to them from religions to which they were previously attached, the full comparative method is essential. As we shall point out in the text, such changes are due to the assimilation of features of the old religion by the new religion. The assimilated features are principally rituals, but the assimilated rituals sometimes carry with them their credential interpretations. Hence, the more we know about the original religions from which the features were assimilated, the better we understand the results. Because of the difficulties we have described, we shall proceed with a minimum of comparison of civilized religion with the religions of savages and semicivilized peoples.

That the psychological problems of religion are primarily problems for group psychology and that the problems of personal religion are secondary in importance should be evident from the principle that is now generally accepted by scholars in the field of the history of religion. This principle, which is explained and illustrated in the text, is that faith develops from ritual, rather than ritual from faith.

The development of faith from ritual, as an interpretation of ritual and with further progressive reinterpretations, is obviously consonant with the fact that ritual is a group product. Hence, although the principles of personal psychology cannot be ignored, the primary requisite for the study of the psychology of religion is the application of the methods of group psychology.

During the more than forty years in which I have been collecting materials for this book, I have drawn heavily on the writings of L. F. Alfred Maury, W. Robertson Smith, J. A. McCullogh, and Sir James G. Frazer. In the more recent period I have drawn much from the works of Arthur B. Cook and Salomon Reinach. These scholars have so well collected and analyzed the materials available on ancient religions that work by an amateur scholar on the sources would not be expedient, except the work of checking on the concepts involved in the disquisitions of the scholars. I have found it profitable, however, to read and reread the works of Homer, Herodotos, Strabo, Pausanias, Aristotle, Diogenes Laertios, Pindar, and the Greek dramatists, using translations, but comparing with the originals to determine meanings the translators so frequently confuse. For religions of unlettered peoples, I have depended on reports of explorers, ethnologists, and missionaries, not depending on compendiums, not even on that of Frazer.

While using the materials collected and analyzed by outstanding scholars, I have not always adopted their conclusions, or their postulates. The comparative study of religion is progressive, and the work of a scholar advances the study to a point at which the scholar's conclusions must be revised, if further progress is to be made. We can honor the scholars of the past more by building critically on their work than we can by naïvely adopting their postulates and their interpretations. Some of the conclusions that Cook drew from the data he collected were based on assumptions that were becoming obsolete while he was working and some of Reinach's postulates even have been discarded. From the point of view of classical scholarship, accordingly, many of the statements in this volume are heretical; but heresy is as essential for progress in the study of religion as it is for progress in religion itself. Application of psychological principles to the materials surveyed by scholars does not, and should not, lead to the conventional conclusions of the past.

Heresies of other sorts will be found in the volume. In the treatment of Judaism and Christianity I have followed in the footsteps of scholars whose findings are irrefutable, especially in the steps of Salomon Reinach. Some of my statements, therefore, may be shocking to a Christian of an orthodox Protestant sect.

Certain typographical features of my composition may need to be explained. In quotations from the Bible, I have placed in parentheses the words which the translators of the King James Version inserted in italics (a method of insertion that has confused many readers). In transliterating Greek names into English, I have usually followed the system of modern classical scholars. In this system *kappa* is rendered as *k*; *iota* as *i*; *omicron* and *omega* as *o*; and *upsilon* as *u*. Some names, however, which have become familiar to English readers in their Latinized forms, I have spelled in the familiar way. In these spellings, *kappa* is changed to *c*; *iota* often is changed to *o*; *omega* is usually changed to *u*; *upsilon* is regularly changed to *y*; and extra *e*'s are sometimes inserted.

Thus, for example, the name of the serpent god of healing is given as *Asklepios*, not as *Aesculapius*, but the name of the early Greek dramatist is given in the popular form as *Aeschylus* not as *Aischulos*. Since classical scholars are not always consistent but sometimes mix the two systems of transliteration in one word, as in writing *Kybele*, the popular spelling is sometimes given in a parenthesis after the preferred spelling.

KNIGHT DUNLAP.

LOS ANGELES, CALIF.,
 February, 1946.

CONTENTS

CHAPTER I

RELIGIONS AND RELIGION

1. The Nature of Religion.—There are in the world today a very large number of what are technically called *cults*,—a term usually applied to a system which includes both faith and ritual—but which are popularly called *religions*. We shall use 'cult' as an abbreviated term for 'religious cult.' During the last four thousand years still other religions have had their periods of flourishing, and have then passed into desuetude, or, at least, have ceased to be recognized as definite cults, although some of them have left their effects in later religions.

It would appear that the human race has been always, and almost universally, religious: that every group in every period has held to some religion or other. We speak sometimes of the 'four great religions,' meaning Christianity, Judaism, Brahmanism, and Mohammedanism. There are, however, a great many other religions to which large groups of Asiatics adhere; and there are religions in great variety in Africa, Australia, and the Americas, among the unlettered peoples of these regions, whom we call 'natives,' 'savages,' 'nature folks,' 'primitives,' and by other inadequate names, properly referring to peoples without written records.

When we examine into these various cults we find striking differences between them; and we are led to wonder why these cults, varying so widely in their characteristics, should be classed together under the generic name of 'religions.' Logically, there should be some common feature or characteristic running through all of them which could be identified as the essential feature of 'religion.' Otherwise, the classification is fallacious. It would seem, therefore, that before we attempt to study religions, we should determine what religion is. If we could abstract a clear and definite concept of religion, capable of being defined, we could apply the definition to the various so-called 'religions,' to determine for each of them the features which are strictly religious and the features which are accidental or extraneous. We might be able to decide whether the social service work of certain American churches is essentially religious or is merely 'secular' activity of religious people, and not actually a religious function. Applying the definition to certain cults, such as Confucianism, Marxism, and psychoanalysis, the status of which has been questioned, we might decide whether these 'isms' are really religions or not.

Superficially, to attempt to discuss religion without knowing what religion *is* would seem an essay in futility. We would seem to be running the danger of putting ourselves in the position of three men discussing the *Peglalium*. One contends that it is the most beautiful object in the world. Another contends that it is extremely pernicious, responsible for much social disorder. The third declares it is completely mythical: a fictitious entity. These three seem to hold conflicting points of view, until it is discovered that the first man understands the Peglalium to be a kind of lily; the second takes it to be a certain political system; and the third understands it to be a winged horse. Situations of this kind actually arise with annoying frequency. The history of ancient philosophy, for example, is chaotic because we may agree as to *what* Aristotle, Plato, and other *sophoi* said about certain things such as *psyche* and *nous;* but there is uncertainty as to what these worthies were talking *about,* and the assumption that they were talking about the same things is unsafe. In some acrimonious disputes over religion, it seems clear that proponents and opponents have been talking about different things.

The importance of having a concept and definition of religion has long been recognized, and for at least twenty-five hundred years intelligent men in European cultures have been attempting to supply the lack. Innumerable definitions have been proposed, but none of the definitions has gained any wide acceptance. The very number of definitions is a proof of the difficulty of the task; and some scholars have explicitly concluded that it is hopeless, though they go on to offer their own definitions. Every definition proposed, would, if it were accepted, lead to a drastic purging of the list of cults commonly included as religions, unless the definition is so vague as to be meaningless; for none of the significant definitions includes more than a fraction of the 'religions' of the world. Each definition has been drawn to fit a particular religion, or particular type of religion, determined by the definer's personal attitude toward religion.

If the definer is proreligious, his definition fits the particular religion to which he adheres, together with some other similar religions, but excludes the great mass of cults that are commonly called religions. At the best, his definition is a statement of what he thinks religion *ought* to be, not what it *is*. This point often is conceded by the definer by designating religion, as defined, as *true religion*, the other so-called religions, which are excluded, being branded, explicitly or implicitly, as *false religions*.

If the definer is antireligious, he picks out a religion to which he is especially opposed, or selects from several religions the features that appear to him the most objectionable, defining religion practically as that form of religion which is most repugnant to him. He may, possibly, succeed better in finding features common to many religions than may the proreligious definer, for he is disposed to consider all religions as bad, whereas the proreligious definer is biased in favor of religion of a certain type, as against all other religions.

The common tendency to define religion in terms of a single type of religion, implicitly rejecting all other cults as nonreligious, may be observed in any group of otherwise intelligent people. If the members of a college class made up of juniors and seniors are asked to write their definitions of religion as the term is understood by them, from 80 to 90 per cent will fall in one or the other of the classes of those: (*a*) who adopt as the basis of their definitions their own religious preferences; and (*b*) who base their definitions on particular doctrines or practices to which they object. If, in advance, it is carefully explained that definitions of religion should not apply to particular religions only, but should cover all systems, good or bad, which in the definer's opinion may properly be classed as religions, the results will not be essentially different.

Among college students, the confusion of *religion* with a *particular religion*, or religions of a limited type, may well be ascribed to lack of information, as the proportion of students who have any wide acquaintance with religions of various types is probably below 10 per cent. Writers on religion who have spent much time in studying religions broadly might be expected to be free from the prejudices: (*a*) that my religion is the type of real religion, and all others are spurious; and (*b*) that religion is merely that which I most object to in the particular religions with which I am acquainted. If we do expect this freedom from bias on the parts of writers on religion we are doomed to disappointment, for the majority do exactly what the majority of collegians do.

There are, of course, exceptions. There are real scholars, who have studied religions comparatively and historically and who have a minimum of bias. It is significant that these scholars are less disposed to construct definitions than are the mere literary men and theologians and that such definitions as they formulate or imply are broader and more inclusive than those of the less scholarly writers. Where scholars are apt to fail is in the hasty adoption of some principle of commonality in religions which cannot be demonstrated to be truly universal even in the 'great' religions. Reinach, for example, defines religion as 'a sum of scruples which impede the free exercise of our faculties,' thus limiting religion to its inhibitory functions.

If it were possible to arrive at an adequate definition of religion that should be universally accepted, then the definition could be used as a criterion for deciding which of the cults existing today, or known in history, that have been classed as religions are properly so classed, and which are not, and for deciding which features of admitted religions are essential. Such a process of elimination, however, can be conducted with safety only when and after we have arrived at a definition through scientific study of the problem. Arbitrary decisions as to what shall be called religion and what shall be denied the name merely block progress toward scientific conclusions. Definitions of religion so far proposed have been, for the most part, merely confessions of faith—useful for personal satisfaction, but not useful for other purposes.

The multiplicity of arbitrary definitions of religion is due, in large part, to the unfortunate, but common, human tendency to insist on a simple explanation for complex phenomena. If, in dealing with a complex subject we can quickly reduce it to a single basic principle, and say, 'This is the root of the whole matter; this is the essence of the thing,' we have accomplished a great deal and perhaps have 'explained' the phenomena. Such an accomplishment is never possible in a hurry; and in most cases, however elaborate the process of deduction, the conclusion is fallacious. It appears that complex phenomena usually have complex roots; and certainly in the field of religions we are dealing with forests, not with a single tree. Simplification of a problem is desirable, where possible; but simplification by arbitrary definition is always misleading.

The complexity of our problem must not be ignored. In speaking even of the great religions we must bear in mind that within each of these religions there are numerous *sects*, which differ from one another in various ways. The Christian religion, for example, includes many sects and subsects, and points that are considered fundamental by some sects are denied by other sects. We speak of Hindu religion; but there are many Hindu sects, and these differ from one another even more sharply than Christian sects differ from one another. Islam (Mohammedanism) also is divided into several sects, from the strictly orthodox followers of the Koran to the Dervishes and revolutionary movements, which differ in important respects. Certain Hindu, Mohammedan, and Christian sects, in fact, resemble one another more closely than they resemble other sects of the 'same' religion.

As a result of the uncertainty as to what is the essential feature of religion, the terms 'religion' and 'sect' are used interchangeably. In conventional classifications of cults we speak of the Roman Catholic, Greek Catholic, and Presbyterian sects of Christianity; and also of the Roman Catholic religion, the Greek Catholic religion, and the Presbyterian religion. The divisions of orthodox Hinduism are called orthodox Hindu sects and also orthodox Hindu religions. If writers seldom call the sects of Islam 'religions,' it is because the writers do not appreciate the actual differences between these sects.

The grouping of minor religions, or sects, into greater religions, has, as a matter of fact, not been determined by similarities of the sects and their differences from other sects, but has been based on historical development. Cults that have developed from a common root, or that are branches from a common stalk, are counted as different sects of a common religion, however great may be the differences between these and other sects. Classification of religions in families is complicated by the fact that the evolution of cults is not a simple arboreal process in which several shoots grow from the same root or several branches from the same stem. Shoots or branches from different roots or stems combine, or, we may say metaphorically, 'anastomose.' A sect, or a religion, usually develops from several earlier religions, combining features taken from all of them. This anastomotic process is exemplified in the growth of Christianity, of Islam, and of Judaism.

The problem of religious origins, of course, is connected with the problem of the nature of religion, and the final solution of each of these problems involves the solution of the other. Hasty inferences from one problem to the other have been sources of illusion and disappointment. This confusion occurs even when the assumptions carried from the one problem to the other are sound; but when the assumptions are fallacious, the confusion is greater. Some theorists have discovered certain factors that appear to have been early in religion and have concluded that these factors remain throughout. Religion, for example, in one stage of its development, involves magic. To conclude further that magic remains forever a feature of religion is comparable to concluding that because a human being, in the embryo stage, is fish-like, he retains gills throughout life.

Lacking a definition of religion, we can proceed to its study only by the logical process of *pointing* to samples, the method of *enumeration*, as it is sometimes called. This procedure has its difficulties, but nevertheless is practicable. *Religion*, we may assume, is something which characterizes all cults that may properly be called *religions*. We may then say that these religions are *such as:* Christianity, in most of its forms; Buddhism, in its modern forms at least; Mohammedanism (Islam); Brahmanical Hinduism; and the cult of the Parsees. Historically, we can add: Zoroastrianism (the religion of the ancient Persians); the leading cults of the ancient Greeks, Romans, and Egyptians; and the cults of the Celts and other early peoples of western Europe. Many cults prevalent among the aborigines of Asia, Africa, and the Americas may safely be included. Regarding various other cults, such as Shinto, Taoism, Confucianism, Babism, and the 'Oxford Movement' (Buchmanism), we can say that they *seem* to be religions, are popularly regarded as religions, and may provisionally be considered as such.

We might then proceed to study these religions critically, tracing their developments, comparing corresponding stages in different religions, and attempting to discover their common features, expanding and/or contracting the list as results might necessitate. Our plans, however, are more moderate and more suitable for the limited time available to us. We shall concern ourselves mainly with the development of religions in the Mediterranean area and the Levant—the religious out of which Christianity developed—with restricted comparisons with the religious developments of other areas. Our present concern is with Western religion, concerning which we shall ask: Out of what did it grow? and How did it grow? If any principles are discoverable that may be applied in other areas in a truly comparative way, such comparative study is a further problem.

2. **Faith.**—Most definitions of religion agree in one respect, although some classifiers of definitions seem to have overlooked this agreement, or, perhaps, have considered it so obvious that it need not be mentioned. Whatever the specific factor a definition of religion assumes, the definer usually assumed faith as an essential feature in religion, although the assumption is sometimes implicit rather than explicit. Such definitions differ from one another in respect to some particularly aspect of faith or belief, which is selected as peculiarly religious. It is admitted that not all faith is religious faith. I believe, for example, that it will not rain within the next twenty-four hours. I believe that one of the candidates for the governorship is a better man for the job than is his rival. I believe that the ratio of the circumference of a circle to its diameter has the value commonly designated as 'pi.' We do not ordinarily call such beliefs religious. The question faced by definers of religion is: What is the difference between religious belief and belief that is nonreligious? On this point the definitions vary widely, for, of course, the meaning of 'religious' is precisely what the definers are attempting to determine.

In popular discourse, *belief* is contrasted with *knowledge;* but the contrast is relative and changeable. If a belief is validated, then it becomes knowledge. That is to say, if a belief fits into the pattern of commonly accepted facts and principles, it is so far true. If it fits into the pattern of scientifically accredited facts and theories, it is scientific knowledge. On the basis of social psychology there is a difference, therefore, between belief and knowledge; but on the basis of personal psychology merely, there is no difference. There is nothing about believing, as a process or response in the mind, that differentiates it from the response of knowing.

Looking backward, from the point of view achieved by later experience and information, that which earlier was considered unfounded belief (which is called 'superstition') sometimes turns out to be true, or valid, and therefore becomes knowledge. Thus, the belief of the Arabs that malarial fevers were communicated by the bites of mosquitoes, reported by Captain Burton in his *First Footsteps in East Africa,* which was regarded a century ago as a curious superstition, is now an item of scientific knowledge. Conversely, what has been socially, and even scientifically, accepted as knowledge sometimes turns out later to be superstition. Astronomers once knew that the sun and planets moved around the earth in a complicated way. This knowledge is now an unfounded belief, that is, a superstition of the past.

Superstitions are sometimes revived, and accepted by some groups as knowledge, without being scientifically validated. Thus, the ancient notion of a daimon or genius possessing a human being and modifying his conscious life and behavior without his being aware of the control, revived by philosophers in the eighteenth and nineteenth centuries as the concept of the 'unconscious mind,' and popularized by Freud in this century, has been considered by certain groups to be an important bit of knowledge. In revamping a discarded superstition as alleged knowledge, a change of terminology is usually necessary to turn the old belief into a new discovery.

Belief and knowledge, in short, can be distinguished in theory, on the basis of the truth or falsity of the belief. A true belief is knowledge; a false item of knowledge is superstition. This distinction is of no consequence in the psychology of religion, for we may have no interest in the truth or the falsity of any religious tenet. From the theological point of view, a religion based on, or involving, false doctrines is a false religion, but it is nevertheless a religion. We must be interested in all religious beliefs insofar as they influence behavior, personal and social. We must be interested in their origins and development and we must compare them with other beliefs. Whether the beliefs are true or false, their psychological effects and psychological importance are the same.

It is obvious that religious beliefs cannot be distinguished from nonreligious beliefs simply on the basis of truth or falsity, for, as we shall show later, one of the characteristics of religious beliefs is that they cannot be proved or disproved by scientific procedures. While this does not necessarily hold for beliefs in ancient religion, we must accept this for religions of the present and future.

That there is no religious test for the truth of a religious belief is obvious from the contradiction of the beliefs of one religion by the beliefs of other religions. Monotheism, for example, is in direct opposition to polytheism. These contradictions are found also between beliefs of cults that are counted as sects of the 'same' religion. Conflicts between orthodox and heterodox beliefs are found in all religions. If the beliefs of one religion are true, then various beliefs in other religions are false. There are few tenets of any religion that are not contradicted by the tenets of other religions.

Definers of religions who make faith the basic feature of religion are faced with the problem of distinguishing between religious faith and nonreligious faith. That is the real point of a definition of religion. Two alternatives are offered. First, the distinction may be based on the affective attitude the person takes toward his beliefs. Those who define religion in terms of 'emotion' seem to be groping for this distinction between religious faith and nonreligious faith. We shall return to this topic shortly. Most of the definers, however, base their distinction on the *contents* of faith. From this point of view, a religious belief is a belief about one thing, or one sort of thing, while a nonreligious belief is a belief about something else. Belief in a god, or a devil, would be typical of a religious belief, while belief in Darwinian evolution would be considered as nonreligious.

If we use the term 'concept' to designate a content of belief, then religious faith, according to this view, is acceptance of a religious concept, while secular, or nonreligious faith, is acceptance of a nonreligious concept. The majority of the definitions of religion seem to have been constructed on this foundation, which leaves the definition of religion up in the air, for the distinction between a religious concept and a nonreligious concept needs to be determined, and the determination is the crux of the definition.

For the popular mind, the discrimination of religious concepts from the nonreligious seems simple, until the question is raised whether belief in magic, in the occult processes of mind reading, in ghosts, or in the unconscious mind is religious faith or nonreligious. Belief in God would be accepted as religious; but is disbelief in God religious? That is an embarrassing question. Naïve discrimination, on the basis of popular concepts, does not solve the problem; accordingly students of religion who have defined religion in terms of belief in a Divinity, or in divinities, have hedged in qualification of their definitions; but the hedging usually fails to bring out the distinction and leaves the differentia of religious faith uncertain.

The universal failure of definitions constructed on this plan, at least the limited acceptance by students of religion of the definitions constructed by other students, indicates that if there are concepts that are specifically religious, as distinguished from concepts that are nonreligious, these are difficult to discover and so far have not been conclusively demonstrated as realities. Before considering other possible differentia, we must investigate another feature of religions as we know them, a feature that appears to be as universal in religion as is faith.

3. **Works, or Ritual.**—In English translations of older religious writings, the term 'works' means ritual; that is, religious behavior, of a systematic sort. That there is ritual which is nonreligious (secular) is admitted; but we are here concerned with the works of religion.

It is generally admitted that belief influences behavior. If, when you are about to leave the house, you believe it will rain shortly, you may, on that account, take an umbrella or a raincoat; you may, on the other hand, decide to postpone your trip. The action in the one case, and the inhibition in the other, is determined to a large degree by your belief. That behavior influences belief is not so obvious to the layman but is admitted by the psychologist.

The interaction of belief commonly called 'religious' with behavior is as evident as is the interaction of behavior and nonreligious belief. In either case, the effective belief is that behavior of certain sorts will secure certain results. One may confess his sins because he believes that by confessing he may secure remission of the sins. One may burn a candle at the shrine of Notre Dame de la Garde because he believes that his sea trip will be safer therefor. The motivation for these types of behavior may not be religious; but the beliefs that effectuate them may be accepted as religious, and so the behavior may be classed as religious behavior. The behavior, moreover, follows a standardized or routine pattern, which the individual has learned, and is similar to the behavior of other persons in similar circumstances. The behavior, accordingly, is *religious ritual*. The significant features of ritual, or works, are: (*a*) The behavior is associated with religious faith. (*b*) The behavior is habitual, a matter of routinized action. (*c*) It is social: one does what others do. The motivation is not essential, and, in fact, much of the 'works' of religion is behavior that continues as mere habit, from which the original motives have long disappeared.

A distinction is sometimes made between works and ritual; this distinction has arisen only in Christianity and is emphasized by the addition of the adjective 'good' to works. In order to clarify this point we must consider the various forms of behavior, including what is commonly called *conduct*, in which a moral (or an immoral) factor is involved. Morality is essentially a matter of social relations and is measured by *purposes*. Conduct (moral or immoral behavior) is behavior that affects the welfare, or the interests, of other persons. If the purposes are benevolent, the behavior is *good conduct*. If the purposes are malevolent, it is *bad conduct*. If, with good purpose, the results for others are injurious, we blame the intelligence or the education for the person, not his morals.

The expression *good works* accordingly means, in Christian writings, works of religion that are intended to help or benefit other persons. Since Christianity has strongly inculcated the duty to help neighbors, 'works' have come to be contrasted with ritual, which includes religious behavior solely for one's own benefit. In translation of oriental writings, and from ancient European languages, these meanings do not hold; for, in most cases, the word translated as 'works' means merely ritual; and 'good works' means merely ritual scrupulously conducted, the moral factor not being implied. Among other terms used by translators of oriental or ancient writings, 'righteousness' and 'righteous man' must be taken critically. To a modern christian these terms mean 'morality' and 'moral man' respectively; but in ancient and oriental usage they more often mean, 'ritual correctness' and 'one who performs the ritual correctly,' with no moral implication.

Even in the translations of the Gospels, the significance of the word translated 'works' is sometimes uncertain. In the second chapter of the Epistle of James, for example, 'works' clearly means moral conduct in verses 14, 17, 18, and 20; but the meaning in verses 21, 22, and 23 is not so certain. Among passages in which 'works' means simply ritual are Galatians 2: 16, Ephesians 2: 9, Romans 3: 27, 4: 6, 9: 11, and 11: 6.

Ritual may be moral, nonmoral, or immoral, and still be religious works. A system of ritual may include works of all three of these sorts. The rules of life laid down in the books of the Hebrew law prescribe some types of conduct that are easily accepted as moral, along with much mere ritual of nonmoral type and some features that would be classed as immoral by modern standards, including modern Jewish standards.

Among the Thugs of India, ritual murder of travelers was conducted in worship of the great goddess called Kali, Durga, and by many other names. From the point of view of the Thugs, these murders were considered as 'good works,' while far from being 'good works' in the Christian sense.

Moral conduct of the highest sort may become ritualized. The good works epitomized as the essence of religion in the Epistle of James 1: 27, 'Pure religion and undefiled before God and the Father is this, to visit the fatherless and widows in their affliction, and to keep himself unspotted from the world,' were systematically organized as ritual by the early Christians, as is indicated in Acts 6: 1 and 9: 39. In the present era, these relief measures are thoroughly systematized, not only as religious rituals by religious groups, but also as nonreligious rituals by city, state, and federal agencies. Benevolent behavior of individuals, ranging from material gifts to the needy to acts of sympathy and kindness, tends to become ritualized as routine types of conduct; and, indeed, these actions are considered as more worthy when they are habitual than when they are occasional or unusual. Definitions of religion in terms of 'works' have been offered, the most noted example being the one quoted above from the Epistle of James, which combines 'good works' and further unspecified ritual as the essential characteristics of 'pure religion,' leaving unspecified the nature of 'impure' religion, but implying that it involves the wrong kind of works or omits the right kind. One might say, of course, that where there is religious ritual, there must be religious faith; and this is true as regards the group of people who have developed and long maintained the ritual. It is not necessarily true of the individual member of the group who practices the ritual, for he may conform to the group's habits from 'religious reasons' or merely from 'social reasons,' or habit.

It is true, nevertheless, that in the religions of ancient civilization, and present religions of uncivilized peoples, observance of ritual is more important than adherence to faith. The essence of religion among Greeks of the classic and preclassic period was participation in civic ceremonies, the observance of the conventional rites of domestic sacrifice, and other ceremonial practices. Such behavior was 'honoring the gods,' but the gods were innumerable. Different people honored different gods, and the beliefs about each of them were confused and conflicting. There were no standardized beliefs about immortality, ghosts, or any other concepts usually attributed to religion, except belief in a variety of manas attached to objects and places, which might hurt men, and in the necessity of observing the common ritual as protection against these manas.

The religious situation in pre-Christian Rome was similar to that in Greece. Bernard Shaw has expressed this very neatly in *Androcles and the Lion*, where the Roman captain tells the Christian captives that all they have to do to escape being thrown to the lions is to burn a pinch of incense on any public altar; that nobody cared what they believed.

It is true that there was, in the ancient world before Christianity, a growing undercurrent of emphasis on orthodox faith. Socrates was condemned to death in 399 B.C., presumably for having taught youths to doubt the popular stories about the gods. While these charges did not represent the real basis for the animus against Socrates—which was probably in part an objection to his private life and his disagreeable personality and in part his reforming activities—but were merely excuses, they could not have been used as such unless the need for uniformity of faith for maintenance of group religion had begun to be recognized.

If we turn to religions of uncivilized peoples of today, we find our best illustrations in the conglomeration of religions known as 'Hinduism.' The only belief which is common to all Hindu religions is the belief that ritual is necessary. Beyond that, there is no common faith, and the range of variations in beliefs is vast. The question as to *what ritual* is essential narrows down, according to Gandhi, to rituals based on the sanctity of the cow, so that the only essential belief is belief in bovine sanctity. In this Gandhi is unquestionably correct, for 'protection of the cow' is a common feature of all Hindu religions, and there is no other common feature. In other words, the cow is the only symbol of unity that Hindus recognize in their diverse religions.

If we consider the distinction between orthodox Hinduism and unorthodox Hinduism, we find ritual even more significantly emphasized. The distinction between orthodoxy and unorthodoxy in India has no relation to faith in any religious concepts, such as gods, souls, or immortality. Some orthodox Hindu religions accept gods as objects of faith, while other orthodox Hindu religions are atheistic. Some orthodox sects maintain faith in one or several souls, while other orthodox sects reject all souls. Some sects teach kindness and benevolence comparable to the teachings of the best Christian sects, while others are bloody, cruel, savage cults. What, then, is orthodoxy among Hindus?

Orthodoxy for Hindus is the acceptance of the Brahmans as the essential priests and of the Brahmanical ritual as the essential ritual. Religions such as Buddhism, which originated in India but has practically died out there, are unorthodox simply because they reject the Brahmanical ritual and the authority of the Brahman caste and have established their own rituals and their own priests to administer it. The religion of the Jains, who still survive in India, is unorthodox for the same reason. Religious faith has nothing to do with orthodoxy. Orthodoxy is simply a matter of ritual. In this respect Hinduism lags in the stage of religious development from which Western religions began to emerge long before the Christian era. Since Hinduism includes unorthodox cults as well as orthodox cults, and since the Mohammedan invasion made the Hindus class-conscious, it is not strange that Gandhi could find no feature common to all Hindu religions except 'protection for the cow.'

It might be theoretically possible, of course, to conceive of religion in its present phases exclusively in terms of ritual, or works. Among Christians there are some who frankly contend that the best religion is that in which 'good works' (good conduct) is paramount, and in which the only faith involved is the belief that the activities carried on are really 'good' for those on whose behalf they are undertaken. This is the religion of social service and benevolence, which is in partial agreement with the principle of religion of ancient Greece and Rome that works matter and faith is inconsequential, although the 'works' of the modern Christians are radically different from the rituals of the ancients. No one would claim, however, that all religion is of this 'best' type, and a definition of religion in terms of 'good works' remains a definition of religion as some persons think it *should be* but not as it *is*. For the vast majority of Christians, and for many non-Christians, correctness of faith has become an important criterion of the values of religion; and the criterion of good conduct is secondary, although correctness of ritual may be considered as the index of credential correctness.

From any point of view, it must be admitted that ritual has played an important part in the development of religion, and religion everywhere involves a pattern of ritual, no matter how much it may emphasize faith. The forms, types, and varieties of ritual are not merely numerous, but are innumerable. Among the rituals conspicuous in ancient religion were: animal sacrifice; incense burning; anointing with oil and washing with water; presenting of gifts to altars; dedicating the altars themselves; chanting of hymns and marching in processions. Every phase of life had its ritual; birth, puberty, marriage, death, and burial were surrounded with religious ceremonials. Elaborate rituals were employed in preparing seed for planting, in the planting, and in the eventual harvest. Eating and drinking involved daily rituals, and every detail of sexual activity was embedded in ritual. There were, further, rituals of the seasons, of the months, and the weeks. The mass of rituals is too great and too complex even for classification.

Among modern Hindus, rituals are even more comprehensive and pervasive than they were among the ancient Greeks and Romans. Every detail of a Hindu's life has its ritual embroidery and limitation. Practically nothing can be done without ritual. In Islam (Mohammedanism), ritual is less pervasive, there being more separation between religious ritual and the routine operations of life than in Hinduism; but the rituals of Islam take precedence over all other activities.

Christian sects vary much in their rituals, but ritual is important in all. There is indeed a great contrast between the elaborate, and often beautiful, rituals of the Greek Catholic, the Roman Catholic, and the 'High' Episcopal church on the one hand and the meager rituals of dissenters' chapels and evangelical churches on the other, but rituals nevertheless are essential in all sects. The vestments, incense, processions, chorals, and genuflections of the High Church are no more truly ritual than are the standardized risings, sittings, gospel readings, and offertory of the Presbyterian. The exclusion of musical instruments from the meetinghouses of the Covenanters, and sects that have replaced them, are strictly ritual exclusions. The 'amens' and other pious ejaculations in religious worship of other sects are definitely ritual, and the groaning, shouting, and leaping in still more exuberant groups or worshipers are standardized rituals. The restraint and formality of the Quaker meeting is a ritual that is as fixed and as important as is the more ornate ritual of the Roman Mass.

Rituals have been built about common operations of all kinds, requiring that these operations be carried on in a prescribed way and with prescribed additions. Thus, in preparing food, members of one cult must proceed in a certain way and must carefully avoid certain things that would make the food religiously impure. In eating the prepared food, certain rituals also may be involved. The eater must turn his back on other people; or he may say grace; or he must offer some of the food and drink to the gods or 'spirits,' pouring a libation of wine and scattering fragments of food. These are examples of rituals built about common operations.

On the other hand, any common operation may be used as a feature of ritual built about something else. From eating and drinking are derived the ceremonial meal, in which one engages not for the purpose of satisfying hunger and thirst, but as a ritual of worship. The Eucharist, in Christian ritual, is a survival, in reduced form, of the ceremonial meals that were common in ancient religions. Almost every type of activity of which man is capable has been employed in some ritual or other, in one or another religion. Dancing, singing, marching, rising, sitting, bowing, and kneeling are common ritual features. Movements and postures of the hands and arms are equally common. Opening and shutting the eyes and noddings of the head occur in some rituals. Votaries of some religions leap and shout; others roll on the ground; others beat their breasts, cut themselves with knives, tear their hair and garments, even tear animals to pieces. Expectoration and urination occur in some rituals, and sexual intercourse has been an important feature of rituals of some ancient religions, as it is still in the Sakti ceremonials of India.

The appeal to the senses is an important matter in ritual. Visual stimulation through colors and forms of vestments, stained-glass windows, flowers, and movements is widespread. Bells, drums, trumpets, organs, and other musical and noise-making instruments are employed, and the human voice is ritually raised in chant and song. The sense of smell is stimulated by the fumes of burning incense, and the odor of burning meat was an important stimulant in the ancient sacrifices, the assumption that it was pleasing to the gods indicating its ritual importance to men. The sense of taste was involved in the eating of sacrificed animals and in other early ceremonial meals. The dermal senses appear to be the only ones that have been neglected in ritual.

It is sometimes assumed that rituals are contrived as symbols of

faith; that faith of a certain sort develops, and then ritual appropriate
to it is adopted. An illustration would be the burning of incense in
Grecian temples. It was believed that the pungent smoke of the
incense contained a life principle or life stuff (*nous*), which, ascending
to the gods of the air or heavens, increased the vitality of these gods.
Similarly, the blood of sacrificed animals was allowed to run into
the ground near the altars; the life stuff which the animal had
extracted from the air in respiration and stored in his blood
being thus contributed to the gods of the earth or of the
underworld.

It has been assumed, accordingly, that the belief in the importance
of giving 'life' to the gods led to the burning of incense; and that the
letting the blood run to waste in the earth was also due to the belief
in the efficacy of the blood for the earth divinities. This assumption
is probably an error. It is more probable that the belief in the usefulness of incense to the gods arose as an interpretation of the ritual of
incense burning, which had developed for quite other reasons. It is
probable also that the interpretation of the ritual pouring of blood
into the ground grew up after the ritual itself had become established.

The theory that faith arises as interpretation of rituals more
often than ritual is devised in the attempt to express faith appears
to have been put forward first by a Paul Regnaud, a French philologist and Sanscrit scholar, and shocked his contemporaries, to whom
the theory seemed absurd. Adopted by Robertson Smith, the
theory was still rejected for a generation, but has finally become
accepted by scholars because the historical developments of doctrines
and rituals can be understood on no other basis. That rituals are
modified to fit modifications in doctrines is of course admitted. It
is plain, however, that as Hopkins pointed out a generation ago,
rituals persist as faiths associated with them fade, and new
interpretations of the persistent rituals constitute new forms of
faith.

The determinative influence of ritual on the development of faith
is due to the development of ritual operations for practical reasons,
which later are given religious interpretations. The burning of
incense was important in the ancient Greek world for several reasons.
At places of sacrifice, the incense helped mask the stench of these
slaughterhouses. In the theaters, filled with unwashed humanity,
the need of incense was great. In domestic usage, the fumes of
the thyme and cedar wood, which were the chief constituents of

domestic incense, helped to keep in check the great curse of ancient man, *lice*. The ritual of incense burning having become established, ascription of religious significance to the ritual was inevitable, and its interpretation was in accordance with the prevailing systems of faith; but conversely, the ritual contributed to modification and development of these faiths. Even philosophy was affected by incense burning, for the word 'nous,' commonly translated as 'reason,' 'thought,' originally referred to invisible life stuff dissolved in the air, and especially evident in pungent smoke, as of incense.

There is always, indeed, a purpose, explicit or veiled, in the construction or development of a ritual, but few rituals appear to have been constructed initially to represent, symbolize, or express a religious belief. They arise, in general, from purposes which are not strictly religious, but which are economic, that is, practical. After they acquire religious interpretations, these interpretations change progressively. The rituals of burial, or inhumation, have changed little in essentials during the last three thousand years, but the significance of the ritual has changed through many phases, and although the conception of a life beyond the grave arose largely from burial rituals and the corresponding rituals of cremation, the same rituals are followed today by many persons with no religious interpretation whatever.

That there are rituals other than those of religion is implied above, and the implication is valid. It has been pointed out that the works of religion include, in various religions, moral actions, immoral actions, and actions that are unmoral, that is, neutral. There are on the other hand moral and immoral actions that are not religiously motivated. And there are routinized patterns of ceremonial action which can reasonably be classed as ritual, but which, apparently, are not religious. As an illustration of such rituals we may point to formalized exercises at commencement and other university public occasions. The processions of faculty members in black robes with gaudy trimmings; the standing of the audience while the procession is filing into the auditorium; the observing of a formal precedence in marching and seating; and the routine program of speeches and music constitute an inflexible ritual, following an ancient, but reinterpreted, pattern. Although a slight religious color is given by the inclusion of a perfunctory prayer in the program, the ritual is essentially nonreligious, in the sense, at least, in which the term 'religious' is usually taken. University functions, however, are no extraordinary affairs, for all public gatherings exhibit, to close scrutiny, unmistakable ritualized features.

The importance of ritual, in and out of religion, is a topic deserving emphasis and study. It seems probable that religion without ritual cannot be maintained and that without ritual religion could not have developed. Individuals trained in an established religion may, indeed, split off from the group, retaining the original faith, or a modification thereof, while not carrying on any ritual or works in connection with the faith. That such bodiless religion could survive several generations without revivification by ritual religion seems improbable.

Religion completely devoid of 'works' would be as near to a purely personal system as anything in human life can be, its social features being reduced to a minimum. It is convenient, therefore, to designate faith as the *personal factor* in religion and works, or ritual, as the *social factor*. These two factors, of course, are inseparable in most religions; but we may, nevertheless, without danger of confusion, speak of religious faith as *personal religion* and of religious works as *social religion*.

Since works and ritual are common features of social life, attempts to define religion in terms of works or in terms of ritual have not been very helpful. A satisfactory definition in such terms would have to specify the exact sort of ritual or works that is characteristic of religion and not found outside religion. If we accept morality as the criterion of religion, the logical requirements are satisfied; but this identification of morality and religion upsets our common habits of thought regarding these two fields and is objectionable to the majority of both proreligious and antireligious persons. The James of the Epistle seems to have recognized that 'good works' alone do not distinguish religion from nonreligion and added a second criterion, 'To keep himself unspotted from the world,' which we may interpret as the following of a further ritual of inhibitions or abstinences, thus perhaps defining the 'best' religion as benevolent asceticism.

This conception of 'pure religion and undefiled' in terms of good works and ritual does not, however, imply that there are no other types of religion. A definition of religion in terms of works, which should include all types of religion, does not seem possible, since it seems clear that some other criterion of religion is required to distinguish the works of religion from activities and conduct that are not religious.

4. The Continuity of Religion.—Attempts to study the 'psychology of religion,' as a specific application of methods and principles of psychology to the problems of religion, commenced about fifty years ago, and since that beginning a considerable number of books have appeared, purporting to embody contributions to the topic. A few of the books have been of permanent value; but on the whole the actual contributions have been slight, as compared with the contributions to the psychology of religion that have been made by scholars who have not posed as psychologists. The reason for the sterility of the work of the psychologists and of others who have tried to work 'psychologically' in this field is quite obvious. The psychological work has been done almost exclusively on isolated phases of particular religions, whereas it is the unanimous conclusion of scholars who have worked broadly in the field of religion that for productive study the *comparative method* is essential.

A distinction is sometimes made between the *comparative method* and the *historical method* in the study of religion, but the distinction is less important that the names would indicate. Some information may be gleaned by the comparison of different religions without regard to the development of any of them, and the study of the development of a single religion, such as Christianity, over a period of centuries, is interesting; but the results from such procedures are meager relative to the results of the full comparative method, which is also historical. Examination of important books with either title shows clearly that the successful work in history of religions is comparative, and the productive work in comparative religion is historical. Adequate investigation requires not merely the comparison of different religions at supposedly comparable stages in their development, but also the comparison of different stages in the same religion, and a comparison of the progressive development (if any) of one religion with the progressive development of the others.

Robertson Smith formulated the principle: *Nothing is lost in religion.* This, in form, is an exaggeration, but conveys a truth that is vital. We might rephrase the proposition simply as: *There is never anything new in religion*, without any fallacy beyond the overgeneralization that is involved in Robertson Smith's maxim. The point is that no religion has an abrupt beginning; no religion is invented by its reputed founder. A 'new' religion grows out of old religions by a process of development such that there is discernible no point at which the new religion actually begins, and the only novelties are applications of new names and changes of emphasis on doctrines. Whatever we find in religion today can be found in older phases, in embryo if not more fully developed; and few features of ancient faiths and rituals are completely eradicated in later phases of development.

On the other hand, religions that continue formally in the same grooves for long periods, with the same verbal formulations of faith and the same apparent ritual, really change in essential features of both faith and ritual, if there is progress in the cultures of which they are parts. Social changes, whether industrial, political, scientific, or of any other sorts, inevitably produce changes in religion. Nevertheless, the modifications of religions are seldom, if ever, substitutions, but are adaptations of the old to new conditions. In some of these remodelings the old materials are preserved in obvious forms, but sometimes they are revealed only to careful study. That which appears in a simple form in an ancient religion may be more complex in a later religion, but often the complex factors become simplified in the developmental process.

Religions, after they have developed into distinct types, are often modified by absorption of the features of other religions. Christianity began as a synthesis of Judaism and Greek religion, evident in the Gospel of John, and the philosophies of Plato and Aristotle were both influential; but it was later modified through borrowings from the Celtic religions of western Europe and from Roman paganism. The Judaism and the Greek religion, in which Christianity had its roots, were both products of religious syntheses; and it is probable that Celtic religion had its roots in still earlier cults. That there is nothing in Christianity which cannot be traced back to the obscurities of prehistory is a fact that has been long known to students of the history of religion.

Religions tend to branch out into sects, but the development is not alone a process of continuously branching stems. The absorption of features from other religions, which we have called figuratively 'anastamosis,' is an important process in religious development, so that, in tracing any religion back from any given point, we are led through a network of converging and diverging factors.

If we turn from the religions of civilized and semicivilized peoples to the religions of savages, we find, superficially, a different story.

The apparent difference, however, is due to the impossibility of tracing the development of a savage religion, because of the lack of written record and carved inscriptions. Changes in the religions of some savage groups (particularly in Africa) are indicated by the tribal traditions; but in most cases a savage religion has reached a stage of crystallization so long before that the group traditions contain no evidence of earlier modifications. Yet, no savage religions are simple, any more than the savage cultures of which they form parts are simple, but have reached the levels at which we know them through long processes of development. Nothing in savage culture is really 'primitive'; from certain points of view our civilized cultures are more primitive (that is, are nearer to the primitive) than are many savage cultures.

Of the 'great religions,' Islam (Mohammedanism) comes the closest to being a religion arbitrarily synthetized. Mohammed, thinking that the Arabs needed an improved religion, considered the possibilities of Christianity and Judaism. He decided, apparently, that neither would be satisfactory; the change to either would have been too drastic to be brought about easily. Moreover, the adoption of either would have given little preeminence to Mohammed. He therefore formulated a religion in which he was the central figure: the founder and the major prophet. The influence of both Christianity and Judaism may, however, be easily discerned in Islam, along with features of ancient Arabian religion.

Jesus and the Jewish prophets were accepted as authentic religious teachers, although their importance was subordinated to that of Mohammed. The ancient holy places of the Arabs, including Mecca, Medina, and Jerusalem, were made holy places of the new faith. Ancient rituals of the Arabs were modified somewhat for the new faith. The Jewish monotheism, with a male divinity, became a central feature of Islam. The elimination of female divinities was a part of Mohammed's program for the reduction in importance of women; but the old gods, and the old goddesses, have continued to be worshiped secretly by Arabs who are nominally pious Mohammedans.

Where Islam has proselyted peoples of other religions, the Mohammedanism of these peoples became different from Arabian Islam. The divergent sects of Islam, differing as sharply as do the most diverse sects of Christianity, derive their characteristics from the original religions of the proselyted groups, on whom Islam was imposed, but modified by the ancient religions. The Persian Mohammedans, for example, are Shiites, and the characteristics of Shiism derive in unbroken lineage from the old Persian religion, of which Zoroastrianism was one phase. The religion of the most important group of Afghans is Islam, officially; but its affiliation with the old Hebrew religion is obvious, which tends to substantiate the claim of this group that they are descendents of Hebrews who were deported from Judea by Nebuchadnezzar.

It would appear that no imposition of a new religion on a people previously devoted to a different religion can succeed unless there is a carrying over of the old religion into the new. We might go beyond Robertson Smith's formula that 'Nothing is lost in religion,' and formulate a principle which, perhaps, is more fundamental, namely: *Religion inherently is resistant to changes, both in itself and in all matters of personal and social life with which it is closely associated.* This is merely a summary generalization of the fact that religion, everywhere, and in all times, is ultraconservative; that it values the antique; that in any stage of its development it considers itself to have reached the ultimate phase; that it lags behind the progress of culture and operates to prevent cultural advance.

The notion that that which is antique is therefore valuable, that the old faiths, and the old ways, are the best, is recognizable in all religions and sects except the very few whose main tenet, as in Unitarianism, is the rejection of this very notion. Such religions succeed only in part; they flourish for a time and then disintegrate. Clinging to the old as of paramount value seems to be essential for the continued life of any religion.

In most religions the importance of continuity and of antiquity is explicitly recognized. Christianity and Buddhism in their earlier years claimed to be not new, but to be the 'fulfillment' of the old. The principles of Buddhism were set forth as the ancient 'noble way,' as the clarified development of the Vedas and Upanishads. The mythical founder of Buddhism, Siddhartha Gautama, was a pupil of Brahmanical scholars and was finally recognized as one of a long line of Buddhas, who preceded and would follow him. Buddhism, in short, claimed to be no more than the ancient tree, pruned of its withered limbs and sapping suckers and reaching a new growth.

Early Christianity emphasized its continuity with Judaism, being satisfied with the antiquity of the cult which claimed Abraham,

Moses, and the prophets while ignoring its roots in the older Greek culture. As Christianity has itself attained a modest age, it has reduced its emphasis on its pre-Christian ancestry. While not glorying in the antiquity of its roots in Celtic religion, Christianity has recognized its practical importance in various ways, for example, by moving the celebration of the birth of Jesus from September along to the winter solstice, the celebration of which had been so long embedded in European cultures that the peoples could not be weaned away from it. The adoption by Christians of the ancient springtide festival, common to peoples of the West and the Levant from ancient times as the period of the resurrection of the god, was another tribute to antiquity.

Some of the modern Christian sects attempt to ignore the ancient roots other than the Jewish, but other sects have prided themselves on the continuity of their faiths and rituals with those of pre-Christian pagan religions. The triumph of the Roman church over rival churches in the early centuries, was due, in no small measure, to the obvious continuity of the Roman ecclesiastical organization with the pre-Christian Roman religious form of organization. The statement of a Roman Catholic theologian a few years ago (in a book approved by the Church) that Jesus was only an incident in the history of the church seems astonishing to Protestants, but not to Catholics.

In spite of the conservatism of religion, changes in religions do occur. Changes occur slowly for the most part, without crisis or revolution. Religion of the present can be understood only through understanding its development from religion of the past. When what appears to be a new religion appears we also look for the features that are but restatements and revisions of features of ancient religions, and we can always find them. Changes in religion, no matter how important, can be evaluated only in terms of *that which* is changed.

We have pointed out that religions, after becoming established, may be modified in several ways; that the changes may be due to borrowing from other religions, or by absorption into the one religion of features of another or of others. We have said also that changes in the primarily secular features of the culture of a group may affect the religion or the religions of the group. This secular modification of religion has certainly occurred in the United States, where the sweeping changes in transportation, communication, industry, commerce, agriculture, and amusements have brought about a social life that is very different from that of even sixty years ago. With these social changes have come changes in religious beliefs, attitudes, and practices, even in the most conservative sects. It is difficult to avoid the conclusion that the religious changes are the results of the other social changes. Certainly, the religious changes have *not* been primary, have *not* been the causes of the other changes.

Whether, without absorption from other religions, and in a fairly static social environment, there would be religious progress is an interesting question. The indications, so far as I can see, are that such progress, if it occurs, is slight. Such evidence as we have from savage cultures is all against the supposition of independent religious changes; but, of course, we do not know what may have gone on in these cultures in their periods of development. Long-established cultures in Asia have been affected from time to time by influences from outside. Among these influences have been not only the secular features of European cultures, but also imported religions. The introduction of Buddhism and early Christianity into China had its effects; and Buddhistic and Mohammedan religions have had discernible effects in other Asiatic regions.

In some cases, groups holding one religion have been forced to adopt a different religion. The Persians, for example, were forcibly converted to Islam by the Arabs. The alternative offered the Persians was: Be converted or die! Some succeeded in escaping to India, where their descendents are called *Parsees*, but the bulk of the population had to adopt Islam or be slain. In this typical case, the new religion is at first merely a dress, or veneer on the old, although in the course of time the new religion may become vital. The old Persian religion still underlies the Islam of Persia, as *Shiism*, which the Arabs consider heretical.

An interesting case of group conversion is that of the Khazars, a tribe of Turki stock, who migrated into southern Russia early in the Christian Era and later moved up the Danube and Dneiper valleys and spread up the tributaries of those rivers. About A.D. 740 the chiefs decided that the tribesmen should adopt Judaism, and so ordered. The tribesmen complied and adopted the Jewish faith, and the Jews of southeastern Europe (the Ashkenazim) are supposed to have descended from them. While the religion of the Ashkenazim is officially not different from that of the Sephardim, cultural differences between Jews of the two branches have probably been responsible for the antagonism between them which is still evident.

A religion can be forced upon a population under certain conditions, but the resultant religion usually shows traces, at least, of the original religion of the group. The Khazars apparently were not averse to accepting the orders of their dictators; and that makes a great difference. The attempt of the Spanish Inquisition to force the Jews in Spain to become Roman Catholics had no such results. In spite of tortures and execution by the Inquisitors, the Jews in Spain were not converted. Some became Christians in form, but secretly remained Jews; and under these conditions there was no assimilation of the new religion to the old.

Persecution of adherents of a religion seems, up to a certain point, to strengthen them in their religion. This has been demonstrated by persecution of Jews in Europe, by persecution of Puritans in England, and by persecution of Quakers by Puritans in America.

Changes in religion may, under certain conditions, be brought about by external influences, but the strongest influences are internal. After individuals within the group have become changed, their influence tends to modify the religion of the group. If, on the other hand, a dissenting group withdraws from the main group and organizes as an independent sect, the influence of this sect on the religious group from which they seceded becomes much lessened. The secession of the Unitarians from the Congregational church, and the secession of members of other Protestant sects to join the Unitarians, undoubtedly retarded the liberalization of Protestantism. The Protestant Reformation, in a similar way, set back severely the 'modernization' of Roman Catholicism.

Reformers, religious and otherwise, proceed more effectively today. They stay in the groups they wish to reform, as 'fifth columnists,' and exert their influence until or unless summarily ejected. Outside the group, their influence on the group would be practically nil.

It seems clear that, in studying the development of any religion, we need to trace it back as far as possible through its actual antecedent stages. We have already noted that what we call a 'religion' is not always discretely separable from other religions which are contemporaneous with it or antecedent to it; and that within what we call a religion there often are distinct differences as great as the external differences from other religions. We have pointed out, also, that when we say of two similar religions, These are different, and that when we say of two dissimilar religions, These are sects of the same religion, the bases for the classifications are historical. Instead of tracing the development of various religions as if they were discrete entities, we can do better by tracing the changes in religious concepts and religious practices in the complexly interrelated groups of religious systems.

The peoples of Europe and of the Europeanized parts of North America are mainly adherents of the Christian religion, although of widely divergent sects. It is true that there are small groups of adherents to Buddhism, Brahmanism, and Islam, especially on the Atlantic and Pacific seaboards; and that voodooism of African origin exists in the Southern black belt and the West Indies. There are a number of other exotic cults represented also; and there is a considerable group of adherents to Judaism, which—let it be noted— is a religion and not a race; but these groups are in total a minority of the population. Our primary task, accordingly, is to consider Christianity, and the religions antecedent, or otherwise contributory, to it.

On superficial scrutiny, Christianity may seem to be merely an offshoot from Judaism, but its actual relationships are more complicated. Judaism made contributions to the development of Christianity, but earlier religions of Greece and the Levant contributed more to the shaping of this religion. The Jewish influence was transmitted largely, but not entirely, through the Hellenized Jewish philosophers of Alexandria in Egypt; but it is not certain that any ancient Egyptian influences were involved. Influence of Persian religion, and of Buddhism, have been suspected, but such influences have not been conclusively proved to have operated. As Christianity spread over Europe, it absorbed much from the religions of the Romans and the Celts; but the savage Teutons, apparently, had nothing to contribute.

Judaism had sources somewhat similar to those of Christianity. Judaism apparently grew out of the religion of the Hebrews, a more ancient people formed from marauding bands in Syria, who preceded the Jews in Palestine. The Hebrew religion was a synthesis of the religions of Syria and adjacent regions, with contributions from Arab and Hittite cultures. An element derived from Egyptian paganism is assumed, and influences from Crete and other Greek islands are suspected; but the Canaanite influence was probably predominant in the formative period.

The evolution of Judaism from the Hebraic religion was stimulated by Babylonian influences, brought to Judea by the Hebrews who were sent back after the captivity. After the formulation of the official scriptures, Greek ideas, emanating from the Jewish philosophers of Alexandria, had effects on the interpretation, if not on the formulation, of Jewish doctrines and were undoubtedly responsible for the ethical aspect of Judaism, as contrasted with the savagery of the Hebrew culture.

Although Christianity arose as a Jewish sect, its appeal was mainly to non-Jews, and its doctrines easily became anti-Jewish. From the conflict between Jewish Christianity and Greek Christianity arose two forces that persist today. (a) The Greco-Alexandrian Christianity, represented by the apostle Paul, by the author of the Fourth Gospel, and by the Catholic sects. (b) Jewish Christianity, represented by the Synoptic Gospels and the evangelical sects of Protestantism. The first is Mediterranean, and the second Levantine, but both have been modified by Celtic cultures.

The sources of modern European religion, accordingly, are primarily in the ancient Mediterranean culture area and the Levant. The most important parts of the Mediterranean area were the southern part of Italy; Greece, from the southern part north to and including ancient Thrace (modern Thessaly and Macedonia); the Aegean coast from the old location of the Philistines northward around Asia Minor; the coasts of the Black Sea and connecting waters; and Crete and other islands of the eastern Mediterranean.

The Levant includes Syria, Asia Minor, and the Mesopotamian valley, with other areas of less importance. Christianity developed from the religions and the cultures of the Mediterranean and Levantine regions we have listed.

It is possible that features of the religions of Persia and India influenced Christianity; but if such influences occurred, they could hardly have been effective before the first century B.C. The prophetic books of the Old Testament contain denunciations of rituals (especially the use of the 'branch'), which may have been of Persian origin, but this is not certain.

Cultural similarities do not in all cases indicate borrowings of features of culture. Often, the similarities are due to the stemming of different cultures from a common antecedent culture; and this seems to have been the source of the slight similarities between Christianity and Eastern religions. It is fairly well known that, in prehistoric times, a culture which may be called 'Pelasgian,' existed not only in the Mediterranean area, but also in the lower region of Mesopotamia, the Nile Valley, and the valley of the Indus River in Hindustan. This culture seems to have been established by groups migrating from the East Indies, who went up the river valleys from the coasts and eventually invaded the western Mediterranean. It has been suspected that this people came originally from China, from which it was driven out by the invading Mongols. In Mesopotamia, this early culture was crushed by invading European autochthones from the north. In Egypt the Hamito-Negroid hosts of the Pharaohs from the south partially extinguished the culture; but the amalgamation of the African culture with the earlier produced the great Egyptian culture of the successive dynasties, in which the negroid features are plainly evident.

It was long believed that early Greek religion drew largely from Egyptian sources, a belief for which Herodotus was largely responsible; but we now know that Herodotus was wrong and that he was misled by the Egyptian priests with whom he consorted. The early religious roots for the religions of modern Europe and America are clearly in the limited areas we have listed. Other roots are conjectural; any Negro influence is limited to that which may *possibly* have been transmitted through Egypt, Colchis, or India. Connections with Asia otherwise, with Africa, with the Americas, and with the Islands of the Pacific are completely negligible. In comparing modern Christianity with the religions of the ancient Levantine and Mediterranean areas, we are comparing early and later stages of growth of the same religion, or rather, are comparing a stem with the roots from which it grew. In comparing civilized religion with savage religions, on the other hand, there is no genetic relationship discernible. If we compare the religion of an Australian Bushman with that of an American Christian or with that of a citizen of ancient Troy, we are comparing two developments from origins which lie back of history and traditions so far that we cannot conjecture any connection. This would remain true, even if we could discover what the Bushman's religion actually is or was.

The actual beginnings of our religions in the ancient areas are lost in the impenetrable obscurity of the remote past. During the long period before the Christian Era, cultural development, including religious development, was influenced by migrations of peoples, political changes, wars, inventions, arts, commerce, and progress in agriculture and animal husbandry. That the primitive civilization common to the Mediterranean, Mesopotamian, and western Indian areas was brought in by an alien people, who dispossessed the autochthones, is a reasonable conjecture.

Still other peoples entered the Mediterranean and Levantine areas in later, but still legendary, times, and while adopting the established culture modified it by features of their own. Among these immigrants were the Achaeans, the 'Thracians' of Greece, and the Canaanites (including the Phoenicians) of Syria. The invasion of the savage Dorians almost extinguished civilization in Greece, as it was extinguished in Mesopotamia by other autochthones from the north and as it was extinguished in the Indus Valley by autochthones and Mongolians. Civilization of Greece was saved only by the migration of the Ionians to the coast of Asia Minor, where Greek civilization made a new growth and from which it was evidently retransplanted to Greece. The Dorians eventually adopted Greek civilization, in part at least, but they had no contributions to make from their own savage culture.

The features of cultures and racial stocks to which we have given passing consideration should now be given more expanded treatment. This involves some repetition, but repetition may be useful.

While the history of the development of culture in the regions under consideration is not entirely clear in respect to the early periods, the consensus of the ancient writers makes some of the important conditions fairly evident. There has been a great deal of agreement among modern scholars on many details of the cultural and racial history of the region; but this was in part a confusion due to the acceptance of the theory that language relationships were valid signs of stock relationship. With the passing out of this confusion of philology with ethnology the problems have been simplified, and it is possible to evaluate the information given by the ancient writers (Herodotus, Pausanias, Strabo, and others), free from the smoke screen of the German philologists.

There were at least three important racial stocks distributed in the area of Asia Minor, Syria, the Mediterranean coast lines, and adjacent territories. These racial stocks appeared in these regions at different periods, and the antagonisms of the earlier groups to the later invaders increased the segregation of the groups and promoted separatist cultural developments. Eventually, however, the cultures combined with one another.

The first group can be called 'autochthonous,' since it was the first population in these areas. This stock, distributed across Europe from the British Isles to Asia, and in southern Asia, was also planted in North Africa. The anatomical conformations of this stock varied in various areas according to climate and nutrition, as we might expect. Head form, shape and size of nose, and stature varied greatly. The characteristics less affected by environment— eye color, hair color, and skin characteristics—identify groups that might otherwise seem to be of different stocks. These are the dark peoples, dark of eye and hair and swarthy of skin. The typical (but mixed) representatives today are the Black Scotch, Black Irish, Welsh, South Germans, Armenians, Riffs, Arabs, Hamites, and Dravidians. They are found all over Europe, even in Norway and Sweden, and in the Levant.

Where this group of peoples originated is a question; but we can well assume that they are the direct descendants of the people of the New Stone Age. That they were established in the Mediterranean area, in Asia Minor, in Syria, and in the Africa north of the Sahara before other peoples invaded these regions seems certain.

A second people who invaded these areas at an early time may be assigned their ancient name of *Pelasgi*, or *Pelasgians*. This name has been given various derivations, but the most plausible interpretation connects it with the later Greek word *pelagos*, the open sea. Other derivations that make the name mean 'wanderers' are connected with this interpretation. The Pelasgi were seafaring peoples, who apparently came along the coast from the East Indies, settled in river valleys such as the valley of the Euphrates and Nile, and finally entered the Mediterranean. Even down to the historical period, the descendants of these peoples were seafaring and especially given to piracy. They invaded the Greek peninsula, spreading as far north as Thessaly and Macedonia. They invaded Italy and areas farther west. They settled in Asia Minor also. From them descended many groups later known as 'Greek,' including the Ionians and Aeolians.

Although it is risky to assume from cultural similarities a common cultural inheritance, or cultural borrowings, it may reasonably be concluded that certain fundamental characteristics of the cultures

of Greece, Asia Minor, Syria, Babylonia, and India are due to
the foundation of these cultures by peoples of the same culture—
the early settlers in the Indus Valley, whose name is unknown; the
Sumerians in Babylonia; and the Pelasgi in the Mediterranean
area and in Asia Minor. The resemblances between these cultures
and Egyptian culture may also be ascribed to the early settlement of
Pelasgians in the Nile Valley. In India and Babylonia the culture
was almost extinguished by invasions of the autochthonous peoples.
In Egypt the Hamito-Negro invasion (Pharaonic) modified the
culture, and gave it a predominantly negroid cast. Glimmerings
of a common cultural foundation appear, however, in all these
regions. In the Mediterranean areas and in Asia Minor, the autochthones came back and almost extinguished the nascent culture;
but before this happened a third group of peoples had introduced
themselves. This group or these groups we may designate as the
'red-haired peoples,' who apparently originated in the Altai region
of Asia. Of this stock were the Achaeans, who settled in the
Peloponnesus and in Argos; the Canaanites (Canaanites of the
Valley) in Syria; and the Phoenicians (Canaanites of the Hills)
on the Syrian coast. Another group of the redheads settled in
Thrace, for we know that the people known to later generations
as 'Thracians' were red-haired and blue-eyed. (We are here not
referring to the area that is now called Thrace, but to the regions
now known as Thessaly and Macedonia, which is ancient times were
known as Thrace.) Other groups of the red-haired blue-eyed
stock streamed across central Europe, reaching eventually the
British Isles. These peoples were known to the Greeks as *keltoi*,
the word from which our name *Celt* was derived. The ancient
Etruscans of Italy were of the same stock, and the physical traits
still appear in the population of Tuscany.

Mixtures of the red-haired people with autochthones and with
Pelasgi took place, in spite of cultural and racial antagonisms.
The Celts in western Europe mixed so rapidly with the dark peoples
of the forests tlat stocks now known as Celtic are described as
having brown eyes and dark hair.

That there were still other stocks involved in the areas we are
considering seems clear, but these other stocks are somewhat
conjectural. The Philistines are believed by some to have been of
the blond 'Nordic' type, and it is possible that the Nordic stock
settled in Crete at an early period.

The puzzling thing about the Mediterranean area is the existence of a type of masonry, which the Greeks of the historical periods called 'Cyclopean' and concerning the building of which there were various legends. It is clear that the Greeks of 2000 B.C. had no valid information about the origin of these stoneworks. The relation of this Cyclopean masonry to the megalithic structures of North Africa, Britanny, Malta, and southern England is unmistakable. Relations of all of these to circles of great stones in southeastern Asia is equally clear.

One theory has been that the Cyclopean structures in the eastern Mediterranean were built by the Pelasgi. This conjecture, however, is not solidly founded. It is clear from the structures in the western Mediterranean areas that the builders feared attacks from the sea. The cities in Greece and the Asian coast were built inland, even when this location made access to the sea troublesome. There would therefore be room for suspicion that the builders feared the Pelasgi. Could the autochthones have built these structures? Must we postulate an additional racial group, Nordics, perhaps? Or does the group we lump as 'Pelasgi' include an earlier and a later flood of immigrants, the first of which established themselves and fought the later? The last of these assumptions appears to be the most reasonable, but there is little foundation for any assumption. Eventually when a comparative study of megalithic monuments has been carried out, and the monuments from England to Manipur have been related to one another and to the legends in the areas in which they stand, a solution may be found to the problem. The trouble so far has been the tendency to treat the monuments in any one area as independent of those of other areas, along with failure to integrate the study of the monuments with the legends and traditions of the areas involved.

We know, in short, that in the areas under consideration there were at least three cultures that developed from sources relatively independent of one another and that these cultures had different racial backgrounds. Of these cultures, only two are important, those of the Pelasgians and of the red-haired people. That both of these influenced the autochthonous cultures is evident, and the close relationship of Celtic religion to Greek religion is no cause for surprise.

5. The Natural and the Supernatural.—Certain terms embedded in modern language are confusing, unless carefully defined, because they represent (designate) concepts that vary according to the points of view that are taken in regard to the phenomena or alleged phenomena that the concepts cover. Among these terms are 'natural,' 'supernatural,' 'magical,' and 'superstitious.'

In the point of view common in the Homeric era, the distinction between the natural and the supernatural did not exist. Nature (the Greek word is *phusis*) was all inclusive, and the gods and their powers were assumed to be as much a part of nature as were the running of water, the sprouting of seeds, the phenomena of the weather and human life. As we shall have occasion to note later, the gods and daimons were not above nature, but were in certain respects as much subject to natural laws as were men. In later periods, distinctions arose between beliefs that could be approved, and beliefs that should be rejected; and the latter beliefs were eventually called 'superstition'; that is, overbelief, or excessive belief. Today the concept of nature and the natural is restricted to matters of this world, as distinguished from the 'other world'; and beliefs and rituals that have reference to the other world are classed either as magical or as religious. In either case, the beliefs are beliefs in the *supernatural*. We classify ancient faiths and rituals retrospectively on this basis, but for ancient peoples the distinction did not exist, for the distinction between natural and supernatural was unknown. 'Magic,' as the term is used today, applies to the class of beliefs and practices that we reject as false, either because scientific tests invalidate them or because we think that such tests *would* invalidate them. The term 'religious,' for the most part, is applied to beliefs and practices that we recognize as not capable of scientific check or for the rejection of which we have no valid grounds, whether or not we accept them.

It is impossible, without clumsy circumlocutions, entirely to avoid the use of the term 'supernatural' and reference to the contrasting concepts of the natural and the supernatural, in discussing ancient beliefs and practices. Where we involve this distinction, however, it must always be understood in the retrospective sense. If we describe a content of belief as supernatural, we mean supernatural from the modern point of view, not from the point of view of those who held the belief. If we call certain practices of the past superstitious, we mean merely that from our point of view they are inefficacious, although among the peoples who maintained the practices the distinction between superstition and sound procedure may not yet have arisen.

6. Praxis.—The relations of science, magic, and religion have been much debated on theoretical grounds. It has been held by some that religion develops out of magic. Frazer and Andrew Lang held that magic and science are twin sisters, both of which are distinguished from religion in that religion is *impractical*, or 'other-worldly,' whereas science and magic are *practical*, or 'this-worldly.' Both of these views have elements of truth in them, but neither is adequate. Religion, science, and magic all develop from a more fundamental human construction which we call 'praxis,' the system of modes of living and of providing for future contingencies which man finds to be more or less successful and which he conserves, enlarges, and passes on to the next generation because it is successful. Praxis is a group accomplishment, by many sessions over many generations.

On this level, man does not know why his methods of procedure are efficacious; he does not even know which details are really effective and which are not. He merely knows that by these methods, without analyzing them, he gets along. Obviously, the great majority of men today live by praxis almost exclusively, with some religion and some magic mingled with the mass. Sometimes we call this 'common sense,' sometimes the 'wisdom of our fathers.' We also call it 'tradition,' that which has been handed down. If the tradition concerns knowledge only, we call it 'legend' or 'folklore.' If it concerns skill, we call it 'art' or 'an art.'

The praxis of every people includes many arts that have developed to a high stage of perfection without any science. The making of pottery, weapons, and ornaments reached a high stage among primitive people. The mingling of copper and tin to make bronze; the smelting and forging of iron; the making of glass; the tanning of hides and weaving of cloth; the painting of pictures and the sculpturing of forms; the preserving of foods, and their utilization through manifold forms of cookery; the evolution of language; irrigation and cultivation of crops; the care of flocks and herds; the making of cheese and butter; manufacture of wine and beer; building of ships and their management; these and a vast number of other arts and products were developed without scientific aid, and to some of them science has added little, while to others it has added much.

Praxes of all sorts include, in general, a conservative and a progressive factor. What has been achieved must be formulated, and passed on; but the old techniques may be gradually improved.

Science has as its chief characteristic the improvement of praxis, for applied science must always be primary. Applied science develops as its chief assistant, however, pure science, the analysis of phenomena regardless of application, which is a paradox. The real function of pure science is to analyze regardless of present or immediate application, trusting that any principle, technique, or fact discovered will eventually be useful. Science is in this sense the ultimate extension of praxis, the provision for future emergencies as yet unknown.

There is no line between science and the simplest improvement of praxis, yet we may draw a line in the transition at the point where science or proto-science certainly deserves the name. This is where it creates, as its servants, accurate analysis, logical inference, and experiment. The prescientific development of praxis involves vague analysis of phenomena and the drawing of inferences that may be of doubtful validity and involves no careful experimental check on the inferences. If a method seems to work, it is adopted. If its failure to work is obvious, it is slowly abandoned. Any progress must be slow, on account of the danger of losing the good we have, and any rejection must also be slow for the same reason.

Praxis is directed to the control of the future. In developing praxis, man necessarily develops a conception of cause and effect. Praxis consists in doing this, in order that a certain other thing may happen. The deadfall is dug, the trap baited, the pottery fired, in order that the game may be trapped, the bowl be made stronger. Man makes or seeks objects, such as flat stones, arrows, spears, poisons, and food plants, in order to use them for certain ends. He thus conceives of material causes, of objects which in certain circumstances will bring about certain desired results. Through the same processes, he conceives of active causes, of activities such as wielding the weapons, eating the food, which are also essential in order to produce the desired effects.

On the level of praxis, man is satisfied if the total of objects and acts he employs achieves the end for which he employs them. When he studies the mode of action, or the structure of the object, in order to discover why or how the effect is produced, he becomes proto-scientific; he is on the road to science.

Generalization is an indispensable part of man's praxis. This particular piece of mineral makes a good spearhead or knife. This other piece of mineral, which looks like the other, will also make a good tool, he generalizes, so he selects his material, and, if his judgment of appearances is good, he is justified by results. This animal with which he fought roared in a certain way. He hears in the thicket a roar that sounds like the other and wisely avoids the beast concealed there. So he reasons in many cases; this, which resembles or is like that in the readily observable characteristics, is also like it in other and more important but not readily observable features. For a large part of man's life this sort of reasoning is successful; but, unfortunately, there are many cases in which objects that resemble one another in one respect are quite different in other and more important respects. Actions, also, may seem quite similar, but may have quite different results. Man, however, tends to generalize rashly and concludes that objects and actions that resemble other objects or actions have the same effects when used in the same way or for the same purpose. He even goes further in his errors, and assumes that causes resemble their effects. Thus, from a feature of praxis, man invents *sympathetic magic.*

Another unfortunate generalization produces *contact magic.* Man notes that he gets no results from his weapons or tools unless he is in contact with them. He notes also that he is harmed only by contact with flints, stones, and thorns and that wild beasts do not harm them unless they touch him. Food is useless unless it is taken into the alimentary canal; that is, is in internal contact with the eater. Some poisons produce damage when in contact with the skin, but others are dangerous only in internal contact. Thus man is prepared, through sound observation, for generalization to the magic effects of contacts of other sorts.

The efficacy of communication also is overgeneralized. By speaking, one man influences another, or even a beast. Even by looking at a person in a certain way, one can influence his actions. The name of a person is easily observed to have especial efficacy. One may call out 'hey!' or 'man!' with no effect; but if one calls out 'John!' or 'M'tesa!' or whatever the man's name is, he stops, or turns, at once. Waving your hand is a form of communication which also is often efficacious in controlling the action of other persons. Thus man is prepared for the magic of words, especially the magic of proper names, for the superstition of the evil eye, and for gesticulatory magic.

Magic and science thus grow out of praxis. Like common praxis, and like science, magic is merely the seeking for the causes that will produce the desired effects. But, whereas dependable praxis utilizes causes that actually do more or less produce the effects, and science discovers certainties in the way of causal relations and determines the circumstantial conditions that modify the causal relation this way and that, magic naively accepts as causes many things that do not actually have any causal relation to the desired effects.

Magic begins thus with illicit inferences, with conclusions based on analogy, with generalizations for which there is no actual warrant. It thus adopts ineffectual practices, and it retains them because it makes no accurate checks on the results. Science, at its best, is apt to make false inferences but can discard them, however, because of its experimental method; for science makes tests of its hypotheses, to determine finally whether they are valid or fallacious. Magic makes no checks. Common praxis, magic, and science, however, agree in their purposes. Each seeks to utilize practical means to accomplish practical ends. The procedures of magic would be sound if they actually accomplished the results that are expected of them.

Science not only analyzes phenomena and checks the causal relations involved, but also discovers new principles and techniques and indicates the method of their application. These things then become a part of either common praxis or of special arts. The radio, for example, was developed through scientific work on radiations and electrical currents. Scientific results in many other directions contributed. The use of the radio, however, has nothing more scientific about it than has the use of an electric coffeepot. It is merely a new feature of common praxis. The making, repair, and adjustment of radio sets, however, is a new art, a specialized praxis. The expert radio repairman, however, need be no more of a scientist than is the garage man or the Navajo potter. A scientific knowledge may be an asset and scientific knowledge may be a value to the householder who uses the radio or the coffeepot, but it is not necessary for the use of either.

We certainly have more scientifically founded praxis today than man had in preceding ages. That we have less magic cannot be so confidently asserted. Fortunetellers, soothsayers, spiritualist mediums, divine healers, palmists, and a vast number of magicians of other sorts prey lucratively upon the public. The borders of psychology are infested with fakers. Courses in character development, character analysis, or courses merely labeled 'psychology,' are given by unscrupulous persons, often working under the plausible guaranty of religious organization, by renting church parlors for the courses. Psychoanalysis, which is really a praxis varying from common sense to sheer magic, with no scientific foundation whatever, has had a great and profitable vogue. Magic even creeps into psychology itself, and we have to be constantly on guard against it. Politics is infested with magic schemes of government, and recurrent economic collapse is due to the fact that our economic system is a product of mere praxis in which there has been little, if any, scientific development, but into which much magic has been introduced under the guise of economic theory. Even in biology, the interest in the transmission of acquired characters is literally an interest in sympathetic magic!—the search for causes of individual determination which shall superficially resemble the results.

The relation between scientific praxis and magical praxis and between science and magic is relatively clear, in spite of the difficulty in drawing separating lines. We might say even that the difficulty of drawing separating lines is the result of the clarity of the interrelationship, for those who have a superficial knowledge of the relationship have no difficulty in distinguishing the two sharply. The relation between common praxis, magic, and religion is more difficult to grasp and can best be understood through a survey of the actual development of religion.

Faith and works are interconnected, in simple praxis as in the magic, the religion, and the science, which develop out of praxis. The practices are undertaken because man believes that they will bring about the desired results. He sows barley after ploughing the ground, at a certain time of the year, in the belief that this is the way to ensure a crop. He shapes the arrowhead in a certain way and attaches it to a staff of a certain type in the belief that thus prepared it will fly farther and straighter and hit harder. He irrigates trees and plants in dry seasons in the belief that the watering furthers the growth. He ties fronds from the blossom of the male date palm in the blossoms of the female tree in the belief that greater numbers of date will set in the cluster if this procedure is followed. These beliefs are sound, and the practices produce results, although the practices were developed many centuries before there was any science.

Praxis, however, often goes astray. Certain practices that have developed do not produce the results claimed, and the faiths involved in them are fallacious. Tying a red string around a child's neck does not prevent nosebleed. Carrying a horse chestnut or buckeye in the pocket does not ward off rheumatism. Throwing pulverized rock crystal over the women will not bring rain, nor does hanging a live snake up by the tail. Yet these and other rituals have been practiced by many people over a long period.

Some procedures that have long been accepted but are now classed as superstitions may have some validity. Men have long believed that the phases of the moon have an influence on the growth of plants, and some still plant root crops in the dark of the moon and top crops in the full moon. That the moon's phases are related to certain features of plant growth has recently been demonstrated, although the full extent of the influence is not yet known. Science has been curiously negligent in rejecting this superstition without investigation, as it has been in its contemptuous ignoring of many other features of praxis that have turned out to be sound. We need to keep constantly in mind the fact that no legend, superstition, or practice that has been developed normally, and has long persisted, can safely be rejected without examination, for there is in most of these some element of validity, however much mingled with error.

In the development of praxis of important types, the explanation of the way in which the procedures work has been unimportant and the explanations for sound praxis has often been erroneous. An illustration of this is found in the practice of planting wild figs near cultivated figs to promote fertilization of the cultivated figs. Knowing that the date palms, with which a similar procedure is necessary, are of two sexes, ancient peoples assumed that the wild fig was the male tree, the cultivated fig the female. While there is an element of truth in this explanation, it is not true as it stands.

Science, we must remember, is a comparatively late addition to man's armament and has done its best work in the sifting of the great mass of praxis that was built up over the long period of time before science appeared. The function of science is to eliminate superstition from praxis and to extend the accomplishments of praxis.

CHAPTER II

FURTHER CONCEPTS APPLIED TO RELIGION

Among the concepts that have been applied to religion in the attempt to define it or to explain it, there are five, in addition to those discussed in the preceding chapter, which have been often employed. These are: (*a*) morality; (*b*) a system of tabus or inhibitions; (*c*) determined by emotion; (*d*) a process of self-development; and (*e*) founded on, and developed from, the belief commonly called 'animism.'[1]

1. Religion as Morality.—Among the principles involved in various religions are some that we call 'moral'; these have to do with man's relation to his fellow men, rather than with his relations to gods or other 'spirits.' Morality has to do with objects and places only in a secondary way and is the antithesis of self-seeking. Moral principles and moral actions are concerned with the promotion of the welfare of, and justice toward, other persons. Principles and behavior that involve taking advantage of other persons, or recklessness of the welfare of others, are therefore 'immoral.'

The concept of morality as an important characteristic of religion is patent in Christianity, but in the religions of ancient civilization, although the group factor was involved, the welfare of 'neighbors,' as Jesus called them, was not so much emphasized. Buddhism officially emphasized morality, but, like the adherents of other Hindu religions, the Buddhists were interested primarily in their own 'salvation.'

Although scholars have attempted to define religion in terms of morality, their definitions usually involve other features. Matthew Arnold, for example, is quoted as defining religion as 'Morality touched by emotion,' but this phraseology does not certainly make morality the primary characteristic of religion.

[1] Hastings *Ency.* (I: 2) contains articles on the five concepts discussed in this chapter. Some of the articles are divided into several sections, written by different authors; each section dealing with the concept as applied to a particular group of religions. Where religious groups are omitted, references are given to the articles in which the concept is discussed.

The definition of religion ('pure religion') in James 1: 27 comes nearer to a definition of religion in terms of morality alone: 'to visit the fatherless and widows in their affliction, and to keep himself unspotted from the world.' This definition was repudiated by Paul, who declared: 'For by grace are ye saved through faith; and that not of yourselves; it is the gift of God: not of works, lest any man should boast' (Eph. 11: 8–9). Paul is here not merely denying that moral conduct can avail man, but more broadly is claiming that religion of a true sort is something quite apart from 'works.'

Definitions of religion in terms of morality encounter practical obstacles. The fourteen million people of the so-called 'criminal tribes' in southern India, to whom we have referred as worshiping the goddess called Kali, Durga, and Maha Lakshmi, by acts of robbery and murder, raise one obstacle. Human sacrifice in other rituals, such as the crushing of human beings under the car of Juggernaut at Puri, raises difficulties. Tearing living animals apart, as in the rituals of Dionysus in ancient times and in present-day religious rites in southern India, is another obstacle. These cruel features of worship are merely striking examples of a vast number of practices which have been considered immoral or unworthy by Judaism and Christianity, but which are accepted in other religions. In ancient religion, as in savage and barbarous religions of today, the relation between religious tenets and practices, and justice, mercy, and benevolence, has been slight. Gross immorality often consorts with profound piety.

Well, we cannot say that these systems which admit and encourage that which is in civilized lands classed as immorality are not religions. We can say that they are bad religions; but a definition of religion must be more comprehensive. The attempt to define religion in terms of morals exemplifies the fact that, as we have earlier said, definitions of religion are most often definitions of what the definer thinks religion should be, not of religion as it actually is. Modern Christians who define, or characterize, religion as morality are defining their particular religions and excluding from the category the religions of large sections of the population of the globe.

2. **Religion As a System of Tabus or Inhibitions.**—Reinach defines religion in terms of inhibitions. For Reinach, the essential factor in religion—that which makes it religion—is a scruple or a system of scruples, developed in human beings, which restrain

them from doing what they otherwise would do. 'Scruples,' of course, are inhibitions of a particular sort; differing from the inhibitions which are physical restraints, from incapacities due to mental conflicts or bad habits, and from physical disabilities. Stammering is the product of inhibitions, but not necessarily of scruples.

A person who is quite able to steal but who is inhibited or restrained from stealing, either because he assumes that the risk is too great, or because he thinks it is something he ought not to do, is said to be restrained by scruples. If he is restrained by the notion that it is something that 'isn't done,' that it is 'bad form' to do it, his restraint is still classed as a scruple. Such restraints are often called 'tabus.' The act which must not be carried out is a 'tabued' act. If the mental inhibition concerns an object or a place, we say that the object or place is tabu or tabued. Reinach's definition of religion really is in terms of tabu rather than in terms of moral principle, and this is exactly as Reinach intends it to be.

The word 'tabu' (also spelled 'taboo' and 'tapu') is from the language of Polynesian natives of the Marquesas Islands of the South Pacific. The concept to which the word applies, however, is not restricted to the Pacific areas, but is, and has been, world-wide. It signifies inhibition or restraint of action on grounds that we today would not consider practical, but which savages do consider practical or which ancient peoples considered practical. Certain objects must not be touched. Certain places must not be entered. Certain persons, objects, and places must not even be closely approached. When contact with or approach to a place, person, or object is tabued, the place, person, or object is said to be tabu, the word thus being used as an adjective. It is probable that the term applied first to the objects and then was extended to the acts of contacting or approaching them. We would, however, hesitate to say that every tabu is specifically a religious inhibition.

Inhibitions that are founded on moral principles, or on hygienic principles, are not properly tabus; but those who are enthusiastically for the tabu doctrine have extended the meaning widely in those directions. No one, so far as I know, has extended the concept to physical inhibitions. A man in jail, or one suffering from a serious disease or a broken leg, has his activity inhibited; but these inhibitions would not be called tabus.

If the concept of tabu is to be employed, the term must be defined
with care. If we agree that tabu is an interdiction that has no
moral basis, nor any other practical basis, we save ourselves from
a great deal of confusion. This does not contradict the fact that
peoples who have observed tabus have believed that the inhibitions
had practical bases. Here as elsewhere we distinguish between valid
principles and superstitions, not from the point of view of superstitious persons, but from that of scientific examination, or of
validity of praxis. Where a tabu is generally observed, it can be
called a 'convention'; but behind the convention there is a motive
that the observers of the tabu consider highly practical, the motive
based on the notion or belief that the tabued act or object or person
possesses a power or potency that may be dangerous.

In ancient Greece there were certain enclosures that no one
could enter. The magic power exerted by the place was deadly.
Certain other enclosures could be entered by a specially consecrated
person, but not by the public. The priestly consecration protected
the priest from the evil effects. A similar system of tabus applied
to Solomon's temple and probably also to the Phoenician temples
after which Solomon's was patterned. In Solomon's temple there
was a court of the gentiles, which anyone could enter, and an inner
court was reserved for the Hebrews. Into the holy of holies, only
the high priest could go, only at certain times, and always with
ritual precaution.

A story that illustrates the deadly power emanating from an
holy object is told in II Samuel 6: 6. When the ark of the convenant
was being taken on a cart to Jerusalem, a man named Uzzah put
his hand on the ark to steady it, and was slain. The power resident
in the ark was effective. To touch the ark was tabued to all persons
except the priest.

In the belief of those who observe tabus, the tabu is practical,
since it is to prevent harm from the tabued place, object, or action.
Violation of a tabu exposes the violator to the danger. Certain
words cannot safely be uttered, since words have power. Names of
certain divinities might be uttered in the proper rituals, but not
otherwise. Usually divinities are referred to not by name, but
by descriptive titles such as 'Baal' or 'Lord.' Names of some
divinities could neither be spoken nor written; the Arcadian goddess
referred to by ancient writers as *Dispoina* (Lady) had a name that
it was forbidden to reveal.

Tabus on foods have been numerous. Adherents of one religion are forbidden to eat certain animals and certain plants or their fruits. The food tabus of the Jews included all animals except those which have cloven hoofs and which also chew the cud. To certain groups of ancient peoples beans were tabu; while for others the bean was permitted as food except in certain circumstances. Animals whose flesh may be permitted as food often are tabu unless the animals are slaughtered in a specific way or unless prescribed rituals are conducted after the slaughter. In no cases can any basis for food tabus that we could consider practical be discovered. Tabus on alcoholic beverages on the other hand, have foundations in practical considerations.

Animals of the species which is the totem of a savage group are sometimes tabu as food; but among some groups, the totem animal may be eaten if the proper ritual is conducted. Attempts to explain food tabus by assuming that tabued food animals or plants were earlier totems of the groups maintaining the tabus have not been successful. That in some cases the tabued animals were sacred animals of peoples in adjacent areas is more plausible, but not all food tabus can be explained in that way.

Among all peoples there are tabus on relations between the sexes. Persons are restrained from marrying within the limits of certain relationships, and coitus within these limits is technically called 'incest.' In some groups maternal cousins may not marry, but paternal cousins may. In other groups, the tabu is reversed. Incest, however defined, is tabu in all groups, and usually this tabu is involved in religion. Are these inhibitions tabus in the true sense, or are they based on practical considerations? Perhaps the answer is that they were originally practical, but eventually some of the inhibitions became mere tabus.

The system of tabus is vast and intricate in all religions, not excluding Protestant Christianity. In considering the universality of tabu, some scholars have seemed to become rabid on the subject and have concluded that all moral rules and principles were merely tabus. Laws forbidding crimes also sink in the estimation of these scholars to the level of tabus. This extension of the meaning of the concept of tabu may be logical, but it does not give much help in our problem. Calling all restraints and inhibitions by the same name leaves us worse off than when we have different names for different types. The important question concerns the distinction between the inhibitions that might properly be called religious, and the inhibitions of other sorts, if any.

If there are restraints that may properly be called religious, the important question is: How did these inhibitions arise? We have not arrived at a fundamental concept of religion by referring it to tabu in a superficial way.

The most obvious defect in the explanation of religion, or the definition of religion, as a system of inhibitions is that the concept, although it may apply superficially to savage religions and to a certain extent to ancient religion, does not cover modern religion. It ignores the positive motivations to conduct which are apparent in Christianity and which are not entirely absent from ancient Western religions. The motivations are not altogether inhibitory. The obligation of the Christian, for example, is not simply to refrain from conduct of certain sorts, but also, in a more important way, to engage in certain activities. Even the Greek had not only the duty to refrain from acts of sacrilege, but also the duty to engage in acts of worship. In savage and barbarous religions, the positive features may be less conspicuous than in civilized religions, but careful examination reveals their presence.

There are many tabus in modern society that can hardly be called religious. It is tabu, for example, in polite society, for a man to wear his hat in the house, to put his feet on the table, or to spit upon the floor. If we follow the common opinion of the group, we do not call these 'religious' tabus. If, however, we make a distinction between religious and nonreligious tabus, it is evident that there must be, in religion, something more basic than tabu.

3. Religion As Determined by Emotion.—Emotion, in the popular sense of the term, seems to be a feature of every religion, and a religious person may manifest at different times every emotion that is included in the popular lists. Popular usage, however, makes little distinction between an emotion and an affect (a 'feeling'), so we may list illustratively affects and emotions that religious persons experience, regardless of the psychological distinction. A partial list would include excitement, depression, pleasure, reverence, anger, fear, hope, sorrow, dread, disgust, approbation, pity, and horror.

Certain philosophers, such as the Stoics in ancient times and Spinoza in the Christian Era, have aimed at the repression of emotion—as if emotion could be ruled out of human life! These philosophers, however, aimed at a state or condition of serenity or tranquillity, which after all is merely another emotion to be listed. Emotion (in the loose popular sense of the term) is inescapable in the religious experience and is involved in experience that may be nonreligious.

There are, in short, no feelings and no emotions that are not experienced by devotees of one religion or another; and in most of the religions of the world the whole gamut of feelings and emotions is involved, each emotion or feeling being experienced in appropriate circumstances.

It is probably recognition of the pervasiveness of emotion in religious experience that has led some students of religion to seek for the essential feature of religion in emotion or to assume, as Matthew Arnold did, that emotion is one of the basic characteristics of religion. Those who have attempted to form a concept of religion on this basis are faced with a dilemma, one or the other horn of which inevitably impales them. Either they must select a particular emotion, or specific group of emotions, as identifying religion; or they must admit that the presence of any emotion in a total experience makes the experience religious. If the first horn is chosen there arises the difficulty of finding the specifically religious emotion or emotions. If the second horn is chosen, the significance of the term 'religion' is lost, since all phases of human life are 'touched with emotion.'

Definers who adopt emotion as the differentia of religion seem to have vaguely in view some particular sort of emotion, rather than emotions of miscellaneous sorts. Matthew Arnold, for example, would hardly have accepted morality combined with hatred, disgust, or even with reluctance as religion. Yet without further qualification, the man who acts morally, while hating or despising the object of his behavior or loathing the moral conduct itself, would have to be accepted, in accordance with Arnold's definition, as acting religiously, and his system of belief, action, and emotion would constitute a religion.

The early attempts to work out a psychology of religion, without necessarily formally defining religion, have proceeded as if some particular group of emotional expressions or experiences, such as those attending conversion, hold the secret of religion. These attempts have been unsuccessful, and it is evident that religion is broader in its scope than these isolated topics. Neither in conversion (which is not by any means a feature of all religions, nor of all religious lives even under those religions in which conversion is a salient factor); nor in the emotional stresses of campmeetings and revivals; nor in the conflicts and struggles of tortured childhood; nor in the repressions of love-starved celibacy; nor in the erotic gratification of some ancient and some present-day religions is there to be found anything essential to religion. The fear of hell, the longing for heaven, the thrill of adoration of divinity, the pain and anguish of self-mutilation, the worry about the 'soul,' the complacent self-satisfaction of being 'saved,' the enthusiasm for the church, and the hatred of infidels and heretics, all are accidents of religion, not essentials, however characteristic certain of these emotional states may be of this or that particular religion.

The campmeeting and the revival, the *sacti* worship (ritual coitus) of certain Hindu sects, the frenzy of those who seek death under the sacred car or of those who castrated themselves in Syria and Asia Minor in olden times, the excitement of whirling dervishes, crusades, persecutions, and witch burnings—these are indeed important materials for the study of religion. None of these phenomena, however, can be considered as characteristic of religion as a whole or as occurring in the life of every religious person. Many religionists today avoid all of them. Even the study of these phenomena, if they are isolated from broader aspects of religion, is useless. They are important only when considered in connection with other phases of religion that are free from them and in connection with social and economic conditions. These manifestations of religion may tentatively be considered as phases of religious pathology or abnormality; and they can be understood only through a sound understanding of the more normal phases of religious life. It is notorious that the attempt of Freud and others to construct a psychology of the abnormal mind in ignorance of normal psychology has been a ghastly failure. The attempt to arrive at a psychology of religion by proceeding from the abnormal alone was doomed inevitably to the same failure.

These are the reasons why the initial interest of psychologists in the study of the abnormal phases of religion has sharply declined. Perhaps it has declined too far.

When we approach the topic of emotion psychologically, instead of popularly, we find still more definite reasons for the refusal to consider emotion as the core of religion.

In some of the writings of those who cultivate fields that are marginal, or subordinate, to psychology, such as educational psychology, psychology of adolescence, physiological psychology, psychology of religion, etc., you will find concepts of emotions as distinct entities, processes, or states, contrasted with intellectual processes or states. Some authors, for example, search for the influence of emotional factors in human personality and in human development, as if these factors were distinct from the cognitive factors, perception and thought. This is, of course, the modern popular point of view, and the history of its growth during the eighteenth and nineteenth centuries is an interesting topic for study.

Psychologists, however, have no such illusions or misconceptions about emotions. The conception of emotions now, as among the important psychologists from the Stoics down, is quite different from the popular view. We cannot set emotion over against cognition, because the characteristics of emotions that distinguish one 'emotion' from another, are cognitive, that is, they are perceptions or thoughts. Failure to grasp the psychological point of view regarding emotion is the one weakness in the theory of emotions of William James and to a less extent in the theory of Lange (whose theory is linked with that of James as the 'James-Lange' theory of emotions). It is also the outstanding weakness of Cannon and lesser opponents of the James-Lange theory.

The application of the psychological consideration of the emotions to the problems of religion is relatively simple. Admitting that emotion is a characteristic of religion, as it is of life in all its departments, the emotion that is religious is the emotion characterized by religious thoughts, including religious belief; and emotion determined by cognitive processes which are not religious is not religious emotion. The religious emotion, in other words, is emotion engendered by religious beliefs; and the differentiae of religion are not to be found in emotion except insofar as emotion is based on belief.

Emotion, as popularly referred to, involves bodily conditions or changes. Yet when we consider fear, for instance, we find that the 'expressions' vary much from individual to individual and in the same individual at different times; and it is evident that emotions cannot be identified by their expressions. Further, attempts to differentiate emotions by their 'feeling' characters eventually show themselves to be equally impossible.

4. Religion as Self-development.—Self-development is sometimes presented as the essential part of religion. 'Development of character' is another phrase for this concept. The concept, in whatever terms it is presented, is a nebulous one, as nebulous as the concept of 'personality' that has of recent years become fashionable in pseudo-psychological circles. I do not know whether any serious attempt has been made to define religion in terms of personality, but certainly a lot of loose talk about personality and its religious importance seems to have crept into popular discourses on religion.

The term 'self-development,' like the term 'personality,' covers a multitude of sins. Often, it is merely another name for morality or for the living of a progressively more moral life. Religion, as self-development or character development in this sense of terms, is merely religion identified with ethics, which we have considered briefly and must consider further before we are through. There is, however, another slant to the self-development concept, in which the self is one or another sort of 'soul,' and the development is the 'saving' of the soul. When religion is presented in this way, it is an intensely selfish thing. In the extreme form, religion has been urged on man, or certain forms of religion have been urged, as a means of saving his own little soul from hell or ensuring its entrance into heaven. This appeal to pure selfishness has been prominent in Christianity since the second century at least, although it is significantly absent from the teachings of Jesus as reported in the synoptic gospels. Morality, as well as worship and other rituals, have been recommended as means to selfish ends. One is bidden to do good works, to be just, kind, generous, not because these things are worthy ends in themselves, but because, by doing them, one gains merit for oneself, saves one's own soul. Whether this sort of selfish seeking is more noble (or less ignoble) than conforming to religious rules for the money there is in it or than going to church regularly because it helps one's business has been doubted by many; but the evaluation of different forms of selfishness is not an important matter for us at this point. It is merely necessary to note well that religion actually has been conceived in terms of self-seeking as its essential feature.

Archer brands Plato's definition of religion as one of the lowest in type. Plato said that religion is merely wanting something from the gods and taking what steps one supposes will be successful to get it from them. We shall have occasion to notice later that in religion man wants many things, if not exactly from gods, at least from some 'power' that can supply these wanted things. Plato was not defining an ideal or admirable religion but was describing religion as it actually appeared; and Plato was not so far wrong as Archer seems to think. The self-development or self-preservation or self-advancement we are speaking of is one particular item of benefit that some modern groups of religious people seem to make paramount. It does not appear that even Plato had in mind such an utterly selfish religion as is held by these groups.

5. **Animism As the Basis for Religion.**—The Latin word for life is *anima*, which means 'life' in the physiological sense, that is, the zoological sense, since this second term is derived from the Greek *zoe*, which meant life considered as a process and which was distinguished from *psyche*. We might expect, therefore, to find that the word 'animism' applies to a doctrine in which life is made fundamental or basic, but that is not what the word means.

The Latin word *anima* meant literally 'breath' and was applied to the life process because it is evident that life is dependent on breathing. Later, *anima* came to mean a daimon, or a 'soul' of some sort; and eventually it designated the soul invented by Plato by combining the old life principle called the *psyche* with the ego, or subject of conscious experience for which Homer's term was *thumos*, and perhaps with the ghost.

The theory of animism, as the doctrinal or credential source of religion, is the theory that 'primitive' man endowed not only the lower animals, but also inanimate objects, with a soul of one of the several sorts attributed to human beings. Sometimes it is implied that the soul so ascribed is the Platonic soul, or at least a life soul—an implication that makes inanimate objects really animate. This soul ascribed to animals and objects is often called a 'spirit,' which does not change the implication, since spirit derives from the Latin word *spiritus*, another name for breath.

The spirit or soul that is involved in animism is a personal entity, which has the human characteristics of perception, feeling, and thought and which further is capable of action, producing effects in the physical world. This indwelling entity is sometimes designated simply as the 'indweller,' but this term is as ambiguous as is the word soul; for there are indwellers of various sorts in the folklores of different cultural groups. At any rate, those who hold to the animism theory of the origin of religion really mean that religion developed from the ascription of a personal entity to animals, plants, and objects commonly classed as inanimate.

That savages do personify objects and organisms, and that our cultural ancestors personified them, is true. Children today are given to personifying objects and animals, although we cannot assume that a child would personify an object if the personification were not suggested by an adult.

Ancient peoples personified rocks, springs, rivers, and mountains; they personified the thunder and the lightning, the winds and the rain. Eventually they personified abstractions, such as victory and justice. A long process of religious development, however, preceded these personifications.

The doctrine that religion developed out of animism is clearly a product of the pseudo-anthropology which assumed that savages are primitive in the literal meaning of the term; that their ideas and their cultures present the aspect of man at or near the beginning of human development. When we grasp the fact that the savage cultures have gone through a process of development as long as that through which civilization has gone, we are protected from this pseudo-anthropology. No intelligent ethnologist today assumes that any savage culture represents a stage in the development through which our culture has passed, any more than a psychologist would assume that a child of inferior mentality represents a stage in the development of a normal individual. Savage cultures may have developed from the same primitive conditions from which civilization developed, but the savage cultures have developed differently.

That the notion of an indwelling spirit, or soul, in the human being is a comparatively late development is evident from the stages of development of our own cultural ancestors. Religion, it seems clear, began its development long before this notion of a personified appurtenance was achieved. It seems probable, moreover, that a certain stage in religious development must be reached before the notion of a soul or spirit is possible. Religion has, in many cases, involved the personification of animals and inanimate objects, although modern religion is free from such personifications. Personification, however, is about the most unlikely factor to call upon as the foundation of religion.

Reinach, who falls back on animism at times, when other explanatory factors elude him, contradicts the animism doctrine in his explanations of totemism, for he points out that the totem animal is at first not any individual animal, but the whole species. That the early totemists personified the animal species as a species is a notion that Reinach would be the first to say is preposterous.

CHAPTER III

CONCEPTS INVOLVED IN RELIGION

In Chaps. I and II we have discussed certain concepts that have been elaborated by scholars and applied by them to religion in the attempt to define it or to explain it. Those concepts are not necessarily formed or adopted by the adherents of any religion. A person may have faith without forming the concept of faith or attempting to discover what faith is. He may engage in ritual, with no concept of ritual. He may be restrained by tabus, while having no conception of the nature of the tabus. In fact, both in religion and in secular life, the average person is carrying on his processes of thought and action, with no regard to the concepts that could be applied to his performances. Those concepts are comparable to the concept of gravitation, which a mechanic does not need to consider in his practical work, although he deals with phenomena that may properly be subsumed under it.

There are, on the other hand, certain concepts which develop in religion, or in most religions, and which are employed by the religious person. It is true that these concepts have been elaborated and clarified by scholars, but they still represent the crude notions of the ordinary religious person. They may be concepts that he accepts as valid, or they may be concepts that he rejects; but in either case, he employs them in his thinking. These concepts are, for the most part, confused notions, and scholars have not completely clarified them. Our task is to examine them and attempt to put them in order.

Concepts that occur in different religions may have different forms in these religions. Such concepts, accordingly, are aids to the comparison of different religions, and critical study of the several concepts is indispensable. Definitions that have been presented are often in terms of one or more of these concepts, and the definitions depend on the relative emphasis placed on the concepts explicitly or implicitly. The study of the evolution of religion is, in part, the study of the origins and the modifications of these concepts.

The list of concepts discussed in this chapter is presented not as complete, but as including those which are of the greatest importance and which occur over a wide range of religions. These concepts are of (*a*) divinities, (*b*) the cosmos, (*c*) daimons or 'spirits,' (*d*) manas or 'powers,' (*e*) souls, (*f*) metamorphosis, (*g*) sin, (*h*) the 'other world,' (*i*) salvation, (*j*) mystical experience, (*k*) holiness.[1]

Having dealt with these concepts in a way suitable for our present purposes, we shall not then be through with them but may revert to them from time to time as we proceed and may further elaborate some of them.

1. Concepts of Divinities.—Most religions, in certain stages of their development, postulate a god, or gods and goddesses. Belief in a single god is conventionally called 'monotheism,' while belief

---

[1] References in Hastings (I: 2), which are useful starting points for study on the eleven concepts listed, are as follows.

1. *Divinities.*
   'God,' in fifteen sections.
2. *The Cosmos.*
   'Cosmogony and Cosmology,' in nineteen sections.
3. *Daimons.*
   'Demons and Spirits,' in twenty sections.
4. *Mana.* Article by R. R. Marett.
5. *Souls.*
   'Soul,' in ten sections.
   'Death and the Disposal of the Dead.'
6. *Metamorphosis.* Article by J. A. MacCulloch.
7. *Sin.*
   'Sin,' in fifteen sections.
   'Original Sin,' by F. R. Tennant.
   See also 'Sin' in *Encyclopedia Britannica,* 11th ed.
8. *The Other World.*
   'The State of the Dead,' in twelve sections.
   'Blest, The Abode of the,' in twelve sections.
9. *Salvation.*
   Article, in nine sections.
   'Soteriology,' by D. Phillips.
10. *Mystical States.*
    'Mysticism,' in fourteen sections.
    'Mysteries,' in seven sections.
11. *Holiness.*
    Article, in five sections.

The reference I: 2 (and similar references throughout the text) is to the classification in the Appendix, pp. 345 *ff.*, where further bibliographical references are given.

in several divine beings is called 'polytheism.' There are types of religion, however, that are intermediate between these extremes, which are called 'dualisms.' Dualistic religions postulate a good or beneficent divinity and an evil personage antagonistic to the good god—an evil divinity, in fact. Zoroastrianism, the religion of the ancient Persians, now represented only by the religion of the Parsees, assumed a good god, Ahura Mazda, and an evil god, Ahriman. Satan plays an important role in Islam and may have been important in one or more of the Syrian religions from which Judaism developed.

In dualistic religions, Satan, the arch devil, is subordinate to the good god, although he persists as an evil power in spite of the beneficent divinity. No religion can be said to be strictly montheistic if it assumes a continuing power or person of superhuman status, who is an enemy or rival of the good god. Christians who accept Satan as a real power cannot be said to be strict monotheists.

Christianity further deviates from strict monotheism, in its orthodox sects, by postulating a trinity; a postulation that theologians have endeavored to harmonize with monotheism. Judaism, on the other hand, is completely monotheistic.

The god of Judaism is definitely male, and the gods of Islam and of Christianity are officially male. In the early period of Christianity, there was controversy over the sex of the Holy Ghost. Some of the church fathers contended that the Holy Ghost should be female, but those who held the male view won out. Since the symbol of the Holy Ghost was the dove, which was an accepted symbol of pagan female divinities, it would appear that the original notion was that this factor in the Trinity was feminine.

In polytheistic religions there are usually female divinities (goddesses) as well as male divinities (gods). But in Brahmanism, and in most other Hindu religions, Brahma, the supreme god, is impersonal and therefore neuter. From the point of view of highly developed religions, it may seem absurd to ascribe sex to a divinity, and this ascription is intelligible only when one considers the actual process of creation of divinities. Divinities, in the stream of development we are considering, were first female, as we shall point out later, and the change from female to male has been a slow process, not always accepted popularly even when confirmed officially. It is not to be assumed, however, that any divinities began as personal beings.

Although the Christian god is officially male, it is difficult to deny the divinity of the Virgin Mary in Catholic Christianity. To many Roman Catholics, in fact, the trinity that is designated as *JMJ* (Joseph, Mary, Jesus) is more real and more venerated than the official Trinity of the church.

In polytheistic religions, the gods usually differ from one another in respect to their benevolence and malevolence, although all have their malevolent aspects—avenging neglect and disrespect and even indulging in cruel whims and in deceit. The God of monotheism also has his dark side, punishing the innocent for the sins of the guilty and visiting the sins of the fathers upon the children to the third and fourth generation.

In moderately late stages of religious development, gods are personal beings, having attributes similar to those of human beings. Being sexed, they have sexual intercourse with one another and with human beings. As the religions evolve further, the divinities become male and tend to delegate their sexual functions to their human representatives, the priests.

In some forms of Christianity, God is an impersonal power, just as in Hinduism Brahma, the supreme god, is impersonal (as well as neuter), being the total reality of the universe. Since the impersonal God is a late development in Christianity, and since Brahmanism claims to be a very old religion, it would appear that there is a progress toward impersonalism as religions become older and more highly developed. This may account for the relatively slight importance of gods in Confucianism, Taoism, and Shinto. It may be that religion progresses from impersonal polytheism, through personal polytheism to monotheism, and terminates in impersonal monotheism.

One of the major tendencies in definitions of religion has been to make belief in a god or in gods essential, to define religion in terms of belief in gods. Such definitions would exclude the original Buddhism, which denied gods or which at least insisted that they are unimportant. Several other unorthodox Hindu religions and several orthodox ones are atheistic in form, although they all seem to assume an impersonal world power or world law, similar to Brahma. If, however, belief in such a universal law system (which the Greeks called the *logos*) is a sufficient characteristic of religion, then there is no clear distinction between religion and science, for science certainly is based on the hypothesis of universal natural law, and some scientists appear to make this hypothesis into a religious belief.   This point will be elaborated in the following section, to which it properly belongs.

2. Concepts of the Cosmos.—If a god is conceived, not as a personal being, but as an impersonal force or system of laws, or principle of reality underlying the universe, religion based on that concept *ipso facto* involves a cosmic principle, or power, which to some extent explains or appears to explain the operations of nature. Religions that involve personal gods, or a personal god, usually involve beliefs about the nature of the world, the secrets of its operations, and its beginnings.   Orthodox Christianity and Judaism, for example, hold that the world is not only regulated and controlled by God, but also that it was created by Him.   In ancient Greek religion, on the contrary, the cosmos, or total universe, is primary, and in the process of its evolution gods appear and flourish, and eventually these disappear and new gods take their places.   Although 'Zeus' and other gods of the classical era had power to control nature, they were themselves subordinate to the great plan or *logos* of the universe. In orthodox Hindu religions, Brahma, the impersonal and divine world principle, is eternal, the other and personal gods having developed from the eternal nature of the universe and being subordinate to it.   While there may have been religions that involved no conceptions of the nature of the cosmos, it is difficult to find them.

On this account, there have been definitions of religion in terms of conceptions of law and order in the universe.   Man, it is supposed, for practical reasons or on account of mere curiosity, attempts to understand the world, its principles of operation, and the laws governing its changing phenomena; and this attempt to explain or understand the universe, or its outstanding features, such as the weather and the growth of animals and plants, is said to be 'religion.'

Some scholars, on the other hand, have attempted to exclude beliefs about nature, and natural law, from religion, classing beliefs of this order under the headings of mythological or magical beliefs, or as philosophy, or as scientific hypotheses.   It is obvious that an attempt to define religion in terms of beliefs about natural law, or of investigations into causal relationships in nature, leaves no distinction between religion, magic, philosophy, and science and is, therefore, useless.   On the other hand, it would seem quite unjustifiable to decide arbitrarily that these conceptions of the nature and origin of the universe, and of its operations, which we find so widely embedded in religions, are extraneous factors and not actually features of the religions in which they occur.

3. **The Concept of Daimons.**—Our word 'daimon' is a transliteration of the Greek word that designated a superhuman person, that which is sometimes called a 'spirit,' but with less precision, as the latter often implies a life principle or else an aeriform implication. The term daimon applies properly to a supernatural person (supernatural from our modern point of view), who is below the rank of divinity. Daimons are supposed to have an integrated conscious life, which includes perceptions, thoughts, feelings, purposes, and memory. In these respects, daimons are similar to human persons, but they possess certain characteristics that human beings do not. The daimon, for example, is invisible and can penetrate into a material object without displacing any part of the object.

These daimons (the plural form 'daimonen' is also used) are not necessarily 'souls,' although some kinds of souls are included under the term. In various religions, the daimons are classified in several categories, in accordance with the powers and other characteristics attributed to them. In Christianity, the daimons fall usually into three classes: angels, human souls, and demons or devils. In Arabic Islam, there are, in addition to these three classes, a class of *jinn* (singular, *jinni*), who are further subclassified. The term *jinn* is sometimes used to include angels and devils, but the usage does not seem authentic.

Angels are usually assumed to be good daimons, that is, to be favorably disposed toward men. Devils are always supposed to be bad daimons—to be inimical toward men. In Greek mythology, as systematized by Hesiod, there was no clear division of daimons into good and bad, but some were more benevolent, or less malevolent, than others, while some had no contacts with the human race and presumably no attitudes toward human beings.

In the conceptions of Islam, and of orthodox Christianity, there are angels of high rank (archangels) and, subordinate to these, angels of one or more lower ranks. In ancient Syrian and Babylonian religions, and in the Hebrew mythology, there were angels (or good daimons), or several grades. Devils also are commonly assumed to be of various grades of power, from Satan, the chief devil, down to the minor devils called 'imps.'

In Greek usage, the term daimon was sometimes extended to include the gods and goddesses, just as Christians sometimes say,

"God is a spirit." On this account, translators of Greek writings often render the word daimon as 'god' or 'goddess'; but this rendering seems, in most cases, unwarranted. When a Greek writer definitely meant a god, he seems always to have used the word *theos* (plural *theoi*) in the proper case form, the word daimon being used to designate a supernatural being of lesser rank than divinity, or when there was uncertainty as to whether the being was or was not a god.

The extension of meaning, comparable to that of the Greek daimon, is found more widely in the sacred writings of the ancient Persians, where the term *ahura* (or *asura*) was applied to the gods, as well as to good daimons, while the term *deva* was applied to the evil god as well as to mere 'demons.' In Hinduism the same class names are used, with the meanings reversed; *deva* meaning a god as well as a benevolent daimon (although some of the gods are predominantly malevolent), while the term *asura* means always a demon. As can readily be seen, the distinction between good and bad daimons is by no means as clear in Hinduism as it is in Islam and in orthodox Christianity.

Daimons are sometimes male, sometimes female, although possibly there are neuter daimons also. In Christian mythology, the angels appear to be considered as male, although some theologians have been doubtful on the point; but in Syrian, Babylonian, and Arabian mythologies of the ancient period, there seem to have been male, female, and neuter angels. Satan, the chief devil of Christianity, is assumed as male; but among devils of lower rank both sexes have been recognized. Among these are the *incubi*, male devils who creep into the beds of women, and the *succubi*, female devils who seek the beds of men. During the Middle Ages, incubi and succubi were objects of widespread faith, and doubtless they are still believed in by some Christians, although I have met with but two persons who claim to have had personal experience with these entertaining devils. No comprehensive modern study of available information concerning the sex of daimons of the various religions has been made, so far as I know.

That daimons both good and bad may enter into or 'possess' human beings and the lower animals, has been a tenet of many religions. According to some Greek views, which possibly were late in developing, the tenancy could be lifelong; but the more common doctrine was that the possession was temporary. In Christianity, and in Judaism, the possessing daimon was always a devil; but in Greek mythology possession by a benevolent daimon, or by a god, was assumed to occur. Possession by a god was ascribed to priestesses who delivered oracles and to other persons who were subject to epileptic, or epileptoid, seizures. Hence epilepsy was called by ancient peoples 'the divine disease,' or 'the sacred disease.' A typical case of devil possession related in the New Testament is that of the Gadarene man who was possessed by a legion of devils simultaneously, which were cast out and entered into a herd of swine (*Mark*, 5: 1–20).

In the early centuries of the Christian Era, there was widely held a doctrine that every human being was throughout life possessed by a *genius*, (the Latin term equivalent to the Greek *daimon*), which guided him. From this notion developed the use in modern languages of the word 'genius' to designate a person of extraordinary talent or the talent itself. The earlier assumption that unusual mental ability was contributed by the person's daimon was thus carried over into modern phraseology. At one Christian period, the belief arose that each person was possessed by two daimons, a good one, or 'guardian angel,' and an 'evil genius.' Accordingly, we still speak of a person's evil genius. This doctrine of guidance by a daimon was derived from Plato, who adopted it from earlier Pythagoreans.

Daimons of some kinds have been associated closely with serpents. The Arabic jinn, when they become visible, usually appear as serpents, and any serpent may be suspected of being a jinni. This association seems to have been common in Levantine religions and may have been responsible for the reverence accorded serpents by Hindus. There seems to have been a similar association among the Greeks, for, aside from the serpent gods, the gods and demigods (heroes) often appeared in serpent form.

Daimons, such as the jinn, have also been associated with the air or the wind. The Arabs assume that a whirlwind is produced by a jinni in travel, and the performances of the whirling dervishes may be motivated by the ancient superstition. It is not without significance that the word 'spirit' is derived from the Latin *spiritus*, which means 'air' or 'breath'; and that *anima*, from which our word 'animal' is derived, also means 'breath.' Our word 'ghost,' like the German *Geist*, traces back to an old Germanic root word for 'air' or 'vapor.'

The concepts of daimon, ghost, and life stuff have been sadly confused with one another. The doctrine of 'animism,' as we have pointed out earlier, took its unfortunate name from *anima*, not in its proper sense of 'life stuff,' but in the sense of 'daimon.' Animism actually is the theory that religion originated in the belief in daimons. It would have been much less confusing if Tylor had called his theory 'daimonism' or even 'spiritism.'

A generation ago, the theory that religion commenced in, and grew out of, the belief in daimons was widely accepted; but it is now generally admitted that a belief in daimons is not essential to religion, however widely it may be involved in various religions. It should also be pointed out that a belief in daimons presupposes a considerable development of religion, which must have occurred before the belief in daimons could arise. For the first point, it is sufficient to note that many devout Christians believe in neither angels nor devils nor any other daimons. As to the second point, considerations will be brought in later.

4. The Concept of Mana, or Power.—Persons, animals, plants, and inanimate objects influence other organisms and objects. In the vernacular, we say that one thing has the 'power' to aid, injure, or otherwise affect another. Powers of sorts that we, from our point of view, call 'supernatural,' or, if we accept them as real, 'divine,' have been features of almost every religion, civilized, semicivilized, and savage. We prefer at present to call 'powers' which we consider to be supernatural by the term 'manas.'

Gods and daimons are conceived as having power to produce effects on man and animals and on the physical operations of the universe. In ancient Western religions, the gods produced, or controlled, the thunder and the lightning, the rain, and all the other phenomena that we lump together as 'the weather' and discuss under the topic of meteorology.

The gods made trees and plants to grow and fish and animals to reproduce. The gods controlled the waves and tides of the sea; they controlled the flowing of rivers and the running of springs. They made men to prosper; they afflicted men with divers diseases and might cure them. The God of Christianity exercises all the powers of the pagan divinities, and more; for he is credited with having created the entire universe, which the pagan gods were not. The God of Christianity, moreover, has power to raise human 'souls' to heaven or damn them to hell. Allah of the Mohammedans has the same power, but in older religions the gods were less influential in respect to the various appurtenances that survived man's death. These are but illustrations of the manifold powers ascribed to gods. Daimons, on a lesser scale, have power to affect human life and in a limited way to modify the course of nature.

To one who rejects gods and daimons, but for whom the world is regulated in accordance with immutable law, there is still the world power, which is in all or above all. Whether man takes a religious attitude toward the world power or a scientific attitude (whatever the difference may be), the power is nevertheless recognized. This world power was recognized, as we have pointed out, by pagan religions and by philosophies developed out of them, as superior to the powers of the gods. This world power was called by the ancient Mediterranean peoples by names that we translate by the English words 'fate,' 'necessity,' 'nature,' or the 'Logos.' Man, in conflict with the gods, might beat them at their own games, or at least might give the divinities trouble in accomplishing their ends; but man could not defeat nature, or evade or impede its operations. Modern science has adopted from the ancient philosophies the concept of infrangible natural law and of uncontrollable cosmic processes; and some scientists have subsumed the cosmic principles under the concept of determinism.

The terms 'power' and 'powers,' as we have employed them in the preceding paragraphs, include influences, or potentialities, of three sorts, which it is well to distinguish. There are influences and potentialities that are capable of demonstration by practical procedures or by scientific tests. These influences and potentialities we may call 'physical,' or 'natural' powers. There are, on the other hand, powers which are assumed, or in which men believe, which are not demonstrably real, and to these we may apply a term that has been adopted into English and that may accordingly be treated as an English word, namely, 'manas' (singular, 'mana') introduced into European languages by Codrington.

Manas, however, are of two sorts, magical manas and religious manas. Magical manas are those powers which are believed in by some persons, but which have been proved nonexistent by practical or by scientific tests or which scientific tests have never yet found to be existent. The powers claimed by mind readers and spiritualistic mediums qualify as magical manas, since careful tests always fail to certify these manas as real.

Religious manas include those which have received wide credence, but which are by the nature of their conceptions not capable of being subjected to scientific tests or even to practical examination. The powers ascribed to the gods are illustrations of religious manas.

Concepts of sin and of tabu have been dominated in the past by the concept of mana. External sin is a taint or injury inflicted on a person by a god, a daimon, or some animal, plant, or object, which has the requisite mana. An object or a place is tabu because there is a deadly mana resident in and radiating from it. Certain acts are tabu because of the manas inherent in the acts, not necessarily manas of any gods or daimons. Spoken words, especially names of persons and gods, exercise manas that may be injurious.

The powers (manas) of gods and daimons and influences exerted by inanimate objects and human beings in these ways may properly be called supernatural, whether we regard them as magical or whether we accept them as real. The term 'supernatural,' however, may be misleading, since no peoples who accepted manas that we call 'magical' considered them as other than natural traits or properties.

Certain men and women are possessed of manas of magical sorts. Magicians and witches who cause persons to sicken or who can heal them, who can change themselves into animals, or who in various minor ways can control the processes of the physical world obviously have the manas that are adequate for these performances. 'Holy men' are men who have mana radiating from them and are therefore dangerous to oppose and even dangerous to touch. The efficacy of the manas of holy men is retained in some sects of Christianity in the laying on of hands to transmit religious authority or to heal the sick.

The line between the powers that we consider to be natural and the manas that are magical is a changing line. With progress in civilization, many powers that were considered to be natural become mere manas of superstition. A generation or two ago, physicians administered many drugs to alter the course of disease and to heal patients. Some of these drugs (quinine, for instance) are still used, since the powers ascribed to them have been certified. Many others are no longer employed, since their alleged powers have turned out to be mere manas. Some drugs, on the other hand, which were once supposed to be merely armaments of magic, have turned out to have the powers ascribed to them. The plant from which ephedrine was extracted is an illustration. Another illustration of a change from the magical to the natural is the verification of what was once regarded as an Arab superstition: the belief that mosquitoes, by their bites, communicate malarial fevers.

No matter where we draw the line between the natural and the supernatural, we must admit that there are powers which are real. Electricity has the power to light our houses and turn the wheels of our machinery; and we commonly refer to it by the simple word 'power.' Every man has varied powers—to walk, to run, to talk, and to digest food. Actions and words have power of a natural sort. The action of the pitcher sends the ball through the air; the word you utter may cause another man to halt and turn around. The power of whispered scandal may bring ruin to its victim, and verbal propaganda has ruined nations. The savage and ancient conception of mana is merely an extension into the region of phantasy of the concept of powers that have been obvious to all human beings.

Beliefs in powers exercised by persons and objects are found in all religions, and sometimes it is difficult to decide whether these powers are mere manas (figments of magic) or concepts of religious faith in the proper sense. The concept of power is involved in all science, as well as in praxis. Fortunately, in studying religion from the psychological point of view, we are not interested in deciding whether a belief is a true belief or a mere superstition.

Through all religion, as well as through science and everyday assumptions about the world, there runs the notion of causation; and we find in religion, at least, all four of the causes described by Aristotle: final causes, formal causes, efficient causes, and material causes. The ascription of a mana to a god, a person, or an object is merely the assumption that it can cause such and such results.

The term 'mana' was borrowed from the language of Melanesian groups who inhabit certain islands in the western and southwestern Pacific. In Melanesian usage, the concept of mana is applied characteristically to the causal efficiency which is believed to reside in animals, in plants, and in inert objects, but it is applied also to the powers of men and of supernatural beings. The savage concept can be understood if we liken the mana-charged object to a wire carrying a high-tension current. The wire is dangerous; if touched carelessly it can harm or kill a person, hence proper procedure in approaching it is essential. Wearing rubber gloves (for lower voltages) or standing on an insulated platform (for higher voltages), one may handle the live wire with impunity. A stone, or a man, charged with a powerful mana must likewise be approached in certain specified ways.

The fact that we consider the savage manas to be mere magical concepts and that we consider the rituals employed to protect one from the manas to be foolish superstitious practices is of no consequence for our consideration of the manas or the rituals.

The characteristics of plant and animal substances that make them suitable foodstuffs and the characteristics of other substances that make them poisonous, are, to the savage, merely manas. From sound experience, magic develops, by unwise extension of a principle of causation that is not understood. While the characteristics of some things are wholly bad, the manas of other things may be used to advantage, if used in the proper ritual way. Just so, certain substances that are poisonous are used as medicines.

The dangerous characteristics of plants and animals are inherent in the species or vary according to conditions of growth or training; but the magical manas may be transmitted from one object to another or acquired by ritual procedures. The mana acquired by an object is not necessarily ascribed to a daimon residing in it (contrary to Reinach's opinion), although the conception of a resident daimon may appear eventually. The error of Reinach, and of some other ethnologists, is due to their assuming that savages are really primitive, in the fundamental sense of the term.

The fetish of the savage, made of bits of animal, plant, and mineral substances, acquires mana in the process of manufacture and remains potent thereafter. Stones may have various manas ascribed to them because of their size, location, or coloration, but when a block of stone is cut into the form of an idol, it acquires new manas. Certain images, for example, have had a mana that, when a barren woman rubs her body against it, enables her to conceive a child. The bones of a saint acquire mana from him, so that after his death the bones have magical healing power. Any object, however, when treated by the appropriate ritual, which in modern religion is called 'blessing' it, acquires mana. Some medals protect travelers; others bring horses 'in the money' at the track—provided they have been properly blessed.

Among ancient peoples, any object which a person habitually carried with him, or which he wore on his body, was assumed to absorb mana from him. On this account, the Greeks and the Romans never used the armor or weapons taken from slain enemies. The weapons had acquired the manas of the enemy warriors, which were inimical to the slayer and could injure him. To counteract their dangerous manas, captured weapons and armor were hung or stacked in the temples of friendly divinities.

The concept of mana, as we have indicated, is indeed world-wide in religion. It was found in ancient religions; it is still prevalent among savages and is found in modern religions of civilized peoples. Many Christians believe in the potencies of amulets, charms, and holy relics. Truly, 'Nothing is lost in religion.'

The belief in manas seems to have arisen through an extension of the concept from potentialities that are demonstrable to potencies that are superstitiously ascribed, the extension being made because ignorant man made no distinction between magical potencies and the actual potencies, which were to him just as mysterious as the manas he invented. The great stone is potent to crush the man on whom it may fall and has the potency to resist the effort to move it. Accordingly, it may have further manas not so easily demonstrable. The tree has the ability to produce fruit that is food for man; therefore, manas that may be helpful or harmful are ascribed to it. Serpents have qualities that make them good food and snakes of some species have a death-dealing power, so manas are ascribed to them. When man starts the enlargement of potentialities beyond the field of demonstrable powers and qualities, there is no limit to the list of manas that may be invented.

Given the concept of mana, and the attribution of important manas to animate and inanimate objects, the eventual development of concepts of daimons and gods may be predicted, unless the culture of the group becomes crystallized too soon. The concepts of divine and semidivine beings and the concepts of 'souls' and of a future life are not starting points for religion, but mark fairly late stages in its development. The concept of tabu, of course, since it is based on the concept of mana, is preceded by the mana concept.

5. The Concept of Souls.—The name 'soul' is freely applied in English to a wide range of concepts, which are found in ancient and modern religions, folklore, and philosophies. Attempts have been made to define religion in terms of belief in souls, but these definitions encounter many difficulties. There are so many kinds of souls involved in the different cults, and these are so confused with one another, not only in popular belief of the present day, but also by anthropologists and historians, that it is seldom clear what kind of soul a definition of religion in terms of soul is presupposing. Furthermore, since the soul concepts of different religions are various, it is exceedingly difficult to demonstrate that any particular kind of soul is essential to religion.

There is perhaps no other term in anthropology, folklore, philosophy, and the discussion of religion that has such confused meanings as has the word soul. Accordingly, it is necessary to proceed cautiously, and laboriously, in discussing the concepts of souls.

We may best begin by presenting some of the various soul concepts that are relatively simple, and then we may consider the various combinations that have been made of these concepts. The only common factor of the various souls is their assumed nature as aspects of the human being, or, we may say for convenience, as human appurtenances, which have been considered as entities, organs, or powers that are relatively isolable from the total human being.

1. The Psyche or Life Principle.—The process of living, or being alive, has been widely assumed to be the result, or the function, of a specific life stuff, or life entity. In early Greek beliefs, this life stuff was designated as the *psyche;* but sometimes it was called *nous.* The original meaning of *psyche* was life, in one of its aspects, life-stuff or life-principle and was so used by Aristotle. The *nous* was the life-stuff considered as something floating in, or dissolved in, the atmosphere; and Aristotle modified this to mean a supernatural influx into human beings who otherwise would be merely natural beings. In later Greek theories, which were adopted by the Hippocratic school of medicine, it was called the *pneuma.* Although the *psyche* was not considered as individuated, or as a property of an individual, translators of classical Greek writings and historians of philosophy render the term too frequently by the word 'soul' and imply that the soul is an individuated human appurtenance.

In ancient Egyptian theories, the life principle, considered as an individuated appurtenance, was called the *Ba.* When in a translation of an Egyptian papyrus or inscription one finds the word soul, it may stand for the *Ba;* but unfortunately, it may be a translation of another Egyptian word, for a quite different appurtenance. In other ancient languages and in savage tongues, various terms are applied to the life principle, which seems to have been conceived of in all religions.

2. *The Ego or Subject of Consciousness.*—The term 'ego' properly designates that which in a human being thinks, perceives, and feels. In Homer's verses, this ego is called the *thumos* (Latinized as *thymus*). The term for the ego in Egypt is somewhat uncertain, but the most probable term is *khu*, which Egyptologists translate sometimes as 'personality.' In Egyptian faith, as in the faiths of almost all ancient and savage peoples, the distinction between the life principle and the ego is maintained.

3. *The personal daimon,* indwelling in a human being, or as we might well say, possessing it. According to the Pythagoreans, such a guardian was assigned to every person, for his lifetime; and Plato accepted this Pythagorean notion.

4. *The Ghost.*—According to Homer, the ghost is an *eidolon* (image) of a human being after death. The image may be visible, but if so, is translucent so that other objects may be seen through it. It is of thin consistency so that if a living person tries to grasp it, his hands pass through it as through a wisp of smoke (see *Odyssey,* Book XI). For the Greeks, moreover, the ghost had a bad odor. It spoke, if at all, in a shrill voice, like the chirping of a bat. Intellectually, a ghost was for the Greeks a feeble-minded person, or the feeble-minded image of a person, deficient in memory, feeble in perception, and thinking as a semiconscious person thinks.

Modern ghosts retain the transparency and unsubstantiality of the ancient *eidola,* but have developed somewhat more robust voices and seem to have lost the offensive odor. It has developed (or some ghosts have) dermal perceptibility, being cold or clammy to the touch. Judging by the messages alleged to be transmitted through mediums, the modern ghost is still as feeble-minded as the ancient ghost. However, modern mediums have not tried the procedure that Homer reports as being effective in restoring intelligence to a ghost, the procedure of providing blood for the ghost to sop up.

5. *The Indweller or External Soul.*—In the superstitions of savages, and in the folklore of European peasants, there is conceived a human appurtenance that may or may not be one of the souls in the list above presented, but which is presented by ethnologists and students of folklore as a soul. This soul has the form of a small animal, such as a mouse, frog, or snake; at least in leaving the person, it takes

such a form. Frazer calls this the 'external soul,' although, since it dwells in a person, we might well call it the 'indweller.'

The indweller may leave the person during sleep; hence, superstitious persons deem it dangerous to awaken a sleeper suddenly, since the indweller might not have time to return. It may leave a person when he yawns; hence, the custom of holding the hand before the mouth when yawning. The nature of the indweller soul is indicated by the belief, common in the folklore of savages and of European peasants, that a person may 'lose his soul' and may still be alive and conscious and may not be aware of any loss. A wizard or medicine man may detect the loss and find the soul and return it to its owner. Obviously this indweller is not the life principle, nor the ego, but is a possession which the owner can lose, just as he may lose his spear, his ax, or his pocketbook. It is usually believed that the person who has lost his soul is vulnerable to environmental features from which the indweller protects him.

In any case, the indweller seems to have the function of a protective daimon, or guardian genius. Frazer would have done better if he had called the indweller the 'separable soul' or the 'dispensible soul' instead of employing the paradoxical designation of 'external soul.'

Expressions that refer to losing one's soul are frequent in Christianity; those who use such expressions are not commonly referring to an indweller that is separable from the body during life, but to a soul similar to that invented by Plato. That the expression harks back to the indweller of early folklore is nevertheless probable.

6. The Man Himself.—In ancient belief, there is a soul that was designated in Greek as *autos*. This *autos* was the man himself, that is, the essential feature of the person. The ancient notion of immortality of a desirable sort did not involve the psyche, or the ghost, but was immortality of the *autos*. In the case of Herakles, his body was burned and his ghost went to the underworld; but Herakles himself (*autos*) was taken to the society of the Olympian gods and goddesses. The appurtenance of the man which was admitted to the Isles of the Blest was likewise the man himself. The ghost persisted, in an underworld existence which was considered deplorable, but the notion of a blessed immortality involved the man himself. Was this an immortality of the ego, or subject of experience? We do not know. All we can say is that the *autos* was the immortal element in some men, for not all men were assumed to attain this blessed state.

These appurtenances—the life principle, the ego, the personal daimon, the ghost, the indweller, and the man 'himself'—are all presented by translators and ethnologists as souls, although ancient peoples did not confuse them. Other appurtenances called souls are found in the superstitions of various peoples and are designated by distinctive names, which only translators confuse. The souls of ancient religions and of the religions of savages are appurtenances that differ from one another in their attributes.

The differences between the different human appurtenances that translators call souls can easily be determined. The ghost, as the Greeks conceived it, did not exist during the person's lifetime, but came into existence at his death. The *thumos*, on the other hand, functioned during life, but nothing is said by Homer about its continuation beyond death; hence the *thumos* may be assumed as ending with the decease of the person. However, since the *thumos* was the ego, or subject of experience, and the 'man himself,' if he survived death, was conscious, there is a possibility that the ego function of the *thumos* persisted.

The life stuff, whether called *psyche* or *nous*, was relatively eternal; but this stuff was constantly being lost be exhalation and in the bodily secretions and constantly replenished by inhaling from the atmosphere, which was the reservoir of *psyche* or *nous*. The personal daimon was conceived as continuing a personal existence before the birth of the person as well as after his death.

Greeks of the Homeric age, and somewhat thereafter, seem to have believed unanimously that every man employed life stuff in his physiological processes, and had a subject of experience; thus, in the confused terminology of translators, a man had two 'souls' during his lifetime. After his death, a third 'soul,' the ghost, appeared. Some Greeks, but apparently not all, believed that the man had a personal daimon, a fourth 'soul.' All ancient peoples further believed that one or more of the many daimons in the universe might temporarily 'possess' a man, in which case, he had an appurtenance, or several of them, of a fifth type, to which the term 'soul' could be applied as reasonably as it is applied to the other appurtenances.

Whether ancient peoples believed in the indweller that Frazer calls the 'external soul,' or whether this 'soul' is a late development, is not certain. The *autos* (the man himself) of a hero, or of a man specially favored by the gods, could survive death; but this was exceptional. Of ordinary human beings only the ghost survived; and this is an obstacle to the identification of the *autos* with the *thumos*.

That combinations of two or more of these souls into a single human appurtenance was conceived is possible. Our first written evidence for such a combination occurs in the dialogues of Plato. Plato's combination of the ego, or one form of ego, with the personal daimon, may reasonably be called the 'Platonic soul'; and since this soul concept was eventually adopted by Christian theologians (with a slight modification), it might be called the 'Christian soul.'

Whether Plato combined the *eidolon* (ghost) with the ego and the daimon is not certain, but Christian concepts of the soul ordinarily make this combination. According to Plato's Socrates in one dialogue, the soul has an eternal existence, both before the birth of the man in whom it dwells, and after his death. All Christian conceptions of the soul agree with Plato in assuming the immortality of the soul after the death of the person; but as to whether the soul existed before his birth, or was created *de novo* at some moment between conception and birth, there has been a difference of opinion.

Plato's Socrates seems not to have been quite sure of the traits of the composite soul. We might suppose that it is the man's soul, and only his soul, which is conscious, which perceives, feels, and thinks. In some statements, however, Plato's Socrates implies that the body, as well as the soul, is conscious. The best notion we can gain from Plato's dialogues is that Socrates had three souls. First, a bodily soul, combining a life principle with an organic ego or bodily subject of experience. Second, a daimon soul, which was conscious and immortal, distinct from the bodily soul. Third, a possessing daimon, or guardian genius, distinct from the ego daimon. This explains why Socrates, the second soul, could talk with his possessing daimon, or third soul.

There are other possible interpretations of the conflicting statements of Plato's Socrates, and such have been offered by scholars who have ignored the discrepancies. From the Platonic uncertainty as to the exact nature of the soul, we may conclude either that Plato invented the composite soul, or that the conception had not occurred much earlier and was not yet standardized. Although Plato called the soul the *psyche*, he does not seem to have identified it with the life principle called *psyche* in Homer's poems, and it certainly has no relation to the *psyche* of Aristotle. This combination of the life principle with the soul is common among Christians, but it is not considered essential. A Christian theologian may relate the life principle to the bodily organism (bodily soul), as Plato seems to have done.

Our terminology would be simpler and clearer if we could use the word soul to designate only the immortal ego-daimon appurtenance and employ other terms to designate 'souls' of other sorts. Established usages, however, do not permit this simplification; we may compromise by employing hyphenated terms for the simple souls. The four simple souls of early conceptions are then: (*a*) the life-soul (*psyche*); (*b*) the ego-soul (*thumos*); (*c*) the daimon-soul; (*d*) the ghost-soul, or ghost (*eidolon*). To these we may add (*e*) the indweller-soul, or 'external soul' and (*f*) the immortal 'man himself' (*autos*).

If we examine Hindu religions, we find still other types of soul; but we need not consider these or the various types of souls in Egyptian religion. The accounts of the various types of souls involved in the beliefs of savages are, at present, so scrambled that, although we are certain that many savage groups conceive of souls of several different sorts, we are unable to determine the specific characteristics of these various sorts.

The foregoing points should suffice to make clear two facts. First, that we cannot define religion in terms of souls. The term has so many meanings that a definition applying to religion in one stage is meaningless for other stages. Second, that psychologists do not discuss the soul in elementary courses in psychology. This is not because psychologists necessarily deny the reality of any of the sorts of souls, but because the concept is so thoroughly confused that it is of no use whatever.

6. The Concept of Metamorphosis.—In the mythology of ancient peoples, and in the folklore of peasants and savages of the present day, we find widely spread the belief that a human being can be transformed completely into a lower animal, such as a wolf, bear, tiger, or snake, or even transformed into a tree or other plant. A transformation of this sort is technically a 'metamorphosis.' This mythological conception must be given attention, since it must be distinguished from the concept of daimon possession.

Some scholars have distinguished between religion and mythology, opining that they are subjects for two different fields of study. The distinction is a tenuous one, since much of our information concerning religion is derived from mythology, and some mythological concepts are so closely integrated with religious beliefs and rituals that it is unsafe to rule them out of consideration.

The metamorphoses of the Greek and Roman gods into animals and into men are familiar to all persons who have dipped even superficially into the beliefs of those peoples. Zeus, for example, became a bull to seduce Europe; a swan to seduce Leda; a cuckoo to seduce Hera; and took on forms of other animals in the prosecution of other amours. Demeter, Athena, and Apollo changed themselves into animals and birds when the changes were convenient. Daimons presumably had the same power of metamorphosis. In Arabian mythology, jinn appear characteristically in the forms of serpents, but may assume forms of other animals or human forms.

The habits of divinities, of assuming human form in endless variety, made ancient peoples especially careful in their treatment of strangers, since any stranger might be a god or goddess or a daimon. That this belief was held by peoples in Arabia and Mesopotamia is shown by the legend of Abraham, Sarah, and the three strangers. Gods, moreover, could transform human beings into animals, and magicians could perform similar metamorphoses. Zeus changed Io into a heifer, and Circe changed her dupes into swine. At the altar of Zeus Lukaios, in Arcadia, men were metamorphosed into wolves and, if they ate no human flesh during their lupine periods, might eventually become men again. Ancient mythology is filled with such legendary stories of metamorphoses.

Even without the action of a god or of a magician, persons might change themselves into animals. This belief still persists among European peasants as the belief in the *werewolf*. The belief in the werewolf has existed in southeastern Europe from ancient times. The werewolf must be distinguished from the *vampire*, which is a corpse that maintains a kind of animation by sucking the blood of living persons; also from the *Zombi* of the West Indies, which is not a bloodsucker but whose activity is maintained by sorcery. A werewolf is a human being who is supposed to be able, at will, to change himself into a wolf and back to human form again. In their lupine forms, werewolves ravage sheepfolds, and kill and eat human beings, while in human form they appear little different from ordinary persons. In some regions of the earth, this picturesque Jekyll and Hyde transformation involves other animals; in India it is the tiger into which men transform themselves.

These metamorphoses are not to be regarded as the passage of some sort of 'soul' out of the human body into an animal; that passage would leave behind a 'soulless' human body. The belief is that the whole man, including his body and all personalized appurtenances, changes into an animal. The man ceases to exist as a man; and a wolf, or some other animal which did not previously exist, comes into existence. The man's body becomes the wolf's body; and the man's soul (or souls) becomes the soul (or souls) of the wolf. One might wonder what becomes of the human being's clothing in such a metamorphosis.

Reports in some cases seem to indicate that the clothing remains where the transformation occurred, furnishing thus incriminating evidence concerning the werewolf. In reports of other cases, there is no mention of the clothing, but the ignoring of the garb does not necessarily indicate that it was transformed into the hairy coat of the wolf or other animal.

Some scholars seem to have confused the ancient belief in metamorphosis with soul beliefs. Early Greeks believed that at death the body of a man, or some part of the body, was transformed into a snake. This metamorphosis, or fractional metamorphosis, has been interpreted as a belief that the snake was the man's soul; an interpretation which is erroneous, at least as applied to the early stages of this belief.

Metamorphosis plays no role in religions of the more advanced types, unless we should interpret the transformation of the elements of the Eucharist into the actual flesh and blood of Christ as a fractional metamorphosis. Many people of groups which are supposed to be civilized, do, however, believe in the possibility of total transformation of human beings into wolves and other animals. The belief is even more widespread among savage and semicivilized peoples.

7. The Concept of Sin.—In almost all cults accepted as religions, there is a concept of a human condition that is designated as 'sin.' These conditions fall into two groups, which we will distinguish as 'internal sin' and 'external sin.' The use of these terms is not well standardized, but we shall explain them and illustrate them as we proceed.

Internal sin is a condition of culpability or guilt that is due to a person's own acts or behavior. The concept is sometimes narrowed further by the stipulation that the guilt is due to voluntary actions, or at least to conscious behavior, in violation of a religious rule

or principle or to conscious failure to act in accordance with a
positive religious rule.   If a man enters an enclosure which he knows
is tabu to him, his entrance constitutes a sin, of the internal sort;
but if he does not know that his entrance is forbidden, the sin is
not internal, although deadly results may follow. For some
Christians, engaging in work or sports on Sunday is sinful, if the
one so engaging knows that the day is Sunday; but if he has mistaken
the day of the week, the actions are not sinful.

Internal sin, in short, is usually conceived as determined by the
intention, purpose, or 'conscious attitude' of the sinner. Jesus,
speaking of this situation (Matt., 5: 27-28) goes so far as to say
that if commission of a certain act is sinful, then the purpose, and
even the desire to commit it, is just as sinful.

The purposes involved are sometimes made the criteria of morality
or immorality of behavior, but sin and immorality are not necessarily
identical.   The principles of some religions make infraction of an
ethical rule, or even the intention to infract it, a sin; but even in
these same religions there are sins that are not immoralities. For
many Christians it is a sin to take communion after eating a meal,
since a religious rule forbids such action; but the action could
hardly be called 'immoral.' Sin must also be distinguished from
crime; for crime is infraction of a civil rule or law, and behavior which
is not forbidden by law is not criminal, even if it is both sinful and
immoral.

External sin is a human condition which is not dependent on volition, knowledge, or consciousness, but is a taint which may be
acquired unintentionally, even unwittingly.   In the same way, a
person may contract tuberculosis or malaria unintentionally, even
without knowing about it.   External sin may even be hereditary,
constituting thus a taint for which the individual is not personally
responsible, since he was born with it.   The best illustration of
hereditary sin is provided by the Christian doctrine of *original sin*,
which is not merely a doctrine regarding the imperfection of human
nature, but a concept of a taint which may lead to the damnation of
an individual unless something is done ritually about it.   The
Christian doctrine might be supposed to be merely an extension
of the Jewish belief that the sins of the father are visited on his
progeny unto the third and fourth generation; but the doctrine
is much older than Judaism, or even the Hebrew religion, being
embedded in the religions of the ancient Greeks.

A man can acquire external sin by his own acts, just as he may become infected with a physical disease by his actions. The man who enters the tabued enclosure unwittingly, becomes infected with external sin as one may acquire typhoid fever by unwittingly drinking infected water. All ancient people were in constant fear lest they should sin unknowingly, for sin is as deadly in such circumstances as it would be if they were aware of what they were doing. Before a dramatic performance in a Greek theater, the seats had to be sprinkled with the blood of pigs, in order to purify the members of the audience from any sins which they might accidentally have acquired. Ancient people regarded a man tainted with external sin as being as dangerous to other persons as is, in our modern opinion, a person infected with a communicable disease. The deadly mana the person has acquired may be transmitted to other persons.

Some scholars have put forth the theory that external sin is a late concept of religion, and that the concept of internal sin is older; but this is the reverse of the truth. External sin is old and universal; while in ancient religions internal sin is scarcely recognized. In savage religion, also, the concept of internal sin is little recognized.

Taking both sorts of sin together, it might seem possible to define religion as including any cult or system involving the concept of sin. Basing religion on sin as its essential and differentiating characteristic seems, however, a drastic step that we can hardly take without further consideration. This point of view would appear to make the teachings of Jesus, as they are reported to us, antireligious, since Jesus attempted to eliminate the concept of sin. It is true that Jesus was in some respects antireligious, since he was opposed to much that has passed, in his day and since then, for religion; but it would still seem an extreme position to assume that the teachings of Jesus were basically antireligious or to assume that there cannot be a religion that does not involve a concept of, and a belief in, sin. Confucianism may eventually be classed outside of religion, but its exclusion because it does not include the concept of sin would seem, at present, too arbitrary.

8. The Concept of the Other World.—There appear to be several different concepts of an 'other world'; and the relations of these concepts to one another are relatively complex. In most of the concepts the other world is contrasted with the world of everyday life.

1. There is a concept which is more often referred to by the adjective 'other-worldly' than by a substantive expression. Sometimes this expression is meant to refer to a world other than the world of sensuous experience, but it is more often metaphorical, indicating merely habits and attitudes of life that are deemed impractical, or as some say, 'idealistic.' Every metaphor, however, is derived from expressions of realistic meaning; the use of the expression other-worldly implies logically the concept of an other world, whether or not the one who uses the expression believes in such a realm.

2. The concept of an other world is often the concept of the realm in which the dead, who have left this mundane life, are still existing. A person, at death, is said to have passed into the other world; sometimes the expression 'passed beyond' or 'passed over' is substituted. A person who believes that some aspect or appurtenance of a person survives death usually believes in an other world, although it is possible to believe that the survival is in this mundane world of our daily life, in an invisible form.

3. The other world is conceived as the residence of the gods, or of God and the angels. This other world may be conceived as bifurcated; Divinity and the demigods inhabiting one section, and Satan and his imps infesting the other section. This concept of a bifurcated other world is characteristic of orthodox Christianity and Islam but is not confined to these religions. One who believes in gods and devils may or may not believe in an other world. Early in the development of concepts of gods and daimons, these beings were conceived as dwelling in this world in which men live.

It is evident that the second and third concepts are basal, and that the first use of the term, insofar as it does not refer directly to one of the other concepts, is a derivative of one or both of them. Obviously, these two concepts may be combined, the world of the gods being also the world of the dead. If there are two 'other worlds,' God, the angels, and the 'spirits of dead men made perfect' may dwell in one, while Satan and his imps may be hosts to the damned in the other. In some religions, there is faith in a third other world (purgatory) intermediate between hell and heaven.

The nature of the other world, in either conception, depends on the assumption, or belief, as to what the condition of the gods, or of the dead, or of both, really is. In the period before Plato in the Mediterranean world, the other world was merely another region of this world. The gods, when they were not down on the surface of the earth, were in the sky, perhaps a little higher than the birds sometimes, but still in our 'mundane sphere.' They were not subject to ordinary human limitations, but in this respect they differed from heroes in degree only, as the heroes differed from ordinary men. From this point of view, the achieving of divine status by men of exceptional merit is understandable.

A distinction was made between the air of the lower levels of the atmosphere, (*aer*), and the substance in the higher regions, which was the *aethir*, (ether). The concept of the ether as an upper stratum of the atmosphere, seems to have been universally accepted. Mt. Olympus, in Thessaly, and high mountains in other regions, were supposed to project through the *aer* into the *aethir*, and so were suitable dwelling places for the great gods, after they became associated with the sky.[1]

Further, in the Greek world there were hosts of daimons and minor divinities who were practically earth-bound; satyrs, nymphs, oreads, dryads, river gods, and a long list of other beings were as much of this earth as were men, horses, and snakes.

The ghosts of the dead, on the other hand, inhabited a region which was sometimes supposed to be a cavern underground, sometimes a far-off region on the surface of the earth. A few men were transported to the Isles of the Blest, where they (not their ghosts) lived forever. These isles, however, were conceived as actual mundane territory, far to the west, where they were lapped by the river Ocean, the description strongly suggesting Salisbury Plain and the adjacent downs in England.

The other worlds for the Greeks, therefore, were merely parts of this world, differing from Greece or Asia Minor not otherwise than did the far northern land of the Hyperboreans (Scandinavians), the regions about the 'Gates of Hercules,' or distant Ethiopa. The realm of Hades, lord of the ghosts, was difficult to find, but Ulysses and others entered it while still alive. The heights of Olympus, where the great gods had their palaces, were scalable, but in ancient times few men would attempt the feat any more than they would wander uninvited into the chamber of a human king. There were other places, closer at hand, which were as dangerous, the reckless or careless entrant dying immediately by the power of the resident god or daimon.

[1] See Cook (ref. VI: 2), *Zeus*, Vol. I, pp. 100 *ff*., and the diagram in Plate IX.

It would indeed be more accurate to say that for the ancient Mediterraneans there was no other world; and, in fact, the people of this area did not use the expression. There were merely regions of this world which were set aside for special purposes; for gods, daimons, ghosts, and exceptional men. These regions, however, corresponded to regions that later men did call an 'other world' or 'other worlds.' The Isles of the Blest corresponded to our heaven, and the realm of Hades approximated our hell. For a long period of the Christian Era, moreover, hell was located under the earth, and heaven in the skies, or on other planets, still in *this world* even if farther off than the Greeks supposed their fabulous realms of the gods and of the dead to be.

It is possible that in India the conception of an other world is more advanced than in the ancient Mediterranean world. It is possible also that some negroid peoples have had a more advanced concept. In Egypt there was, apparently, a basis for a different concept, but the underworld, and the sky world of the gods and men who chose the 'better way,' were, to the end of the Egyptian culture, parts of this world, being merely lower and higher parts of it. The region in the west, to which went Egyptians at death by the 'worse way,' was a region on the earth's surface.

The first suggestion of an other world which is not just a far region of this world is found in Plato, although, for all we know, earlier Pythagoreans may have had the concept. While not contrasted with this world in a clearcut way, Plato's description of the world in which the daimon-psyche lives before its incarnation, and after the death of the body, marks a definite step toward the conception of an other world that is not merely a different region of this one. Christianity, taking over Plato's daimon-psyche as the soul, was influenced strongly by Plato's conception of the other world, but yielded to popular conceptions and brought the other world into this one. With the passing of the centuries, and the popularization of the results of the great advances in geography and astronomy, the other world, for many Christians, has become more and more remote from this world. There is no doubt, however, that, to Christians of many groups today, heaven is in the skies and hell deep in the earth; while to others, slightly more sophisticated, these other worlds are vaguely located on remote planets, a notion tellingly burlesqued in Mark Twain's account of *Captain Stormfield's Trip to Heaven.*

The final conception of the other world as not in space at all, but completely free from spatial limitations, is probably held today by few persons, although the conception of the other world as timeless—transcending time—is accepted more widely. It is significant that while the word 'eternal' is understood by many as signifying timeless, we have no corresponding word for spaceless. That the concept of the other world, or other worlds, as timeless and spaceless is the ultimate form of the concept, which will be reached universally if religious progress continues, is certain. The progress of the last 3000 years in European religion has been steadily in that direction, and some of the many Hindu religions have already attained it, so far as the literate among their adherents are concerned. Although for the bulk of Hindu religionists the other world is much like the other world of the Greeks before Plato's times, the implications of the other world as timeless and spaceless are clear in Brahmanism and in some of the religions that have developed out of it.

The advanced Hindu conception, however, is somewhat startling in the naïveté of its logic to one who is not familiar with the Eleatic philosophy of Greece and Italy. The other world, being timeless and spaceless, is never and nowhere. It doesn't exist. One who enters it, therefore, attains salvation by ceasing to exist. The technical term for this goal of nonexistence is 'nirvana.' Some philosophies, like the Sankhya system, and some heretical religions, like early Buddhism, have struggled to escape from this logical conclusion, but the irresistible tendency of the systems founded on the Vedas is toward it.

Consideration of this Hindu conclusion raises at once the question of the gods of Hinduism. Are they in this same other world, and therefore nonexistent? This question can be answered. The gods, with one exception, are in a world similar to this world; in fact, they are practically in this world. In this respect, Hinduism is in the stage in which Greece was in the Homeric era. The exception is Bráhma, who is distinguished from the Brahmā of the Hindu trinity, which consists of Brahmā, Vishnu, and Shiva. Bráhma, of course, is a paradoxical figure. It (the name is neuter) is the central reality of the universe; we might say, the Logos. It has no qualities whatever—no sex or any other traits that can be described. Bráhma, in short, is nonexistent; it represents the finality of divinity, the nothingness into which man also can be absorbed.

The nothingness of Bráhma explains the fact that little worship is directed to it, and Brahmā is so associated with Bráhma that he is little worshiped, there being only two temples to Brahmā in all India. Orthodox Hindus are divided into two great groups: the Vaishnavites, who worship Vishnu, and the Shivaites, who worship Shiva. The worship in each group may be directed more to the goddesses associated with the gods, but the classification is official. There is no Hindu name for worshipers of Brahmā, for there are no devotees of Brahmā; at least there are none among the orthodox Hindus.

When we trace the concept of the other world backward in its development, we have no difficulty in concluding that in a really primitive religion there was no concept of an 'other world' in any sense. The Mediterranean peoples of 2,500 years ago were barely emerging from this primitive stage. The conception of the dead as existing in a special region of this world is a step from the notion that they continued in the region in which they had lived and in which they were buried or cremated.

The gods, walking the earth, or on the mountaintops, or flying through the air, are but a step from the manas which were assigned to the animals, trees, and other objects among which man lives. It was a step, nevertheless, in the progress toward the conception of an 'other world.'

The concept of the supernatural as contrasted with the natural depends upon the concept of an other world. Ancient man believed in events that *we* class as miracles; he held many beliefs that *we* class as superstitions. There was, however, nothing in his world which, from his point of view, was supernatural; for the distinction between the natural and the supernatural does not arise until there is a concept of a super-nature—an 'other world'.

9. **The Concept of Salvation.**—'Salvation' may be loosely defined as the process, or the condition, of being saved; that is, of being rescued from, or protected from, some harm, danger, risk, or hazard. In religious usage, and the in usages of equivalent words in other languages, salvation means the rescue of the person, or of some appurtenance of the person, from some danger or threat to his existence or his welfare. In some religions it is the person's 'soul' which is saved or protected, either in this world or in an 'other world.' In Islam and Christianity salvation is the prevention of a state of misery which threatens the person or threatens his 'soul' in the other-worldly period which follows death and the guaranty of a state of felicity in the other world.

Hindu religions generally regard personal life in this world as unavoidably miserable and felicity as unobtainable. Life beyond the grave is assumed to be miserable, whether or not the person is reincarnated. Salvation for the Hindu, accordingly, is the ending of conscious life. According to some of the orthodox Hindu religions, salvation is attained through absorption into the impersonal Bráhma, thus ending personal existence and danger of rebirth. That which is absorbed is, for some religions, the soul, but this is not true for all orthodox Hindu sects. On the other hand, Buddhism, an unorthodox religion which rejects the soul, teaches that salvation can be obtained through reaching nirvana, the state of nothingness. One branch of orthodox Hinduism, represented by the Sankhya system of philosophy, assumes the reality of a 'soul,' and denies that the soul can ever be absorbed or annihilated. Salvation, as viewed by the Sankhya system, is the attaining of eternal unconsciousness, for a soul that is unconscious cannot suffer. All Hindu religions, orthodox and unorthodox, agree that salvation is the ending of personal consciousness.

Hindu religions reached their present forms, so far as we know, just before the Christian Era, but we cannot trace their courses of development. We assume that all religions, savage, barbarous, and civilized, have developed over long periods from primitive concepts, but some religions have developed more rapidly than have others. The stages in the development of savage and barbarous religions can be guessed only by comparison with the stages of development of the religions of the Western world, the histories of which are better known. These comparisons give us some light on the development of the concept of salvation.

In the period from 600 to 400 B.C., in the Mediterranean world and Asia Minor, the Orphic mysteries, the mysteries of Demeter, the Dionysiac mysteries, and various other mystery cults offered a salvation much like that of early Christianity. These mysteries were increasing in popularity during the first century of the Christian Era, and Christianity was able successfully to contend with them only by adopting the salvation they offered. The mysteries were elaborate rituals, into which candidates were initiated. The details of these rituals we do not know, for initiates were sworn to secrecy. Pagan writers who had been initiated, as for example, Herodotus and Pausanias, carefully avoided revealing any information. 'I know,' says Herodotus, 'but I cannot tell.' 'This is a matter it is not proper to relate,' says Pausanias. Even Clement of Alexandria, converted to Christianity and bitter against the pagan rites, merely hints at them.

We do know, however, what the purposes of the mysteries were, in their later forms. Initiation into the mysteries assured happiness or an alleviation of misery after death. In some cults, apparently, this happiness was for the ghost, which had a less deplorable existence in the underworld than did the ghosts of the uninitiated. For other cults, probably it was a possessing or indwelling daimon or an 'external soul' which was benefited in the other world. For still other cults, perhaps it was the 'man himself,' vaguely conceived as an integrated person, whose future welfare was assured by initiation.

Before the rise of the mystery cults, in the Homeric age, salvation was bestowed on a few heroes by special act of a god. Herakles was transported to the Olympian home of the gods, although his ghost went to the underworld. Some others were transported to the Isles of the Blest. Rituals of cremation and burial contributed to other-worldly welfare, by releasing the ghost, which, however miserable in Hades realm, was even worse off if compelled to hang about the decaying body. Whether, for ordinary men, cremation was considered as sending a 'spiritual body' to the celestial abode of the gods, is a question, but the body of Herakles was burned.

When, from the early concepts of ghost, life entity, indwelling daimon, and the even more nebulous concept of the 'man himself,' the synthetic concept of the soul developed, salvation was the saving of this soul. Plato's view was that this salvation was attained through wisdom—the understanding of the facts about this world and the other world. It is probable that some such notion had begun to form in the Pythagorean cult before Plato. Knowing the truth, and regulating one's earthly life thereby, could end the succession of incarnations of the soul; and the soul (not the man himself, but a certain part of him) could dwell eternally in the other world of pure 'ideas.' Escaping from the body, the soul escaped from pain and from pleasure (both of these, with all other feelings, being attributes of the body ego, not of the soul) and lived a life of pure thought.

Prior to the rise of the notion that something could, in this world, be done about the other world, salvation was freedom from danger in this world and the securing of happiness and mundane prosperity. Protection is required, not only from physical hardships and handicaps of natural occurrence, but especially from the malevolence of the gods. Actual assistance may be secured, if the gods are properly approached, for the gods may bestow good as well as evil. The means to this end is 'righteousness'; but righteousness meant merely conforming to rituals of sacrifice and worship approved by the gods.

Zeus, Athena, and other divinities were worshiped under various of their aspects, among which the aspect of *Savior* was highly important. Shrines to Zeus Soter (Zeus the Savior) and Athena Savior were plentiful in the Greek world. There were other savior gods and goddesses, however, such as Artemis Savior and Kore (Persephone) Savior.

In Christian usage, the term salvation is restricted to other-worldly protection and blessings, although the ancient concept of this-worldly benefits to be obtained through religion still persists.

10. Mystical Experience.—In many religions, and in some philosophies that do not claim religious status, there is the concept of an experience which, for most purposes, can be called 'mystical.' The belief that such experience is possible is 'mysticism.'

This mystical experience, and that which is experienced therein, are held, in the philosophies that have developed the most advanced mysticism, to be incapable of description. The mystic experience is not perception, nor is it thought; it is something above these. It is not consciousness, in the ordinary sense of the term. Since knowledge, in the psychological sense, is a matter of perception and thought, the mystical experience is referred to as the 'third kind of knowledge.' The indescribability of the experience and its content follows from the fact that words refer to, and are developed from, sense perception and thought and so are not directly applicable to the third kind of knowledge, which transcends perceiving and think-ing. Any verbal explanations about the mystic experience, we are warned, are misleading; but by a variety of descriptions we may be given some notion of its ineffable nature.

The mystical state or experience is also called 'union.' It is as if, in knowing, the knower and the known become identical. Instead of being contrasted, as in psychological experience, they are *one*. The relation between knower and known which we call 'being aware' or 'being conscious' is thus completely excluded. The 'knower,' for the time being, *is* that which he 'knows.'

Discriminating the knower from the known, as they are before union, the object to be known is, for most philosophical mystics, either God or Ultimate Truth.   In union with the divine, one is identified with the ultimate principle of the universe and so may be said, in inadequate metaphor, to know all truth.   For some mystics, however, that which is 'known' is another human 'soul.'   The outstanding formulation of the doctrine is given by Aristotle, who elevated the ancient Greek concept of *nous* into that of super-knowledge, super-knower, and super-known.   *Nous* is the divine element in man; it is divine knowledge, and its object is itself.   A close paraphrase of Aristotle's formula is: *Nous nouses nous.*

The technical term for the state in which the mystic is when he has the mystic experience is 'ecstasy,' which means, literally, a 'standing out.'   The person 'stands out' from himself, from his ordinary condition, becoming other than himself because he is absorbed into the divine reality.   In common parlance, we use the term ecstasy for an emotionally exalted state; but when we use it in reference to mysticism and mystics, we must avoid confusing it with the same term as loosely or metaphorically used.   Mystics deny that ecstasy is an emotional state; for they claim that the mystic experience is above feeling, as it is above knowledge.   Although to psychologists, ecstasy as described by the mystics really is a state of pure feeling (and therefore not an emotional state at all), we must constantly bear in mind the mystics' denial of this conclusion.

In the usages of religious persons who are not philosophically oriented, a wide range of experiences that are, strictly speaking, not mystical at all are included under the heading of 'mystical experience.'   Seeing of visions and hearing of voices is not really mystical; for the contents of these experiences are thought contents and are describable in words.   A supernatural message or revelation of fact or doctrine is not mystical.   There is nothing mystical in messages given by spiritualist mediums.   Thought reading and 'extra-sensory perception' may be superstitial, but they are far from being mystical as is the watching of a horse race, or thinking about the war.   Saint Theresa is commonly called a mystic; but there is little in her report of visions of other-worldly visitants; tactual contacts with them; or hearing of their voices which could properly be called mystical.   The effects of these perceptual and ideational experiences of supernatural beings upon her, as described, are strictly emotional.   Such experiences and states we distinguish as 'pseudo-mystical.'

In various sects of the Christian religion, there is some mysticism and a great deal of pseudo-mysticism. No sect has denied the possibility of ecstasy, but the use of mystical phraseology does not necessarily indicate a mystical meaning. The Roman Church is truly Catholic in regard to mysticism, neither denying nor endorsing it. Outside of religious circles and philosophical schools, the terms 'mystic,' 'mystical,' and 'mysticism' have no meaning, but are commonly mere terms of reproach hurled by one 'scientist' at another whose theories or postulates he dislikes.

Etymology, here, is completely misleading. Our word 'mystic' is derived from the Greek word for persons initiated into a mystery cult, but, paradoxical as it may seem, there was nothing mystical about the ancient mysteries, so far as we can tell. We must distinguish carefully between the terms 'mystery' and 'mysterious' on one hand, and the noun 'mystic' and adjective 'mystical' on the other. Mysticism is a belief in a supernatural principle, but otherwise the vast range of beliefs in the supernatural that have held through the ages are not mystical. Belief in mind reading, astrology, spirit communications, extrasensory perception, ghosts, and various other alleged 'occult' phenomena and objects is superstitious, but not mystical. In addition, certain religious beliefs that are not to be classed as superstitions, whether the beliefs are or are not valid, are beliefs in the supernatural but are not necessarily mystical. The belief in God and the belief in the other world are of this order.

11. The Concept of Holiness.—Holiness, or sanctity, in all religions, attaches to persons, places, actions, and material objects. The priest is a typical holy man. A temple or sanctuary is a typical holy place. Sacraments such as baptism are typical holy actions. Crucifixes, amulets, and the bones of saints are typical holy objects. The range of holy persons, places, rituals, and objects is an extensive one. The concept of sanctity runs broadly through religion everywhere and in all times, and the concept is intelligible only when the range is surveyed. For convenience, we may best consider the personal, local, ritual, and objective aspects of holiness separately, and attempt to bring these several aspects together in a final synthesis.

1. Holiness of Person.—In some sects of Christianity today, the concept of personal holiness is a conception of moral value, or personal worth. This concept, of course, involves notions of social relations. A moral man is one whose life is exceptionally full of the virtues of justice, truth, generosity, gentleness, and love. Even a god is deemed holy only if he evidences these moral qualities. This concept of holiness has evolved from the concepts held by ancient people, for nothing appears *de novo* in religion, but the evolution has been a process of considerable length, and the modern concept, as held by the more advanced religionists, differs sharply from its antecedents.

In other religions of the present day, and in ancient religions generally, holiness and morality are not so closely connected, and in fact, in some religions they seem to have no bearing on one another. In Hindu and Moslem religions, a holy man is one who follows a prescribed mode of life, in which neither what we would consider morality, nor even decency, is essential. Holy men, in these religions, are devoted to selfish ends, seeking their own salvation or welfare. This is true also of Christian monks of some types, although others devote themselves to the service of their fellow men. In non-Christian religions of the present and past eras the conception of holiness as a characteristic apart from the social virtues has been almost universal.

Herakles, the greatest of the heroes, who was taken to dwell with the gods at his death, was guilty of every important crime in the catalogue, but his murders, larcenies, rapes, seductions, mendacities, and varied injustices were, apparently, conducted with ritual holiness. Herakles was revered as a man of great power and accomplishment. Kleomedes also was powerful physically. Odysseus (Ulysses) was a hero of lesser rank, greatly admired for his skillful lying and trickery, as well as for his physical exploits.

In all religions, the real characteristic of the holy man is his possession of mana. This power may be nothing more than the ability effectively to conduct rituals that are inefficacious when conducted by unqualified persons. The Brahmans have that power and are holy men, as compared with men of other castes. The mana of the Brahman is hereditary but can be lost by failing to observe the caste distinctions. Other holy men in other religions have the power of prophecy or the power of discerning truth. This power is usually assumed to be a special gift from a god, but may be dependent also on ritual preparation, such as abstaining from certain foods, self-mutilation, or the hermit life, or, as in the case of the pythoness of the oracle at Delphi, intoxication by drugs or the inhalation of vapors. In some holy men, the mana manifests itself in the production of miracles of various sorts or in effective blessing or cursing. The miracles are not always voluntary productions but may be produced by mana radiating from the holy man automatically. The miraculous mana does not cease at the holy man's death. The bones, hair, or nail clippings of Christian, Mohammedan, and Hindu saints work miracles for centuries. A sick, person, for example, may be cured by touching a holy man, or touching his clothing, as in the story of the woman who was cured of a disorder of twelve years' standing by merely touching the hem of Jesus' garment, after which Jesus realized that virtue (mana) had gone out of him and asked, Who touched my clothes? Touching the bone of a dead saint, or being in its immediate vicinity, may be just as effective.

The newer concept of holiness has not been completely adopted by all sects of Christianity. In some sects, the manas possessed by the priest are valid even if he becomes a dissolute person, until the power is taken away from him by higher authority of the church. Sacraments administered by an officially authorized priest are efficacious, however sinful or heretical the holy man may be, unless his power has been officially revoked. The priest is, in any case, but an instrument through whom power is transmitted or in whom it is manifested. Most Christian sects recognize, however, that it is not proper that a person should be classed as holy unless his life is moral, or at least free from vice.

The contrast between this concept and the more ancient concepts is brought out sharply by the fact that most ancient religious approved certain groups of prostitutes, ritually selected and controlled, as holy and provided these holy women in the temples. The custom is still kept up in some Hindu temples. Intercourse with sacred prostitutes was, and is, a religious ritual. In some ancient religions of the Levant, sacred male prostitutes, for homosexual relations, were provided or approved. The term in Semitic languages for such prostitutes, *kadesh*, or *kadesha*, is translated in the King James Version of the Bible by the word 'dog.' Consideration of prostitutes and sex perverts as holy persons is excluded from the modern concept of holiness as strongly as is the consideration of thieves and murderers. Holy men of Islam, however, may be sex perverts.

2. *Holy Places.*—In modern times, as in late pagan times, a holy place is a locus in which the power or mana or god or daimon, or of a

holy man or woman, is manifested. In Christianity, Islam, and Hinduism, the characteristic holy places are temples, churches, mosques, tombs of saints, and similar enclosures or unenclosed shrines. In the Mediterranean area, as in countries farther east, wells, springs, and streams were sacred in ancient times and in some religions still are. Some streams and water sources were especially holy because routes of travel passed by them and pilgrimages were made to them. Among the more important sacred wells in the Near East were those at Aphaca, Dan, Beersheba, Mamre, and Mecca. The Pool of Siloam along with these others was holy long before the rise of the Hebrews. The Zem-zem well at Mecca is still important in the pilgrimages of Islam, but in earlier times the other wells above listed were just as holy. In the Greek world, practically all springs giving out an appreciable volume of water were holy, although some were especially sacred. Sometimes holy men created springs, as did Moses in the wilderness. Holy animals such as the winged horse, Pegasos, also created important springs. Presumably the mana of the holy man or animal continued in the spring, but more probably the sanctity of the animal was derived from the spring.

Some rivers, such as the Adonis, were sacred throughout their entire lengths. Others were sacred at certain parts of their course, like the Alpheus, which was sacred in Elis, where it flowed by the temple of Olympian Zeus, but which may not have been sacred in its smaller branches in the mountains of Arcadia. The Jordan, and the Barada, the chief river of Damascus, which Naaman the leper thought as full of mana as the Jordan (II Kings, 5: 12) were sacred throughout, and their sources were more holy still. The source of the Jordan remained holy down into the period of Roman control, when under the name of *Paneas* it was sacred to the old Arcadian god Pan. The important temple of the Syrian goddess at Baalbek (Heliopolis) was at the source of the river Leontes.

In regions where springs ('living waters') were not found, wells and pools were holy; but otherwise, the living waters were primarily the sacred sources. The symbolic use of the term 'living waters' is widespread in ancient literatures. From the practical point of view, springs and headwaters are freer from contamination than are wells, ponds, and rivers in their lower courses and so are more palatable and better for drinking. In desert areas, wells, although usually contaminated and tasting of minerals and decaying vegetation, are nevertheless precious sources, indispensable for human and animal life. The lower courses of rivers, however, are indispensable for irrigation and household purposes. The sanctity of water supplies is based on factors that are exceedingly practical.

The manas of waters easily became extended beyond the limits of actual functions. Waters of sacred springs and rivers were used not only for drinking, washing, and other natural purposes, but also for ceremonial drinking, bathing, sprinkling, and other ritual uses. Pilgrims took away bottles of water for the ceremonial uses at home. Moslems still carry water from the well Zem-zem, and Christians from the Jordan, deeming it especially potent for sprinkling in baptism or for the exorcising of demons. In general, however, Christians consider any clean water to be filled with sufficient mana for ritual purposes if consecrated by the priest or minister, who contributes the requisite mana to the water.

In some places, it was believed that a divinity or daimon lived in a sacred pool or spring, in the form of a serpent, water lizard, or fish, constantly communicating its mana to the water.

In the Greek world, important rivers were not merely assumed to be the habitations of divinities, but were themselves assumed to be gods. Since the river gods were represented in statuary in human form, often with animal characteristics, indicating an earlier animal divinity, it might be supposed that the consideration of the river *as* a god was merely a metaphorical way of considering the god *of* the river. On the other hand, there is some basis for the supposition that the rivers as such were really believed to be gods. Perhaps both beliefs may have been held in different places and different times. The oft-recurring legends of a river begetting offspring by a human mother may have meant that the god of the river, in human form, had intercourse with a woman; or it may, in some instances have embodied the belief (familiar in many areas) that a woman might become pregnant simply by bathing in a river endowed with the mana of a male.

Offerings were made to the springs and rivers, or to the divinities haunting them, by casting articles of actual value or of symbolic meaning into the waters. Statuettes of gold, silver, bronze, or clay; money and jewels; weapons; and articles of many other descriptions were thus offered. Oracles were consulted at some springs. One form of divination was through the casting in of offerings; if the offerings were cast out, the sign was unfavorable.

Ordeals were carried out by causing the person under test to drink of the water. If, for example, he were guilty of perjury, the draught would be fatal to him.

Among places held to be holy, mountaintops occupy an important position, and so mountain areas were favorite sites for temples. The houses of the major gods and goddesses were believed to be on the tops of the higher peaks and ranges, such as Sinai, Parnassus, Olympus, Ida in Crete, and Ida in the Troad. Around these peaks the clouds clustered, the lightning flashed, and the thunder roared. Power of great magnitude was thus manifested on the peaks. From the peaks, the rains spread out to water the thirsty soil, and the streams had their sources in the mountains. These were places of danger, to which ascent would be safe only for holy men, with due ritual.

On the lesser peaks, altars were consecrated and sometimes temples were built. Sanctuaries, consisting of open enclosures of masonry or upright logs, were common on level areas below the peaks themselves. Sacred areas were sometimes recognized without enclosure. That these sacred heights below the storm levels had their origins in the early usages of elevated places for lookouts against enemies and for signaling, as well as for encampments rendered safe by their relative inaccessibility, is indicated by similar developments in western Europe.

Although early holy places were for the most part mountain heights, or precincts of water, there were many other sacred areas. Wherever a temple was erected, or an altar built, it became holy. Shrines, sanctuaries, and temples were in many cases placed at spots already holy; but wherever erected, these became holy places because they were seats of a divinity or daimon, whose manas were there manifested. The tomb of a holy man or saint is holy ground in all religions, for some mana of the saint continues to emanate from it. Dens of serpents, such as the snake pits at Eleusis, might become very holy. Caves were the dwelling places of powers, and a large rock, especially if of peculiar form, might be a Beth-El (house of god). Any place in which power was manifested was holy ground.

The practical importance of trees was early evident to man, not only of fruit trees, but of others. As the forests on the mountains and plains are denuded, large trees standing alone are valued for their shade, in which a traveler may rest, or in which Socrates and his friend might discuss philosophy. The holy areas around specimen trees (rowan trees) in hot countries are easily explained. Dense thickets, in which wild animals lurked, also became holy ground through their importance. The holiness of fruit-bearing trees was an important factor in religious development that we shall consider later in detail, along with the holiness of food animals.

The outstanding feature of holy places, holy objects, and holy persons is their dangerous or inimical nature. Unless one comports himself circumspectly in sanctuaries, and with regard to holy men and holy objects, one will be injured. The holier the place or the object, the deadlier its mana. The man who put his hand on the Hebrew ark with the best of intentions, was struck dead forthwith, for this was the holiest place of the Hebrew religion. The boys who reviled Elisha, the holy man, were devoured by bears. These stories can be matched everywhere in the ancient world, and among savages.

On the other hand, benefits were to be derived from holy places and holy persons, by those who understood the techniques. The altars, shrines, temples, and sanctuaries were places where supplication of the divinities and ritual sacrifices to them were most effectual, as soon as divinities were conceived. Sleeping in the sanctuary of Asklepios cured diseases, although it was the presence of the holy snakes in the sanctuary which was of major importance. On the other hand, the cures performed at the grotto of Lourdes were done by virtue of the power of the Virgin, who once manifested herself there. The mana infused into the holy place continued. Bathing in holy streams and springs was not considered sacrilegious, but gave benefits from the manas of the waters. A holy man approached reverently and with gifts in the ritual way may give healing and prosperity. He may bless, as well as curse, and so may the gods and daimons.

Some divinities and some places were completely inimical. They exercised manas that could not be turned to good use for men. Some divinities, however, were both malevolent and benevolent, according to the way in which they were approached, or according to their feelings at the time. No divinities were wholly well disposed toward man.

The manas exerted by holy places are of various sorts. To enter into certain sanctuaries produced instant death. Unauthorized entrants into others were struck blind. In other cases, death came to the violator within a year. Into some sanctuaries an authorized priest could go, but for a layman to enter was presumed to have unfortunate consequences. In many Greek sanctuaries, as in the Hebrew temple, there was an inner holy place forbidden to laymen, although they might with impunity enter the outer court. In temples or sanctuaries that were open to laymen, and in the vicinity of shrines in general, circumspect behavior was necessary and previous ritual cleansing was required, in order to avoid evil effects of the mana of the place or of the divinity residing there.

The best that could be hoped from any god was that he would be persuaded to be generous and benevolent toward his devoted worshippers and do his evil only on other people. The Hebrew view of Jehovah was, in this respect, quite in accord with the beliefs of the Greeks and other Mediterraneans toward their gods.

To holy places and holy objects, the same considerations apply in part. Some are dangerous and nothing but dangerous. Some are sources of benefit if properly used; damage if improperly used. It is possible, however, that some places were believed to exercise no evil in any case. Whether this is the case in modern religion, it is not possible to decide.

A somewhat similar situation surrounds some holy animals, such as the pig. A holy animal for the Mediterraneans and Syrians, it was an accursed animal for the Hebrews. In both cases, it was holy in the basic sense of exerting or emitting a powerful mana. Students of comparative religion have long accepted the view that the destinction between that which is accursed and that which is sacred is a variable, both being tabu because of their manas, the actual line being drawn in accordance with the assumption that the power may be in the one case beneficial as well as evil and totally evil in the other.

There is a peculiar practical aspect of holy places, which is important for two reasons. In the first place, it probably had influence on the development of the concept of holy places. In the second place, it undoubtedly had influence on the development of the concept of holiness as morality. All holy places in the ancient world were sanctuaries, in the sense that they were places in which conflicts between groups and punishment for offenses or reprisals resulting from combats were forbidden. In war, refugees who entered the temple of a divinity were safe. If the enemies violated the sanctuary and killed the refugees, dire results accrued to them eventually. Individuals who had committed crimes sought 'sanctuary' in holy places. In later periods, only those who were guilty of manslaughter and lesser crimes were thus protected, but earlier, murder was included. In the Levant, areas around springs and wells were areas in which fighting was prohibited. Enemies might find refuge there; in times of drought, flocks of peoples at feud with one another could be watered there. Those who violated the holiness of these neutral areas were, presumably, visited with punishment later.

Runaway slaves could not be recaptured and even stray camels could not be retaken by their owners if they reached certain of the Arabian sanctuaries.

The holy springs were subject to the same rules. They were open to the use of all, and no controversies could be carried into their precincts.

The advantage of having these sanctuaries scattered throughout the land is inestimable. Travelers could count on water, supplies, and resting places, from which they could not be driven by enemies and in which robbers dare not enter. In especially dry seasons, there were certain areas in which the remnants of the flocks of various tribes could be kept alive and thus the tribes be prevented from perishing. In these scattered spots, few though they were relatively, the brotherhood of man under the common fatherhood of the god was recognized, and there was a demonstration of the advantages of peaceful relations between peoples, contrasting sharply with the general situation, in which the brotherhood was restricted to the clan or tribe, while all hands were against all other tribes.

3. Holy Objects.—Objects, as well as persons and places, may be holy. The mana of a holy man may cling about his relics. Scapulars and medals may be ritually infused with mana, which preserves the life of the wearer or in other ways contributes to his welfare. In some cases it is the ritual treatment that creates the mana. In other cases the form of the object itself (as the crucifix) or its construction is partly responsible for the mana. The medal of St. Christopher that protects the traveler has a representation of the saint and his name upon it. The medal that helps the racing fan to pick his horses, or brings in the one picked, bears the image and superscription of the appropriate saint. This is not enough, of course; the ritual of 'blessing' the medal is essential. So, the composition of the fetish of an African native, from various materials, cooperates with the ritual process of its making, to produce a powerful mana.

The concept of mana inherent in certain objects, or communicable to certain objects, is ancient and world-wide. In modern religions these manas are beneficial only. In ancient religions and savage religions, they may be baleful to those against whom they are used and may be even disastrous to the user if used unskillfully.

4. Holiness and Uncleanness.—We have described sin as a taint or evil mana attaching to a person. It is otherwise designated as uncleanness, or defilement. In highly developed religion, sin is the antithesis of holiness. Satan, powerful as he is, is not holy, but is unclean. A wicked man cannot be holy. This contrast, as we have pointed out, is relatively modern and is not fully embodied in all modern religions. Even where a sharp distinction is made between God or gods as entirely moral, and Satan, or devils, as thoroughly immoral, the same distinction is not necessarily applied to men and women. In few religions has even the distinction between good divinities and evil divinities been fully developed. In philosophical forms of orthodox Hinduism, and in some unorthodox forms, such as Buddhism, the distinction is made, but in popular forms of Hinduism the holy gods are beings whose malevolence is feared while their good will is sought. Justice is not one of their characteristics, and they delight in cruel rituals. The God of the Israelites was appeased by savage treatment of tribes who did not accept him. Zeus of the Greeks, in one of his forms, was entirely malevolent, and the name *Meilichos* ('gentle' or 'benevolent') was applied to him in not too subtle flattery, in the hope that, by thus being addressed in worship, his evil disposition might be lulled and his evil power might be turned aside from his worshipers. In other forms, Zeus was a mixture of benevolence with malice and mendacity. This was to the Greeks no inconsistency, because the distinction between helpful power and hurtful power was not conceived. Power was potentially good and also potentially bad. Holy places, like holy supernatural beings, exercise power that might have hurtful or harmful effects.

Human beings who are wicked, in the modern sense, might be holy; but if they were ritually unclean, that is, if they had contracted external sin, their manas were wholly bad, and they were a source of danger to other peoples who might come near them. They were accursed, the antithesis of being holy.

Animals and objects might also be unclean, accursed, and so dangerous. Contact with the unclean animal or object might infect a person with sin, .which is specifically the uncleanness of a person. As we trace this contrast between holiness and accursedness back toward the beginnings of religion, however, we find it disappearing in the undifferentiated concept of mana. Animals and places that appear in later times to be divided into those which are tabu because they are holy, and those which are tabu because they are unclean, earlier were not so distinguished. They were tabu because they had powerful manas.

The notion that hygienic purposes were involved in the tabus on uncleanness in ancient religions, and that the rituals of purification had hygienic bases, is quite unfounded. Only one of the tabus has so far been proved to have a possibly real basis, the tabu on menstruating women, since the menotoxin to be found in different secretions at that period is poisonous to growing plants. But no hygienic significance has been found in any other forms. Contact with dead bodies is no more dangerous than contact with living; ritual hand washing does not protect against infection. There may be, however, if not hygienic at least practical bases for some of the tabus, as in the removal of offensive odors.

CHAPTER IV

THE EVOLUTION OF DIVINITIES

1. The Final Pagan Divinities.—Gods are not essential for religion; for religions that have discarded gods have survived, for a time at least. Buddhism is an instance of a religion that, in its original form, considered gods as of no importance, which is practically the elimination of gods. All religions, however, in their normal course of development reach a stage in which gods and goddesses appear and multiply; and some religions have gone into further stages, in which the goddesses are eliminated and the gods reduced to a single one. Information concerning the evolution of divinities throws much light on the development of religion, and even on its primitive origin, the most important information being supplied from the ancient religions of the Mediterranean area, although comparison with the religions of the Levant, of western Europe, and even of India is helpful. Our information concerning the development of divinities in these areas is, of course, less complete and less reliable than is the available information concerning the Mediterranean area, in which the population became *grammatikos* in a prehistoric period.

The evolution of divinities in the Mediterranean area seems to have reached its final stage somewhere near 500 B.C., but was nearing completion by 1000 B.C. The primitive stages are lost in the obscurity of the remote past, but from the early processes which left their evidence in the final religious conceptions, and from comparison with other religions, we may, with reasonable certainty, infer the early parts of the development. We may even conjecture the further developments that would have taken place if the Greek culture had not been destroyed.

In the Homeric and classical periods, there were twelve major divinities—seven gods and five goddesses—organized mythologically into a royal family and assigned to a seat of government on the stormy heights of Mount Olympus, in Thessaly. There were, however, many other divinities who were not included in the royal

98

family. Some of these divinities who were not included in the Olympian group were, nevertheless, of primary importance; some, on the other hand, were secondary divinities who were rated as progeny of the major twelve.

In the period of Roman domination, the Greek divinities were equated with the gods and goddesses of the Roman pantheon, and in translations of Greek writings the Roman names often are substituted for the Greek ones. Such equations and substitutions, however, are not valid and are avoided by modern scholars. The Olympian twelve (with their Roman substitute names) were Zeus (Jove), Hera (Juno), Poseidon (Neptune), Aïdoneus or Hades (Pluto), Hephaistos (Vulcan), Ares (Mars), Apollo (*idem*), Artemis (Diana), Aphrodite (Venus), Hermes (Mercury), Athena (Minerva), and Demeter (Ceres).

The family relationships of the Olympian gods and goddesses differ in different legends, but the most widely accepted account is given by Hesiod. Zeus and Hera are brother and sister, progeny of an earlier pair of divinities, Kronos and Rhea. Zeus and Hera, nevertheless, were husband and wife—an incestuous relationship that some later Greeks rejected. Apollo and Artemis were children of Zeus by Hera or by the goddess Latona, who preceded Hera on Mount Olympus. Hephaistos (Hephaestus) and Ares were considered as sons of Zeus and Hera, although Hephaistos seems to have been an ancient god of the Mediterraneans while Ares was probably a later importation from Asia. Hermes was the son of Zeus and Maia, an ancient Arcadian goddess. Aphrodite, the wife of Hephaistos and the mistress of Ares, was the daughter of Zeus by Dione, an ancient goddess. Demeter had no connection with the Olympian group by birth, but she bore one or more children to Poseidon or to Zeus. Hades was regarded as a brother (or half brother) of Zeus, and so may be considered as a member of the Olympian twelve, although his residence was not on Mount Olympus, but in the underworld over which he ruled.

Persephone was an ancient Arcadian goddess, hardly to be distinguished from Demeter, but was later differentiated as the daughter of Demeter. She was commonly called 'Kore,' a name that meant virgin, or maiden, until she was captured by Hades and taken to the underworld to be his queen. The Arcadian goddess whose name was secret and who was called 'the Lady' was probably Persephone. Eros (Cupid) was either the son of Ares and Aphrodite or the son of Hermes by an unspecified mother. Asklepios (Aesculapius), the serpent god of healing, was a son of Apollo by a human mother. Hygeia, the goddess whose image always was stationed in the sanctuary of Asklepios, was figured as the daughter of Apollo or as the daughter of Asklepios. Kastor and Poludeukes (Castor and Pollux), the Dioskouri (Gemini), who were important gods of mariners, were sons of Zeus by a human mother, Leda. Dionysos, who became one of the most important of the later gods, was, in one of his aspects, the son of Zeus by the human Semele.

Athena, the great warrior goddess, who may have derived her name from the city of Athens, or *vice versa*, has a peculiar relation to the Olympian family in that she was born directly from the head of Zeus, with no mother.

The artificiality of this system of divine relationships is obvious. Athena, Demeter, Kore, Artemis, Hermes, Maia, and Poseidon were ancient Mediterranean divinities, of Pelasgic or Celtic origins. Both Aphrodite and Ares are generally assumed to have been Asiatic divinities, imported into the Mediterranean area. Apollo is considered by classical scholars to have been a god imported from the northern area of Europe. Dionusos (Dionysus), also is often held to have been an importation from the region north of Greece proper. Classical scholars are apt to go to extremes, but it can be admitted that some of the aspects or features of Aphrodite, Apollo, and Dionysus in their later conceptions were importations, assimilated to Mediterranean divinities; and it seems fairly certain that Ares was an ass god, originating in Asia Minor, for whom there was no Greek god to which he could be assimilated. The promiscuous sexual relations of Zeus are to be explained by the obvious fact that Zeus was a synthesis of various earlier gods, each of whom had his goddess.

The attempts to systematize the divinities of the Mediterranean peoples began before the Homeric era and was evidently a plan for the bringing of some order into the confused and chaotic polytheism that had developed. Similar systematization was attempted in Egypt, Mesopotamia, and India. In the first two areas, the work of the priestly class is obvious. In Greece, there were multitudes of priests, but no organized priestly castes, the priests of each shrine being independent or under the control of the local civic government. The systematization of divinities, accordingly, appears to have been the work of the poets, such as Homer and Hesiod.

Some of the ancient divinities, who retained their prestige to the end of Greek culture, were not taken into the royal family or assimilated to any of its members. Among these were Pan, the Arcadian god of the woodland and of goats, and Maia. While there are indications that Dispoina (the Lady) was merely a descriptive epithet for Persephone, it is possible that the indications are misleading. If this is the case, Dispoina, who remained to the last an important Arcadian goddess, should be added to the list.

2. Processes in the Evolution of Divinities.—In the production and modification of divinities there are six processes recognizable. These processes occur in combination but are analytically distinguishable.

1. Primitive Origin, or Creation of Individual Gods and Goddesses.—This process we shall consider and explain in later sections.

2. Migration of Divinities.—The adoption in one area or by one group of a divinity that had originated in another area or among people of another group. In many cases, the immigrant divinity was not adopted as a total individual, but certain aspects of a foreign divinity were imported and added to a native divinity.

3. Assimilation of Divinities.—The merging of an immigrant god or goddess with one of native origin. In some cases the result of the merger was called by the name of the native divinity; in other cases the name of the alien divinity was imported and applied to the synthesis. In most cases, the assimilation was more nominal than real—the synthetic divinities being distinguished thereafter from the original native component. Sacred animals from one region were sometimes assimilated to sacred animals in another region, although the animals had not attained to divinity. Symbols of divinities migrated freely, sometimes, apparently, without migration of other aspects.

4. Multiplication of Divinities.—Occurring through migration and incomplete assimilation in most cases, although it is possible that creation of new divinities in the local area may have been involved.

5. Systematization of Divinities.—In default of assimilation, divinities were arranged in families such as the Olympian or grouped in trinities as in Egypt and Mesopotamia and partially in India.

6. Change of Sex of Divinities from Female to Male.—There is no doubt that divinities in the areas we are considering, as well as in Egypt, Mesopotamia, and India, were created first as goddesses and that some were later changed into gods.

The creation of divinities came first in time and may well be called the 'primitive' factor in the evolution of divinities. The other processes listed above have not been uniformly consecutive and have followed different patterns in different areas. Migration of divinities seems to have begun early, but the migration continued to the end of the religions, except for those religions which became monotheistic. Synthetic divinities produced by assimilation continued. Change of sex seems to have come rather late in the religions of most areas, and this change contributed further to the multiplication of divinities. Creation of new divinities apparently ceased in the Western world before the Christian Era but has not ceased in farther Asia.

In western Asia, the goddesses were supreme down to the period of Roman domination, although the change of sex commenced earlier and was continuing. The goddesses of the Levant were associated with the earth, as the mother of all plant and animal life. These goddesses were especially worshiped on high mountains, and the goddesses may have been their mountains personified. When, later, male divinities were assigned to the mountains, the goddess of the mountain became the wife of the god.

Goddesses of the same types, with similar attributes, had various local names, of which two or three are typical. In Phrygia the mother goddess was Kubele (Cybele); in Cappadocia and the Pontis, her name was Ouris. In other parts of Asia Minor she was called Ma (mother). The Thracian Bendis and the goddess at Ephesus designated in the King James Version of Acts 19: 28 as 'Diana of the Ephesians' seem to have been similar to Kubele in attributes and in rituals employed in their worship. In Crete the mother goddess was Rhea; but Britomartis, an ancient goddess of the fisherman, had an important place. The Arabian and Babylonian goddess Ishtar was introduced into Syria and adjacent religions as Ashtart or Ashtoreth, from whom later developed Aphrodite. In Assyria and in Armenia there were goddesses of the same type as the ones we have named, and the Anaïtis of the Persians may have been borrowed from the Armenians.

With many of these goddesses were associated male divinities, as their husbands, lovers, or sons. With Kubele was associated Atys (Attys or Attis); with Ishtar, Tammuz; with Aphrodite, Adonis. The names of these gods varied locally, and the male associate of a goddess in one area might be assigned to a different goddess in

another area. Thus, Paris, the villain of the Trojan war, is assumed
to be a symbol of Atys, although Helen is interpreted as representing
Aphrodite.

The Greeks, coming in contact with the peoples of Asia Minor and
other parts of the Levant, applied the names of their divinities to
those of the Asiatics, as did the Romans later. Thus we have a
long list of Asiatic goddesses called 'Artemis'; and a long list of
gods called 'Zeus.' In some cases, as in that of the Artemis (Diana)
of Ephesus, the name of the city was attached as a surname, to
distinguish the divinity from others to which the same name was
applied. In other cases, the original local name of the divinity
was attached as the surname. We find, for example, a long list of
Zeuses distinguished by their native names as surnames.

3. **The Local Origins of Divinities.**—Each god or goddess appears
to have arisen as the divinity of a particular group of people. Traces
of this origin persist in the myths and legends of European and
Levantine religions, but we perhaps come nearer to the primitive
in the religions of nomads of northwestern Asia. The divinity of the
nomad group at first is not attached to a locality, but follows the
group in its wanderings. If and when a previously nomadic group
settles in an area and begins an agricultural life or a localized
pastoral life, the god settles with them and becomes the 'lord'
of their area. In the Semitic languages that were spoken by peoples
of various racial stocks, these localized gods were called *Baalim*
(singular, *Baal* or *Bel:* lord or ruler). Having become attached
to the soil, the gods remained as local divinities after the population
was destroyed or removed, and new populations in the areas were
subject to the rule of the *Baalim* and were required to worship
them (see II Kings 17:24–28), although the newcomers might
worship also their own gods.

The early populations of Europe created or adopted gods, but
whether these peoples were nomads in their remote period, we do
not know. On the other hand, we are unable to conclude that the
autochthonous populations developed gods before they became
attached to the soil. Whether the Celts, Phoenicians, Achaeans,
and others of the red-haired, blue-eyed immigrants into Europe
and the Levant brought their divinities with them or created
them after settling is another problem for the solution of which we
have no basis. Although the religions of the nomads of interior
and northern Asia may be regarded as nearer to the primitive than

are the religions of Europe, inferences from the nomadic conditions to those of settled populations cannot be made *simpliciter*.

Among settled populations, divinities are developed mainly from economic necessities and economic practices. A hunting or a fishing people may develop gods of a sort, but with the adoption of an agricultural or a settled pastoral life, the development is more rapid and more important. This principle has been accepted by all scholars who have dealt with the development of religion, because it is obviously sound.

To the practical features of life that determine the creation of divinities we shall give further consideration in the proper place. For present purposes, it suffices to warn that the conception of a goddess or a god as the mother or the father of the group or the association of the divinity with a tribal 'totem' gives no indication of the processes through which the divinity actually was created.

Gods, or rather goddesses, are first conceived as trees, plants, or animals and later arrive at human status. Reinach has sagaciously indicated that the first step in the creation of a divinity is the ascription of sanctity to an entire species or variety of plants or animals and that the selection of a single specimen to represent the species is a later step.

The deification of springs and rivers (to which we have referred in Chap. III, Sec. 11) seems at first glance to complicate our problem regarding the creation of divinities, but, as we shall see, this offers no real difficulties. The occurrence of deified abstractions is more of a puzzle. Abstract divinities were frequent before the classical period of Greece. According to Pausanias, there were at Corinth images of Terror, Necessity, and Force. At Athens there were images of Modesty, Reputation, and Effort, with, curiously enough, images both of Demos (the people) and Democracy. At Olympia, Pausanias reports images of Struggle, Opportunity, and Truce, while at Aegina in Achaia he found an image of Safety.

Although abstract divinities, such as those we have mentioned, were probably of relatively late development, they are obviously products of the final form of the process of abstraction, which commenced by considering the manas of objects and of living beings in abstraction from the objects or organisms in which or through which the manas are exerted. The generalization of manas, which is a form of abstraction, began early in religious development, even before the differentiation of religion from praxis. When the mana of an animal is conceived as residing in all animals of the same species, an abstract concept of the mana has been formed. The deification of an animal possessing a certain mana is not in any sharp contrast with the deification of the mana abstracted from the animal; and, from this to the deification of more complex concepts such as Truth and Justice, the step is not difficult.

4. **The Ways of Divine Migration and Consequent Multiplication of Divinities.**—When a people not attached to the soil migrate into a new region, they take their divinities with them, but even divinities that have become attached to the soil as *Baalim* may be induced to break their roots and migrate with their people. This is easier for a pastoral people than for an agricultural population, but it is not probable that all the gods can be thus transported. The Hamito-Negroid invaders of Egypt brought with them from Ethiopia their hawk god, Ra, and their cow goddess, Hathor. But Ra flies and is not soil-bound, and the hordes of the Pharaoh apparently brought cattle into Egypt with them. Other African divinities, of whom traces persisted in Ethiopia, had become *Baalim* and were left behind.

A conquered group may adopt the divinities of the conquerors, and even with some assimilation the multiplication of divinities is promoted by such adoption. On the other hand, the conquerors, if they settle in the conquered areas, must adopt the divinities of the conquered population. Both of these effects were produced in Egypt, and the multiplication of divinities was tremendous.

When several groups, previously more or less independent of one another, combine into a nation, there is the tendency, often the necessity, for each of the local groups to adopt the gods and goddesses of all the others. This also is exemplified in Egyptian history; for when the Nomes were consolidated into the two kingdoms of Upper and Lower Egypt, the divinities of each Nome were added to those of the other Nomes in each kingdom, with some assimilation of the new gods to the older.

Even without conquest, colonization, or settlement in new areas, gods are imported from one group to another. This migration is promoted by trade relations between groups, by recognition of a common cultural basis of the groups, and sometimes by mere contiguity. The adoption by the Romans of the Asiatic gods Adonis, Mithra, and Ma may be explained as the adoption of the gods of conquered peoples; but the migration of gods into Greece was not a matter of conquest of the peoples from whom these gods were borrowed. Greek gods migrated to Asia Minor with no factor of conquest involved. Athena probably developed in Athens, but before the end of the classical era there were shrines and temples of Athena not only in various parts of the Greek world, but also in Asia Minor. This migration of Athena, Artemis, and other Greek divinities to the Levant may be said to have been largely nominal, the names alone having been assimilated to Asiatic divinities, but apparently other aspects of the Greek divinities were assimilated to some Asiatic gods and goddesses.

5. **Forms of Divine Assimilation.**—Assimilation of divinities, as we have already said in brief, may occur in either of two forms. An immigrant divinity may absorb a local god or goddess, or the local divinity may absorb the immigrant. Hera, originally the chief divinity of Argolis, probably furnishes an illustration of the second form. Hera was primarily a cow divinity who absorbed other cow goddesses or cow heroines such as Io, reducing them to the rank of mere heroines. Hera seems also to have absorbed a cloud goddess whose name may have been Euruphaessa (Euryphaessa), and the cloud goddess did not even persist as a heroine, but disappeared completely. Traces of still other goddesses absorbed by Hera are indicated.

In most instances, the form of assimilation is intermediate between the two extremes. Apollo, the oracular god of Delphi, included as his primary feature the snake god Puthon (Python), but he had also the aspects and symbols of a swan god, an apple god, and possibly a wolf god. In a later period, Apollo assimilated some of the aspects of a sun god, although there remained a number of sun gods, such as Helios and Phaëthon, whose identities were permanent. The apple god and the swan god were evidently immigrants from the northwestern region of Europe, where the people called by the Greeks the 'Hyperboreans' (probably the Nordics) lived, and were both completely assimilated to the original snake god of Delphi. According to some legends, Apollo slew the Python; according to other legends, the Python slew Apollo. In either case, the snake god survived as the principal feature of Apollo, who consequently was a god of healing, and the priestesses who gave the oracles at Delphi were called 'pythonesses.'

Demeter presents a peculiar case of assimilation. Demeter was a synthesis of a mare goddess, a sow goddess, a snake goddess, and a barley goddess. In her rituals, myths, and symbols, she retained all these aspects, but eventually the barley aspect became paramount and the other aspects were assimilated to that one. It is probable that the relative importance of the various aspects of the divinities assimilated in Demeter had changed progressively in earlier periods. It is possible that the barley goddess originated at Eleusis and that the other goddesses were immigrants who were assimilated to the goddess of the barley, but there is no certainty as to this.

According to scholars, most of whom have been prejudiced by too much dependence on philology, Dionysos was an immigrant into Greece, and the place of his foreign origin has been a topic for much scholarly disputation. The assumption that the various gods called 'Dionysos' in different areas were all the same divinity, imported and naturalized on the 'all-or-nothing' plan in the several places, does not, however, seem to be borne out by the evidence that these scholars have collected. The variety of aspects ascribed to Dionysos in different areas and the variety of plastic representation and pictures all support the interpretation that these gods were various local divinities who assimilated the name Dionysos, which possibly was imported, and who absorbed some other characteristics of different foreign and domestic gods.

The outstanding illustration of the assimilation of divinities of a wide range to a basic concept and to a single name, with little else, is supplied by the Greek 'Zeus.' The concept is that of a supreme divinity, at least of a divinity more or less supreme over other gods and goddesses—to use Homer's phrase, 'King of gods and men.' It is noteworthy that the various gods called Zeus in the Greek tongue were never identified completely as a single divinity, but each retained his individual traits and was worshiped by his special ritual. The name Zeus can be accepted as a dialectical form of the word for god, which in classical Greek is *theos*, the name Zeus being eventually reserved for the great gods. As gods multiplied, the tendency to rate one as more powerful than another was natural. With the ascendancy of the male, there were gods called Zeus in various places, and the identification of these gods with one another was nowhere complete. As we have pointed out above, the various gods called Zeus were distinguished by surnames, which in many cases indicate the original god. Zeus Melosios was a protector of herds. Zeus Lukaios in Arcadia was a god of the daylight. Zeus Asterios was probably an ancient form of Pan.

The Zeus of the oak grove at Dodona is allied to Peruna and other oak gods of Slavic peoples. Zeus Pelasgikos was, without doubt, Poseidon.

On this basis and no other, we can understand how Zeus was born in so many different places. We can understand also the various metamorphoses of Zeus as a combination of legends about a variety of gods. The Zeus, for example, who assumed the form of a swan to seduce Leda was evidently a swan god; the Zeus who took the form of a bull to seduce Europa can easily be identified as the Cretan bull Zeus.

Some of the ancient great divinities escaped assimilation into the nominal Zeus. These include Pan, Hephaistos, Hermes, and Poseidon. Hermes, however, became the messenger of Zeus, or, as has been said, 'the executive aspect of Zeus'; and Apollo was reduced to being the son of Zeus. These gods were too great and had themselves assimilated so many other divinities that they could not be taken into the nominal Zeus. For somewhat the same reason there was no female counterpart of Zeus. Demeter, Athena, and Artemis were far too important to be assimilated to Hera who, although she ranked as the queen of the gods, was actually of lesser importance than these great goddesses.

In the process of assimilation some curious myths were produced, in which the various god elements appear as actors in the drama. In the myths about Apollo, the god slays himself, for he (the synthetic Apollo) is the combination of the snake god (*python*) and the apple and swan gods from the north. In the Phrygian legends, Attis is slain by a wild boar under a pine tree; but the boar is Attis, and the pine tree is Attis, so Attis slays Attis under Attis. This feature of a myth is technically called 'reduplication,' but the real explanation is that Attis is the result of assimilation of a pine god and boar god. The persistence down to the end of paganism of the pine tree and the boar as symbols of Attis (often designated as Adonis) is thus comprehensible. In the less complex reduplications, Attis is slain by the boar, with no mention of the pine tree, or Attis emasculates himself under a pine tree.

An instance of reduplication due to the coalescence of two traditions is presented in the Gospel account of the crucifixion, in which Jesus and Barabbas (*Bar-abbas* meaning 'son of the father') seem to be the same person. In this story are combined the legend of a religious teacher, the legend of a leader of an insurrection against the

Roman government, and traditions of an older Syrian ritual of human sacrifice in which a victim was selected, crowned, and worshiped as the son of god, and finally killed that he might carry messages to the father god.[1]

6. Further Factors in the Multiplication of Divinities.—Migration of divinities with incomplete assimilation results inevitably in multiplication of divinities, which eventually produces a chaotic polytheism; but there are other factors that contribute to the multiplication. The change of divinities from female to male did not always eliminate the goddess, but left her merely reduced in status, thus increasing the number of divinities.

Assimilation of an immigrant divinity to a native one usually did not abolish the immigrant. When a god or goddess was imported into an area in which there was already a divinity of the same name, the native and the imported divinities remained distinct. To the original Athena at Athens were added by importation at least six other Athenas; these Athenas were never combined, but remained different Athenas. This is an illustration of a divinity migrating from her original home, acquiring a differentiating surname and some changes in attributes, and then migrating back to her original place. In other instances, foreign divinities were imported under the name of a native divinity, with a distinguishing surname. In Arcadia, various alien goddesses, which were identified as Artemis, each with a distinguishing surname, were borrowed from their original cults and remained separate goddesses.

In some cases the surnames were not derived from the place of origin but signified characteristics ascribed to the divinities. Of this order were the names of Zeus Savior, Artemis Savior, Zeus the Friendly, and Artemis Brauronia (of the bear). The nature of the surname, however, was not important for the keeping of various divinities given the same name distinct from each other.

It is possible that if Mediterranean paganism had continued for another thousand years, the chaos of polytheism would have been reduced. The organization of the greater gods and goddesses into a family was a step in that direction, and the nominal identification of a number of great gods under the name of 'Zeus' was another step. Earlier assimilation of divinities had helped a little but not much. The tendency in all religions is first to multiply divinities and later to reduce the number by systematization. It is possible

[1] J. M. Robertson, *Pagan Christs*, p. 138.

that Greek paganism might eventually have arrived at monotheism, but this is conjectural. Monotheism may be officially endorsed, but usually polytheism continues as the religion of the common people unless a social catastrophe intervenes; in most cases the polytheism under cover is eventually recognized officially.

7. The Personalization of Divinities.—According to the theory of animism, which happily no longer troubles students of religion, religion began with the ascription of daimons, or spirits, to animals, plants, and inanimate objects; from these daimon divinities developed. Since we are disposed to date the beginnings of religion far earlier than the rise of the concept of daimons, the development of personal divinities cannot be so easily explained.

It is evident that early in the development of religion animals of a given species were all credited with the same manas; that plants of a given species were all likewise assigned the same manas. This is a consistent extension of the facts of common observation, although not a sound one. Plants and animals of given species do agree in their characteristics, but not completely. Eventually particular plants and particular animals were selected as representing the species, in respect to the manas assigned, whether the manas were natural or supernatural. Bulls, for example, have certain characteristics, natural and supernatural; but one particular bull in Egypt (the Apis bull) became the center, or at least the important representative, of the manas that were, from our point of view, superstitiously ascribed to the species.

Ascribing supernatural manas first to a plant species and then to a particular plant is designated as 'thallomorphism'; likewise, ascribing supernatural manas to an animal species and finally to a particular animal is 'thieromorphism.' From either of these stages in the development of religion, the next step is obvious. The animal or plant divinity is anthropomorphized, that is, has human traits ascribed to it. Inverting Genesis 1: 27 (with due respect to Xenophanes), man creates gods in his own image, but this is only a final step in the long course of development of divinities. It is a final step since the further transformation of divinities into abstract powers, which occurs in some religions, is really a regression toward the primitive stage of religion.

Representation of divinities in animal forms may begin in the use of such images as symbols of the animal manas, but, if the course of development is not interrupted, the animals represented, if not the representations themselves, become the actual divinities. That idols in animal form were, for the populace, actual divinities is evident in ancient Egypt and the Levant. The idols are not mere symbols of gods and goddesses, but are the divinities, the manas ascribed being resident in, and exercised by, the image itself.

The transition from animal divinities to divinities in human form is clearly recorded in the representations of the gods of the Egyptians. The transition was through animal images with human heads, and human figures with animal heads, to human figures to which the symbols of the original animal deity were affixed. Hathor, for example, is represented as a cow, as a cow with a human head, as a woman with a cow's head, and as a woman without any bovine trait. In the latter images, however, the cow's horns or the equivalent lunar crescent are always represented somewhere in connection with the statue or the painting. Gods of other animal types—crocodile gods, ibis gods, hippopotamus gods, etc.—were represented, in their intermediate stages, as human bodies with animal heads, less often as animals with human heads.

It is probable that some divinities were created in the anthropomorphic stage, without having gone through the thieromorphic or the thallomorphic stage. Such creation could be possible only after other humanized divinities had developed through the plant or the animal stage. It seems clear that after divinities had become anthropomorphic, no further plant or animal gods or goddesses were created.

8. The Sex of Divinities.—Certain traits and potentialities of human beings and of the lower animals are obviously male, and certain other traits are female. In the plant world, the separation of the sexes is less obvious, but, from the remote past down, man has known that in certain species of trees, such as the date palm, some trees are of one sex and some of the other. This separation of male traits from female traits in trees and animals is especially important in and for the reproduction of the species, for which man in all cultures has well known the cooperation of the male and female is essential. In view of these facts, we cannot regard it as strange that divinities when they were created were endowed with sex.

In the religions of the areas to which we are giving primary consideration, the divinities were created first as goddesses. This fact is accepted by all serious scholars of religion, and while the scholars do not agree in their explanations, there is a consensus as to the factors involved in the later change of divinity from female to male.

MacCulloch in his article on the Celts (Hastings, I: 2) assumes the importance of agriculture in the development of religion, which is sound, although MacCulloch overemphasizes the principle. He further assumes that agriculture was developed by women, who began with the gathering of wild fruits, seeds, and roots (an assumption for which there is little proof). MacCulloch then concludes that religion, developed by women from their agriculture, inevitably produced female divinities, the women creating divinity in their own images. MacCulloch, unfortunately, ignores the religion of hunting and fishing peoples and of the nomadic pastoral groups. He ignores also the thieromorphic and thallomorphic stages through which divinities progressed, seeming to assume divinities as created in the anthropomorphic stage.

Other speculators have assumed that agriculture was the product of male activity and have given attention to the religions of hunting, fishing, and pastoral peoples, among whom the labor involved in providing the means of subsistence is done chiefly by the men. These theorists consequently have concluded that religion is a creation of men primarily. The explanation offered for the origin of divinities as female is then found in the extreme interest of the male in the female, both for satisfaction of erotic desire and for reproduction of the human species, and in the fear of the female because of her mysterious menstrual cycle. The female reproductive function was an influential factor in the determining of divine sex, and the menstrual cycle, so curiously related to the lunar phases, has had religious importance. The inferences of the theorists, however, are much too simple regarding both of these female functions.

Increased importance of the human male was undoubtedly an important factor in producing the changes from male to female divinity. Change from the matrilocal and matrilineal family systems to the patrilocal and patrilineal systems were in part responsible for the increase of male prestige and authority. These were primarily economic changes; other economic changes that increased the food supply were also influential.

The known changes from the matrilocal system to the patrilocal system, and from the matrilineal to the patrilineal, have given rise to a theory that there was, in early times, a matriarchal system that gave way to the patriarchal system. As a matter of fact, no evidence for a matriarchate (government of a group by a head woman) is discoverable in ancient history or traditions. A valid picture of a system that was matrilocal and probably matrilineal, but patriarchal, is given in the story of Jacob and the family of Laban (Genesis 28–31). Jacob joined the family in which his two wives were born, and, although he was free to leave, he had no right to take with him his wives, his children, or any group property.

The converse system, patrilocal and probably patrilineal, is pictured in the story of Isaac and Rebecca (Genesis 24), in which Rebecca joins the family of her husband.

Another social change that contributed directly to the raising of the prestige of men and which also contributed to the development of the patrilocal and patrilineal systems was the rise of war and the organization of armed military forces. Informal aggression and mass migrations into the territories of other peoples are phenomena of one order; assault and aggression by organized armies and organized defense are of a different order. The male, as a soldier, is highly important in his group; men organized as a warrior group become superior to all other group members and especially to women, who are relegated to inferior roles.

The change of divinities from female to male has seldom been a simple process of modification of characteristics, although the occurrence of Arabian gods carrying the name of Ishtar indicates that this simple change did occur sometimes. One of the more common processes was exemplified in Mesopotamia. The goddess, previously supreme, was given a consort, probably an immigrant god in most cases; but in some cases a male divinity was created as an analogue to the goddess. The goddess was thus reduced to a secondary position and in some cases was eventually eliminated, as Ashtoreth was eliminated from the Hebrew religion. The accounts in Kings and Chronicles of the long struggle to build up the worship of Jehovah are stories of the subordination of the goddess to a male divinity and of her final ousting.

In Asia Minor, the goddesses remained primary; the gods, for the most part, were secondary; male divinities did not evolve beyond the stage of paramours of the goddesses. In Syria, masculinization of divinities was apparently due to Hittite influence; in Mesopotamia, the change in sex was imposed by the Assyrians from the north. The masculinization of divinities apparently occurred earlier among the Armenoid autochthones of the interior of Europe and of the regions north of Mesopotamia than among the southern groups.

Whether or not divinity began as female among savages we cannot say, since we have no information concerning the development of savage cultures and religions. Among the Mongolian nomads it is possible that the divinities were male from the beginning, since among nomads the males are dominant and possibly were so in the earliest periods. Concerning the development of the religion of the Mongolian nomads, which has never advanced beyond a crude stage, we have little more information than we have concerning the development of savage religions.

In Greece, the rise in power and staus of male divinities was probably influenced by the 'return of the Dorians' from the Balkan region, since masculinization was least in the regions that were least affected by the Dorians. In this connection it is worthy of note that the divinities who were imported into Greece from the north, Apollo and Mars, were male. Exclusive of the influence of the men from the forests, however, changes are indicated. Hera, the old goddess dominant in Argolis, became the secondary aspect, or wife, of Zeus. Dionysos apparently supplanted goddesses in various places and became associated with Demeter. Mare goddesses, of whom traces were left in Demeter, Kore, and Athena, were supplanted by Poseidon. Artemis became the subordinate 'sister' of Apollo. In the long list of heroines, nymphs, and minor goddesses who were ascribed to the synthetic 'Zeus,' as his paramours, we have the shadows of the goddesses who reigned before the rise of the Zeus gods.

It is necessary to take a critical attitude toward the myths that have grown up in Hindu culture and to the theories of scholars who have naïvely accepted these myths as historically valid. We may assume that all myths of natural development, that is, those which are social products, and not the work of inventors or editors, have some bases in facts. Even in myths and legends that have been distorted and confused by later editing (as in the case of the Jewish Scriptures), the original features and their significance may be discerned if there are sufficient historical, archaeological, and anthropological data with which to compare the legendary material.

In Hindu religions of the orthodox group the concept of divinity has reached the stage approximately parallel to that of Greek religion between 1000 and 500 B.C. Among some groups the goddesses have been reduced to secondary status, but for the popular belief they are still paramount, although paramours are assigned to them. In Buddhism, the female divinity has been completely eliminated, while in the religions of some other unorthodox sects the elimination is less complete.

In Egypt and in Babylonia, an attempt was made to settle the conflict between the male and female concepts of divinity by organizing trinities of the father-mother-son type, a ratio of two to one in favor of the male. The trinity of Osiris, Isis, and Horus is typical. Osiris was apparently a native divinity, identified with the grain called 'spelt' (a grain related to wheat); Isis was the synthesis of the Pharaonic cow goddess Hathor and various native fertility goddesses. Horus, made the child of Isis and Osiris, is practically the hawk god Ra brought in from Ethiopia by the Pharaonic hordes. Similar divine trinities, with the male ratios two to one over the female, were composed in Babylonia. In Greece, the tendency to the composition of trinities was checked, apparently by the organization of the royal Olympian family. Some incipient trinities are recognizable, nevertheless—some with two goddesses involved, as in the relation of Poseidon, Demeter, and Kore, and some with two gods and a human mother, as in the case of Zeus, Semele, and Dionysos and that of Apollo, Koronis, and Asklepios.

Two more factors in the evolution of divinities remain to be mentioned. One is the influence of kings in determining the traits of divinities. Frazer, throughout the *Golden Bough.* (ref. I: 3), makes much of this factor. Kings, of course, have greater actual power than do their subjects, and these powers are easily extended into the magical domain of manas by addition of supernatural manas to the real powers. Among such manas have been power over the weather, control of the growth of crops, and power to heal the sick. The influence of kings in the development of divinities, however, is possible only in the later stage of development of the divine concept, when divinity has become not only humanized, but also masculinized. That in this stage aspects of royalty, such as imperial moral irresponsibility, and symbols of royalty, such as crowns, thrones, and scepters, should be attributed to gods is quite intelligible. By most Christians of orthodox sects, God is conceived, even today, as a great king or as 'King of Kings,' and the references to crowns and other symbols of imperial majesty are widely scattered through church hymns.

The second factor is the creation of demigods or 'saints' from among the ranks of persons who, during their lives, were revered or to whom were ascribed extraordinary powers. After death, these persons are elevated to semidivine rank. In a thoroughly masculinized religion, these saints or demigods are of the male sex only, the occurrence of female saints being evidence that masculinization of divinity has not been complete.

The real point of importance in regard to sex and other traits of divinity could be expressed as an answer to the question, What sort of divinity is most useful to mankind? This question may be formulated also as, What sort of divinity does man really want? That man wants a divinity of the sexless type of the Hindu Brahma or the *nous* of Aristotle has so far not been demonstrated.

To become a saint, a person after death must be canonized by ritual procedures. A somewhat similar procedure was followed by early Mediterranean peoples for the elevation of a popular hero to the rank of minor divinity, the endorsement of the hero and recommendation that he be worshiped as a god emanating from a recognized oracle.

9. The Gods Leave the Earth.—Edward Rowland Sill in his poem on 'The Venus of Milo' wrote: 'From our low world no gods have taken wing.' This statement, however, is too broad. Some of the ancient divinities took flight from the 'low' part of our world to the skies. Others, indeed, remained earth-bound until their cults died out. If the poet had specified 'goddesses' instead of 'gods,' his statement would have been more accurate, for most of the ancient goddesses were earthbound until their ends. Some divinities who originally lived on the surface of the earth took, eventually, to the underworld of ghosts, from which they emerged occasionally and temporarily. Such were Aïdoneus (Hades), and Hekate. Persephone, originally an earth goddess, came to spend the winter season as queen of the underworld and the spring and summer above ground. Tammuz, Attis, and Adonis died in the fall and went to the underworld, returning in the spring. The Babylonian Ishtar went down to the underworld annually to bring back Tammuz, but there is no evidence as to whether a goddess went down to bring back Attis and Adonis. This part-time dwelling in the underworld, as we have explained, was a representation of the death of vegetation in the fall and its revival in the spring. Persephone, Tammuz, Adonis, and Attis, in other words, were the divinities of the growing things, although the goddesses associated with them were obviously the divinities of vegetation in earlier periods. Demeter, Artemis, Despoina, Kubele, and Aphrodite remained earth-bound to the ends of their cults along with many lesser goddesses and female daimons.

Divinities having their dwellings on the mountain tops—on Mount Olympus in Thessaly, on Mount Ida in Crete, on the other Mt. Ida in the Troad, and on numerous other peaks—may be counted as still on earth, although the point is a minor one as compared with the evident fact that divinities evolved from plants and animals on earth before they winged their ways to the heavens. The point might be made that a pious Roman Catholic genuflecting to the Host really identifies the Host with God. The Host, however, is believed to be a part of God on earth and the identification is thus akin to the identification of a particular animal or tree with a divinity, ascribing the manas of an animal or plant species to a particular individual, which is a symbol of the species.

The ascription of the production of meteorological phenomena to divinities is a simpler case, but akin to the personification of the manas of the sun and moon. Thunder, lightning, rain are produced by a divinity (a 'Zeus' eventually), and the production of these phenomena is a result of a mana of the god. The phenomena are not the god himself. The mana to produce heat and light are included in the personification of a sun god, but that does not mean that the sun and the god are necessarily identified.

The manas of the gods were sometimes personified as their children. Thus, Eos, a personification of the dawn, was a daughter of Zeus. Eos was, in short, neither the dawn as such nor an independent divinity of the dawn. Zeus, in his meteorological aspect, brings the dawn, and Eos is merely a personification of that power of Zeus. Helios was a personification of the power of the sun to spread light and heat, but the power of the sun to travel through the heavens was thieromorphically represented by the divine horses who drew the sun's chariot, and anthropomorphically personified in Phaeton, the Sun's charioteer. These personifications are strangely like the personifications of courage, democracy, and panic.

If, as some scholars have maintained, religion had its beginnings in human awe, fear, and reverence for the heavenly bodies and for meteorological phenomena, we would have expected to find these bodies and phenomena actually worshipped and the gods identified with them at the earliest period of religious development. It is evident that religion did not begin this way, but that the personification of the heavenly and meteorological powers came late in religious development. It is evident also that personification of divinity is not a simple matter, that the manas of objects, plants, and animals are really what are first personified.

To clarify the relations of the divinities to the forces and powers of the weather and to the heavenly bodies, it is necessary to examine into a concept that was held by all ancient peoples from western India through the Mediterranean area. This is the concept of what the Greeks called a '*stoicheion*' (plural, *stoicheia*) and the Latins called an '*elementum*' (plural, *elementa*). These *elementa* were four in number, but a fifth was sometimes added. Earth, water, air, and fire were the four; ether was the fifth, which was added by some speculators. We still speak of the 'elements' in this sense in modern times, especially in regard to storms, which we describe as the 'raging of the elements.' But we do not view them in the same way as that in which they were viewed by ancient peoples. The four elements were accepted as the fundamental stuffs of which all earthly things are composed. The four were holy, especially in the East, but even in the Mediterranean area a certain religious coloring attached to them. We sometimes describe the ancient Iranians (Persians) as 'fire-worshipers'; but actually they held all four of the *elementa* sacred. A corpse could not be buried unless it were encased in wax, for otherwise it would pollute the holy earth. It could not be thrown into a stream or into the sea, for it would then pollute the holy water. It could not be allowed to decompose on the surface of the ground, for it would thus pollute the holy air. If it were burned, the holy fire would be polluted. The whole situation seems to have been quite impractical, for the wax supply, of course, could not have been sufficient, and we must assumes that there was a great deal of pollution of the holy earth. Eventually pollution of the *elementa* was minimized by the institution of the 'Towers of Silence,' in which vultures stripped the flesh from the bones of corpses, the pollution of the air being thus minimized, and the disposal of the bare bones was a matter of little trouble. This institution was carried to India by the group of Persians who fled from Iran when the Mohammedans conquered the country and is still maintained by the 'Parsees' (a name corrupted from 'Persians').

In India down to the present time the four *elementa* are holy, and in the Brahamical rituals the four products of the cow (milk, ghee, dung, and urine) are symbols of the four *elements*. In Greece, where both cremation and earth burial were practiced, it would appear that the sanctity of the *elementa* was less than in the eastern regions.

Philosophy, in all its origins, grew out of religion, and the early philosophers of Greece never doubted the fundamental nature of the *stoicheia*. Even Aristotle built his philosophy about the four *stoicheia*. Corresponding to the four primary stuffs, there should be four senses, and Aristotle achieved this fourfold scheme by identifying taste as a special form of touch. He assumes for each sense an organ, a medium for transmission of the stimulus to the organ, and a receptor or sensitive element in the organ. His scheme finally worked out as follows.

Sense	Organ	Medium	Receptor
Vision	Eye	*a.* Air *b.* Water	Fire
Audition	Ear	*a.* Air *b.* Water	Air
Olfaction	Nose	*a.* Air *b.* Water	Fire
Touch proper	Heart	Flesh	?
Taste	?	Flesh of tongue	?

Acceptance of both air and water as media for the three cranial senses was due to Aristotle's knowledge that one can both hear and see under water and that fishes have a sense of smell. Since taste was assumed as a form of touch, it is probable that the heart was assumed to be the organ. We might suppose that the receptor for touch was, for Aristotle, air in the heart, but this is not explicitly stated by Aristotle.

In popular thought, each of the *stoicheia* had a specific attribute. Earth is dry; water is wet; air is cold; and fire is hot. In the writings that have come down to us, these *stoicheia* are commonly designated by their attributes. 'The dry' means earth. 'The wet' means water. 'The cold' means air. 'The hot' means fire. This ascription of a single attribute to each *elementum* did not suit Aristotle, who attempted to assign to each of the four *elementa* two of the four attributes. His schematization is not clear, and different students

of Aristotle have come to different conclusions regarding his assignment of attributes.   According to A. W. Benn, for example, Aristotle
schematized earth as dry and cold, water as wet and cold, air as
wet and hot, and fire as dry and hot.   This seems to be a departure
from traditional notions greater than Aristotle would have made.
Another scheme, which is somewhat more plausible, makes fire hot
and dry, air cold and dry, water cold and wet, and earth hot and
wet.   The fact seems to be that Aristotle played around with
various permutations of the *stoicheia* and their attributes and never
found a suitable combination.   Air was so generally accepted as
cold and earth as dry, that neither of the two schemes presented
above would have been accepted by Aristotle, who leaned heavily
on the past.   The safe assumption is that Aristotle played with the
binary combinations of attributes but gave up the attempt.

In the beginnings of philosophy in Ionia, we find a school of water
philosophers originating with Thales, a school of air philosophers
represented by Anaximander, and a school of fire philosophers
founded by Heracleitos.   It is not to be assumed, however, that
philosophers of these schools rejected the other *stoicheia*, for they
accepted them as naively as did the populace.   The problem for the
philosophers was simply to determine which of the *stoicheia* was
'first' in the evolutionary scheme.   Did earth, fire, and air evolve
from water?   Did earth, water, and fire develop from air?   Or did
earth, water, and air develop from fire?   It may seem strange that
there was no earth philosophy; but we must remember that for
popular belief earth was fundamental and the other *stoicheia* supplementary, not in the evolutionary sense, perhaps, but in relative
importance.   Philosophy indeed develops from popular notions and
accepts popular concepts but seeks to alter the notions with which
it starts.

The Eleatic philosophy in Italy, which possibly started from the
teachings of Xenophanes and which was elaborated by Parmenides,
accepted the four *stoicheia* as naïvely as did the Ionian schools.
Their problem was the problem of *being*.   Being of what?   Why,
the being of the *stoicheia*, of course.   For the Eleatics, there was no
problem of primacy of one over the others, but the problem of the
existence of all was their concern.   We might point out that in the
fire philosophy of Heracleitos there was no question of primacy,
since for Heracleitos there was an endless succession of transformation of fire into air, air into water, and water into earth, with the

reverse process of transformation of earth into water, water into air, and air into fire. Fire, for Heracleitos, was of primary import-ance, not in the evolutionary sense, but because the life stuff was identified with fire, and life is the important thing.

Empedocles, the Sicilian medical faker who is counted as a mem-ber of the Eleatic school, abandoned the problem of primacy in all senses, reverted to the ancient popular notion that the four *stoicheia* are equally primary, and taught that the life stuff is composed of a mixture of all four just as everything else is.

In religious development, earth had a position of major importance because man lives on the surface of the earth and the earth produces the plants that provide food for him directly and also indirectly through the flesh of the animals that feed on the plants. On earth the gods developed; and it is not strange that Mother Earth herself was made into a divinity as Ge, Gaia, Maia, Demeter, and with other names. Fish and water animals were sources of food, but the men who took fish still lived on land. The importance of water for the growth of plant life and for the drink of men and animals was recognized, but water is useful only if land is fertilized by it and if the animals who drink it have food also. The development of fresh-water divinities and sea divinities in great number was inevitable but was secondary to the development of earth gods and earth goddesses.

That air divinities developed is evident. The importance of air for breathing is unmistakable, and air was the first life stuff assumed. The 'breath of life' is an expression found in various forms in all ancient languages. That this assumption of air as the life stuff influenced the development of air divinities is probable. Among the later divinities who had assimilated air divinities, Hera is conspicuous, for her name literally means 'air.' Athena also is believed to have assimilated an air goddess.

The flight of some of the divinities to the mountaintops is in a sense a moving from earth to the air, although, as we have pointed out, the mountains are parts of the earth. High mountains such as Mount Olympus were supposed to project through the air into the ether. The ancient concept of the ether, however, is not clear. Apparently for some types of thinker the ether was the dry stratum of the atmosphere, the lower strata being assumed to be moist, as they really are. For others ether was identified with fire. In either case, the ether was merely a special form of another *elementum*, either a form of air or of fire.   The sky was thought of as a metal surface to which the stars were fastened; the atmosphere extended from the surface of the earth to the starry dome.   The ether, in all views, was the upper layer of the atmosphere.

The early gods moved about on earth much as men and animals do, but later they were believed to fly through the air, although not needing wings like those of birds.   Even Pan, the most earth-bound of the gods, seems, in the classic period, or shortly before it, to have flitted from one place to another without walking; but he could not have done that in a more primitive period.   Demeter, on the other hand, seems never to have been able to move from place to place without walking or riding in a chariot.   Apollo, in the myths, flew on the back of a swan or in a chariot drawn by swans. Triptolemos, the messenger of Demeter who took barley to men in various places, is represented as riding in a chariot drawn by serpents.   Apparently the notion of a god or goddess flitting from one place to another without a vehicle was a late development and was most characteristic of the divine dwellers on the mountaintops.

CHAPTER V

THE ROLE OF DESIRE IN RELIGION

1. The Importance of Desire.—We have suggested earlier that religion develops from man's praxis, as do magic and science. This is no startling idea, for few modern scholars in the field of comparative religion take an opposed point of view. (The philological school of a generation ago, addicted to solar theories of religious origins, was the exception.) The differences between the various theories of religious origin and development have concerned the order and details of the process of emergence of religion and the psychological and culture factors that have been most important in causing, promoting, or directing the emergence and the further development of religion.

The development of praxis in its simplest forms is motivated by desires, which man attempts to satisfy and does satisfy through the procedures he undertakes. The praxes involved in hunting and fishing, in agriculture and animal husbandry, the making of clothing and the construction of fortresses and dwellings are procedures for the satisfaction of desires. The making of tools, weapons, pottery, and innumerable other artifacts is motivated by desires, since these artifacts are important aids to the carrying out of the final processes.

We may assume, therefore, that in the further development in which praxis includes elements that retrospectively we discriminate as magical or religious, and that in the still further evolution in which religion emerges as a system of activities and beliefs contemporaneously distinguishable from praxis, desire was still the moving power. That magic, when it becomes distinct, is still motivated by desire is easily demonstrated; for man, when he practices magic or witchcraft, does so because there is something he wants. We shall attempt, in this chapter and in further chapters to justify the principle that religion, even in its late stages, is directed by desires. To this end we shall first pay attention to the influence of desires is earlier stages of religious development.

If we consider any fully developed religion, and as we consider one religion after another, we find everywhere the implication or the explicit admission that there is something or are some things that man wants and that he deems it possible to secure through religion. The works of religion are activities designed to secure these goods; the beliefs of religion concern the validity of the procedures, the nature of the goods desired, and the powers and personages involved in the system to which the goods pertain. Religion, like the secular phases of life, revolves around desire, and the activities of religion are accredited as means to the satisfaction of desires.

The particular desires that man hopes to satisfy through religion vary from cult to cult, and in what we call the 'same' religion the desires vary from period to period. In the same period of a given religion, the desires may be evaluated differently by different groups of adherents, some emphasizing certain desires, and some emphasizing certain others. 'Give us this day our daily bread' is the expression of a desire that has been and still is literally significant to some Christians. For other groups, the expression is merely formal or understood to refer to desires other than those for food. 'Lead us not into temptation' is the expression of an urgent desire on the part of some sorely tried persons, but an empty formula for others who are more self-assured. The desires expressed in the prayers, litanies, hymns, and scriptures of Christianity are innumerable and evident, but the interpretations and emphases vary. The moving power of desire and the variability in the specific desires are as evident in other religions, both ancient and modern.

2. Desire and Needs.—That which man *needs* is that which would benefit him and which he has not. Unfortunately, man does not always really need what he desires. There is, sometimes, a confusion of these two concepts, which is partly due to the dual sense in which the word 'want' is used. Sometimes want means desire, but sometimes it means lack or need. For this reason, the term want is best avoided if we are to keep our terminology significant and our discussion clear.

Desire is an actual psychological process in which a person thinks of an object which he has not or of a condition in which he is not. In addition to the cognitive element in desire, there is an affective, or feeling, element that distinguishes it from mere thinking. One may think of another person who is absent without in the least desiring his presence, but one cannot desire the other person's presence without thinking of his absence. Both the ideational and the affective factors are essential in desire.

Need, on the other hand, is a condition that may or may not be known to the person who is 'in need.' Need, if a person becomes conscious of it, may give rise to desire, although the need may have been as real before it was known to exist. People have needed vitamin A for years, but, not knowing that they needed it, they did not desire it. Thought of the need, however, becomes a motive for the desire, which in turn is the motive for the obtaining and applying of the vitamin. Thinking that one needs a certain medicine may, on the other hand, produce the desire for it when the need really does not exist.

Human praxis does not grow simply out of needs but is based on conscious desires. Simple desire for food (appetite) may cause a person to take and eat food if it is perceived, but the procedures involved in human praxis that indirectly provide food are results of desires upon which man has reflected—that is, about which he has thought further. Not mere lack of the means of satisfying desire, but recognition of the lack, leads to the praxis which, carried out in advance, provides the means or increases the provision. Where food is abundant and always available, food praxis is simple. It is where the lack occurs and is foreseen as certain or probable that the most effective techniques of praxis are invented through observation of the ways in which the means (the foodstuffs) are produced and the reflection on these processes.

In the lower animals, needs are relatively simple and, in most cases, appear to produce the activities requisite to fulfill them by simple processes not rising above the perceptual level. The tiger needs food; this makes him restless, perhaps arouses unpleasant feelings. He wanders about guided by visual and olfactory clues, finds his prey and eats it. If he thinks of food, or of getting food, his thought is obviously of a low or crude order, perhaps restricted to simple imagination. He develops no praxis for promoting the production of food animals or for securing them.

It is true that rats, apes, and other animals in experimental situations develop some types of simple praxis, such as pulling strings, jumping on treadles, etc., to secure food. These praxes never become complicated or involve foresight over any considerable period. The hoarding of nuts by squirrels probably does not involve foresight, certainly not reflection, but is produced by the combining of perceptual and affective processes to which, without analysis, we have in the past applied the misleading (pseudo-explanatory) term 'instinct.' On the whole, there are no grounds whatever for supposing that any animals below the human level develop anything that could be called religion. Their praxes do not develop anything beyond simple processes. We make an unjustified assumption even if we ascribe motivation to animals, for motivation involves desire, which is a complex process probably above the mental level even of the ape.

3. The Primary Desires.—There seem to be no desires that are not, or have not at some time been, items in religions. Prayer certainly is an expression of desire, and there is nothing which man could desire that some man does not or has not prayed for. Many desires, however, are ephemeral. Man today desires many things of which men did not even dream a few years ago. On the other hand, many objects desired in the past are no longer desired. If we propose to trace the development of religion over a long period, and relate this development to future conditions, it would seem that we should pay particular attention to those desires which have long endured and which promise to endure further. We must consider desires which have been present in man's life universally, from the remote past to the present day, and which man will probably retain. Such desires we may call 'fundamental' or 'basic.'

It has been charged in the past that the desires listed are merely 'instincts' under new names. This charge is due to failure to understand the nature of a desire and the nature of an instinct. Instincts are classes of behavior, classified not in accordance with any conscious processes in the animal to whom instincts are assigned, but in accordance with the ends or purposes which, in the opinion of the classifier, the behavior may attain. Since any analysis or discussion in terms of, or with respect to ends or objectives is properly teleological, we can describe instincts correctly as 'teleological constructs.'

A desire, on the other hand, is an actual psychological process, a conscious process which involves thinking and feeling. It is in no sense an abstraction or a construction, but an actual occurrence which is to be found in the conscious life of every human being. In classifying desires, we are proceeding abstractly, but the desires classified are not abstractions.

We may well repeat that man does not desire what he has, but desires what he has not. He may desire to continue in the possession of what he has, for this continuance is 'not yet.' We have pointed out that he desires not only what he needs, that is, cannot do without, but also many things that he does not need; and that things may be needed but not desired, especially if the need is so abundantly supplied that there is no lack or if man does not recognize the need. We need air, for example, but under ordinary conditions there is no lack of air, hence it is only under the exceptional conditions of suffocation that man desires air. Man long needed sanitation, but he did not know he needed it, hence did not desire it.

Desire, in other words, involves the *recognition of lack*, either of lack as existing or as a distinct possibility or threat for the future. The primary desires, accordingly, are the desires for those things which have always been problematical or contingent, or which over long periods and for man universally have been frequently lacking or insufficient in supply.

The primary desires may usefully be classed under nine headings.

1. *Alimentary* desire. Desire for food and drink or for substances substituted for these.

2. *Protectional* desire. Desire for protection from any or all of the objects, forces, and conditions that threaten injury, suffering, or death.

3. Desire for *rest*. Under this heading relaxation, relief, and recreation may well be included, since there are no lines between these several benefits insofar as they involve cessation of muscular tensions.

4. Desire for *activity*. In some cases this is opposed to the rest desire but usually the desire for rest is desire for relief from forced activity. In many cases, however, as in recreation, the two desires may have a common motivation.

5. *Excretory* desire. This is typified by the basic desires for defecation and urination, but various other removals of annoying factors may be desired in different circumstances, as, for example, the removal of sweat and dirt from the skin. In some cases, the desire may include in its total content relief of muscular tensions as in the basic excretory desires, but relaxation does not account for the contents of the desire in all instances.

6. *Erotic* or amatory desire. In its normal occurrence, this is the desire for association with, and stimulation by, a member of the opposite sex, culminating typically, but not necessarily, in the specific erotic desire for coitus. The desire may be particularized, that is,

directed to a particular individual of the opposite sex, or may not be particularized.

7. *Philopedic* desire. This is desire for association with children, with, in many instances, desire to care for them or to promote their welfare. This desire may have a generalized form or a limited form directed to children of one's own procreation. It may lead to a desire for procreation which may at some future time become a primary desire, if procreation ever becomes completely a matter of choice and planning. In the past, however, this procreative desire has been incidental, not primary. Philopedic desire has, by pseudo-psychologists of the past, been confused with erotic desire, and needs careful discrimination therefrom. Either may be highly developed in an individual in the absence of the other.

8. *Preeminence* desire. This, in its basic form, is the desire to be attended to, to be conspicuous. This may involve desire to be admired, respected, or imitated, but preeminence often is desired even though it may arouse the envy, antagonism, or hatred of other persons. Desire for leadership is one type of desire in this class and is often combined with desire for activity. The preeminence desire is so universal that its absence from an individual is a sufficient basis for his being rated as abnormal.

9. *Conformity* desire. This is the desire to follow a leader, to adhere to group standards, to follow fashions, or to obey conventions. This desire is in no wise contradictory to the preeminence desire, for the same individual may be strongly developed in both respects. Lack of the conformity desire is seldom found, for although an individual may be highly contemptuous of certain conventions and conformities, he is at the same time bound by others. General lack of this desire, or general low development thereof, renders an individual so abnormal that his confinement is unavoidable. It has been said that there is really never a conformity desire, except as a means to an end. The objections amount simply to the emphasis of the fact that desires are motivated by other desires, or may be so motivated, a principle that is thoroughly approved by psychologists. We are here concerned with the factual nature of desires, and their results, rather than with their motivation.

The classification of primary desires is a practical one, determined by the contents or objects of desire, that is, by *that which* man desires. Concerning the desires themselves as conscious processes, there are several possible views. We might assume that desire is the same in every case, except for differences in urgency or intensity and in duration. From this point of view, the desire for one thing is the same as the desire for another thing, except for the difference in the object or content. On the other hand, we might assume that each class of primary desires entails a specific and distinct sort of desire, varying in its content within the class, but different, as a conscious process, from the desires included in the other classes. Or we might adopt the assumption that every desire is *sui generis*, different from every other desire, quite aside from differences in content.

Ultimately, the choice between these three hypotheses or assumptions may be important. For present purposes, however, it is not necessary to adopt any one of the three, provided that we are careful not to adopt one of them illicitly and, in particular, that we carefully avoid seeming to adopt the first while implicitly adopting the second, identifying all desires with a particular class of desires.

It will be noted that desires of certain of the foregoing classes are essentially individual, in the sense that they are not directed toward other persons and that other persons are not *necessarily* involved in their satisfaction. These are the alimentary, rest, activity, protective, and excretory desires. A Robinson Crusoe on his island may experience these desires and may satisfy them. Some of these, such as the alimentary and the protective desires, may be better satisfied in conjunction with or in relation to other persons, although other persons are not essential.

Certain other desires, on the other hand, have as objects other persons or relations to other persons and cannot be satisfied *normally* except in conjunction with other persons. These are the erotic, philopedic, preeminence, and conformity desires. These desires, accordingly, are sometimes designated as *social* desires, in a loose meaning of the word 'social.'

In the long run, however, all desires become social. *Protection* is best secured by group organization for defense. *Food* is secured, prepared, and eaten by organized group activity. Satisfaction of *excretory* desires is socially regulated and group provisions are made for their satisfaction. *Activity* normally becomes group activity, as in games and sports. *Rest* can be ensured only through the protective function of the group.

The other desires, erotic, philopedic, preeminence, and conformity, early become social in the full sense, being directed by group habits and satisfied in accordance with group ideals.

Various other classes of primary desires, in addition to those in the foregoing list, have been suggested, but when scrutinized critically these desires are found to be merely aspects of one or more desires of the nine classes and not primary in the sense of being indispensable for the continuation of the person or being universal in occurrence in all human groups. The desire for *ownership*, for example, applies to ownership of food, mates, children, and implements for production of food, for protection, and various other objects and rights and privileges pertaining to the gratification of the desires of the several classes. Desire for *accomplishment* is for accomplishment leading to satisfaction of any desire. Desire for *knowledge* likewise applies generally, for knowledge of techniques and conditions is necessary for the satisfaction of any desire. The desire for *life*, to continue *living*, also is an aspect of various desires and is, in effect, the generalized form of all desires.

There are, of course, innumerable secondary desires that are important in one age or one group but unimportant in other ages and other groups. Desires for automobiles, radios, and dramatic entertainment are examples, along with desire for ornament. Even when these desires are particular forms or derivatives of primary desires, they are nonessential.

There are malicious or malignant desires that might at first seem to require a class in addition to those listed as primary. A person often desires to harm another or wishes that evil would befall him, and such desires often lead to acts designed to harm the object of the hatred. Physical assault and slander are common results of malicious desires. The services of witches are even today invoked to bring illness upon an enemy or to ruin his crops. In the main, these desires are outgrowths of one or more of the primary desires, the satisfaction of which the hated person has thwarted or obstructed or is believed to have thwarted or which he threatens. In the latter case, the malicious desire is clearly for protection. In the former, revenge for injury is sought, but the injuries are interferences with the satisfaction of primary or secondary desires.

Any of the primary desires may be purely selfish or may be altruistic. We may desire food, protection, rest, or any other good for ourselves, with callous indifference to the desires, even to the needs, of others. Or we may desire that others may share in the satisfaction we enjoy or hope to enjoy (moral desire). For this reason some philosophers have divided desires into two groups, the egoistic and the altruistic. This division may be judged artificial on two grounds. First, all desires take both forms. There is no good or benefit that may not be desired for oneself alone or for other persons. Second, the distinction has been, and still is, relative. In one stage of moral evolution the individual has moral desires as regards his family, but none regarding those outside the family circle. In the second stage, moral principles apply to the tribe or clan, but for those outside the tribal group the individual has no concern. In the third stage, the limits of altruism are extended to the national group, although usually a distinction is made between one's own caste and other castes in the nation, whether these castes are economic or religious. Whether the fourth stage, in which moral desires extend to all men, regardless of caste of any sort, is attainable is an important question.

The desire to attain ideals might seem to be something not covered by our nine classes, but it is not really an additional desire. Ideals range from the particular to the general and may be defined roughly as any objects of desire thought of reflectively. When one thinks of an article of food, and desires it, the particular food is a particular ideal. When one considers means of obtaining food of any sort, or desires a dependable food supply, this object of concern is an ideal a little above the particular sort. A somewhat higher generalization is the ideal of provision for satisfaction of all desires. In short, we can make no fundamental distinction between a desire, general or particular, and the desire that that desire shall be satisfied, without involving an endless refrain (the desire that the desire that the desire . . . shall be satisfied).

Abnormalities, or aberrations, occur in all classes of primary desire. In the main, these take three directions: (*a*) deficiency, as in anorexia (deficiency of food desire) and frigidity (relative lack of erotic desire); (*b*) excess, as gluttony, sluggardy, nymphomania, and satyriasis (excessive erotic desire in the female and male respectively); (*c*) perversion, the substitution of some other object for the normal one, as in desires for chalk and other nonfoods, homosexuality, and zoophilia (desires for animal pets in lieu of children).

If we should attempt to rank the primary desires in order of their importance to the individual from the point of view of preservation of his life, we would put the alimentary and protective first. Without food, man cannot live long, and, even when he is well fed, adverse conditions of climate or the physical force of an animal enemy may quickly terminate his existence. In some environments, the dangers from which man desires protection may be small, but food is always imperative. Next in order would come the excretory and erotic desires, with perhaps the excretory the more vital. The alimentary, rest, activity, protective, and excretory desires have to do immediately with the preservation of the individual, and through him of the race. The others have to do immediately with the preservation of the race and through that, of the individual.

Now, all these desires appear over and over again in religion. We might suspect, however, that the alimentary and protective desires would be the most influential in the early development of religion, for reasons that we shall now present.

However important excretion, rest, activity in general, and erotic activity may be, these, in a primitive and even in a somewhat later stage of development, are not problems requiring forethought and planning. The man has the desire to excrete, and simply excretes. He is tired, and rests. He desires activity, and does something. He desires sexual intercourse, and that is easily arranged, unless the preeminence of one male inhibits the satisfaction of other males. For protection, however, he must be constantly on guard, and he is never certain of the security of even the immediate future. Food, for primitive man, and for later man down to the present century, has been the great topic of uncertainty and the most undependable variable. Man's constant worry, in most environments, has been his protection and his food supply; his most constant activity has been the search for food. As regards the care of his children or the children of his group, protection and food, again, have been the most vital issues. As for preeminence and conformity, their early importance apparently has been in regard to the securing of the individual's share of the food supply and the securing or limiting of his erotic satisfaction, and in social organization for protection.

On the whole, therefore, we come back to alimentary and protective desires and the means of their satisfaction as paramount in the concern of early man, as well as in man down to the present era, with erotic desires running well behind, in third place at the best.

So far, our procedure has been analytical. Let us now proceed to the practical features of praxis and religion from which alone we can validate our analysis.

In seeking for the evidences of the importance of the primary desires in religions such as Christianity, we must expect to find that the recent emphases are reinterpretations of older emphases and that the specific contents of the desires themselves have changed. Many formulae have become symbolic that were earlier understood in a more literal way. Many ancient symbolisms have been retained, but with new implications.

CHAPTER VI

RELIGION AND THE FOOD SUPPLY

1. The Importance of Food and of Lack of Food.—As we have pointed out in the preceding chapter, the desires that have the greatest influence in the early stages of human life are those classed as alimentary, since food and drink are essential for the life of the individual man, therefore, for the persistence of groups and the development of culture. The prominence, in the early stages of development of religion, of food animals and of food-producing plants and trees is no accident but is the predictable result of man's concern for his food supply.

Within the last half century, food has become abundant in most regions, but in earlier centuries conditions were quite different. The introduction of food plants and food animals from one area into another, improvements in the growing, harvesting, and preparation of food material, improvements in preservation of foods, and improvements in transportation have increased the food supply in civilized lands to the point at which starvation is not feared.

Even within the half century, it is true, seasonal failure of crops in certain countries has produced famine, and millions of persons have died from mere lack of food. Famine, however, was a recurrent condition in ancient times and menaced most savage groups up to recent periods. The diversification of the food supplies of uncivilized peoples by bringing to them food plants and food animals from other areas, and so making the supply more dependable, has been a service rendered by the 'white man' as great as the improvement in economic methods that has gone with these introductions or the contribution of medical services that has followed.

These contributions to the welfare of uncivilized or semicivilized peoples do not always produce the alleviation of misery that might be expected, because in many groups the increase in the food supply and the lessened danger of starvation is compensated or neutralized by an increased birth rate, which leaves the population where it was before. The ingratitude of the peoples to whom these contributions

134

have been made and their resentment against the white man for his obvious superiority are probably due to the factor here indicated, namely, the improvements do not relieve the misery of the population, since the increase in the population takes up the slack that the increased food supply might otherwise produce.

The original life sequence of savages has been described as 'a feast and a famine,' a phrase that describes as well the lives of civilized men not many centuries ago. In stages of culture near the primitive, in which man has depended on game, fish, wild fruits, and roots, the danger of food shortage was constant. Failure in the chase might be produced by drought causing the herds of game animals to desert their customary feeding grounds. Drought or other climatic conditions might result in failure of the wild fruit crop. Fish often desert the shores where they ordinarily run.

Grains, nuts, and some other fruits that can be kept after the harvest were especially valued, and it is not surprising that the introduction of such foodstuffs was ascribed to great heroes. The drying of fruits was practiced by some groups, and in favorable climates meats were dried. Dried fruits, nuts, and grains, however, are subject to damage by moisture, as well as by insects and rodents, and must be protected against such damages.

Mere desire for food does not stimulate the praxes for its production and conservation; hence, mere desire would not cause the development of religion. Thinking about the undependability of the food supply—concern over the food problem—leads to praxes for increasing the food supply and for conserving food materials. Praxes for increasing the satisfaction of alimentary desires develop from concern and planning.

Domestication of food animals and the development of agriculture and horticulture were great steps ahead for early man. While some praxes were developed from hunting and fishing and from the use of wild fruits, there appears to have been no great religious or magical development among peoples such as the Australian Bushmen and the Bushmen who formerly inhabited South Africa. Religion, among people depending entirely on wild products, may well be described as religion in its primitive form or not far advanced from the primitive stage.

In the few favored regions of the globe in which fruits grow wild in abundance and in which fish are always available, religious development appears to have been proportionate to the extent to which man has supplemented the natural abundance by care given to trees and by cultivation, as well as by development of tools and techniques for fishing and of methods of protecting foodstuffs.

Rituals have been built up not only around the processes of procuring food, but also about the preparation and eating of food. Ceremonial meals have been conspicuous, the Eucharist of the Christian churches being an attenuated form of the more substantial repasts of earlier religions. Sacrifice of an animal, in its earliest forms, was a feast to which the gods were invited and in which shared every member of the family of the person conducting the sacrifice. Among some nomadic peoples, the whole tribe or encampment participated in the sacrificial feast. When the priesthood was instituted, the priests of the shrine at which the sacrifice was offered received their shares.

Feasts were held in honor of the dead; in the Egyptian ritual the mummies of ancestors were often brought out to grace the feasts, participating thus by their presence, if not in partaking of the food. Bread, fruits, and wine were conventional offerings to the gods in all areas and were placed on or near tombs as offerings to the dead. When food became more abundant, it might be allowed to spoil, just as an entire sacrificed animal might be burned, but in the earlier period the food was not wasted but was consumed by human beings.

Almost every animal, plant, tree, or fruit that was important for the food supply has figured in religion, and derivatives or by-products of foodstuffs have also had religious uses. Olive oil was used for ritual annointing. The blood of domestic animals was the great purifying agent that cleansed from sin. Libations of wine were poured to gods and daimons. Barley meal was sprinkled on the head of the sacrificial victim before it was slain. Bread, oil, and wine are still employed in Christian rituals and along with blood figure verbally in Christian liturgies and hymns.

Tabus on the eating of the flesh of certain animals have been numerous, and the animals which were tabu to the Jews are still tabu in Islam. Although Christians have abandoned the tabus on particular animals, some sects accept a tabu on the eating of any flesh on Friday and during the forty days of Lent. Mohammedans are prohibited from eating any food, animal or vegetable, during the month of Ramadan, except between sunset and sunrise. Outside of civilized and semicivilized cultures, tabus on food are complex; in some savage groups, certain foods are tabu for women but may be eaten by men, and age-class distinctions also are drawn.

Attempts have been made to explain the tabus on the eating of the flesh of certain animals as hygienic rules, the flesh being banned because it is really dangerous for eating. This mode of explanation is not acceptable to scholars, because there are no hygienic objections to the eating of the meat of most of the tabued beasts which are not valid for animals not tabued, even if there are one or two exceptions. Ancient man had no more information on hygienic matters than do savages and avoided only those things which were clearly poisonous or to which religious or magical manas were ascribed. Since in areas adjacent to those in which certain animals were tabu, the peoples ate those animals and thrived on them, it is evident that the tabus were not based on hygienic principles.

The tabus, moreover, were usually not alone on the eating of the animals, but even on touching them and often on killing them. In the ancient world few fruits, plants, or grains were forbidden as food. The exceptional tabu on the eating of beans and on touching the bean-plant may have had a practical basis, but this was not hygienic. Many fruits that actually are detrimental, such as acorns, were used for food. Aside from religious (or magical) tabus, man seems to have eaten everything that did not manifestly poison him. We cannot find the basis for religious tabus in rules of hygiene, regarding which early man was completely ignorant.

To take an example, there is no evidence that ancient peoples recognized trichinosis or any other disease that could be attributed to swine. The most intelligent peoples of the ancient world, such as the Greeks and the Philistines, continued, to the end of their cultures, to eat pork and to thrive on it. If any bad results had been produced by eating pork, it would have been observed and would have been reported by some writings. The attempt to explain the tabu on the pig as due to recognition of trichinosis is anachronistic.

That the slaughter of some domestic animals was prohibited because reckless slaughter would be detrimental to the group of human beings is true. In especial, the females were protected by tabus, as today we prohibit the killing of female deer. These tabus are, of course, intended to promote the multiplication of the animals.

Some tabued animals were deemed accursed because they were

sacred animals for other groups of people. The sanctity of the pig, the dog, and the hare for ancient peoples may explain the tabu on these animals for the Hebrews, whose leaders wished to make a sharp distinction between Hebrewism and surrounding religions and to wean the Hebrews from their old rituals. This explanation has been offered by some scholars, while others have opined that the origin of the tabus was in the sanctity of an animal which at first was benevolent and could not be eaten or touched for that reason, passing eventually from the state of sanctity to that of accursedness. As a matter of fact, these two explanations do not contradict one another.

It is now necessary that we pay detailed attention to food animals and food plants, especially to those which furnished sustenance to man in the early periods of religious development. We must pay attention also to animals that contributed indirectly to the food supply by protecting food materials. We need to consider the praxes which were developed in connection with these sources of food, the sanctity which came to be attributed to these plants and animals, and the divinities which were enate from some of the species or families.

Information on the natural history of the animals, trees, and plants discussed in this chapter may be obtained by consulting articles correspondingly titled in the *Encyclopaedia Britannica*, ninth or eleventh edition. One might expect to find in Hastings (ref. I: 2) information on the religious functions of these plants and animals, but one would be disappointed. Except for incidental information given in articles on certain religions or on certain divinities, the food plants and food animals are ignored. For this information one must turn to writers such as Cook, Reinach, and Maury and comb through many volumes of exploration and travel.

2. Sacred and Divine Food Animals.—In the Levantine and Mediterranean areas, a number of food animals attained sanctity, and from some of these divinities developed. The expressions 'sanctity,' 'sacredness,' and 'religious importance' may be used as synonymous with one another, but must for the present purposes be understood as designating a position of respect in the views of men, due to actual characteristics or to certain manas ascribed to them, which would be retrospectively designated as 'magical.' Since, however, these animals, or representatives of their species, became in some cases divinities and in other cases associates or symbols of divinities and were in other ways involved in what we must for the present recognize as ancient religion, we should recognize these associations as 'religious,' and admit the concept of the animals' manas as that of their 'sanctity.'

Wild animals (game) were important not only for their flesh, but also for their skins as sources of leather and clothing; their bones, from which awls and other tools were made, and with which arrows and spears were tipped; their sinews, used for making bowstrings; and their horns, hoofs, and claws, which were useful for many purposes. These products contributed indirectly to the procuring of food and to the satisfaction of protective and other desires. From the ruminant domestic animals milk also was obtained.

Among the wild quadrupeds, the deer, wild boar, bear, cattle, wild ass, goat, antelope, and possibly the bison were important. Of animals lower in the scale, fish and serpents were food sources, and, in some areas, mice were relished. Of wild fowl, we have no information, except concerning the goose and swan, which, so far as we know, were not game animals.

Domestic animals were apparently introduced from Asia, none, so far as we know, having been domesticated in Europe, although it is possible that geese were domesticated in the Scandinavian or Baltic regions. The important domestic food animals were the dog, pig, sheep, goat, and 'ox' (a name applied in the literature to cattle of both sexes, as well as to the emasculated male). Among fowls, the goose appears to have been the earliest, the chicken coming later. The domestic duck was not brought into the Western world until after the beginning of the Christian Era.

Domestication is not mere taming. Individual animals of many species have been tamed to a certain degree and have been taught to do tricks. Bears and lions have been so trained but have never been domesticated. Domestication involves breeding in captivity, but that is not the whole of the procedure. The animal must be subjected to the conditions of a household (domus) and must become accustomed to those conditions or to the conditions of a farm, which is a part of the *domus*. Handling or herding is usually involved.

So far as can be ascertained, no animals have ever been domesticated in Africa, although domestic animals have been introduced from Asia and Europe. In America the animals domesticated were limited to the llama and alpaca, and similar animals allied to the camel, which were domesticated in Peru, and the turkey, which was domesticated in Mexico. It is uncertain whether or not any animals or fowls were domesticated in Europe.

In general, animals can be domesticated only if the young of the wild species are captured not long after birth and brought up in captivity in close association with human beings. For domestication of wild-fowls, it is usually necessary to take the eggs from the nests and hatch them artificially. Ducks and geese, which in the wild state nest in northern regions, could be domesticated only in those regions.

Not all species of animals are capable of domestication; the failure to domesticate animals in Africa and Europe and the limited domestication in America may therefore have been due to the absence from these continents of animals suitable for the procedure. On the other hand, it is possible that certain Asiatics developed a special technique or an 'aptitude' for domesticating animals that was not developed by peoples in other continents.

All these animals (except, of course, the duck) attained sanctity in some degree. Some arrived at divinity, but others appear to have been assimilated by divinities before reaching the divine stage themselves.

3. **Game Animals.** *1. Deer.*—Deer, of many varieties, have been important food animals in Asia, Europe, and the Americas. In Greece, the deer is associated with Artemis and is represented with her in paintings and statuary. Although she figures in the myths as a huntress for whom the deer were prey, she is also the protectress of the deer and was undoubtedly originally a divine deer. The sanctity of the deer in Celtic areas is indicated, but there is no clear evidence for the occurrence of a male deer divinity anywhere.

2. Wild Boar.—The name 'wild boar' is conventionally applied to the wild pigs of both sexes. These animals ranged over practically the whole of Europe and the Levant and attained sanctity in the Levant and the Celtic and Germanic areas, if not in the Mediterranean region. In Phrygia the wild boar was associated with Kubele and with Attis, who assimilated in his late form an ancient boar god. Although in Greek areas the boar was associated with Aphrodite, she was a goddess imported from the Levant and the boar association was perhaps imported with her. Evidences of sanctity of the wild boar in Gaul and in northern Europe are clear, and the use of the boar's head at the Yule festival survives as an attenuated symbol of the earlier religious importance of the animal, which in

Nordic regions was associated with the sacred oak. To what extent the wild boar contributed to the sanctity of the domestic pig is uncertain.

The 'wild boar' was found from an early period down to the present day in Asia and in Europe. In Africa there is an animal, the wart hog, of the same family. According to some classifications the American peccary is of the Sus (swine) family, but some classifiers rate the peccary in a separate family of the Dicotylidae. Domestic pigs tend to run wild and revert to the type of the wild boar, and the 'wild pigs' in some regions, as in the East Indies, are suspected of having descended from the domestic pigs that were introduced from Europe.

3. Bear.—Bear abounded in Europe, although they were less common in the Levant. The flesh of the bear has been esteemed as food in Europe, Asia, and the Americas. Artemis in one form, Artemis Brauronia, is evidently the result of an assimilation to Artemis of an ancient bear goddess Brauronia; she was worshiped in Arcadia as a sacred bear, served by priestesses in her rituals who called themselves 'bears' and wore bear pelts. Callisto, who is now in the heavens as the 'Great Bear,' was apparently another Peloponnesian bear goddess. There were, apparently, a number of bear goddesses in Celtic areas, among whom Arctio was perhaps the most important. Whether the Swiss city of Berne received its name because of bear cult there is disputed, but all of these words (Braunonia, Arctio, Berne, and Verona, the latter another form of the Celtic word 'Berne') in different tongues mean 'bear.' Bears are worshiped today by peoples in northeastern Asia and sought for their meat.

4. Wild Cattle.—That wild cattle were hunted in the Levant we know, and we may assume that they were valued for food in Europe, where they ranged from the east to the west of the continent and in the British Isles. Bull gods may have been derived from the wild bull originally, but this is not certain, since the cow goddesses evolved from domestic cattle. The wild bull, however, attained a degree of sanctity, as is indicated by the representations of winged bulls (Cherubim) in Assyrian reliefs and statues. In the Mediterranean area and in Europe otherwise, no such monsters seem to have appeared, and the evidence for sanctity of the wild bull is absent, although bull gods assimilated to Zeus and Dionysos may have developed initially from the wild bull.

5. The Wild Ass.—The ass occurred in the wild state only in the Levantine area, in which it was valued for its flesh and admired for its speed of running, in which it could outstrip the fastest horse. The ass was apparently domesticated in Asia and introduced from there into Europe. The original wild ass is extinct, the present wild asses in Asia being descendants of domestic asses that escaped from captivity. These animals, however, were eaten by Persians and Arabs down to a late period of the Christian Era.

The sanctity of the ass evidently was derived from the wild ass, not the domestic ass. It seems probable that Ares, who was assimilated by the Romans to their Mars, originated in Asia as an ass god. The best evidence for the sanctity of the ass, however, is presented by the pictorial representations on ancient vases of Marsuas (Marsyas), the seilenos (silenus), who challenged Apollo to a musical contest. Marsuas was defeated and, in punishment for his temerity, he was flayed alive. Reinach held that Marsuas was originally an ass god, but whether or not Reinach's conclusion is accepted, there is no doubt that the flaying of Marsuas is connected with ritual uses of the skins of asses.

Marsuas is pictured in human form but with the characteristic pelt and tail of an ass. In Greek pictures, the seilinoi are associated with Dionysos and are represented as horse men, rather than as ass men. Some scholars have confused the seilinoi with the satyrs, but the distinction is clear.

6. The Wild Goat.—Wild goats were plentiful in Arcadia and in various other Mediterranean areas, and species were probably found in Asia Minor. They were hunted for their flesh and probably for their pelts and doubtless achieved a degree of sanctity, which contributed to the development of goat divinities. This development, however, was mainly from the domestic goat, although the divinities took on some of the characteristics of the wild animal.

The satyrs (often confused with seilinoi by modern writers) were conventionally represented in human form except for their feet, which were goats' hoofs, and for the horns and tails of goats which were attached to them. The satyrs are always male, and it is evident that the sexual prowess for which the he-goat had a reputation was the mana that led to the conception of the satyr. The ancient notion of the satyr as extremely lascivious is retained in our word 'satyriasis' for pathological erotic desire in males.

7. The Antelope.—The majority of the numerous species of

antelope are African, but several species occur in Asia and two in Europe, the chamois of the Alps and the ibex of the same region and the Apennines. These European antelopes seem not to have arrived at any sanctity, but there are myths about Levantine animals that penetrated the Greek world. The Greek name from which our word 'antelope' is derived was first applied to a mythical animal of Mesopotamia which had the power to cut off trees by sawing them with its horns. The flesh of antelopes, of course, was, and still is, highly prized for food, but it nowhere attained much sanctity. The habits of the European varieties, which frequent mountainous areas relatively inaccessible thus making hunting difficult in ancient times, would explain this in those areas but not in Mesopotamia.

8. Fish.—Fish have always been important in the diet of peoples living near fresh and salt water. The early settlers in Babylonia near the point of entry of the Euphrates into the Persian Gulf seem to have depended on fish as their staple food; they developed as their early divinity Ea, a fish goddess. Ea was later assimilated to Ishtar, and the fish was carried over to that goddess as a symbol. On the Mediterranean coast, Dagon, an important god of the Philistines, seems to have been a fish divinity. In Syria, Derketo, or Attargatis, was a fish goddess. Although fish were important in the diet of the Greeks and were imported from the Black Sea region to supplement the local supply, no fish divinities seem to have appeared in Greece, although it is possible that fish divinities developed in an early period and passed into oblivion later.

Fish had a certain religious importance at some places, but not universally. In Cyprus, they were sacred to Aphrodite. In a pool at Myra, in Lycia, they were employed to predict the future. Fishermen offered tunny fish and eels in sacrifice to Poseidon. On the other hand, eating of fish was tabu for initiates into the Eleusinian mysteries and for the priests of Poseidon at Megara and Leptis.

In Egyptian religion as it is described to us by Herodotus, fish were tabu as food for priests; but there was a more general tabu on the eel and on one species of fish, which was probably the Lepidopus. Herodotus, however, derived his information from the priestly caste of the highly Negroid Upper Egypt, and we know that in the Delta fish were the principal food of the population, but our information concerning the rituals of the Delta is meager.

Fish cults have existed, in modern times, in the lacustrine region of Africa and on the West Coast and in the islands of the Pacific.

Fish divinities were on the wane in the Levant by the beginning of the Christian Era, but the fish has not yet been discarded. The early Christians revived the fish as their secret emblem, and the explanation of this by the Greek word for fish, *ichthos*, which is made up of the initial letters of the words translated, 'Jesus Christ, the son of God,' was undoubtedly invented to explain the use of the fish symbol. The fish's head still figures in modified form as the bishop's miter, and fish are religiously eaten on Fridays. This dietary ritual has been handed down from the worship of the fish goddess, for whom, after the Babylonian seven-day week was established, the sixth day of the week, as we reckon it, was set apart, and in whose worship fish were eaten on that day.

In addition to the use of the fish as food, the enormous fertility of the fish, well known to the ancients, enhanced the veneration for it as an outstanding representative of the mana of fertility. Other factors that have been suggested by various writers as enhancing the importance of the female fish divinity are the supposed resemblance of the odor of fish to the odor of the human female and the resemblance of the mouth of the fish to the external genitalia of the human female. This latter suggestion is supported by the use of the pointed oval as a symbol of the goddess, even after her assimilation to other goddesses.

Although the basis of the fish rituals probably was in the praxis of fishing, the control of the schools of fish to bring them near the shore in coastal areas was a matter of vital importance. Rituals (which we call magical) are still employed in various parts of the world for this purpose.

9. The Serpent.—Snakes are found in all temperate and tropical regions of the world. In Greece and Asia Minor they were abundant. The valleys of the Nile and the Euphrates were full of them. Even in modern times, snake meat has been relished in various parts of the world, and for early man the snake was a lifesaver, since the only weapons needed for taking serpents are stones and clubs. The hunting techniques required are simple; we may well assume that in ancient times these techniques were much the same as those employed in modern times in river valleys of China, in the East Indies, and in the Americas.

Snake meat (of American varieties), can hardly be called delicious, but it is palatable. Up to recent years Chinese in the coastal cities made dishes of snake meat which were relished by tourists, especially by those who did not know the ingredients. Some of the American Indians ate rattlesnakes, and in 1930 rattler meat began to be canned in Arcadia, Florida. The canneries for a long time were unable to fill the commercial demand for this meat.

The snake attained sanctity among all ancient peoples and among most savages it continues to be venerated and to be employed in rituals we can hardly avoid calling religious. In India, the cobra is worshiped today, and the 'snake charming' by music that is done by certain men as a public exhibition is said to be primarily a religious ritual. The sanctity of the snake, however, has roots in the dangerous aspects of the poisonous varieties, as well as in the food value of other species.

Serpents had religious importance in almost all parts of the world, in ancient times, and still maintain their ritual positions among some of the peoples of America, Asia, and Africa. How much of this religious importance stems from the ancient food value of the serpent, and how much from the dangerous features of poisonous serpents, it is difficult to say. The need and desire for protection against serpents will be considered later.

There were evidently many snake cults in the Mediterranean area in ancient times, and a number of snake divinities seem to have appeared. For the most part, the snake divinities were assimilated to other divinities of alimentary origin, and snake rituals, which may not have produced snake divinities, were added to other rituals.

Snakes were not eaten in the Mediterranean areas, at least in the periods as late as those to which our sources of information extend. In classical times, although snakes of many varieties, both poisonous and harmless, abounded in Greece and in Asia Minor, they were small and probably of inedible sorts. The myths and legends of dragons (great serpents) and pythons (of uncertain types) indicate, however, an earlier supply of larger snakes. The snake attained major sanctity in Greece, a number of serpent divinities having evolved. Although most of the early snake divinities were assimilated to Apollo, Zeus, Athena, Demeter, and Dionysos and other divinities of otherwise nonserpentine origin, one important snake god of healing, Asklepios, maintained his independence down to the end of Pagan culture. Orpheus, the legendary hero who charmed all animals with his music, was evidently originally a snake god. Pythagoras, the legendary founder of the Pythagorean cult, was a snake hero.

The snake dances of American Indians and of Bantu groups in the lacustrine regions of Africa had their parallels in the ancient mysteries of the Mediterranean. Female votaries of Dionysos carried snakes in their rituals at night on the mountains, and some of these serpents were poisonous. Figurines and paintings of ancient date representing votaries carrying snakes indicate a similar ritual use of snakes in various parts of the Mediterranean area.

In Egypt there were several snake divinities, and the symbol of royalty was the African cobra (uraeus) which was also widely represented in charms and on medals. Here the poisonous snake had become paramount, the earlier food value having been lost completely.

It is noteworthy that an especially sacred serpent in Greece, peculiar to the region about Epidaurus, was small and harmless, and that there was in Egypt, according to Herodotus, a small sacred serpent, which was harmless and had two horns growing out of the top of its head. Representations of horned serpents from Celtic areas of Europe dating from the Gallo-Roman period have been found, but the horns are those of the ram. Serpents with beards are represented in connection with barley in Greek religious scenes, although no bearded serpents are known ever to have existed.

10. The Mouse.—The mouse probably was not eaten in Europe, but was esteemed a choice tidbit in the Levant. The mouse for the eating of which the Jews were denounced by Isaiah (46: 17) is assumed to have been the jerboa, which was eaten by Arabs. Apollo Smintheus in the Troad was a mouse god; in his temple there was a golden mouse and a colony of live mice. The golden mice sent to the Hebrews by the Philistines to quell a plague visited upon the Philistines by the Hebrew god may be fictional, but the legend indicates a recognized cult of the mouse among the Philistines. The legend of the defeat of the army of Sennacherib in Egypt because of the gnawing of their bowstrings during the night by an army of mice sent by an Egyptian god (Herodotus, ref. VI: A3, Vol. II, p. 141) indicates a mouse cult in Egypt.

Fraser explains mouse cults (*Spirits of the Corn and of the Wild*, Vol. II, Sec. 2) as propitiatory rituals to avert plagues of mice, but although such rituals were conducted and Apollo Smintheus became a protector from mice, the influence of early eating of mice cannot be arbitrarily ruled out. The persistence of the mouse in European folklore, as a form in which the 'external soul' is visible, indicates an ancient sacred status of the mouse as something more than an enemy.

4. Domesticated Food Animals. *1. The Dog.*—The dog was apparently the first animal domesticated by man and may indeed be said to be an animal created by man. The various breeds of dogs are the results of hybridization of various varieties of wolves and foxes, with perhaps bear strains in some breeds. In the wild state, crossing does not occur, even between wolves of different varieties. When wolves have been domesticated, however, the females breed readily with wild wolves, and when descendants of one breed are transported to other areas, hybridization is easily brought about. After the hybrid type is established, further crossing is easy. Asiatics migrating into Europe and America took dogs with them in very early periods. Further crossing with European and American wild canines occurred in these continents. There were no wolves in Africa, but the imported dog probably was crossed with the jackal, but not with the hyena, which is not canine and which eats dogs at any opportunity. Some of the wild 'dogs' in Africa are probably descendants of domestic dogs which have run wild. A native animal resembling the hyena, but which is neither a hyena nor a dog, is sometimes called 'wild dog.'

The motives for domestication of wolves in the first place are obscure, but, after the dog was developed, he was maintained as a food animal. Dogs are still eaten in various parts of the world, but, with the addition of other domestic animals whose meat is more palatable, the dog declined in importance as a food animal.

The dog was an excellent food animal, since he is attached to his owners, does not run away or need herding, follows the group when they move camp, and provides a part of his own food supply by scavenging and hunting. He has been eaten down to recent times by some tribes of American Indians. Some African tribes eat dogs, although among some Bantoids the dog has become too holy to be eaten and is used only in ritual sacrifices, as it is employed by American Indians.

The domestic dog gives warning of the presence of enemies or strangers, as do geese, and eventually the dog was trained for hunting, although the use of dogs for hunting came late in Europe and western Asia.

The sanctity of the dog in the areas into which it was introduced in early periods is unmistakable. It was a holy animal to the Syrians, and the blood of dogs was employed in rituals of purification by the Corinthians down to the classical period of Greece. The sanctity of the dog diminished when pigs and other domestic animals that furnished more appetizing meat were introduced.

The sanctity of the dog has increased in modern times. Although not an actual divinity in America, he is held sacred by many persons, who not only maintain dogs as pets and associate with them as equals, but go to great lengths to protect the 'rights' of dogs against the rights of human beings. In Hollywood, there is a Tail-waggers' Club,' which is organized to 'protect' dogs and to persecute persons who attempt to protect themselves against the dog nuisance and dog danger. Legal protection of human beings against dogs is obstructed by dog lovers, to whom the dangers to children and the constant menace of hydrophobia are insignificant as compared with the protection of the sacred dog and its 'rights' to freedom.

The insanitary nuisance created by dogs has been somewhat abated, but dog lovers in city houses and apartments 'walk' their dogs, to enable them to deposit ordure on the lawns of other persons. Since legal protection against the stray dog and the dog walkers is practically impossible, because of the strong political influence of the dog worshipers, sufferers often resort to illegal measures, including the cruelty of poisoning. The fact that sheep, pigs, and goats are not given equal rights with dogs can be explained only on the ground that the dog is a sacred animal. It is relevant to note that the antivivisectionists are interested in the protection of only one animal, the dog.

That the dog attained sanctity is not surprising. He is ritually employed by many groups of savages and continued down to the Christian Era as a sacred animal in Corinth and among the Dorians of the Peloponnesus, where he was sacrificed to Ares and other divinities and where his blood was used for rituals of purification. The tabu on the dog among the Jews indicates that he was a sacred animal for other Syrians. He figures in the reliefs and statues of the Celtic areas and apparently was sacred in some degree to the Celts, who probably brought dogs with them when they migrated from Asia into Europe and the Levant.

No dog divinity appears to have developed anywhere, although the hero Actaeon, slain by his dogs in punishment for having spied on Artemis bathing, may have been originally a sacred dog associated with the goddess. He may even have been a dog god, a counterpart to Artemis Huntress, for the slaying of Actaeon at the behest of Artemis is parallel to the slaying of Attis by the boar.

2. The Pig.—The domestic pig, introduced into Europe very early, became for Mediterraneans and Levantines the food animal that for a while was of paramount value. That strains of the wild boar of the West were introduced into the domestic stock is possible, but in general the ancient representations of pigs deviate little from the familiar types of the Asiatic domestic hog.

Use of the blood of hogs for rituals of purifying was extensive. Persons guilty of manslaughter were cleansed by pouring over them the fresh blood of swine. The seats in the theaters were sprinkled with the blood of pigs as a prophylactic measure against any taint of 'sin' on any member of the audience. Similar purification was necessary for any place of civic assembly. Oaths were taken on the flesh of pigs. Before a 'great' sacrifice (cattle) the officiant purified himself with the blood of a pig.

We have pointed out that Demeter, in her late form, had assimilated an older sow goddess; Hades, Lord of the Underworld, *may* have been a pig god originally. The pig was associated with the earth because of his rooting habits and could easily transfer to subterranean regions.

The introduction of the pig marked a transition in Europe from the use of acorns as the staple human food to the use of meat. Instead of eating acorns, men let the pigs eat these nuts and then ate the pigs. Apparently this transition occurred in prehistoric times in most parts of Greece, but in Arcadia it did not happen until shortly before the Christian Era; in Britain, acorns were the staple food until the eleventh century.

3. Sheep and Goats.—Domestic sheep and goats have been important food animals wherever they have been introduced. In some areas the milk, as well as the flesh, of goats has been an item in the diet, although sheep's milk has been less widely used. Sheep divinities developed in Egypt where Amen, the sheep god, was ultimately assimilated to Ra, the hawk god; but there is no clear evidence of any sheep divinity in the Mediterranean or Levantine areas. The goat god, Pan, however, appeared in Arcadia, and in fairly late times was imported to Athens and into other areas. A goat god seems to have been assimilated to Dionysos in some of his forms, but this may have been the assimilation of the manas of the goat, rather than of specific goat divinities. Various associations of the goat with the vine (grape) may have been due to the goat's fondness for nibbling the tender shoots. The reputation of the he-goat for lasciviousness has already been mentioned, and it is probable that the satyr was suggested by the domestic goat, rather than the wild variety.

Goats were associated with Aphrodite, probably for the reasons which gave rise to the satyr, and goats were sacrificed to various divinities, male and female; but no goat goddess can be identified unless one was assimilated to the goddess of Argolis in her form of Hera.

Seers, augurs, and priests who practiced semantics depended largely on the entrails of sacrificed sheep for their omens, although pigs and dogs were occasionally employed. It was customary for armies to take with them a flock of sheep for semantic purposes, sacrificing them before an engagement to determine from the intestinal omens the favorable time and place for giving battle. Such a flock of sheep was led by a she-goat, and we may infer that, for herding sheep to and from pasture, goats were employed as leaders.

The goat was an important milk animal in Syria, the hilly regions being more suitable for goats than for cattle. The description of Palestine as a 'land flowing with milk and honey' (Josh. 5: 6) is to be understood as referring more to goat's milk than to cow's milk. That the goat acquired a special mana in Syria is indicated by the Hebrew ritual of the 'scapegoat' and by the prohibition of 'seething a kid in its mother's milk.' This ritual was a magic process of regeneration, highly regarded in the Levant and practiced by Medea in the regeneration of the old man Aeson. This ritual should not be confused with the superstition current in central Africa that the boiling of milk 'dries up' the animal which gave the milk.

The religious association of the goat and the sheep undoubtedly had its main roots in the values of these animals for food. The domestic sheep and goats contributed their flesh to man's diet, and there are some references by ancient writers which imply that goat's milk was used. Wild goats were abundant in the Peloponnesus and in other parts of Greece and were actively hunted. The goat, accordingly, had a start on the sheep in religious development, although the important stage of the development commenced with the introduction of the domesticated goat.

4. Domestic Cattle.—Two types of domestic cattle have been conspicuous, the commonly called 'European,' and the 'Indian' cattle. These two varieties have been hybridized in modern times. In Asia, Europe, and Africa, cattle have been important animals, mainly for their flesh and milk; but in the Mediterranean and Levantine areas, the 'ox' was the animal which, along with the ass and mule, was used for drawing plows, carts, and wagons.

In all areas where cattle were bred, the cow attained a high degree of sanctity. In the Mediterranean and Levantine areas and in Egypt and India, the bull achieved sanctity; in Africa outside of Egypt, while the cow was sacred, and still is, the bull attained only a minor sanctity, if any.

In regions where cow's milk is the staple food, the cow cannot be killed. In India still, neither males nor females may be slaughtered by Hindus. In cattle-raising areas in Africa, the males may be killed sacrificially, but their flesh can be eaten only by warriors. Old men, children, and women cannot partake of the flesh nor of the blood, which is drawn from the living bullocks. In Greek areas, cows were not killed for meat in early periods, although in the later periods they could be sacrificed to certain goddesses. The tabu on killing cows is obviously a means of protecting the milk supply and the reproduction of the herds.

Cattle achieved divinity in all cattle-raising areas. Bull gods may have evolved from the wild bull, but this is not certain. Cow goddesses certainly evolved from domestic cattle.

In Egypt, Hathor was an important cow goddess later assimilated to Isis, who in some inscriptions is designated by the hyphenated name, Hathor-Isis. All cow goddesses were eventually associated with the moon, with the crescent moon as their symbol. Where a cow goddess was represented in human form, cow's horns were attached to her head. Where worshipers of Hathor-Isis came in contact with Mesopotamian cults, she was identified with Ishtar, the date goddess.

In Egypt, in addition to the bull Apis, considered as the incarnation of Ra, the bull was identified with Amen ('Bull of his Mother'), Osiris ('Bull of Amentet'), Seb, and with Onuphis (Unnefer) the divine bull at Hermonthis. The cow was sacred to the goddesses

Nut and Meh-urt, as well as being identified with Hathor, which might indicate that there were a number of early cow goddesses, most of whom were finally assimilated to Hathor.

Early Brahmanical religion grew up in the Indus Valley and was centered around the domestic cow. Krishna, an important incarnation of Vishnu, who is identified with Rama in the Vedic scriptures, was associated with cows in multiple ways. Among his titles are Go-pal (cowherd), Go-pinath (lord of the milkmaids), and Go-vinda (cow finder). The occurrence of the syllable 'go' (cow) in the name of the legendary last Buddha, Siddhartha Gautama (or Go-tama) may be significant. The cow was important in ancient Persian religion, and Zoroaster, the Persian equivalent of a Buddha, may have been a cow priest or a bull god. There is but one obvious bull god (Nandi) in India at present, but both Shiva and Vishnu appear to have bovine aspects. Where Brahmanism is supreme and also among adherents of the unorthodox sects, the cow is sacred, and the sanctity is in a measure shared by the bulls. No orthodox Hindu can kill a bovine animal or taste beef. When a cow becomes decrepit and is no longer a milker, the Hindu sells her to a Mohammedan to be butchered. Among the Dravidian peoples of southern India whose religion is only superficially colored by Brahmanism, cows are somewhat sacred, but male cattle are sacrificed in religious rituals, often being hacked to pieces while alive, as were animals in the Dionysiac rituals in Greece.

In the Greek area, cattle figured extensively in myths and legends and both bull gods and cow goddesses developed. Hera included as one of her principal factors an ancient cow of Argos, and her conventional descriptive title was 'cow-eyed Hera.' The bovine type of face was considered by the Greeks a high trait of human female beauty. The priestesses of Hera at Argos were conventionally called 'cows.' Chryses, in the island of Lemnos, was originally a cow goddess, and there are indications of other cow divinities in the Mediterranean area. Some of the legendary heroines associated with cows may have been cow divinities, but the conclusion is not always warranted. Io, who was turned into a cow by Zeus to protect her from his enraged spouse, who discovered him carrying on with the girl, was chased by the gadfly sent by Hera, and finally went to Egypt, where, according to one legend she gave birth to Apis, the incarnation of Ra. Other legends place the birth in Greece (Strabo, 5: 5). Pasiphaë, the Cretan queen who con-

cealed herself in the wooden cow to attract the bull of which she was
enamored, and who gave birth to the Minotaur, certainly assumed
the role of a cow goddess.　Whether or not either Io or Pasiphaë
was originally a cow goddess, however, is not a question to be
arbitrarily answered.

The Zeus who seduced Io, and the Zeus who seduced Europa,
were clearly bull gods.　Dionysos, in various of his cults, was
represented as a bull or with a bull's head, or as clad in a bull's
hide.　Among his descriptive titles were 'cow-born,' 'bull,' 'bull
shaped,' 'bull faced,' 'goodly bull,' 'horned,' 'two-horned,' and
'horn bearing.'　The title 'Bromios,' which means 'roarer,' was
evidently drawn from the bull.

In Thrace, the bacchantes celebrating the rituals of the Thracian
Dionysos wore bull's horns.　The tearing to pieces of a bull and
eating the raw flesh was a characteristic ritual in several of the
Dionysiac cults.　From this rite grew the myth that Dionysos, in
the form of a bull, was dismembered and devoured by the Titans.
These assimilations, however, do not entitle us to decide that Semele,
the mother of Dionysos, was a cow goddess.

The bull was associated also with Poseidon (Pausanias, ref. VI:
A4, Vol. X, viii, p. 2) and with Ares (*ibid.*, Vol. I, xxiv, p. 2), indicating that in certain places these divinities assimilated local bull gods.

As a rule, in the greater sacrifices, cows were sacrficed to female
divinities and bulls to male divinities, although there were exceptions.
This does not conflict with the assumption that in the early period
cows could not be killed and eaten.

Cow goddesses were eventually associated with the moon and in
some areas bull gods became sun gods.　Hathor in Egypt was a
moon goddess, and Hera had some lunar associations.　Pausanias
(Vol. VI, xxiv, p. 6) describes a statue at Elis representing the
moon in human form with cow's horns.　In Egypt, Ra the sun
god (earlier a hawk) was identified with the bull Apis.　In the
Levant bull gods became sun gods.　In the Greek area, however,
this flight of the bull to the heavens did not take place, but the
horse was associated with the sun.　Cows, however, were in some
Greek places sacred to the sun god Helios, herds sacred to him being
maintained (Homer, *Odyssey*).　The sacred cow that guided
Cadmus to the site in Boeotia where he founded the city of Thebes
was marked with a white disk, which is commonly interpreted as
representing the full moon, but more probably it was the sun.

The curved shape of the horns of the Indian cow undoubtedly was influential in Egypt in suggesting the crescent moon, but the horns of European cattle were not so suggestive. The lunar period, corresponding roughly with the menstrual period, of course, tended to make the moon female and to retard the replacement of the moon goddess by a male divinity. The gods developed on earth before they took to the skies; lunar and solar attributes are secondary, not primary, as some classical scholars have assumed.

Numerous statuettes representing women with cow's horns have been found in the Mediterranean area, and it is sometimes assumed that these are images of cow goddesses. Bearing in mind, however, the priestesses of Dionysos with cow's horns and the 'cows' of Hera, we must admit that these statuettes probably represent priestesses of a cow goddess or votaries of a bull god.

In northern and western Europe, evidences of the appearance of cattle divinities and of the sanctity of the cow are slight. This lack of development may be due to the introduction of cattle too late, after the formative period of religion was over. The lack supports the assumption that no cattle were domesticated in Europe, but that the domestic stock was introduced from Asia. The cattle figured on monuments of the Gallo-Roman period are quite similar to modern domestic cattle of various breeds.

The importance of the cow and the bull in the Levant is unmistakable. On Assyrian monuments the winged bulls are significant. In Asia Minor, Atargatis was represented as a cow, and the God of the Caananites, Moloch, was conventionally represented with the head of a bull. Bulls were associated with Ishtar and her prototype, Ashtart, and with Teshub, the Hittite prototype of the Jewish divinity. Both cows and bulls seem to have been sacred in the early Hebrew religion.

The association of an anthropomorphic divinity with the cow or the bull is, in some cases, clearly based on the earlier bovine form of the god or goddess, who, on emerging into human form, still retains the old associations. This interpretation applies to Hera, to the Zeus of Crete, and some forms of Dionysos. In some of the other cases, however, we must admit the possibility that the sanctity of the bovine animal was added without the assimilation of a specific bovine divinity. That is, an animal which had become divine, but not anthropomorphized, assimilated to one which has reached the human stage.

5. The Domestic Goose.—Geese were associated with Asklepios, and at his temple at Epidarus geese were maintained along with dogs and snakes in the building in which healing was practiced. The indications are that these sacred geese were allowed to bite the patients. The healing power of geese undoubtedly was based on the snakelike neck and head and the habit of hissing like a snake. The goose was associated also with the serpent hero or god Trophonios at Lebadeia in Boeotia. In Brittany, according to Caesar, flocks of geese were bred, but the goose was not eaten. How early the goose was introduced into Brittany, we do not know, or how early it was introduced into the Mediterranean areas. The legend of the flock of geese on the Capitoline Hill in Rome, who gave warning of an attack by the Celts, indicates clearly the maintainence of a flock of sacred geese at the Capitol.

In Egypt, geese were sacrificed, and it is probable that they were sacrificed in Greece. As a food animal, geese seem to have been important in all but a few regions in the ancient world.

Geese were domesticated in Asia, and possibly in northern Europe, where the wild geese nested. The domestication of fowls, as well as of quadrupeds, is possible only if they are secured shortly after hatching or after birth. Failure to domesticate waterfowl in Egypt is explicable by the fact that the waterfowl did not nest there.

There is no indication that wild geese were ever taken for food by Mediterranean or Levantine peoples. Such captures could have occurred only in exceptional circumstances, when flocks of wild geese were forced down by storms into areas that normally they did not frequent.

The source of ancient admiration for the wild swan and wild goose was undoubtedly appreciation of the power of these fowls to make long flights, although the admiration was probably enhanced by the observation of the military formations in which they fly.

6. The Chicken.—Chickens seem to have been introduced into Europe in relatively late times. They were domesticated either in the East Indies or Malaysia, where the wild fowl from which they have descended occurred. That they were sacrificed by the poorer folks who could not afford sheep or goats we know. They are still sacrificed today in southern India, and the blood of a chicken is drunk by priestesses to inspire them. The sanctity of the chicken, however, seems not to have risen higher than the ascription of an

especial mana to its blood.   There was an association of the chicken
with the serpent, which is indicated by the fact that a cock was a
conventional offering to Asklepios.

5. Animals Indirectly Important to the Food Supply.—Where
barley, wheat, or other grains are staple articles of diet, the food
supply is seriously threatened by mice, rats, and otherr odents.
Animals which destroy these enemies are therefore of great importance, and may achieve sanctity.   Among such rodent destroyers
are cats, serpents of certain varieties, owls, and hawks.

1. The Domestic Cat.—In what part of Asia the cat was first
domesticated we do not know, but several different varieties have
come from that continent.   Introduced into Europe and America,
the blood of native wild cats has been introduced into the imported
strains, giving rise to the 'tiger cat' breeds; but we do not know
what the wild ancestors of the domestic cat in Asia were like.   One
variety was imported into Egypt at an early period for the specific
purpose of destroying mice.   The physical characteristics of this
breed are well presented in Egyptian statues and statuettes and crop
out in the mixed breeds of our cats.   The cat, because of its services
in protecting food, became so sacred that to kill a cat was a capital
crime, and the felines that died natural deaths were mummified.
Several cat goddesses developed in Egypt, of whom the most important was Bast, at whose temple in Bubastis the mummies of cats
were interred.   Cats, of course, were not eaten in Egypt, although
I have been informed by Chinese friends of my youth that young,
fat cats are good eating.   The cat is the outstanding example of an
animal that became sacred simply because it protected the food
supply.

2. The Owl.—The owl was a sacred bird in Athens and was one
of the symbols of Athena, to whom Homer conventionally refers
as 'Owl-eyed Athena' (*Glaucopis Athena*).   In paintings and statues
of Athena, the owl regularly appears.

That there were great numbers of owls in Athens we know, and the
expression, 'To take owls to Athens,' was the ancient counterpart
of the modern one, 'To take coal to Newcastle.'   Although the
mere abundance of the birds, who probably infested the Acropolis
on which the major temple of Athena was placed, may have been
the basis for its acceptance as the symbol of the goddess, the greater
probability is that the service of the owls in destroying rodents was
responsible for its sanctity.

3. The Hawk and Eagle.—The important god of the Pharaonic hordes that invaded Egypt from Abyssinia appears to have been Ra the Hawk, although Horus later was an important hawk god and was always represented as that bird or in human form with the head of a hawk. The source of the sanctity of the hawk in Egypt may have been its association with the sun or its devouring of poisonous serpents, but we cannot exclude the possibility that its service in destroying rodents may have been a factor.

In the Mediterranean area, the hawk was less important except insofar so it was confused with the eagle. That a mana of some dangerous sort was ascribed to the hawk, however, is indicated by the myth of Kirke (Circe), the sorceress who transformed men into pigs, for the name Kirke apparently represents the cry of the hawk.

The eagle, frequenting the mountaintops where the gods eventually resided, was the associate of these divinities of the thunder and storm, and it is probable that this had much to do with the eagle's being the 'bird of Zeus' after the various gods called 'Zeus' were assimilated to one another. The strength and flying ability of the eagle doubtless contributed to this achievement of sanctity; his being a danger to lambs and kids may have had its influence.

6. The Horse in Religion.—The horse occupies a peculiar position in the history of early religion. The early sanctity of the horse is unmistakable, and there were horse gods and horse goddesses. Poseidon, was a horse god who long held sway. Mare goddesses were assimilated to Demeter and to Athena. The mare goddess absorbed into Demeter had two children by Poseidon, one of whom was admitted to have been a colt, while the other appears to have been the 'Lady,' that is, Kore (Persephone).

Although the wild horse was the principal food animal of men in one period of the Old Stone Age, we cannot ascribe the sanctity of the horse in later periods to his ancient food value, since the flesh of the domestic horse has not been widely appreciated, and the wild horse is thought to have disappeared from Europe and the Levant shortly after the New Stone Age. The concepts of horse divinities and real reverence for horses as animals persisted down into the classical period.

The sanctity of the horse is further indicated by the legends of Kentauroi (Centaurs), hybrid monsters that were described as part horse and part human, sometimes represented with the body and four legs of a horse and a human torso with arms and head replacing the equine neck and head. The seilenoi, represented in Asia Minor as men with the pelts, ears, and tails of asses, were in Greece represented with the corresponding horse attributes. The legend of Pegasus, the winged horse, contributes further evidence of the religious importance of the horse.

The horse was bred in the ancient world for two purposes. He was used, after the invention of the wheel, to draw war chariots, but never for menial labor such as plowing or drawing carts or wagons for transporting goods. Asses, mules, and oxen were employed for these purposes. Occasionally a man traveled in a horse-drawn chariot, but this seems to have been exceptional. Equitation (the riding of horses) was a late achievement in the Mediterranean area, although it was an early accomplishment for the tribes in southeastern Europe and the Steppes of Asia.

The horse was bred also for racing; the greatest public service a wealthy man could give his city was to maintain a stable with which to win races at the Olympic and other games. The prestige of the horse is further indicated by the fact that any Greek name containing the root *ip* was an aristocratic name, borne only by a member of an aristocratic family. Thus, we know that Chrysippus ('golden horse'), Leucippus ('white horse'), and 'Hippocrates' (ruling horse) were of noble lineage.

For this great sanctity of the horse there are several possible explanations. It may have descended from the remote period when the horse was a staple food animal, although that is doubtful. It may have been due to the association of the horse with springs and running streams, where the wild horses congregated to drink and so were seen at close range, for springs and streams were holy in their own right. That the satisfaction of the desire for preeminence through victory in racing was the source is eliminated because the sanctity of the horse antedated the games. The protective function of the horse in war may be ruled out for the same reason. These functions undoubtedly contributed to the prestige and religious importance of the horse, but appeared after the sanctity was well established. The probable explanation, even if we cannot rule out the food association completely, is to be found in part in the association of the wild horse with fresh-water supplies. Admiration for the wild horse because of his speed (exceeded only by that of the wild ass, elephant, and camel) and because of his strength and handsome appearance may be assumed, however, to have been important in enhancing his sanctity. Anyone who has seen and heard a troop of horses running and has felt the tremor of the ground from their thundering feet can understand the ancient title of 'Earth Shaker' which was applied to Poseidon.

Down to and in the classical era, horses were sacrificed not only to Poseidon, but also to certain other gods in the Mediterranean area. Several of the heroes associated with horses were doubtless conceived as human horses, although they may not have been actual divinities.

That the sanctity began with the wild horse is evident in the antiquity of the myths. We might assume that the equine characteristics of Ares, Athena, and Hera were assimilated after the domestic horse was imported, and the horse heroes, Hippolytos, Lycurgos, and Diomedes, obviously were based on domestic animals; but the association of horses with water sources and the myths of Poseidon, Demeter, and their offspring probably could have arisen only from the wild horse. Although we have suggested Poseidon as an ancient Ionian (Pelasgian) 'Zeus,' the blue eyes ascribed to him raise some doubt. The possibility that Hippos, from whom Poseidon developed, was an Achaean divinity in his origin cannot be completely excluded. If this possibility were validated, the struggle between Poseidon and Athena for Attica could be interpreted as the ousting of the Achaeans from Attica by the Ionians, for Athena was never represented with blue eyes (Pausanias, ref. VI: A4, Vol. I, xiv, p. 6) except by modern translators, some of whom render *Glaucopis Athena* as 'Blue-eyed Athena,' avoiding the literal rendering of 'Owl-eyed.'

7. **Extension of Food-animal Praxes.**—There is a uniform characteristic attaching to all food animals, wild or domestic, and to some of the animals that assisted in the protection of the food supply. *Something had to be done about them*—praxes had to be developed for making use of these animals. Such praxes were never totally satisfactory, but only in part succeeded in providing and protecting food. Something more remained to be done; hence, the extension of the praxes from the sound to the magical or the religious was inevitable.

Where and when game is abundant the major need is for the development of techniques of hunting and fishing and for the making of suitable weapons for the chase and for fishing. In most regions, however, the game supply has not been uniform. Even in areas where game animals are not migratory there are seasonal variations, and successful hunting may diminish the herds. Hunting praxis, accordingly, extends not only into rituals designed to make spears and arrows fly truly and strike vital spots, but to rites designed to protect the game from nonhuman enemies, to increase its fertility of reproduction, and to bring the wild herds into the hunting areas. That such rituals were practiced in remote antiquity has been inferred from the paintings in the caves of paleolithic man, as interpreted by magical practices that have persisted down to the present day.

Similar rituals were necessary for the successful taking of fish and for the bringing of the schools of fish near shore. These rituals were later addressed to the power of the animals—to help them to reproduce, to draw them into areas where they could be taken, and to make them vulnerable to the hunters. No praxes for taking serpents appear to have developed far, since snakes are easily located, and a club or stone is a sufficient weapon.

With the introduction of domestic animals, the meat supply is made much more dependable, but new praxes of breeding and caring for the livestock are necessary. These are never 100 per cent efficient, and so they are extended into rituals. A great impetus is given to religious development by the use of domestic animals, so that it is not astonishing that the food animals that become sacred include all domestic animals. It is not the use of animals as food that produces ritual, but the concern about them and reflection on ways of making the supply dependable to avoid famine that leads to ritual and so to religion.

From the survivals of rituals and myths of remote periods into later rituals and myths with which we are acquainted, it can be inferred that in the earliest stages of development of an animal cult all animals of a given species were sacred, in the sense of sharing a mana peculiar to the species. Rituals for promotion of the reproduction and welfare of a food animal were directed toward all individuals of that species, at least all those in a given region. An early form of ritual was the impersonating of animals of the species by participants wearing the skins or conspicuous features, such as horns, tails, etc. Rituals for ensuring success in the hunt were also mimetic, consisting in going through activities similar, in form, to those of the chase. It is suspected that the superb paintings of animals in the caves of Altamira had some connection with rituals of one or the other of these sorts, but we are not certain of this. That imitating an animal may work in either of two ways, to promote the lives of the animals, or to enable the imitator to kill the animal, involves no contradiction. The purpose of assisting the animals to multiply and thrive has the further purposes involved in it. The man dependent on game wants the game to flourish solely because he wants to kill it for his own use.

If ritual stopped in this stage we would call the system magic rather than religion. Among some savages the rituals have not proceeded further, and they would not progress further in any case without the domestication of animals.

Domestic animals (except dogs) require care: herding, protection from carnivorous animals, and other sorts of personal attention. Rituals extended from this praxis accordingly involve doing something to, for, or about the animal itself. Elaborate ritual for each animal individually is impossible, and the problem is solved at a low level by rituals for the particular herd or flock collectively. Cattle-raising Bantus in Central and East Africa had such rituals before the tsetse fly devastated the herds. The nature of the active portions of the ritual are obscure, as they were solicitously concealed from Europeans, but they undoubtedly included formal procedures when letting the cattle out to graze, returning them to the kraal, etc. The negative parts of the ritual are better known. Women were not allowed to touch the cattle or to eat the flesh of one if killed or to drink the blood drawn from the living animal. This was in no wise to protect the women, but to protect the cattle, which would sicken if the tabu were broken.

Where the ritual for domestic animals is collective, no individual animal is picked out for special ritual treatment. In European and Asiatic countries, on the other hand, there seems to have been a selection of a particular beast to represent perhaps a limited herd, at first, but eventually to represent the whole species. Ritual conducted for its benefit vicariously applies to the group. The idea eventually develops that the life power or mana of the species centers in this individual, which becomes, in effect, an animal god, and religion has really commenced. It might be assumed that the selected animal represents the species because it is a god; but the development is probably in the other direction. The animal is conceived as a god because of the ritual that has been built around it.

A feature of the sanctity of a species of domestic animals is that there is restriction on the slaughter of the animals. When milk is the primary consideration, females must not be slain. When animals are few, even if milk is not the product but meat is desired, females are not to be killed because they are necessary to produce young. The males are subject to slaughter because they are mostly superfluous for breeding purpose, but an ox broken to the plough cannot be slain. These restrictions are embodied in rituals, and, if the tabu is broken, the whole species in the community suffer. Even when domestic animals are more plentiful, they must not be killed except ritually, as sacrifice. All over the ancient world a sacrifice was a feast, and meat originally was not eaten otherwise. This restriction was loosened, first for small animals (sheep and goats), last for cattle. Whether pigs and dogs were ever subject to these restrictions there is no evidence, but among the Arabs down to the early Christian centuries, camels were not to be slain except as sacrificial victims.

The same restriction persisted among the cattle-raising Bantus until the breakup of their culture less than a hundred years ago. Cows were not killed and bullocks were slain only in secret ceremonies in the forest remote from the camp, and the flesh eaten by the warriors. Hindus, orthodox and unorthodox, do not kill either female or male cattle, the cow being valuable to them for her milk, although the tabu on killing the male is less easy to explain, and in the Christian Era the orthodox Hindus have extended the tabu on slaughter to all animals.

The eating of a domestic animal except a dog or a pig in early cultures was always a group affair. No one might kill an animal of his own flock privately, but in some cases the whole encampment and in others all blood relations had the right to participate in the feast. These conditions protected the flocks and herds from reckless slaughter. A man possessing large numbers of domestic animals might slaughter for his immediate family; but if every poor relation or every member of the tribe had the right to partake of the feast, he would be more conservative.

When animal gods evolved, another custom grew up—that of sacrificing individual animals to the god of the species, for which explanations are more simple than reliable. This custom persisted down to a late date in Mediterranean religion in the worship of Dionysos. The animal was torn to pieces alive, and from this ritual myths concerning the god arose that were credited after the original animal god had become humanized. Other more savage rituals regarding domestic animals, such as the boiling of a kid in its mother's milk (forbidden in Exodus 32: 19), are difficult to trace to their original intentions, although their later interpretations are more evident.

Where religion, based in part on pastoral pursuits, has progressed, the animal divinity has eventually been humanized. The power of the animal is represented by, and concentrated in, a divinity conceived as human (or rather superhuman) in form and attributes and not identified with any actual human being, although it may appear in human form at times. In this stage, the original animal divinity appears as the companion, or symbol, of the goddess, or some feature of the animal is attached to the divinity. This leads, as we have pointed out, to duplication and reduplication; the divinity figures in myths in its human aspect and also in its original animal aspect.

As we have already warned, association of an animal with a god or goddess does not prove that that animal actually attained divinity, but merely that it had attained a degree of sanctity and might eventually have achieved divinity. Such animals were apt to be assimilated to divinities developing from other sources. The association of the pig with Demeter in the rituals at Eleusis, for example, does not prove that there was a sow goddess earlier, although from the total evidence from rituals and myths we may reasonably conclude that there actually was a sow goddess as representative, not merely of the pig species, but also of the earth power, and that, by the addition of a male consort to Kore, Hades, the lord of the underworld, was created.

The wild boar attained divine status in Asia Minor, but in Greece and Celtic lands probably attained only a lesser sanctity. That there were deer goddesses in Arcadia and in Celtica, before the deer was absorbed as a symbol of Artemis and other goddesses, is probable, but not certain. The evidence for a bear goddess in Arcadia and in Switzerland is stronger.

8. Trees and Plants Producing Food.—Among the trees that had sacred associations because of their contributions to man's food supplies, the oak and olive were especially important in the Mediterranean area. Farther north in Europe, the apple as well as the oak seems to have been of religious importance. The name

'Apollo' apparently is derived from the same root as our word 'apple,' and although the apple does not thrive in southern areas, the apple god from the north absorbed the earlier divinities at Delphi. The acorn was an early staple food throughout Europe and was the main food of the Arcadians in Greece down to a late period. In England, prior to the Norman conquest, the acorn crop was the most important food crop. The 'Zeus' at Dodona in Epirus in the northwestern part of ancient Greece was originally an oak-tree divinity, and various oak gods are known to have flourished in the areas of Europe farther north. The importance of the oak in Celtic religion is well known; the word 'druid' is apparently connected with the Celtic name for the oak.

In ancient times the greater part of Europe was a vast oak forest. The 'English oak' (*Quercus robur*) grew as far north as Norway, south into Sardinia, and eastward to the Caucasus and Ural Mountains. In these areas, the acorn was the staple food of the peoples. When the domestic hog was introduced, men preferred to feed the acorns to the swine and eat the pork, but the poorer folk continued to eat acorns, boiled or roasted, especially in times of food scarcity. In England, down to the Norman Conquest, acorns constituted the most important food crop for the proletariat.

The European oak is especially liable to being struck by lightning, which explains the 'oak god' being a 'thunder god.' The mistletoe was sacred only when it grew on an oak tree, on which it seldom appears in Europe. Its growth on the oak seems to have been ascribed by the Celts to the tree's having been struck by lightning. It is not surprising that many of the gods and goddesses throughout Europe were evolved in their primitive forms as oak divinities, to whom other divinities were assimilated. Since the early Europeans were *agrammatikoi*, we have no records of the progression from goddesses to gods of the oak divinities but know them only in their final male forms. Among the oak gods were Donar of the Teutons, Thor of the Scandinavians, Perun of the Slavs, Perkun or Perkunas of the Lithuanians, Taara of the Esthonians, and the 'Zeus' of Dodonian Thessaly. In Boeotia there was a Hera, as well as a 'Zeus,' identified with the oak.

In ancient Italy every oak tree was sacred, and the sacred fire tended by the Vestal Virgins was fed with oak wood. It is probable that the Roman Dian and Diana were originally oak divinities, to which animal divinities were assimilated. Zeus Lukaios (Lycaeus) in Arcadia is marked as an oak god by the ritual in which his priest 'made rain' by sprinkling water from an oak branch.

The association of the boar with the oak can be explained as due to the animal's feeding on acorns. This association was long maintained by the ritual burning of the sacred Yule log at the mid-winter festival and the gracing of the festal board with the head of a boar.

1. The Oak and the Acorn.—The oaks that grew in Asia Minor in ancient times produced acorns that were inedible; even rodents could not eat them. No oak divinity developed in that area. There were, however, great pine forests producing edible nuts, so that the development of pine divinities in Phrygia is what might be expected. Attis, later identified with Adonis, was an assimilation of a pine-tree god to a boar god, or *vice versa*. It is possible that Ma, the Great Mother, who persisted as the chief goddess of Asia Minor, was the original pine divinity, and that this divinity easily developed male characteristics because of the analogy of the pine cones to the male testicles, and the analogy of the harvesting of the crop by cutting off the cones to the early method of castration. This is why the priests of Ma and Attis castrated themselves. The substitution, in the worship of the grove, of the pine cone for the original pollen frond of the male date-palm blossom apparently occurred under the influence of the Assyrians, who were already devoted to the pine god.

2. The Olive.—The olive, which flourishes in the coastal areas around the Mediterranean, furnished food, which took the shape of pickled and dried olives, and oil, which was used for cooking, for lamps, and for oiling the body for the purpose of discouraging lice.

3. The Fig.—The fig, and its related tree the sycamore, were important food trees in the Levant and in Egypt, where the fig attained a considerable and somewhat confusing sanctity. The fig tree (or the sycamore) was associated with Hathor, the cow goddess of Egypt (later assimilated to Isis). The great goddess of Ephesus in Asia Minor, who was referred to by Romanized writers as 'Diana of the Ephesians,' was evidently a fig goddess in origin. That the fig did not become an important fruit tree in Greek areas may be explained by the absence of the wild fig from these areas, since the figs cultivated in the Levant required fertilization by the pollen of the wild tree. However, figs were of some consequence in southern

Italy in ancient times, for the legend of the nursing of Romulus and Remus by the she-wolf locates the scene under a fig tree. While the shape of the fig suggests the dugs of a she-wolf, this does not supply a certain explanation for their conjunction. It may be a duplication in which the fig tree and the she-wolf are identical, or it may indicate that Romulus and Remus were children of a fig goddess by a wolf god. We may assume that the story of Adam and Eve making aprons of fig leaves has reference to the sanctity of the fig in Babylonia and that the legend of Zacchaeus climbing a sycamore tree to see Jesus is no mere accident. The association of the fig with charms against the evil eye in the folklore of southern Europe in modern times has been explained from the supposed resemblance of the male testicles to the fig; but the full history of this symbol is still as unexplained as the name 'sycophant' ('presenter of the fig') for the professional informers in Athens.

4. The Date.—Although the date was of no economic importance to the Greeks, a ritual that in Babylonia grew up around the cultivation of the date palm gave a divinity to the date and to a cult that has erroneously been described as the 'worship of the grove.' The word 'grove' in the English is not to be understood as a plantation of trees, but as a conventionalized representation of a female date palm. 'Tree' would have been a better English rendering, but the translators of the King James Version of the Bible went astray.

The separation of the sexes in the date palm was influential as a factor in promoting the importance of the female; and the necessity of artificial fertilization of the female blossoms emphasized the importance of the female still more. The ancient praxis of tying fronds of the male blossom in the female blossoms is still followed by modern date growers. New procedures were introduced by California date growers a few years ago, but I understand that they have gone back to the ancient procedure.

In certain areas in Mesopotamia, Arabia, and North Africa, the date was and still is the staple food. Men perhaps cannot live on dates alone, but with the addition of a little green stuff or milk, a completely balanced diet is provided. Domestic animals in the Great Oasis are fed nothing but dates, but perhaps pick up enough brushwood to form a supplement. The ensuring of the date crop for these areas consequently has been a matter of great importance. In some areas irrigation is practiced, for the date grows best, as the Arabs say, 'With its feet in the water and its head in the sun.'

Without artificial fertilization of the blossoms, the 'hands' of dates do not set fully. But even with irrigation and pollination, the results are not always perfect. Hence, it seemed, the praxis should be extended; more should be done. The obvious extension is by analogy, with ceremonial impressiveness. Accordingly, a ritual, portraying in elaborate form the pollination procedure, was devised. Selecting a particular tree as the representative, the chief or king, together with the priest of an earlier divinity (a fish divinity in Babylonia), ceremonially presented to the tree a symbol representing the male blossom. For impressiveness, of course, the king wore his royal robes and the priest wore a magnified copy of a fishskin with the representation of the fish's head forming a cap or beret on his head (the original from which the bishop's miter is derived). What other ceremonials were added we do not know, but perhaps processions and music were added. Eventually, an artificial and elaborately designed representative of the tree was substituted for the living tree in Babylonia, such a symbol seeming more impressive; under Assyrian influence the symbol of the pine god was substituted for the frond of the male blossom in the ceremonial. Before this change occurred, however, the ritual of assistance to the date trees had given rise to a date goddess (Ishtar) to whom, in Babylonia, the older fish goddess had been assimilated.

Once inaugurated, the worship of Ishtar spread to other areas, even those in which the date does not thrive, with the goddess' name appearing in the variant forms of Astarte, Ashtart, and Ashtaroth. The pillar representing the goddess in her temples before images were made in many cases is formed or marked in ways that plainly identify it as the trunk of a date palm.

The date palm did not fruit well in Greece, even in places where it would grow, so that no date goddess arose in the Greek area, and Ishtar never was imported, although a derivative goddess, Aphrodite, was borrowed from the Levant.

The date goddess had her manas extended beyond the initial production of the date crop and became the goddess of vegetation in general and apparently the promoter of animal life and the protector of human life in various ways. The tree as a symbol or representation of the goddess did not spring entirely from the date. The cultivated fig tree was regarded as female (which, in a sense, it is, since the blossoms of the Smyrna fig are defective), and the pine and oak divinities were probably female at first, as the olive divinity was throughout.   Pillars, whether of wood or stone, representing divinity, were derived from the tree trunk, and the notion sometimes presented that wooden pillars were female and stone pillars male does not represent the actual facts.   With the addition of a male divinity as a consort of the goddess, pillars were employed as symbols of the god also.   Hence, we may be certain from the erection of twin pillars before Solomon's temple that it was a shrine of both a male and a female divinity, as were apparently other Phoenician temples of which Solomon's was a replica. As in other instances, the goddess (Ashtaroth) was ultimately ejected.

Pillars have been erroneously interpreted by modern pseudo-ethnologists, from whom Freud drew his 'phony' symbolism, as representing always a male principle.   The Latin cross has also been interpreted as a male symbol, but this cross was originally a conventionalized tree, and the early Christians well knew this and spoke of Christ's dying on the 'tree.'   The early Christians apparently were not unaware of the analogy of the crucifixion to the death of Tammuz in the arms of Ishtar and to the death of Attis under the pine tree, although they refrained from elaborating upon it.

5. The Grape.—The grapevine was an important producer of fruit for consumption, fresh and dried, and for the making of wine, which was the common drink of the peoples of the Mediterranean and Levantine areas.   Whether the *vinifera* grape of certain varieties was native to southeastern Europe, or whether the stock was introduced from Asia where there certainly were native varieties, is uncertain.   That any grape god or wine god, as such, ever developed anywhere is problematical.   However, in the cult of Dionysos, under whose name various gods of vegetation and animal gods were assimilated in the Mediterranean area, the grape eventually became one of the chief symbols of the god.   This is undoubtedly an instance of the assimilation to a divinity of a plant that had acquired a certain sanctity, but was assimilated before it had quite reached the stage of divinity.

6. Food Cereals.—The cereals that have been most widely used as food for human beings during the centuries are wheat, barley, spelt, and rice.   Oats have been eaten in some areas but have not been of world-wide importance.   Maize (Indian corn) was cultivated in America long before 1492 and was for the American Indians a staple food. In the ancient world, spelt and barley were the principal food cereals, although wheat was grown and eaten in some areas. Religious rituals and religious concepts developed in connection with the growing of barley and spelt, but the comparison of these religious developments with those of the peoples who for long periods cultivated and ate rice and maize is illuminating.

Demeter, in the Greek world, included in her make-up aspects of a barley goddess as well as those of a sow goddess, a mare goddess, and a snake goddess. Whether her barley characteristics were primary or whether some other divine nature was primary, we cannot determine, but in the view of the Athenians of the classical period, the barley feature of Demeter was paramount. For the Athenians, the barley was a staple food and the sowing of the barley as well as its harvesting were conducted under the auspices of Demeter, with rituals and festivals in her honor. The processions from Athens to Eleusis at the Thesmorphoria were parts to the rituals that were believed to promote the growth of the barley.

According to the legends, Triptolemos, under the direction of Demeter, carried the seed of barley from Eleusis to peoples in other parts of the world.

Spelt was the grain of the Egyptians. Spelt may be described as an inferior kind of wheat, and some botanists have classified it as a species of wheat, although others have given it a separate listing. Spelt was used and perhaps cultivated by the ancient lake dwellers of Switzerland and was widely cultivated in various European areas in the period of Roman domination. Eventually the true wheat took its place.

In Egypt, Osiris was the god of the spelt, and the myths about him are clearly dramatizations of the planting, growth, and harvesting of the spelt. Osiris, like Demeter, was associated with the pig, but the relation was one of antagonism, not of cooperation. The god Set in Egypt, who in the myths represents the pig, was not assimilated to Osiris. The slaying of Osiris by Isis represents the growth of the new grain in the next season. The planting of the grain was by scattering it on the damp soil and letting a herd of pigs tramp it in. Pigs also were turned into the field after harvest to pick up scattered kernels. It is not strange that the priests of Osiris were prohibited from eating pork.

Wheat was cultivated in Mesopotamia in early times, and it is assumed that it was indigenous in that region. Doubtless the wheat acquired sanctity, but no clear evidence for this has come down to us.

Maize was cultivated in the Americas, as we have said, long before the white man arrived and was an important crop for the Indians. Since the fifteenth century maize has been introduced into Europe, Asia, and Africa, and, apparently, uncivilized groups have transferred to the maize rituals and concepts which they had developed from the use of other cereals. There were in Africa other cereals related to maize, cereals such as sorghum, which bear their kernels in the blossomhead or 'tassel,' so that, when Frazer describes rituals practiced by African tribes in the planting and growing of 'maize,' we cannot be certain that he is really referring to maize.

The Indians in North and South America developed various rituals around the growing and the use of maize. In some groups, these rituals included the preservation of stalks from the harvest until the next planting, in order to conserve the life principle of the corn. In the northeastern areas, the maize was personified as an old woman; in Mexico, as a little girl growing up. In Mexico a maize goddess, Chicomecoatl, was evolved, and a maize god, Cinteotl, also appeared. In other words, the religious development characteristic of civilization appeared in America also.

Rice has long been the staple food of peoples of eastern and south-eastern Asia. In rice-growing regions religious rituals and religious concepts grew up around the rice and its cultivation, as we might expect. Eventually, a life principle or life stuff was assigned to the rice. The Malays and the Dyaks called this psyche the *semengat*, which is the conventional Malay name for the life soul. Some of the rice peoples, however, distinguished between the plant life stuff and the animal life stuff, applying different names to them. Some rice-growing groups had a special name for the life principle of the rice.

The blossoming of the rice was associated with human pregnancy by some groups, who have applied rituals derived by analogy to promote the production of the grain. Some groups developed a ritual of capture of the rice life principle, analogous to the capture of a small animal, and imprisoned the rice life in a granary. In Borneo, the Kayans set aside a small area as a ceremonial rice field and conduct therein all religious ceremonies, including symbolic processes of planting and cultivation, which are later carried out in the actual rice fields. In many groups a rice mother and a rice child are represented by bundles of rice heads in which the rice life is supposed to be concentrated.

As might be expected, the tabus associated with the planting and cultivation of rice are numerous and varied. The complex of rituals, tabus, and concepts is centered around the notion of a life principle of the rice. The life principle is often referred to as a 'bird,' which relates it to the ba of the Egyptians. A rice goddess has appeared, but evidently the concept was imported from Hindu religion, since the goddess is identified as the wife of Vishnu, and it is improbable that this goddess developed in India from the rice.

The religious developments around the rice in Asia and around the maize in America are, as Frazer points out in the *Spirits of the Corn and Wild*, similar to those of European peasants about the wheat. Wherever there is a staple foodstuff, religious rituals develop in a certain period of religion, designed for the promotion of the production of the foodstuff. From the rituals, religious concepts evolve in the process of interpretation or explanation of the rituals.

In Europe and Africa, cereals were used not only for food, but also for the making of beer. Beer was an invention of natives of east-central Africa, from whence it was introduced into Egypt and from Egypt into other lands. The Africans made beer by fermenting bread in water, employing bread of two kinds, that made from meal of cereals (principally millet) and that made from plantains dried and pulverized. The Egyptians used the bread-fermenting process also. Malting grain for the brewing of beer seems to have been a European invention.

Ritual uses of beer grew up in central Africa, but there is no evidence of religious associations of beer in Egypt or in Europe. The late introduction of beermaking into Europe precluded the development of religious features of beer in that area, but this explanation is not applicable to Egypt.

7. Leguminous Plants.—Various legumes were eaten in the ancient world, but of these only the bean attained sanctity. Beans were offered to Apollo, as the protector of food plants, in the month Pyanepsion, which is reported by ancient writers to have derived its name from the offering, the bean being, in Greek, *puana*.

To the Pythagoreans the bean was forbidden food, although Diogenes Laertius says that the Pythagoreans held the bean as sacred. At any rate, it appears that a powerful mana was ascribed to the plant and its fruits.   The offerings of beans to Apollo suggest that the plant was associated with the serpent, and, since Pythagoreanism was a serpent cult, this may possibly be the explanation of the sanctity or the accursedness of the bean.   No worship was developed about the bean, so far as we know, unless the Pythagorean tabu may be interpreted as a ritual of worship.

Outside of the Pythagorean cult, the bean was tabu to persons who were about to engage in religious rituals.   Initiates of the Eleusinian mysteries were prohibited from eating beans for a certain period preceding the ceremony.   Priests of most divinities were prohibited from eating beans before offering sacrifice to the divinity. Similar tabus on eating of beans are reported by Herodotus as enforced in Egypt.   Apparently, tabus were laid on beans in Asia Minor, but there is no report of similar tabus in Mesopotamia, unless the 'pulse' which was eaten by Daniel and his companions, to the horror of the Babylonians, is assumed to have been beans.

Various explanations have been offered for the tabu on the bean, of which two are plausible.   (*a*) The association with the serpent, which was an early earth divinity or earth daimon, easily associated with the growth of plants from the earth.   The tabu on beans for initiates at Eleusis comports with this theory, since sacred snakes were kept at Eleusis and associated with the growing of the barley. (*b*) The production of flatulency by eating of beans, which was as well known to ancient peoples as to moderns.   Diogenes Laertius relates an anecdote which demonstrates that knowledge.   For a person or a priest who participated in a religious ceremony, the effects of flatulency would be insulting to the divinity, as well as to participants in the ceremony.

Beans were grown and eaten in America before the advent of the white man, but, so far as we know, no rituals or tabus were developed about the beans.   The Old World bean belonged to the genus *Vicia*, which includes the horse bean, sometimes called the field bean or tick bean, and which is believed to have originated in Asia.   The American beans were numerous species of the genus *Phaseolus*, from which have come most of our garden beans.

Aside from beans, the only important edible legumes indigenous to America were peanuts.   It has been reported recently that excavations in Peru have unearthed evidence of religious associations of the peanut, but full information is not yet available concerning the discovery.

8. Questionable Plants.—There were two wild plants which acquired, in the Mediterranean area, sanctity for which explanation is difficult. These were the ivy and the wild celery. The ivy was sacred to Apollo at Delphi and sacred to Dionysos wherever orgies were held in his honor. The assumption that the pythonesses at Delphi and the Bacchantes in the worship of Dionysos chewed ivy and swallowed the juice to produce frenzy is not demonstrable. The ivy, however, was a symbol of Apollo and of Dionysos, and their worshipers often wore ivy wreaths. Ivy is eaten (one writer says 'greedily') by deer, horses, cattle, sheep, and goats, these animals seeming to derive neither frenzy nor harmful effects from its consumption. That its consumption by these animals about whom religious rituals arose caused it to be associated with the animal gods assimilated by Apollo and by Dionysos is the most plausible explanation of the sanctity of the plant.

Wild celery grew all through the temperate regions of Europe and was associated with heroes. Whether or not the wild celery was eaten by ancient peoples, we have no information. It is obvious that the people who first cultivated celery must have eaten the wild plant, but we do not know where celery was first cultivated although it almost certainly was not Greece.

The bestowal of a crown of wild celery on the winner of an athletic contest was customary at the Nemean games in Argolis and at the Isthmian games near Corinth. As neither of these games was associated with a particular divinity we have no indication from this usage as to the source of the sanctity of the wild celery.

There were numerous Greek myths relating the foundation of the games, myths that are highly conflicting. The fact seems to be that the actual development of these games was not known to the Greeks of later periods. It might be assumed that the Nemean games were originally instituted in honor of Hera, and we could go on from that assumption to the further supposition that the wild celery derived its sanctity from the eating of the plant by cows. This, however, would be indulging in mythology of the same sort as that to which the Greeks were addicted. It is possible that celery was first eaten because of a medical virtue ascribed to it. If we should find that the wild celery was associated with Artemis or with Apollo, or with the serpent, this possibility would become a probability, but we are completely in the dark.

CHAPTER VII

PROTECTIVE AND OTHER PRIMARY DESIRES IN RELIGION

1. Desire for Protection.—Man is vulnerable to many external agencies, many of which are directed against his skin but which endanger deeper tissues. Protection against these agencies is needed, and the need has long been consciously recognized. Hence, a lively protective desire became a normal feature of human life, apparently at a very early period, if not as soon as man became man. Protection involves concern, fear, foresight, and planning, as is evident from the various protective devices that man has developed through the ages.

The methods, and even the implements, of protection have been woven into the faiths and rituals of religion, and the religious importance of protective desire is displayed in the liturgies and rituals of present-day religion. If we turn again to the Ninety-first Psalm, we find it written in verses 5–10:

Thou shalt not be afraid for the terror by night: (nor) for the arrow (that flieth) by day; (nor) for the pestilence (that) walketh in darkness; (nor) for the destruction (that) wasteth at noonday. A thousand shall fall at thy side, and ten thousand at they right hand; (but) it shall not come nigh thee. Only with thine eyes shalt thou behold and see the reward of the wicked. Because thou hast made the Lord (which is) my refuge, (even) the Most High thy habitation; there shall no evil befall thee, neither shall any plague come nigh thy dwelling.

There is a great range of physical dangers against which protection is promised to the votaries of Jehovah. Threats of physical damage to the heathen and the unfaithful are conspicuous all through the Jewish scriptures, and promises of protection for the faithful are equally numerous. These promises and threats are often interpreted symbolically by Christians, as promises and threats of 'spiritual' protection or loss thereof; but it is obvious that in the original conception the protection was physical, or that no distinction was made between physical injury and 'spiritual' damage.

In the Lord's Prayer, the petition for 'daily bread' may be given a symbolic interpretation, but it was a plea for food in a literal sense in early Christian usage. The petition: 'deliver us from evil' which follows the petition for bread, is interpreted usually as a plea for protection from both physical and spiritual evil. If further evidence of the religious nature of physical protection were needed, the extensive use in some Christian sects of holy amulets to protect from physical injuries would supply it.

The threats against which man needs and desires protection in this world can be classified under seven headings as possible injuries: (*a*) of a mechanical nature, (*b*) by insects, (*c*) by wild beasts, (*d*) by other men, (*e*) by climatic conditions, (*f*) by disease and poison, (*g*) by occult forces. We will consider these dangers in the order as listed, with some cross references.

2. Protection against Mechanical Injury.—Physical damage can be inflicted by an inanimate object, such as a falling stone, or by a falling tree. By tripping over a root or other obstacle, bones are often broken. Thorns and brambles, which are abundant in some regions, pierce the skin and may cause deeper injury. Protection against thorns has long been afforded by leg wrappings and arm bandages made of animal skin, or by more comprehensive coverage such as that afforded by the *chaparejos* of the modern cowboy. To protect the feet against rough surfaces and sharp stones, as well as against thorns, sandals and shoes were invented. These protective devices marked stages in the development of clothing and acquired religious value almost as soon as they became common. From the Jewish legends we find that shoes and sandals had to be removed when the person entered 'holy' areas (Exod. 3: 5; Josh. 5: 15; II Sam. 15: 30), as well as in other ritual circumstances (Deut. 25: 9; Ruth 4: 7). A Mohammedan entering a mosque leaves his footgear at the door. This removal of foot coverings, of course, is a symbolic act of submission, indicating that the person places himself completely at the mercy of the power of the holy place.

Among many African tribes a rear apron of animal hide is worn by men when in camp. Apparently, the real purpose of this apron is protection of the skin of the buttocks when the wearer sits down. Other types of savage clothing are for protection against the weather or against annoying insects.

3. Protection against Insects.—Biting, stinging, and clinging insects have been persistent enemies of mankind through the ages in almost all regions. The chief insect pests have been mosquitoes, flies, and lice. Fleas do not seem to have been so widely annoying, and bees and wasps are usually avoidable. The insect enemies attack the skin or through the skin.

Mosquitoes annoy man, even if he does not know that they communicate fevers, since the bite causes swelling and itching. The enveloping robe of the Arab and his face covering protect to some extent against mosquitoes, as well as against the sharp sand carried in the blasts of the wind. Mediterranean peoples used veils in religious rituals in early times; but whether or not they knew about the danger from mosquito bites, we have no information. It is more probable that the religious use of the veil arose for protection from flies, which, as we shall note shortly, were serious pests at animal sacrifices. Apparently no mosquito gods or mosquito devils developed, even among the Arabs.

Flies of many species, including the common housefly, abound in all warm and temperate regions and have abounded through the ages. Some flies, such as the 'stable fly' and the tsetse fly bite and infect animals with disease germs. The housefly, although it does not bite, is annoying, since it seeks the moist membranes of the eyes and the genital organs and crawls over foods. Infection by flies and gnats with inflammatory diseases of the eyes and transmission of typhoid fever by houseflies were dangers of which our insanitary ancestors had no knowledge; but flies were annoying to them, both personally and religiously.

Clothing of all types developed as protective covering, and, in the warmer areas of the world, protection from flies seems to have been an early and important purpose of clothing. Protection for the eyes is not simple, but protection for the sensitive membranes of the genital organs is relatively simple. Some of the types of clothing that were developed for protection from flies still persist among savages, for whom clothing has no connection either with sexual modesty or with immodesty. Bandages, loincloths and G strings are widely worn by savage men and sometimes by women. More efficient, and less uncomfortable in warm climates, have been aprons of flimsy materials suspended in front of the crotch. These sketchy aprons may be strips of bark, strips of fur, or woven fabrics. Similar aprons or tassels of fiber or tails of animals are often suspended in the rear. The flapping of these aprons and tassels discourages flies, just as did the 'fly nets' that were used for horses in the 'horse-and-buggy days' of yore. In lieu of aprons or tassels, bunches of leaves are worn suspended from the waist and probably are as effective as were the bunches of leaves formerly attached to the bridles of horses to keep the flies out of their ears. Grass skirts and sarongs wrapped about the waist and hanging to the knees seem also to be excellent fly excluders suitable to areas where the climate is not too warm.

Various theories have been advanced to explain the origin and evolution of clothing, including the theory suggested in the book of Genesis, namely, that clothing began to be worn for purposes of sexual modesty. The opposite theory, that clothing began to be worn to increase sexual stimulation, has been ascribed to several authors, but no one seems actually to have adopted it.

The search for explanations other than the one based on protection has been due to two factors: (*a*) neglect of the importance of protection from insects. Much clothing that approaches the primitive in type is not protective against mechanical injury or against cold weather; hence, the theorists ignore its real protective value. (*b*) The social values of clothing, once wearing of clothing has become established, have been mistaken for the original foundations of the habit of wearing it.

Religious rituals addressed to the flies developed in Mediterranean and Levantine areas, and from these rituals emerged at least one fly god, *Baal-zebub* (lord of the flies), from which name is derived our 'Beelzebub.' When an animal sacrifice was offered, the flies, already numerous about the places of sacrifice, were attracted in swarms and covered the meat before it could be roasted. This was offensive to human beings, even if they had no sanitary notions, and it was construed as an insult to the divinity in whose honor the sacrifice was offered. Hence arose the ritual of a preliminary sacrifice to the flies. Gorged with juices of the preliminary offering, the flies then retired into crevices to digest, and according to some stories the flies left the scene *en masse*, the ensuing sacrifice therefore not being befouled. It is not surprising that from this ritual of sacrifice to the flies a fly god should arise in some areas.

Lice were pests to our ancestors, as they still are to savages and semicivilized peoples today. Reports of Greek writers inform us that lice were a serious menace in the Mediterranean area, even in classical times. Men died of a disease which, in later medicine, was called *morbus pedicularis* (louse disease). According to reports by ancient writers, a number of eminent persons died of this louse infestation, among them the philosopher Plato.   In modern times, after it was discovered that typhus fever is communicated by lice, the old disease was assumed to have been typhus, but recent experiments seem to show that it is produced by lack of a specific vitamin, a vitamin that is not yet on sale.

Various techniques for partial protection against lice have been developed.   In various parts of Africa, where dwellings are simple structures of sticks or brush, the huts are abandoned when the 'cooties' become too numerous, and new huts are built.   A more widespread technique is that of oiling or greasing the skin and greasing of clothing made of skins.   Among the Bushmen of South Africa, before they became extinct, buchu and other strong-smelling herbs were mixed with the grease, apparently to increase its louse-repelling properties.

In Greek areas, olive oil was used for greasing the body, and it is probable that the ritual called 'inunction,' for which the corresponding verb is 'anele' (to oil), owes its origin to the protective oiling of the skin.   The application of oil having a slight protective value against lice, the extension to other manas followed the usual pattern of religious development.

Infestation of houses by lice was not so easily handled in the Mediterranean area as it is in Africa.   The houses were at first dugouts, or sod houses, replaced later by structures of stone or timber.   Such houses could not simply be abandoned when the infestation became serious.   Hence arose the custom of daily burning of incense in homes, which later became a religious ritual.   Domestic incense consisted largely of the plant thyme or of the wood of the incense cedar, perhaps sometimes of the two combined.   When these plants are smoldered, some of the thymol or some of the cedar oil is vaporized and condensed on the walls and furnishings of the house, both thymol and cedar oil being well-known insecticides.

The incense burned in temples and in theaters was of different composition and was burned to disguise foul odors, a protective ritual of a slightly different sort.   From these two practical protective functions of incense burning, the religious feature emerged and had great influence on the development of religion and of the philosophy that grew out of religion.

4. Protection from Ferocious Beasts.—Animal enemies of man were more numerous in early times than they are today, and protection against wild beasts was important. Against the claws and fangs of the quadrupeds and against the bites of serpents shoes, leg wrappings and arm bands give some protection, and further defensive clothing seems not to have been developed for protection against animals. Man seems to have depended largely on the implements of the chase—stones, clubs, axes, spears, and arrows—and on dexterity in the use of these tools. By day, these implements seem to have been man's best defenses against animal enemies, while by night he found protection by secluding himself in caves or huts or within stockades. To some extent nets, traps, and deadfalls, devised primarily for the capture of game, helped in man's protection from wild beasts of prey.

The divinities that emerged from food animals and food plants were extended in their manas from the powers of protecting man from starvation to manas protecting from mechanical injury, from animal enemies, from human enemies, from disease, and eventually to protection from occult dangers in this world and the next. In a monotheistic religion, all manas are exerted or at least controlled by the one divinity. In a polytheistic religion, although there may be a god or a goddess superior in authority to all the others, the lesser divinities may be appealed to for protection of specific sorts. Thus, in the Mediterranean world, Apollo and Asklepios were more often appealed to for healing than was the great Zeus. Similarly, in Catholic Christian sects, one saint is especially potent in healing; another more important for protection of travelers; another is especially appealed to for the finding of lost articles; and another brings horses 'in the money' at the tracks.

The supreme divinity in a nominally monotheistic religion may delegate protective functions to daimons, the reason for the potency of saints in special fields. In Jewish theology, protection, although controlled by Jehovah, may be delegated to daimons of the angel class. Thus, in the Ninety-first Psalm, from which we have quoted, verses 11 to 13 read:

For he will give his angels charge over thee, to keep thee in all thy ways. They shall bear thee up in (their hands), lest thou dash thy foot against a stone. Thou shalt tread upon the lion and the adder: the young lion and the dragon shalt thou trample under feet.

As contrasted with the beneficent divinities who protected mankind, there were in various ancient religions divinities that developed from species of animals that were not food animals but were enemies of man. These divinities were malignant, and rituals arose for protection from them, or from the animal species the manas of which the divinities represented. There is, of course, no malignant god contrasted with Jehovah in Judaism; but Jehovah presents certain malignant features that may have been due to assimilation of evil gods of religions from which Judaism developed.

The rituals for protection from malignant divinities were mainly rituals of *propitiation*, that is to say, of *flattery*, although there seem to have been features of the ritual designed to give more direct protection from the enemy god or from the animals of the species he represented. Flattery of a malignant god, by rendering homage to him, praising him, and by other rituals of adoration, was supposed to render him less malignant; this leads to the conclusion that the evil divinities were believed to be less intelligent than the beneficent deities, less able to see through the pretenses involved in the propitiation.

The most widespread animal enemies of man were the wolf and the serpent, which were found generally throughout Europe and Asia, although there were no wolves in Africa. The origin of wolf divinities is somewhat clouded by the fact that the wolves, in addition to being dangerous to man directly, were also threats to the food supply, devastating flocks of goats and sheep and killing the young of the cattle. The development of snake divinities is less clouded, since the serpent had ceased to be a food animal, in the areas in which civilization developed, at a very early time, although it remained a food animal down to modern times in other parts of the world.

Wolf gods were created by the Celts in central and southern Europe and probably were created in India also. In the ritual worship of the wolf god, the participants wore wolf-skins on their shoulders, which indicated their claim of kinship with the wolves. Whether this was entirely propitiatory, or was in part designed to give the worshipers greater power in combating wolves, is uncertain. The Romans seem to have adopted their wolf god, whom they identified with Mars, from the Celtic Etruscans; but against this conclusion is the fact that the Romans worshiped also a wolf goddess, while there is no evidence of a wolf goddess anywhere among the Celts.

In Greece there was an *Apollo Lukaios* in Arcadia, apparently the result of assimilation of an early wolf god to the synthetic apple-serpent-swan god. There was also a *Zeus Lukaios* in Arcadia, but this Zeus was the result of a confusion of two Greek words that had similar sounds. *Zeus Lukaios* was really the god of light, but the word *lukos* (wolf) was confused with the word for light, and, as a result, legends grew up of wolf rituals and of transformation of men into wolves on Mount Lukaon (Lycaon).

Poisonous serpents were numerous throughout the Levantine and Mediterranean areas, and from tales that have come down to us it is evident that there were many deaths from snake bite. Protection from snakes involves either of two techniques, avoidance of snakes or killing snakes, but, since the serpent lurks in hidden places and bites unexpectedly, these techniques are not sufficient. Rituals therefore grew up, and rituals of propitiation seem to have predominated.

Whether the brazen serpent that Moses set up in the wilderness (Num. 21: 8, 9) to cure the 'Israelites' of bites by poisonous serpents was intended as a propitiation of the serpents or a serpent god, we are not told; but that the mana of the serpent was respected in Solomon's time is indicated by the replica of the legendary brass serpent that Solomon installed in his temple (II Kings 18: 4). It is to be suspected that a deadly serpent was originally kept in the Ark of the Covenant, and the suspicion is strengthened by the explicit statement that when the ark was placed in Solomon's temple, there was nothing in it but two tablets of stone (II Chron. 5: 10), implying that the deadly agency had escaped or had been removed.

When from a poisonous serpent species a snake god is developed, rituals develop for protection from snakes of that species, then from snakes of all species, and eventually from diseases that are as mysterious as are the effects of snake bites.

One of the snake gods which, as we have mentioned, was eventually assimilated to the Zeus of Mount Olympus, was known by the surname of *Meilichios*, which means 'friendly' or 'benevolent.' This name was applied in flattery (propitiation), for he was regarded as really malicious rather than as friendly. We do not know what particular species of snake he represented, but it was obviously poisonous. The late representations of the *Zeus Meilichios* present him as a gigantic snake; but that is merely in accordance with the notion that a god great in power must be great in size. Undoubtedly, by worshiping the god, the danger, at least from the species he represented, was reduced.

The healing power ascribed to the serpent may possibly have derived from the nutritious character of snake meat, as we have suggested earlier.   On the other hand, it may have been a primitive theory of homeopathy.   The deadly effect of snake bite was mysterious.   If ancient man knew that the snake injected a poison, he must have known also that it is slight in quantity.   It is indeed probable that primitive man conceived of the deadly effects of the snake as a mana projected in a general way from the snake.   At any rate, the effects of snake bite are analogous to those of disease.   If the snake can produce disease, then, when properly propitiated, he could remove disease.   The representation in Babylonian mythology of the source of all evil as a serpent, and the theory in Genesis that death is the result of the machinations of the old serpent, the devil, are ascriptions of disease and death to the snake.

On the other hand, it is possible that the snakes used in healing were nonpoisonous, although poisonous snakes certainly were kept in the temples of the healing gods; hence the notion involved in the snake cults *may* have been that, since poisonous snakes produce disease, the nonpoisonous ones may cure disease.   If the Greek writers in the first two centuries of the Christian Era, a period in which the cults of Apollo and of Asklepios were still flourishing, had not been so reticent in their information, we might be able to settle this point.

That snakes were first worshiped and propitiated as actual snakes rather than in personified form is evidenced in India, where deaths from cobra bites are numerous, where religion is still near the primitive, and where cobras are worshiped today.

The most dangerous of all wild animals is the wild 'ox.'   It is possible that the evolution of the sanctity of the cow and bull was in part determined by protective desire.   Wild cattle were hunted in Mesopotamia and probably in Europe.   The bull seems to have achieved divinity in various regions, the bull gods being assimilated eventually into others; but we are not certain that the divinity developed from the wild bull.   The wild cow is more deadly than the wild bull, but did not achieve divinity anywhere, the cow goddesses being developed from the domestic milk-giving cow.   This seems to indicate that the sanctity of the bull was not derived so much from his dangerous aspect as through admiration of his strength and his impressive bellowing and through the use of his flesh as food.

How far the dangerous character of the wild boar contributed to the sanctity of the species is another problem of the same sort. It is possible that the rituals of boar gods were designed in part as protective—to promote the safety of the hunter in the taking of that vicious animal. Another problem is raised by the bear. Although bear flesh has always been valued as food, and the bear does not wantonly attack human beings as do wild cattle but minds his own business when let alone, he or she is a formidable antagonist when wounded or cornered. It is possible, therefore, that the rituals of the bear goddess in Arcadia, in which the participants were females who wore bear pelts and called themselves 'bears,' were protective rather than alimentary in purpose.

Certain animals, especially certain birds of prey, we have pointed out are directly protective to man by destroying his animal enemies. Among these fowls were the sacred ibis and the hawk in Egypt. The hawk devours rodents as well as serpents and does not disdain poisonous snakes. Before the domestication of fowls the hawk was not an enemy of the food supply. Domestic fowls came late in history, but the hawk was a holy bird in Egypt in remote antiquity.

The sanctity of the sacred ibis in Egypt obviously rested on the activity of that bird in destroying poisonous serpents. According to Herodotus, who derived his information from the Egyptian priests, Egypt was at an early period subject to incursions of winged serpents, which flew in from Arabia. The ibis met these flights near the Red Sea and destroyed them. This tale is obviously a confusion of the proclivity of the ibis for eating poisonous serpents with a legend of the pterodactyl. The sacred ibis is now extinct. The common ibis, which Herodotus describes, was not sacred, probably because it restricted its diet to nonpoisonous snakes.

The eagle became a symbol of 'Zeus' in Greece at a relatively late period. There may have been earlier an eagle god, assimilated to Zeus, but this is not certain. In any event, the sanctity of the eagle, as we have indicated, probably derives from his strength and flying ability and his destructiveness to lambs and kids. Since the eagle was an adjunct to, or a messenger of, Zeus, propitiation of Zeus was propitiation of his eagles.

The lion has long been a denizen of Africa and of the Near East. In Europe it was historically known only in a small area east of the Balkans. In Egypt a lion goddess, Bast, emerged, and was later associated with the domestic cat. In Asia Minor, the lion was represented as an attendant of gods and goddesses, but there is no evidence of divinities of the lion family. In Crete, the lion was a guardian or heraldic supporter of the goddess, but the lion idea was probably imported from the Levant. The lion is a rather cowardly animal, not especially dangerous to man. The lions to whom the Christians were thrown in the Roman arena had to be starved beforehand to make them attack the victims; hence the direct effect of protective desire in promoting the sanctity of the lion is not assumed, although danger to the food supply may have been an important factor, leading to propitiation. Apparently, the strength of this largest member of the cat family, and its impressive roar, led to its association with divinities as their suitable guards.

5. Men as Foes.—It is probable that primitive men engaged in personal combats for the possession of females in the rutting season and for possession of items of food in times of scarcity. As groups increased in size, group rivalry for the possession of caves, of hunting grounds, and of fishing shores can be presumed to have occurred. War, however, as distinguished from mere casual brawling, was not possible until weapons were devised.

Weapons were made first as implements of the chase or for fishing. Eventually, weapons in the true sense, more suitable for combat with other men and less suitable for the chase, were devised. From the hunting javelin evolved the war lance; from the hunting knife, the sword. This development was late, and even today many savages use in war the same implements they use for hunting. Some of the tribesmen of central Europe, in the period of Roman domination, employed their fishing nets and spears (tridents) in warfare and were skillful in the technique of first entangling an adversary in the net and then finishing him with the spear. When captured by the Romans and compelled to fight as gladiators in the arena, these warriors were known as *retiarii* (net men). The civilized Greeks, after the Trojan War, were easily overcome by the savage Dorians, who had developed the long military lance (*doru*), from which the Dorians were named. Against these 'spearmen' the Greeks could not succeed with their light hunting-type spears and their swords.

For defense against attack by other men, the main dependence, down to early historical times, was on counterattack, which still remains an important factor in defense. However, in or just preceding historical times, devices to protect against the weapons of antagonists were invented: breastplates, shields, and bucklers. When heavy swords for slashing were introduced, helmets, which were of slight use against arrows and javelins, were devised. Greaves for protection of the legs later were added, and at long last full armor appeared.

Defensive armor, along with weapons, acquired religious values. This is indicated by the custom of dedicating weapons and armor of slain foes in the temples of the divinities. Thus custom, as we have explained, began in fear of the manas of the original users of the arms, but it acquired ritual importance over and above the primitive purposes. Armor and weapons of war became associated with divine protection and are still symbols of this protection in Jewish and Christian hymnology. Reverting to the Ninety-first Psalm, we find in the fourth verse:

He shall cover thee with his feathers, and under his wings shalt thou trust; his truth (shall be thy) shield and buckler.

Among some ancient warlike peoples, the actual object of worship was a spear or a sword. These represented the manas about which the cult was developed. Where weapons did not become divinities, special manas were ascribed to them. The sword, in particular, had its manas widely extended. Not only was it effective for cutting or thrusting, but magical powers were ascribed to it—the power, for example, to daunt or repel ghosts and demons. In medieval superstition, this occult power was deemed to be due to the cross formed by the hilt of the sword, but the notion of the magic power of the sword came in long before Christianity. Ulysses drove away, from the pool of blood he had prepared, the ghosts that came eagerly out from the gate of the underworld, until the ones he wanted to interview had drunk. The physical damage the sword could do to the ghosts, of course, was nil, but the sword had occult manas. These manas were due to the fact that the sword was of bronze, the holy metal. Iron, which was an evil metal, would have been without effect against ghosts, although in later folklore iron became a protection against vampires and werewolves.

As dwellings and fortifications became important means of protection against human enemies, these structures acquired sanctity. One of our poets has declared that 'the groves were God's first temples,' but, if this theory had any validity, it was in application only to nomads, whose religious development never went so far as to produce any structure that could properly be called a 'temple,' or to men of the forest, who found protection from human enemies by losing themselves in the remote woods. Actually, temples and sanctuaries seem to have developed mainly from protective fortifications, although dwellings may have contributed somewhat to the development.

Caves, dolmens, sod houses, and finally structures of timber and masonry were used as dwellings, but these places, while they afforded some security for families, did not provide adequate group protection, and other defenses were needed. In an early period, these fortifications took the form of stockades made of logs set on end and of arrangements of great stones, which are conventionally known as 'megalithic monuments.' Eventually, there appeared structures of masonry in the true sense of the term, but the antecedent structures were great stones that were not in contact with one another.

The megalithic monuments still existing almost encircle the globe, from England eastward through the Mediterranean islands and North Africa and through southern Asia into the Pacific islands. The culmination of these structures was in the cromlech known as Stonehenge, on Salisbury plain in southern England. From the monument type, there was a transition to masonry structures that are represented on the island of Malta, and by further masonry developments in the eastern Mediterranean islands and the mainland of Greece. The most primitive type of megalithic monuments is represented in southern Asia, east of India; but the primitiveness of these monuments does not prove their antiquity. The stone arrangements in Manipur may be the latest of all, in spite of their primitive type.

The megalithic monuments are of four types, conventionally known as (1) menhirs; (2) alignments; (3) cromlechs; (4) dolmens. All of these except the dolmens were for defensive purposes, that is, for protection against human enemies.

1. The menhirs are single stones of huge size, standing near the seacoast or on relative eminences further inland. The principal menhirs still standing are in Brittany. Obviously these stones were places where sentries watched for enemies. Their stations command the coast or overlook plains across which invaders would have to pass in order to reach the encampments of the natives. These menhirs are all located at strategic points, in or adjacent to the

areas of the great settlements of ancient times. Lurking behind the menhir, the sentry was protected reasonably well.

2. Alignments are of two sorts. One sort is represented by the 'great alignment' near Carnac, which originally consisted of nine rows of great stones, extending from the encampment back into the forest. Unfortunately, some of the rows were broken up for use as building materials before the French Government took over the monuments and protected them from vandalism. The purpose of this alignment is clear and is further indicated by the ancient legends. If an attacking party landed from the sea, which is near, or from the bay to the south, and if the people of the encampment could not fight the invaders off, an avenue of escape was provided by the lines of stones. The women and children could escape to the forest, while the warriors, fighting as a rear guard from behind the stones, protected the retreat.

The group life of the people centered in the encampment, which may have been fortified, although no evidence of fortification remains. What temple existed is not known, but the mound of debris which had accumulated in the encampment is now occupied by a Roman Catholic chapel. The location of this church indicates that the spot was holy in earlier times, since the tendency of a new religion is always to take over the holy spots of the former religion.

Concerning the great alignment at Carnac there is a legend, which has two forms. In one form, St. Corneleys was a Christian who was pursued by Roman soldiers from Italy across France into Brittany. When he came to Carnac, close to the sea, further flight was impossible. The saint turned and cursed the soldiers, who were turned into the stones of the alignment. In the other form, the legend is that the saint was a missionary who tried to convert the Bretons, and the stones are the heathen who pursued him. The legend, like most legends, contains a basic truth, for each stone does represent a warrior fighting from behind it.

Alignments of a second sort are found facing beaches on which enemies might land or protecting defiles leading from the coastal region into the interior. These alignments are single rows of stones, smaller and closer together than the stones of the great alignment. In one place, at least, the stones are flat, with their surfaces arranged roughly in the same plane. Defenders obviously lurked behind the stones, launching their arrows and javelins between them.

3. Cromlechs are circles of stones. Sometimes there were several

concentric circles, as in the cromlech called 'Stonehenge.' Although the outer circles have disappeared, the plan of the arrangement has been discovered, and the inner circle is mostly standing. Stonehenge represents the last word in megalithic monuments; the stones of the inner circle were dressed and connected at their tops by lintel stones doweled to the upright ones.

Surrounding the cromlech at Stonehenge was a great encampment, probably the greatest living place of early man. The cromlech itself was a place of refuge for the people in case of attack, and the inner circle was the place in which religious rites were conducted. The assumption that a large stone, more or less flat, which lies inside this inner circle, was an altar stone may be accepted as correct. That human sacrifice was offered there is quite possible. Another great cromlech at Avebury, a little farther inland, was destroyed before archaeologists were able to interest the public in saving the monuments.

The utility of fortifications consisting of huge stones spaced at some distance from each other might be questioned, but for men fighting with javelins or with bows and arrows the type is ideal, and solid barricades and trenches would not be suitable. The question of the manner of transportation and erection of the stones has never been answered. Some of them, we know, were brought from a considerable distance, and the weights of the stones are great.

The cromlechs in Brittany, at least those which remain, were not centers of encampments but seem to have been intended for emergency use. Some of the cromlechs are double circles in the form of a figure eight. One in particular, partly on an island in the bay of Morbihan in Brittany, has one circle on land and the other in the water. Obviously, men caught by an invasion while out in boats could take refuge first in the water half of the cromlech and from there escape to the land half in which to defend themselves.

Pausanias describes groups of stones, monuments of minor size, which were still existent in Greece in his day. The significance of these rough stones had been entirely forgotten by that time and they were reinterpreted, each stone being assumed to represent a god or a goddess of a later period.

4. Dolmens approach the structure which we call 'masonry,' in which stones are in contact with one another. A dolmen is, in effect, an artificial cave. In a shallow excavation, walls were formed of flat stones, and a roof, consisting of a stone slab, was covered by

a mound of earth heaped over it. They were originally dwellings, rather than fortifications, although the protection afforded at night from animal and human enemies may have been involved in their purposes.

The temple is a development from the dwelling and the fortress, but the fortress was the most important structure in respect to the development of temples. The Greeks erected their first sanctuaries in their fortified citadels, and these sanctuaries were the forerunners of churches. In the areas near the Baltic sea, the 'Nordics' erected, for defense, stockades of logs, and, as we might well expect, their temples were similar stockades.

It is not surprising to find that the religious rituals of the ancient people who erected the megalithic monuments were conducted in and around those monuments, whose protective value made them sacred. It is not surprising that in Brittany, some of the menhirs have become 'calvaries,' with the emblems of the crucifixion carved on them. A holy monument, in a land where traditions are tenacious, easily becomes a holy spot for the new faith that supplants the old.

When buildings of masonry and timber took the places of megalithic monuments and log stockades, the erection of a temple or public building was marked by human sacrifice, the victim being buried under the foundations, or under the cornerstone, of the structure. This ritual persists in an attenuated form as the ceremonial laying of a cornerstone, which has degenerated into a rather stupid mummery but furnishes opportunity for lengthy orations. Someone has said that instead of immolating a single victim, a whole audience is victimized.

6. **Protection from Disease.**—Early man had no practical means of protection against sickness. After the medical art appeared, it was for a long period a matter of religious rituals, for medicine began its course in the serpent cults of Asklepios. Disease, mental and physical, was evidently a mystery, the work of deadly manas, eventually personified as a daimon or a malignant god. Against these there is no defense, until techniques of protection against visible and tangible enemies are ritualized and applied to the condition of sickness. Eventually, men discovered herbs and other substances that allay itching of the skin and relieve ulceration. By analogy, other substances should cure more deep-seated ailments; and eventually, some simple remedies that actually work were found.

Medicine, in this sense, however, is a very late development, and before it arose, the mysterious enemy was associated with wild beasts, especially with poisonous serpents, which for man are the most mysterious of animals in their ways, as well as the most deadly. Gods of healing were originally snake divinities, and the ritual of cure seems to have involved snake dances similar to those performed by natives of America and Africa today. In the cult of Asklepios, in Greece and adjacent lands, patients slept in the sacred enclosures where snakes were kept; possibly this was a naïve form of homeopathy. By recourse to, perhaps propitiation of, the malignant sources of diseases, diseases might be cured. The brazen serpent traditionally supposed to have been made by Moses to cure his people of snake bites in the desert probably belongs to the same therapeutic system. In the Grecian world, the best health insurance for a man who was still sound was to present a serpent to one of the temples of Asklepios. As we have said above, serpents of many varieties, many of them deadly, were numerous in Greece, and apparently there were many serpent divinities in the early period, which were assimilated later to Zeus, Apollo, Athena, Artemis, Asklepios, Demeter, and other divinities.

The serpent achieved a reputation for wisdom, based simply on the observed fact that it lives on and in the ground, in the bosom of Mother Earth. It was assumed to be bred in the earth, and consequently was called the 'earth born.' It is thus in intimate contact with the fount of wisdom and with the source of the food supply. The retiring of the serpent into the earth in winter and his return in the spring with the rebirth of vegetation is symbolized in the myths of Herakles and of Orpheus. The fact that diseases were healed at the temple of Herakles at Hyetta, in Boeotia (Pausanius, ref. VI: A4, Vol. IX, xxiv, p. 4), is evidence of the connection of Herakles with the snake cult. It is possible, but not certain, that Tammuz, whose return each spring from the underworld brought renewed life to vegetation, was originally conceived as a divine serpent. The wisdom ascribed to the serpent, and its symbolizing the life of vegetation emerging from the earth, probably contributed to its reputation for healing.

In the early historical period of the ancient world, mental disorders, with the exception of epilepsy, were universally assumed to be due to possession of the person by a demon or by a group of demons, as in the case of the Gadarene man and the swine, and religious rituals for the exorcising of the demons were developed. These rituals, however, are not related to serpent cults in any simple way.

7. Protection from Climatic Factors.—Man, in various climates, suffers from heat in summer and from cold in winter. Aside from the temperature, the direct rays of the sun may be damaging. Rain and snow afflict man, and winds may be sources of trouble if they are chilling or are filled with sharp sand. Clothing protects against these climatic factors to some extent. Headdresses protect from the sun; cloaks of skin protect from cold and wet; for polar climates jackets and trousers of fur are suitable protection. Although clothing develops in warm climates mainly for protection against insects, it develops also for protection against climatic factors and against abrasive and puncturing objects.

The habit of wearing clothing continuously produces sexual modesty and immodesty, which eventually become associated with religious rituals and subject to religious regulations. Along with clothing, personal ornamentation and adornment develop, and garments themselves in the course of time become decorative and become also badges of status and occupation. Tattooing and scar patterns are primarily decorative, but these also become badges of social status, along with clothing and detachable ornaments.

If we use the term 'attire' to include both clothing and personal ornamentation and decoration, we can say that attire has been an important feature of religion from the earliest time down to the present day. For participants in religious rituals in the past, specific vestments, fillets, chaplets, and veils were prescribed. Today, religious attire is prescribed mainly for priests and acolytes, but laymen must garb themselves in conventional ways for attendance at ordinary church services and must don special raiment for confirmation.

The fillets and garlands worn by ancient worshipers have passed out of the picture, along with the fawnskins worn by bacchantes in the worship of Dionysos; the bearskins of the devotees of Artemis Brauronia; the wolfskins worn in the rituals of the wolf god; and the fishskins worn by the Babylonian priests; but the conservatism of religion is still evident in ecclesiastical vestures. The priestly vestments of most Christian sects still follow the pattern of the Roman vestures of the pagan period.

For protection against climatic factors, clothing is important but not sufficient. A major protection is afforded by houses and the more primitive dwellings out of which houses developed. The earliest human dwellings were caves, in the larger of which men probably lived, in the sense of conducting all their domestic operations therein. At most of the sites of the Old Stone Age, however, men seem to have lived around the caves, into which they probably retired at night or in inclement weather. The cave, in short, was a fortress rather than a dwelling in the modern sense of the term.

When, with increasing number of the population, the caves were insufficient in number or when changes in the food supply necessitated migration to new areas in which caves were few, artificial caves were constructed. These artificial caves were the *dolmens*, which we have described. Dolmens are obviously too small to have been living places in the complete sense; men lived around the dolmens, keeping their prized possessions in them and retiring into them for protection.

In the Japanese Islands, before the Ainus dominated them, the earliest inhabitants lived in pits, which were probably roofed over with wood covered with earth. In some areas in southeastern Europe, 'gipsies' have lived in similar pits in modern times. The huts of native families in the open regions of North Africa between Tunis and Algiers are little larger than the ancient dolmens, and obviously the families do not conduct their domestic operations in them, but keep their important possessions in them and, in bad weather, sleep inside.

Dwellings of any substantial type afford protection against rain and cold. In stormy weather a group of people can crowd into a space in which they could not actually 'live,' in the sense of conducting all their domestic affairs, but in which they can wait until the weather improves. The number of people of a crude culture who can sleep in a small space is astonishing.

There is a strong tendency among savage groups in certain parts of the world to bury their dead in the houses in which they have lived. In parts of New Guinea the natives bury the dead in shallow graves under the floor, and the rest of the family continue to inhabit the hut. The British have found it difficult to restrain the natives from this practice. Men of the Old Stone Age seem to have had the same tendency. In some of the caves, and in some of the dolmens, there are found skeletons of corpses that had been buried in those dwellings, although such burial was not universally practiced. Possibly, use of a dwelling as a place of interment develops an attachment to the dwelling which contributes to its sanctity, the remains of the dead, and eventually their ghosts, making it a holy place. Greater sanctity, of course, is contributed to a tomb by the corpse of a holy man or to a shrine by a fragment of the body of a saint, but the ancestors of a family are holy to the family. The lares of Roman belief, which were appurtenances persisting from ancestors lurking about the house, were probably derived from earlier customs of burying the dead in, or close to, the dwelling.

Protection from floods in valleys, such as that of the Mississippi River in America and that of the Euphrates in Mesopotamia, was attained by heaping up great mounds of earth on which people could take refuge when the surrounding country was under water. Camps were adjacent to the mounds, for convenience in emergency, and the lives of the population centered about the mounds. The dead, or their burned bones, were buried in the mound, and insofar as religion developed it centered about the place of refuge. The tendency characteristic of religious development to carry over into the impractical that which originally was practical is evidenced strikingly by the building of mounds in areas in which floods did not occur, by peoples who had migrated from flood areas.

After temples had evolved from structures that were practical in purpose, temples as such began to be built for purely religious use. When temples began to be constructed in flood areas, they were placed on mounds. This was not merely for the protection of the temple, but because the temple was conceived as a place of refuge, or a source of help in time of need, just as the mound itself was a place of refuge.

The placing of temples by Greeks and Asiatics in inland areas on high land was a carry-over from the fortification of these high places for refuge from attack by invaders. Each city, if not built entirely on the heights, had its *acropolis* or citadel, strongly fortified, on the highest point of the city site. Location of temples in the acropolis was a natural sequence to the fortification custom.

The early inhabitants of Greece, who built the fortifications of great stones, which the later Greeks ascribed to the 'Cyclops,' built these largely in the interior on mountains. The citadels of the cities which were eventually built at lower altitudes were at first called *larissae*. Pausanias (ref. VI: A4, Vol. II, xxiii, p. 9) avers that this name was taken from the goddess Larissa, daughter of Poseidon;

but this legend probably reverses the actual development, in which from the *larissa* developed the protective goddess who was the personification of the fortification. The name *larissa* is associated with so many citadels in various parts of Greece that this explanation seems sound.

Whether the Greeks ever buried their dead in or on the acropolis of the city is not known, although, as we have said, the mound builders interred their dead in, or adjacent to, the mounds. It is a long step from the sacred fortresses to modern churches, although the development of the latter from the former is obvious. The custom of burying the dead in churches or adjacent churchyards apparently derives from the notion that the church symbolizes the home of the populace, rather than from the custom of burying the dead near fortifications.

8. Protection from the Unseen.—For early man, in the development of his religious beliefs, many of the dangers against which he desires protection are occult. Disease, as we have pointed out, was assumed to be an occult affliction, produced by manas that may emanate from natural objects, but that may be from a god or a demon. Against a mana the only protection is through religion or magic. This religious protection is invoked against ghosts or other human appurtenances that may survive a person's decease. The fear of ghosts was universal in ancient times and persists among many savage groups, the Negro peoples being the exceptions. The fear, in fact, persists among civilized peoples of the class that skeptics call 'superstitious.' In some areas it is difficult to find a tenant for a house that has acquired the reputation of being 'haunted.' For many persons a graveyard is a fearsome place at night, since ghosts are reputed to walk during the darkness more than in daylight.

Against ghosts, of course, there is no protection of a practical sort. Nothing can avail, in the place where the ghost appears, except magical or religious ritual. Since ghosts are supposed to be dangerous, rituals have long been employed to protect the living from the ghosts of the dead. Among the Mediterranean peoples, it was believed that cremation or burial of a corpse with religious ritual enabled the ghost to leave the place in which the person died and to go to the underworld in which it belonged. This ceremonial disposal, accordingly, removed from the living the danger of being annoyed by the ghost. This, clearly was a ritual of propitiation of the ghost. Propitiation of the deceased survives in an attenuated form in our eulogies pronounced over the corpse. Among savages of most groups, it is tabu to speak the name of a dead person, since the utterance of the name might call the ghost back to his old haunts.

The powers that protect man against injuries of other sorts are those which protect him from ghosts. The rituals protecting against the unseen manas of natural objects, against gods and daimons, also unseen, are easily extended into protective rituals against ghosts. The rituals for each purpose are different, but they fit into the total pattern of religion. Protection of a person's 'soul' in the future life also fits into the pattern. In Christianity, 'saving one's soul' is a form of protection against the perils of the other world, the occult or unseen world.

Protection by religious procedures is not merely a matter of eliminating threats to the organism, not even protection against death, the last of enemies. Beyond the threats from insects, from ferocious beasts, from climatic conditions, from disease of body and of mind, religious protection extends to the realms beyond the grave. The same powers or divinities that are invoked for protection in this world are invoked also for protection in the other world. The manas of rituals, of amulets, are assumed to be efficacious not only for present needs but also for the needs of the occult future. Religion thus involves the whole life of man, including the existence after death. Man may need no food or drink in the other world, but he needs protection and, needing it, or thinking he needs it, he desires it.

9. Desires Involved in Religion, but Not Essential to It.—Religion originated, as we have been trying to make clear, in the attempt to provide satisfaction of the alimentary and protective desires. Concern about food and adverse features of the environment leads to planning to increase the food supply, to make it dependable, and extends to planning to obtain the best protection. Praxis expands into ritual, and ritual is the beginning of religion.

The other primary desires, along with innumerable secondary desires, some of which have been ephemeral, have been taken into the fabric of religion after its development but do not seem to have been essential to religion or to have been foundations from which it developed. When satisfaction of a desire, or regulation of the satisfaction, is taken over by religion, the religious rituals and faiths may be modified by the assumption of authority over the satisfactions; but the promotion of satisfaction by religion, and the religious control of satisfaction, for all primary desires except the two from which religion developed, requires that religion shall be in existence and in operation in order that it shall promote and regulate.

The relation of the other primary desires and their satisfaction, the desires for activity and rest, erotic and philopedic desires, desires to achieve preeminence and to conform to the group will be considered briefly in their relations to, and involvement in, religion. Excretory desire will be considered at slightly greater length, since it is connected with the concept of sin.

1. *Desire for Activity*.—Man in a really primitive stage of development had no lack of activity. His incipient praxes for the procuring of food from wild plants and game animals and for protecting himself and his family from the weather, from enemy animals, and possibly from human enemies undoubtedly kept him busy enough. If at times he had leisure, and desired activity, the desire could hardly have been for him a matter of concern. His concern was about the alimentary and protective satisfactions for which constant activity was necessary.

When man emerged into savagery, or into the proto-civilized stage, the desire for activity became more important. As religion evolved, the activities that were not essential—that were, in other words, not economic—were promoted by, and regulated by, man's religion. In ancient civilization, the need for activity beyond that required for the satisfaction of the desires for protection and alimentation became important. This desire was satisfied through sports and games, which religion took under its wing. The Isthmian, Olympic, and Pythian games, which involved foot racing, chariot racing, prize fighting and other sports and poetic contests were religious festivals. Sports today are mostly secular activities, but they were important features of ancient religion. To a large extent, the social features of these games were of paramount importance, but the spectators derived the same vicarious satisfaction from watching the contests that the bleacher crowds today derive from watching the activities of a small group on the football field.

The general excitement of the games, and the travel to them, were outlets for pent-up energies of that section of the population for whom the activities of work and of religious performances at home were insufficient. These activities, however, although they were taken under the wing of religion, cannot be ascribed a function in the original production of religion. As we have said, any function that religion assumes may modify religion, but the sources from which religion springs are not to be identified with the functions it assumes later.

After religion has established itself, activity in religion becomes an important concern. The activity desire may be satisfied through religious activity, but there can be no religious activity until religion has appeared.

2. Desire for Rest.—In early Christianity, the satisfaction of the desire for rest was an important concern. In Christian hymnology the notion of 'rest for the weary' is still conspicuous. That the early Christians were for the most part of the laboring classes we know. The offering of rest to the overworked, whether the rest was in this world or in the next, was apparently an attractive feature of the new faith to the oppressed classes.

In earlier pagan religions, the rest motive was lacking. There is no indication that in pre-Christian religions anyone sought rest. The concept of a heaven as a place of eternal rest seems to be a novel feature of religion, which was introduced by Christianity. That in ancient religion a certain placidity and satisfaction was achieved through the consciousness of religious duties well done is doubtless true, but such contentment is not possible until religion develops and the duties are formulated. Even Christianity cannot be assumed to have developed from the rest desire, although the promise of rest made it attractive.

Primitive man could have had no great concern about the satisfaction of the rest desire. If he became weary in his endless search for food, in making weapons for the chase, in making clothing and building shelters, undoubtedly he rested. If he became exceptionally fatigued, he desired rest, but we cannot suppose that there was such constant deprivation that rest became a matter of serious concern for him. Yet it is from concern for future satisfaction of desire, and planning for such satisfaction, that rituals develop.

3. Preeminence and Conformity.—Conformity to ritual and to faith is an essential feature in organized religion, and opportunities to achieve preeminence are offered by religious organizations. The religious person may become a priest or minister and in some sects may advance to still higher stature, and there are, in most Christian sects, offices below that of priest or minister. The need for conformity does not await organization, but is vital in the early stages of religious development, since all rituals are essentially group procedures in which the several members of the group do the same things in the same ways, except, of course, those who, as priests or other officials, are set apart for specific functions.

In Christian sects, any young man who has the requisite intelligence and industry may achieve high rank in the ecclesiastical organization, although women are not yet permitted achievement of the same preeminence.   In ancient religion there were limitations, even for men, certain religious positions being restricted to members of specific families or tribal groups.   Laymen and laywomen, however, achieve preeminence of a sort in modern religion by heading church societies and committees, and a congregation is sometimes dominated by a lay leader to whom the minister is really subordinate.

Religion offers satisfaction of the desires for preeminence and conformity, but these desires cannot be assumed to be sources of religion, although in its stages of organization the preeminence desires of a few, and the conformity desires of the many, make the organization strong and persistent.

4. Erotic Desire and Satisfaction.—Before the beginning of the Christian Era, and periodically since that time, theorists have brought up the explanation of religion as a production of the thwarting of erotic desires; or, as the terminology goes in the latest revival of the age-old theory, 'repressed sex desires,' meaning vaguely by 'sex desires' what should be more definitely designated as *'erotic* desires.'   This is, and has been, mere armchair theorizing, for examination of the course of development of religion shows plainly that erotic desires and their thwarting or their satisfaction had little to do with the early development of religion and have been of very minor importance in later stages of religious development.

Votaries of a well-developed religion attempt to satisfy all desires, primary and derivative, through their religion, or to supplement their satisfactions.   A Christian in love is apt to pray that his affection may be returned and his yearning satisfied.   He may pray also for success in the stock market, for new clothes, for healing from disease, or for a bicycle.   These attempts to satisfy desires through religion have no bearing on the explanation of religion and its development.

Organized religion, in ancient times, did attempt to promote the satisfaction of erotic desires of men by providing great numbers of prostitutes at the temples of the goddesses.   In later periods, organized religion has tried to regulate marriage and to regulate extramarital coitus, just as it has tried to ban drinking of alcoholic beverages. These economic functions of religion give no information as to the origin of religion.

Monks and nuns may substitute religious interests for normal erotic desires, but this is properly regarded as a feature of religious pathology. Libertines have used the associations of religious groups in furtherance of seduction, but, as we shall point out, use of religion for nefarious purposes is even more extensive. Church groups promote social relations of young men with young women in the interest of normal living and successful mating in marriage. These misuses and proper uses of religion are but details in the vast range of applications of religious control to human affairs.

From the time of Paul on, Christianity in its various forms has attempted to promote chastity and continence, but this was a relatively late feature of religion for the layman. Ancient religion was much more concerned with reproductive functions and human fertility than with erotic matters, although it did promote prostitution, which cannot be assigned an important role in the development of religion. Tabus on extramarital coitus, it should be noted, are of fairly late introduction into religion.

Satisfaction of erotic desires was not a serious problem for early man as compared with the difficulties in obtaining food and protection. As culture became more complex, the food problem became less pressing, while erotic satisfaction became increasingly difficult. The theorists who have picked on erotic desire as an important factor in early religious development have made the mistake of projecting late social conditions back into earlier periods.

Failure to distinguish between reproductive desire and erotic desire has been the main source of the confusion in which the theorists have been plunged. That erotic desire may lead to reproduction is of course a truism, but the desires involved are different. There may be desire for children of one's own procreation, but this desire is more closely connected with other desires than it is with the erotic desire.

The failure to distinguish between erotic and reproductive desires, and further confusion of philopedic desire with erotic desire, has misled the theorists in regard to the ancient symbols of religion, many of which, as we shall explain in detail, are 'sexual' but are sexual in the reproductive sense, not in the erotic sense.

5. *Philopedic Desire.*—Whether child divinities and child forms of divinities such as Dionysos, who were figured in both childish

forms and in adult forms, arose from yearning for children we cannot tell. When divinities arose, however, they were appealed to to promote conception, and rituals of various sorts were employed to that end. It is possible that these rituals had their roots in an earlier stage of religious development before godesses had been evolved. When a priesthood had arisen, the priest's direct offices as the representative of the god were sought by barren women and seem usually to have been efficacious. (Eli 'blesses' Hannah, who conceived Samuel: I Sam. 17). Aside from priests, however, strangers who might be gods in disguise were deemed potent (Sarah and the three strangers: Gen. 18).

Goddesses whose special functions were the safeguarding of women in childbirth were rather numerous, and some of the great goddesses of the later period seem to have assimilated earlier obstetrical goddesses.

6. *Excretory Desire.*—The desire to excrete waste products from the body includes also desire to cleanse the skin and to keep it clean. Excretion is ridding oneself of materials that are annoying, disagreeable, dangerous, or inconvenient. The desire to excrete has easily been extended to the desire to rid oneself of sin and guilt through rituals of cleansing. Avoidance of contamination through dangerous acts, or through contact with materials deemed to be either physically, morally, or 'spiritually' contaminating, were prescribed in ancient religion. Contact with a dead body, or with the menstrual secretion of women, were specifically contaminating, and such contacts were religiously banned (tabued). Contamination may occur, however, without the person involved being aware of the taint. Avoidance of contamination developed into a praxis of avoidance, but since accidental contamination may occur, rituals for the removal of contamination also grew up to supplement the praxis. Washing with water, and with blood, were the common rituals. Since water cleanses the skin, it has a mana that is easily extended into the removal of sin and guilt. Baptism, in its several forms, was the eventual type of that ritual. Immersion in a sacred river was a ritual for the healing of external diseases such as leprosy. Blood was held to be a more efficient remedy for guilt and sin than was water. Absolution from the guilt of murder required the pouring over the culprit of the blood of a pig. The use of oil on the skin was undoubtedly first a praxis for the discouraging of lice, possibly as treatment for skin diseases also; but

inunction with oil persists today, as a religious ritual. Of just what the person is ridded when oil is dabbed on his forehead is not clear; but it is evident that the ritual is deemed efficacious in some way.

Numerous ritual avoidances of contaminating materials were enjoined upon the Jews. Among them are avoidance of menstruating women and women after childbirth, women in these periods being designated as 'unclean.' In the ancient Mediterranean religions and those of Asia Minor, excretory tabus were perhaps fewer; but everywhere in the ancient world a dead person was considered to be a source of danger, and a person who touched a corpse, or even was in the same room with it, had to be cleansed ritually. This tabu on the dead of course had no hygienic basis, since the sick one who may communicate an infectious disease was not tabued, and the ritual of washing with water does not eliminate disease organisms.

In Islam and in Hinduism there are many excretory tabus, and a comparative study of these with the tabus in proto-Christian and Christian religion would undoubtedly be highly informing.

CHAPTER VIII

RELIGIOUS SYMBOLISM

1. Symbols and Symbolism.—We might define a symbol as an object, a pictorial design, or an item of behavior that represents a concept, or a system of concepts, or that represents a more nebulous pattern of thought and feeling that we vaguely designate as an 'attitude.' The cross, for example, may be an object made of wood, metal, ivory, or some other material, or it may merely be a pattern of lines drawn on any surface, but what it symbolizes, or means, is the same in either case. The gesture of 'crossing' oneself by touching the two shoulders, the forehead, and the chest in a particular order may have the same significance as the material or pictured cross. The symbol may also be formed by moving the hand as if drawing the cross in the air.

The cross is an example of a symbol that has had religious meaning in many lands and for many religions, but it has been adopted by Christians as the symbol of the Christian religion. It is more than a symbol of a religion, however, for it has in popular usage a protective use, protecting especially against the unseen dangers. Other religions have their symbols. The Jewish symbol is the six-pointed star, which is sometimes called 'Solomon's Seal' and sometimes called 'David's Shield.' The symbol of Islam is the crescent, and the symbol of Hinduism is the cow.

The words 'symbol' and 'symbolism,' with corresponding adjectives and verbs, are not terms that can be technically employed with precise meanings, but are highly fluid in their significance. A symbol, it is obvious, is merely something that means something else; and there is nothing in nature, in art, or in behavior that does not, in some circumstances, mean something else. All words, spoken or written, are symbols, for they have meanings or may have meanings. If we could restrict the terms to entities or actions that signify abstractions, our use of the terms would be more precise, but such restriction is impracticable.

If we confine our discussion to religious symbols we shall be on fairly safe ground. By a religious symbol we shall mean any object, animal, tree, or plant, or any production of plastic or pictorial art, or any gesture or verbal formula, which has been employed to represent a group concept of religious or quasi-religious sort, or about which ritual has developed.

Most religious symbols have had specific meanings. The *ashera*, for example, symbolized the female divinity. The thunderbolt, crudely or artistically represented, became the symbol of the gods of the mountaintops, about which the clouds gathered and the lightning flashed. The crescent moon originally symbolized the female divinity but eventually became the symbol of the religion centering around the male Allah. The descriptive formula, 'Queen of Heaven,' however, has persisted as the symbol of a female divinity or a female saint.

Most of the symbols employed in modern religion are of great antiquity and have been passed on from phase to phase of religious development, with continuous reinterpretations. Some ancient symbols have become mere charms of magic, their earlier religious significance having been lost, while others retain their religious significance. Some symbols persist as verbal formulae, the objects or the actions to which they refer having been discarded. Christian hymns are full of references to the 'cleansing blood'; but the ritual washing with blood has ceased. The 'Rock of Salvation' and the 'Rock of Ages' are formulae that are well understood, but stones are no longer employed by Christians as symbols of God.

2. **Sex Symbols in Religion.**—Many of the symbols that are retained in modern religion were originally drawn from the sex organs, from sexual processes, or from concepts based on sex and its manifestations. Some of these symbols signified the male, some the female, and some were conventional representations of human coitus. The fish was an ancient symbol of the life power or life source, conceived as female. The tree first represented female divinity, so the tree trunk became the pillar symbol of a goddess. The cross was referred to as the 'tree' and still is so described in Christian hymns. Eventually, male pillars were introduced. The 'stable' triangle (triangle with base down) has been from ancient times a symbol of the male, and the triangle with one point down has been the conventional symbol of the female. These symbols have been explained in various ways, but the simplest and most plausible explanation is that the symbolism is determined by the characteristic forms of the area of pubic hair in the two human sexes.

The spear and the arrowhead are symbols of the male, which are in little need of explanation. The crescent moon, as we have said, was the symbol of a goddess—probably in origin the symbol of a virgin goddess because of its suggestion of the unruptured hymen. The crescent, however, was employed as the symbol of mother goddesses, along with the circle, the pointed oval, and the fish, which were the appropriate symbols for a mother.

Combination of the symbols of the two sexes in a way that naïvely suggests coitus produced some of the symbols of reproduction that are often called 'symbols of perfection.' The employment of designs drawn from sexual union as symbols of perfection developed from recognition of the incompleteness of the male and female organisms by themselves and the knowledge that the union of a male and a female is necessary to form a complete organism, capable of reproducing its kind. Paul expressed this knowledge when he said of the married couple, 'They two shall be one flesh' (Eph. 5: 31). Among such symbols are the six-pointed star, formed by super-posing the male and female triangles; and the five-pointed star, formed by superposing the arrowhead on the female triangle. The six-pointed star must always be placed with one point down, and the five-pointed star must be placed with two points down to agree with their symbolic values. Artists and designers who employ these symbols in their designs continue to place them in the ancient way, although in most cases they are merely following conventions, the significances of which are not known to them.

Not all symbols of perfection are made in this simple way. The 'tah-gook,' which apparently originated in southeastern Asia, is a conventionalized representation of two fish in the act of spawning, the mouths and eyes of the fish being sometimes represented. Appropriately, the tah-gook is sometimes said to symbolize the 'generative power in nature,' while it otherwise symbolizes perfection.

The swastika, which may have been religious, but which today in India symbolizes coitus ('good luck'), is a symbol that has been found on ancient coins and pottery from various parts of Asia and Europe. This symbol, in some areas, may have resulted from attempts to make simple linear designs; but it may, in other areas, have been intended to represent the primitive positions of the male and female in coitus—positions which are still employed by some savages. Reinach (ref. III: 4) presents the theory that in eastern Europe and western Asia the swastika was intended to represent a stork in flight. Some of the ancient designs do indeed present swastikas with recognizable birds' heads, and others present swastikas definitely associated with birds. We know, however, that all symbols, when they become conventional, are subject to decorative variations at the whims of artists; hence a decorative addition to a symbol does not give evidence as to the original derivation of the symbol itself.

Among other symbols of the male and the female which have had religious significance are the first and the last letters, *alpha* and *omega*, of the Greek alphabet. The letter *alpha* was not derived from the male genital organ but probably from the Semitic letter *aleph*, which represented the head of a bull. *Omega*, however, may have been originally intended as a crude representation of the female genital passage. The form of *alpha*, as the male triangle, and the form of *omega* obviously suggested the human male and female, whatever may have been their original derivations. The reference to these letters as the 'first and last' comports with the ancient legends of creation, in which man was created first and woman last.

The design that is conventionally named the *crux ansata* (cross with a handle) and also called the 'key of life' was an important religious symbol in ancient Egypt. This symbol has been interpreted as a symbol of coitus by persons unversed in Egyptian religious history; but Egyptologists well know that it was the symbol of the female, considered as the source of life. The actual Egyptian symbol of the union of the sexes was a conventionalized combination of the female pubic area with the male sex glands, which seems not to have become a religious symbol.

Although not all religious symbols are drawn from the realm of sex, the prevalence of such symbols, their transfer from one stage of religious development to another, and their persistence down to the present day are unmistakable facts. All the ancient sex symbols, with the exception of the pillar, are employed in present-day Christianity, suitably reinterpreted, of course. This persistence of sex symbols has confused many theorists because they have confused the two common meanings of the word 'sex.'

Primarily, sex means simply the characteristic of an animal or of a tree of some species, which classes the animal or the tree as male or female. Since reproduction by sexed organisms requires the cooperation of the male and the female, reproduction is obviously a sexual process. Contributory to the reproductive process are the processes, including thoughts and affects, which should properly be called 'erotic' or 'amatory.' Although the erotic features of life are closely related to the reproductive features, they ought to be distinguished from, not confused with, one another. Beginning before the Christian Era, however, theorists have confused the erotic with the reproductive and have sought for the origin of religion in thwarted satisfaction of erotic desire.

The development of religion, on the other hand, indicates clearly that the sex symbols are to be taken as symbols drawn from the reproductive process and from the male and female organs as organs of reproduction. Erotic desire and erotic satisfactions have had little to do with the origin and early development of religion. The same factors that determined the early divinities as female gave rise to symbols drawn from the female as symbols of the life power or the life principle, which produces animals for food and which produces the growth and fruiting of trees.

The female animal, as a source of progeny, is more important than the male simply because one male may fertilize many females, so the actual number of young animals produced in any season depends on the number of female animals available. Of further importance is the carrying of the young offspring by the female before its birth and the nourishment of the young after birth by the milk of the female. The reproductive function of the female animal continues for a relatively lengthy period, while the function of the male is brief.

For species of trees in which the sexes are separate, as they are in the date palm and as they were supposed by Levantine peoples to be in the fig tree, the same considerations are valid. The fruit develops on the female tree, so that the major limitation of the crop is the number of female trees. Since early man assumed that all reproduction is sexual, the importance of the female in reproduction was evident to him.

That the female sex symbols usually were drawn from the human female, and not directly from the female food animals or food-producing trees, is a fact that does not conflict with the principle that early man applied. Not only were the symbols of the life force drawn from human genitalia and from the process of human coitus and applied as means of promoting the production of plant and animal food, but actual coitus was engaged in for the same purpose. Even in the Christian Era, farmers, after planting their crops, had intercourse with their wives in the field, and sometimes general promiscuity of the unmarried was permitted as a ritual to assist the work of the life forces in growing the crop. The Roman Saturnalia and similar festivals in midwinter were maintained by the tribes of western Europe were probably instituted for the same purpose. These practices, which we class in the category of 'sympathetic magic,' cannot be denied the title of religious rituals among the people who employed them.

The importance of the fish as a symbol of the female life power rests on observations that early peoples could not fail to make. Fish furnished an important part of the food supply for ancient people in the Babylonian and eastern Mediterranean areas, and the great number of eggs produced by the female fish makes her an obvious symbol of fertility (see Chap. VI, Sec. 3, 8). That fish goddesses would develop and that the fish would become a religious symbol was inevitable.

The imperfection of the human sexes is emphasized in the myths, current apparently among all ancient peoples, that human beings—or the first human beings—were created as bisexual organisms (androgynes) and later separated into the two sexes. This myth is presented in a crude form in Plato's *Symposium* and in a modified form in the biblical account of the creation of Adam and Eve (Gen. 2: 21–24), where the taking of a 'rib' from Adam is a veiled account of the splitting of the bisexual organism into two organisms. It is said in the legend that God breathed into Adam's nostrils the breath of life (Gen. 2: 7), but nothing is said about the infusing of life into Eve—a process that was unnecessary, since Eve was half of the organism that had already been made alive.

The acknowledged imperfection of the human male and female easily made the sexual union of the two a symbol of perfection, since man has always considered himself superior to all other animals. The representation of coitus thus became a derivative symbol of perfection.

3. **Symbols Other Than Sexual.**—In preceding chapters we have discussed animals and plants that became symbols of particular divinities. When an animal or plant species gave rise to a divinity, animals or plants of the species remained associated with the divinity after she became anthropomorphized, and sometimes after her sex was changed. These animals or plants were conventionally added to statues or pictures of the divinities for purposes of identification.

Thus the deer indicates Artemis; the olive, Athena; the swan, Apollo; the barley, Demeter; the date palm, Ishtar; and both the pine and the boar, Attis. Other symbols, which we will shortly discuss, were used in some representations.

The serpent was always represented near the statues of Asklepios and of Hygeia, since the serpent was the symbol of both. The serpent figures also as a symbol of Demeter and of her lieutenant Triptolemos. The association of the serpent with the barley was due, apparently, to the drooping habits of growth of the barley, which suggests the head and forepart of a snake protruding from a hole in the ground. The bearded snake, often pictured, is obviously a symbol of the barley or of the barley goddess. The serpent, as we have earlier said, was also a symbol of Athena, indicating the assimilation to her of the earlier snake divinity Erechtheus—hardly distinguishable from the hero Erechthonios, who was conventionally represented either as a serpent or with a human torso and with bodies of snakes in place of legs.

The poisonous serpents of Apollo at Delphi, which were kept in the pits over which the priestesses sat when delivering oracles (Diogenes Laertius, Vol. I, V, p. 91), might be considered as symbols of Apollo drawn from the ancient snake god (or goddess), assimilated to Apollo. If, on the other hand, we consider them to have been the living representatives of the god, through which his power was transmitted to the pythoness, they are still symbols of the god.

In ancient Babylonian myths the serpent figures as the symbol of evil, or an evil divinity. The story of the temptation of Eve by the serpent (Gen. 3: 1–6), which is identified by the author of the Apocalypse as the devil himself (Rev. 12: 9 and 20: 2), was evidently patterned on the Babylonian myths. The legend of the brazen serpent erected by Moses in the wilderness and reproduced in Solomon's temple may have been taken from Mediterranean sources and substituted for a Syrian or Mesopotamian myth of which the editors disapproved.

An important symbol at Delphi was the *omphalos* (navel), which represented Delphi as the center of the earth, analogized to a human body. There were two of these symbols at Delphi: one, which was kept in a secret chamber in the temple of Apollo, was in the form of a large stone with rounded top, which was covered by a network of fillets of wool; the other, displayed to the public, was constructed with simulacra of fillets carved on its surface. The significance of the wool fillets may possibly have been drawn from the sanctity of sheep or goats. Since sheep were employed in semantics, and the oracle at Delphi was the chief oracle in Greece, the sheep is the most probable basis for the fillets. Fillets of wool were conventionally bound about the heads of those who officiated at sacrifices or in other rituals.

The knotting of the fillets into a network over the top of the *omphalos* was a symbol of the effect (religious or magical, as you please) which has long been ascribed to the tying of a knot. Whether the knotting was originally intended to restrict the operations of evil manas or to promote the effects of beneficent manas remains an unanswered question.

Other important symbols arose from the invention or devising of tools and weapons and from other inventions that increased man's power over his environment. Almost every invention that added to human power became a religious symbol, and failure to recognize the basis of religion in praxis has led scholars to the formation of tenuous conjectures as to the sources of these symbols. Among these inventions are the hammer, ax, ladder, spear, bow and arrow, sword, boat, and wheel. All of these seem to have had properties that man could employ, and all of them became religious symbols.

The *hammer* was first made by binding an oblong stone to a handle of wood or bone. Hammers were useful for a variety of practical purposes, including the killing of animals. Eventually, a groove was cut around the stone to facilitate the attachment of the handle. Such hammer heads are found in various parts of the world and are conventionally called 'celts.' Magical powers were ascribed to them by later people, who did not understand their original purposes. In Africa, natives insert celts at a certain stage in the enlargement of the ear lobes, but this is a practical procedure—not a magical one.

The *ax* is an obvious development from the hammer, made by attaching an edged stone to a handle. Eventually a hole was bored through the stone and the handle inserted through it. The double ax has a twofold practical importance: in the first place it is more easily attached to the handle and is better balanced; in the second place a second edge is provided against the dulling or breaking of one edge. It is not without significance that double axes have been used by modern woodmen and probably are still in use.

The progress from stone axes to bronze axes enhanced the religious importance of the ax rather than diminished it. Bronze axes were mounted on altars, and divinities were represented carrying axes as symbols of divine power. Miniature axes were employed as charms or talismans. There is no mystery about the religious and magical significance of the ax; the ascription of manas to it over and beyond its practical utility is a part of the normal process of religious development.

The importance of the invention of the *ladder* is sometimes overlooked. The ladder gave man removable adits to caves in cliffs, as well as means of climbing trees to gather fruits. Eventually, the building of houses and temples was facilitated by the use of the ladder. We can easily understand why the ladder became a religious symbol, although we know it mainly in the later stage of religion, in which the conception of another world had emerged and in which the flight to the other world was symbolized as the climbing of a ladder. The ladder that Jacob saw in his dream (Gen. 28: 12–16) is one instance of this symbolism, but eventually the Milky Way was conceived as the ladder along which the dead passed to the other world.

The *spear* and the *bow and arrow* greatly increased man's power in the chase, and the spear also was useful in fishing. Ultimately, these implements were applied to war and greatly increased its deadliness. The *sword* developed from the knife that was used to cut the throats of animals or perhaps from knives used for domestic purposes. Its offensive and defensive uses in war were undoubtedly the factors that made the sword a religious symbol and gave it manas as a talisman.

In a picture or statue made in ancient times, a person who carries a sword or a spear is usually to be identified as a divinity, although heroes (demigods) were sometimes represented with these arms. The symbolism of the bow was restricted to particular divinities or heroes. Artemis and Apollo were depicted with bows, or with quivers for arrows, and Herakles often was represented as so armed, but no pictures of other divinities or heroes armed with the bow have come down to us.

In a late period 'Zeus' is represented as carrying a wand or scepter instead of a spear or a thunderbolt. Presumably the power of Zeus was so great that no active might was required of him. According to Homer, the world trembled at his nod and a mere blink of his eyes was sufficient to produce effects. Hence a scepter symbolizes his power and authority as greater than that of the other divinities.

Before implements of the chase were invented, men used clubs and threw stones. Herakles is sometimes represented as carrying a club, and the thunder gods are depicted as carrying bolts, which they were supposed to hurl like stones. The greater advantages of edged and pointed weapons, however, caused these to supplant clubs and stones as symbols of divine power, although among the Teutonic peoples the mere hammer remained the symbol of thunder gods, such as Thor, for a long period. The stone celts, which we have said above were supposed by later peoples who found them to have magical manas, were called 'thunder stones,' while in the Greek area bronze axheads were respected as thunderbolts.

When bronze weapons were made, the alloy itself acquired manas, which may be ascribed to the practical superiority of bronze weapons and tools over those made of stone. Bronze became the holy metal while, on the other hand, iron was regarded as an evil metal endowed with pernicious manas. The fact that iron was called the 'African metal' indicates that men in the period of transition from the Bronze Age to the Iron Age knew that the smelting, working, and use of iron was discovered by African Negroes and was transmitted to Europe through Egypt.

That iron was considered by Mediterranean people to be an evil metal is evidenced by a story that Herodotus relates in Book I of his *History*. The Lacedaemonians, at war with the Tegeans, were informed by the oracle at Delphi that in order to win the war they must find the bones of Orestes and bring them to Sparta. Inquiring where the bones were, they were given the following oracular answer.

> Level and smooth is the plain where Arcadian Tegea standeth;
> There two winds are ever, by strong necessity, blowing,
> Counter-stroke answers stroke, and evil lies upon evil.
> There all-teeming earth doth harbour the son of Atrides;
> Bring thou him to thy city, and then be Tegea's master.

Lichas was one of the men sent to find the bones during a truce with the Tegeans. He went to Tegea and entered a smithy, where the smith was forging iron. The smith told Lichas that he had started to dig a well in the smithy and had dug down to a coffin in which there were the bones of a man who was about seven cubits (nearly eleven feet) tall. Lichas surmised that these were the bones of Orestes, that the two winds were those of the two bellows in the smithy, and that the evil lying on evil represented the iron lying on the iron anvil. Eventually Lichas dug up the bones and took them to Sparta, whereupon, of course, the Lacedaemonians began to win against the Tegeans.

The *wheel* made possible the cart, wagon, and chariot, which made transportation more rapid for both persons and commodities and revolutionized trade while adding to the deadliness of war. The mounting of divinities in chariots, accordingly, symbolized the power of the divinities over distance, as well as their general superiority. The wheel, however, appears as a religious symbol detached from any vehicle. Ignoring the practical importance of the wheel has led some scholars to the interpretation of the wheel as symbolizing the sun in the daily circuit that it was believed to make around the earth. The wheel, as a religious symbol, has been called by these scholars the 'solar wheel.' We have no information as to the period in which the wheel was invented, but the invention was probably made before there was a concept of a circular course of the sun. The association of the wheel with the sun undoubtedly arose from the assignment of a chariot to the sun god—after the invention of the wheel, of course.

Ancient barbarians destroyed enemies they had captured, not only by dragging them after their chariots but also by binding them to the chariot wheels. The wheel, therefore, became a symbol of torture and death. The myth of Ixion, who was punished for his infatuation with Hera by being bound to a wheel, should be interpreted in the light of this fact and not as a mere 'solar myth.'

Not all religious symbols that had practical bases were inventions in the mechanical sense. Some were derived from discoveries of new praxes. In the Mediterranean area, *horses* were used to draw chariots before they were ridden, and the development of 'equitation' (riding on a horse) led to the mounting of divinities on horses, as a symbol of divine power. Not all gods, therefore, that are depicted as equestrians can be assumed to have been originally horse gods or to have assimilated horse gods. Some of the divinities that are known to have been of equine origin—such as Epona, the Celtic goddess—were conventionally represented on horseback; but on the other hand, Dionysos, who had no equine history, is also depicted as mounted. Whether the mounting of *Zeus Sabazios*, of Asia

Minor, indicates that he developed from a horse god cannot be guessed.

Persistent desires that were not gratified have given rise to myths in which heroes are said to have achieved the gratification. The devices and processes employed by those heroes might be said to be symbols of the group desire. It is evident that man in an early period envied the birds and wished that he, too, could fly. We have pointed out that man's admiration for the swan, wild goose, hawk, and eagle probably was based, in part at least, on this envy and desire. The myth of Ikaros (Icarus) and Daidalos (Daedalus), who escaped from Crete by the use of wings fastened to their bodies with wax, is an indication of what man long wanted to do and has finally achieved. The power of flight for which man longed, but which he had not achieved, gave rise to the myth of Pegasus, the winged horse, and to conception of other flying animals such as bulls, serpents, and griffins. Not all myths, however, can be explained as 'wish fulfillments.'

Wings were freely employed as symbols of divine power but were seldom presented as attached to the bodies of the greater divinities. Minor divinities such as Eros (Cupid) and small daimons which come in the class of *keri* are shown as flying with wings, and wings are represented as attached to the shoes and the cap of Hermes (Mercury), but none of the great divinities were represented as winged. Apollo was shown riding in a swan-drawn car and as riding a swan, but he was not shown as flying. Wings, however, were frequently attached to the chariots in which the divinities were depicted as riding. The winged animals depicted on Assyrian monuments in Mesopotamia did not represent gods but were assumed as lesser daimons. The winged bulls and winged serpents may be assigned their proper rank through noting that these were respectively the cherubim and seraphim, which were anthropomorphized as 'angels' in Christianity.

In Egypt wings were the symbols of divinities who had taken flight from earth—divinities such as Hathor-Isis. A single feather was often the symbol of a heavenly divinity. As in the Greek depictions, the Egyptian representations do not show any important divinity in human form with wings, not even the divinities who developed from sacred birds.

Some inventions and discoveries of great importance did not become religious symbols. The *plow* was a great invention, but its use gave rise only to metaphors and myths; the plough never became a religious symbol. The *mill* for grinding grain was another invention that had verbal effect on ancient culture but that did not become a religious symbol. Whether the determining factor was the period in which the inventions were made, or whether inventions, the use of which was especially laborious and which consequently devolved on slaves and other inferior members of society, were excluded as religious symbols, is a question of interest. That the mill was a symbol of drudgery is indicated by the Syrian legend of Sampson; but as to the plow, we have less information.

The building of *boats* evolved from two practices that preceded the use of boats, the use of swimming logs and of rafts. The swimming log, which was still in use in recent times in central Africa and in northern Australia, was a pole in which usually a short lateral peg was inserted near one end. In use, one arm of the person was hooked around the peg, while the other arm was used for natation. The first rafts were made of rushes, sticks, or logs, but were satisfactory only for floating cargoes or persons with the current. Rafts were in use on the Euphrates and Tigris rivers, to carry cargoes to Babylon, down to the time of Herodotus, if not later. When the destination was reached, the cargo was sold, the raft broken up for sale as firewood, and the raftsmen trudged home on foot.

The first boats appear to have been of three sorts: one made from a log hollowed out; another made from rushes or stalks of other plants formed into a hollow structure and sometimes daubed with pitch or bitumen; and a third sort made from skins of animals. The Africans never went beyond these forms, and the Australians never progressed even that far. The building of boats, and eventually of ships, from boards was an invention of the Egyptians, Mediterraneans, and Levantines. The boat became in Egypt a pictorial symbol of the gods and of the other world; but in Europe and the Levant it appears to have figured only in verbal symbolism. The anchor, which gave great aid to navigators, was probably invented too late to become a direct religious symbol, although it figures extensively in Christian hymnology as a verbal symbol.

4. The Manas of Symbols.—It is difficult to draw the line between a symbol of divine power or a symbol of a religious concept and a representative of the power that it transmits directly. This we noted in connection with the snakes at Delphi, which can be considered either as symbols of Apollo or as transmitters of the power of Apollo; and we may add that in many cases the distinction is negligible. The brazen serpent erected by Moses in the wilderness was obviously a symbol of the deadly serpent power, but it also exercised or emitted a healing mana. Belief in the manas of symbols was not only characteristic of religion in its early phases but is retained today by Christians of various sects.

That which represents or symbolizes a divine power actually exerts the power. The use of images of divinities has been explained as merely the use of a symbol of the god or the goddess, who was conceived as being elsewhere or at least as being other than the image itself. Nevertheless, it appears that the rituals of worship were believed to be more effective, and the benefits more certain, if those rituals were conducted at the place where there was a symbolic representation of the divinity than if they were conducted elsewhere. As the symbols of divinity were progressively modified from special trees, living animals, rough blocks of stone, and rudely shaped pieces of wood to statues—some of which eventually were great works of art—these representatives of divinity continued to be more than mere symbols. They involved and exercised the manas of the divinities. A man accepted as the representative of a divinity likewise was infused with the mana of the divinity he represented.

This notion is quite consistent with the belief that the representative of a power is in direct communication with the power, even if it is believed not to be localized entirely in the representative. The symbol being in dynamic contact with the power, the power manifests or expresses itself through its symbol; and, conversely, rituals addressed to the symbol, or in its presence, are more influential than they otherwise would be. Anointing the symbol, tying fillets on it, laying food or flowers at its base or on an adjacent altar are approaches to the power itself. It probably was not assumed that the image of a god actually smelled the odor of the incense burned before it, but, since the smoke came in contact with the image, it was in contact with the divinity whose manas were resident in the image.

To assume that the cross, when worn on the person or when laid on the body of a sick person, is employed as a mere intellectual symbol of faith would be to make a serious error. It would be equally erroneous to assume that the making of the sign of the cross with the hand is merely a symbolic gesture. These symbols are believed to be directly efficacious, just as Odysseus' display of the sword directly daunted the ghosts.

That medals ritually blessed and the bones and relics of saints are infused with manas that have effects directly we have already noted. We have pointed out also that shrines and other holy places are not mere symbols of religion, but are filled with manas. Verbal formulae too, while they are symbols of faith, transmit manas.

It is claimed that the efficacy of the Host in the Eucharist is not that of a symbol but is due to its being an actual part of the body of God; but there is only a gradation, with no line of demarcation, between this and the efficacy of medals, relics, scapulars, and symbols of other sorts.

The manas of symbols can be communicated to objects that come into contact with them or that are ritually associated with them. That the early Christians believed that a dangerous mana was communicated from idols to meats offered to them is evident from the exhortation by the author of the Acts of the Apostles to Christians to abstain from such contaminated foods (Acts 15: 29). Ordination of priests and ministers by the laying on of hands embodies the belief that manas which have been communicated to one representative of divinity can by him be transmitted to others, especially by contact. Such transmission is analogous to the magnetization of a piece of steel, which in turn can magnetize other pieces of steel. Carrying this analogy further, the mana transmitted to a person who is not ritually prepared is like magnetizing a piece of soft iron, which quickly loses its magnetization. The manas that heal disease or otherwise benefit persons can be effective only if the recipient is in the proper attitude, involving faith. This is analogous to the fact that some metals can be magnetized, while some other metals cannot. On the other hand, it is held by some that the manas of the medals of some saints operate even for heretics, which is the point at which our analogy breaks down.

CHAPTER IX

FUNERARY PRAXES AND RITUALS

1. **The Importance of Disposal of the Dead.**—Of all the cultural features of past ages, the practices of disposal of the corpses of the dead are of the most outstanding importance for several reasons. (*a*) Such practices are universally obligatory; every man dies, and at his death something must be done about his corpse. (*b*) The disposal of a corpse is bound up with the emotional results of bereavement, with fears for the living as well as for the dead, with the system of family life, and with group integration. Funerary praxes therefore have a significance for group life that few other praxes have. (*c*) Funerary praxes are always parts of group religion, whatever may be our criterion of religion—features of religion in its simple form, which we have called 'proto-religion,' as well as of religion in its complex, more highly developed form. (*d*) Although some of the more evanescent products of religion are lost, insofar as later study is concerned, if they are not preserved in written or carved records or in authentic legends, the results of burials may be preserved for thousands of years.

For the study of peoples of cultures that disappeared more than a few centuries ago, the bones and other objects preserved in tombs or in accidental inhumations constitute often the sole materials. Archaeology, except for the relatively late periods in which writing and architecture and art forms were employed, is almost exclusively a study of results of burials; while even for the later periods, funerary archaeology has been far more important than the architectural. Among the inscriptions that have been preserved, the funerary inscriptions are the most informative. These statements apply, of course, only to the type of disposal that we call 'burial,' and not to the various other forms of disposal, which we shall shortly discuss.

(*e*) Funerary praxes began to develop very early in man's progress from the primitive stage of culture, and, in spite of modifications that have occurred in later stages, these praxes furnish us with the few cultural threads that connect us with the primitive.

The development of ritual from praxes, and the formation of concepts of faith as interpretations of rituals, is more strikingly illustrated by the building up of funerary rituals and their credential consequences than by rituals of any other sorts. The rituals evolved about the disposal of the dead are accordingly of great importance for the study of religion.

It might be supposed that the death of a member of a human group would be immediately terrifying to the surviving group members, since it would be a reminder of the inescapable fate of all persons, but there is no evidence on which we could base the classification of such fear as either 'primitive' or primary. That fear of death does develop in some persons is to be admitted, but man seems to have built up the tendency to have such fear, and we have no grounds on which we could base the assumption that the first observations of death produced it.

There are, however, effects produced on the living by the death of a group member which are unmistakable and which we have no reason to suppose were not produced in man near to the primitive stage. The death of a person with whom one has been associated affects one's thinking and one's feeling. The dead person may have been an enemy or a rival, in which case there will be an emotion of relief over the simplification of one's life. On the other hand, if the deceased has been an ally and companion, the thought of loss and the emotion of bereavement are produced. In either case, a person with whom one has reckoned has passed out of the reckoning. If such a deprivation does not impress a person at once, it may impress him after the disposal of the corpse.

Death eventually becomes something that is popularly called a 'mystery,' but it does seem probable that this mystery develops quickly. Prior to reflection on deaths, and speculation as to their causes, there would be no more mystery about the death of a person than about the death of the deer, the fish, or the snake that man kills and eats. We cannot assume a 'mystery of death' in man's thinking until a religious complex has been built about death or a religious feature of thought and feeling, which later becomes complex.

Feelings and emotions of bereavement, sorrow, and grief are inevitable for the man who has social relations with his fellows. Family relationships, such as those between parents and children and between home mates more generally, are especially productive of these emotions. Recollection of the dead person persists and adds to the emotional states. Man enjoys his relations with his family and with the social group, and we can assume that this enjoyment was found in men of primitive groups. Regret for the loved one who has passed from the scene is regret concerning a deprivation and is often poignant.

The regret and the emotion over loss may occur when an animal companion dies, but, since man did not domesticate animals in his primitive stage, man was familiar with human death long before he had any animal companions.

In all save the most nearly primitive stages of human development there was one consequence of human death that was of immense importance for religion. When a human being dies, something must be done about the corpse; in fact, something must be done *with* the dead body. For man as a member of wandering groups, this need may not arise; but when men have abodes or habitations, even temporary abiding places, the need is inevitable. This need is recognized and affects man's desires, producing the desire to dispose of the cadaver; and from this need and the consequent desire, funerary praxes have arisen.

The disposal of the corpse has taken a variety of forms, which we must briefly survey. While it is well to consider the forms of disposal that have been developed in the world at large, including those which still persist among savages, our chief concern is with the forms that have influenced the development of our own methods of disposal and have influenced the religious rituals and the beliefs that have grown out of them.

2. **The Forms of Disposal.** *1. Abandonment.*—Abandoning a corpse may take one of two forms, in theory at least. (*a*) A wandering group may leave the corpse where it lies, abandoning it to scavenger birds and beasts and the action of insects, bacteria, and the weather. It seems reasonable to assume that primitive man, wandering in small groups, employed this praxis, but we have no proof of the assumption. (*b*) Some peoples today, who have fixed residences, pursue the plan of shutting the corpse in the hut in which the person died and in which he had previously lived and then abandoning the hut. In some cases, the entire encampment may be abandoned, the group establishing itself elsewhere. In theory, caves could have been so employed by cave dwellers, the corpse being shut in a cave and the cave being abandoned. That this was

done, however, is improbable, since caves were not plentiful, but dolmens may have been used in this way.

2. Exposure Away from Camp.—Exposure away from the settlement takes three forms. (*a*) The corpse is taken to a place in the forest, and there exposed to the action of scavenger beasts, as in simple abandonment. This praxis has been maintained by some tribes in central Africa, where the hyenas are the undertakers. (*b*) The corpse is thrown into the sea, to be carried off by the ebb tide, or thrown into a stream to be carried off by the current. (*c*) The dead body is placed on a raft or in a canoe or boat and committed to the water. This praxis is said to be carried out by the Sea Dyaks of Borneo and may have been the original praxis of the Norsemen.

3. Thanatophagy, the Eating of the Dead by the Living.—In various parts of the world this praxis takes one of two forms. (*a*) The corpse is eaten by the group to which the person belonged before death. Various explanations for this praxis have been offered, one being that the eating of the body keeps the manas of the dead person within the group. It is to be suspected, however, that this explanation developed from the praxis, and not the praxis from the belief. The most plausible explanation is that the custom developed simply from the scarcity of food. After man has begun to eat animals of relatively large size, the corpse, in time of food shortage, would be another animal to be eaten. Anthropophagy (cannibalism) was world-wide in ancient times, and in Europe it persisted among the 'Nordics' down to the Christian Era, if not into this era. The transition from the eating of the bodies of those who had died 'natural deaths' to the slaying of human beings for food is not difficult. The custom having been established, it would persist as a ritual after the urgency of the food problem was lessened; and the explanation mentioned above would appear as other interpretations of rituals have developed.

(*b*) The corpse may not be eaten by the members of its groups, but is presented to a neighboring group for consumption. The neighbor group returns the favor when one of its members dies. This custom has obtained among African tribes and among tribes in South America.

4. Cremation.—Burning a corpse may be a primary praxis or may be carried out in conjunction with one of the other forms of disposal. (*a*) In conjunction with the abandonment of the body in a hut, the hut may be burned, together with the corpse. What practical consideration or considerations led to this praxis is unknown. Certainly the body would not be consumed to the point where no other form of disposal would be required, unless the settlement were abandoned. (*b*) In conjunction with the placing of the corpse on a boat, the boat is set afire when it is set adrift. This procedure would be useful only when the boat were set adrift on the sea, and it seems to have been followed only in that circumstance. The burning of the boat would hasten the falling of the corpse into the water, and so lessen the danger that the tide would bring it back. (*c*) The corpse has been burned on a funeral pyre, made of a pile of wood or brush sufficient in quantity to ensure the reduction of the body to charred bones. In Mediterranean countries oil was added to accelerate the combustion and make it as complete as possible. The 'ashes' (charred bones) required further disposal, which took different forms among different groups, as it does in modern times. The common forms were burial and enclosure in an urn placed in a tomb.

5. Elevation.—The body may be fastened in the crotch of a tree, or elevated to platforms supported on poles, as by the Plains Indians, or it may be placed on a platform built in a tree or on a platform supported by stakes. In many cases the 'platform burial' has been for a brief period only, followed by burial or cremation. The corpse fastened in a tree, on the other hand, may be left until it falls to pieces. The practical considerations that led to elevation of the corpse are unknown.

6. Burial.—For convenience, and in accordance with common usage of the term, several forms of disposal are included under the heading of 'burial.' (*a*) Inhumation, or 'burial proper,' is the placing of the corpse in a pit dug in the ground, and filling the earth in upon the body. The earth may be in contact with the body, as in war burials; or the pit may be lined with boards or matting and a protective covering of stakes or branches placed over the body before the grave is filled. The use of coffins to protect corpses is a later practice, which savages have not adopted. (*b*) Entombment. Tombs are of two sorts, surface tombs and subterranean tombs. The surface tomb may be a mere heap of stones or brushwood piled upon and around the corpse to protect it from beasts. On the other hand, it may be a heap of earth of some size, which is called a 'tumulus.' From these tombs of relatively primitive types are developed eventually structures of masonry. In central Africa the tombs of kings were structures built of sticks, with thatched roofs; but the Egyptian pyramids, which were tombs of kings, were stone structures patterned after the wooden tombs of the African kings.

Subterranean tombs were cells dug in the earth and sometimes lined with masonry. The dolmens, insofar as they were used as tombs, approximated to this type, although some dolmens appear to have been partly above ground.

Tombs have sometimes been individual, only one corpse being entombed in each. Some, however, were group tombs. In the Scandinavian area, large rooms were built by neolithic peoples, and a number of corpses were placed in each tomb. At Carthage, subterranean chambers were excavated, with smaller chambers arranged around the central one, and a corpse was deposited in each of the small chambers.

Mounds, such as those extant in the Mississippi Valley, were places of group burial, of inhumation, although they were not constructed primarily as tombs. The persistent tendency among savages of certain groups to inhume corpses under the floors of houses is a carryover from the cave men, who sometimes buried their dead under the dirt floors of their caves.

7. Dismemberment and Mutilation.—Dismembering a corpse is not a primary form of disposal, but has been practised as a preliminary to burial. The arms and legs, and sometimes the head, were severed from the corpse prior to inhumation. Such mutilations did not precede cremation, but graves have been found in which dismembered corpses show signs of partial cremation. Obviously, the corpse was first partially burned, then dismembered and the parts buried. While it has been conjectured that dismemberment was a praxis designed to reduce the danger that a corpse would become a vampire and while it is true that skeletons have been unearthed the bones of which had been broken, but not separated, the most plausible explanation for dismemberment would be that it reduced the size of the grave and made its digging less laborious. For men with crude tools for excavating, this would be a great practical advantage.

Among some savage tribes, the flesh was stripped from the bones and separate disposals were made of the flesh and the skeleton. While this suggests an earlier praxis of thanatophagy, the indication is not certain.

Mummification, of the Egyptian sort, might be considered as a form of dismemberment, since the visceral organs were removed from the corpse. That this mummification developed from the dismemberment praxis applied to Ethiopian kings, in which praxis actual mummifications did not occur, is fairly certain. The mummification praxis of South Americans in Chile and Peru was a different procedure, in which there was no dismemberment, but in which the corpse was merely desiccated (dried).

It is possible that the removal of the intestines from the corpse began in Egypt, or in central Africa, as a means of preventing the long intestine from turning into a snake, but this is merely a conjecture. That the praxis began with thanatophagy, and persisted as a ritual after the eating of the corpse ceased, is another possibility. In any case, the ritual was eventually interpreted in terms of the resurrection of the body.

Inhumation, entombment, and cremation have been praxes of many groups throughout the ages and throughout the world. The funeral pyre was the preferred means of disposal in ancient Greece and ancient China and is the means still customary in Hindu India. The pyramids of Egypt are the most impressive tombs of which we know, but the tumuli scattered over the five continents and the wooden tombs of Ethiopian kings are reminders that man built surface tombs before he made them of masonry. The dolmens of Europe and North Africa, which were dwellings in which the dead were sometimes buried, as they were in natural caves, marked the transition from the earlier tombs to the later.

Structures of these sorts were tombs only for kings, heroes, and men of wealth, just as masonry tombs are today. For the common people, inhumation was the normal method of disposal of the dead, as it is at the present time. Even cremation, in ancient times, seems to have been restricted to the upper crust of society and is a minor praxis among modern civilized people.

Aside from the three praxes just mentioned—inhumation, entombment, and cremation—the other funerary procedures we have discussed are found only among the savage peoples of Africa, Asia, and the Americas. The religious developments from disposal of the dead seem to have come from these three alone, at least so far as the evolution of the religious concepts of civilized religion is concerned.

3. Further Aspects of the Rituals.—Inhumation and entombment are complicated by three important factors: the position of the corpse; the orientation of the body; and *dona mortuis data* (gifts to the dead). The last two of these factors have had important effects on the development of religious concepts, and it is possible that the first also may have had religious results.

1. Burial Positions.—A corpse may be buried or entombed in an extended position, stretched out to its full length, or it may be forced into a bent or contracted position. In the latter case, the position is usually one that suggests the fetus in the uterus, the knees being drawn up to the chest, the head bent forward, and the arms either folded on the chest or wrapped about the knees. Burials in the contracted position were common in pre-Pharaonic Egypt and in ancient Peru. Some burials of this type were made in western Asia. Several theorists have concluded that this contraction was a deliberate imitation of the fetal position, symbolizing the belief that death is a rebirth into another life. This interpretation must be rejected as being overly sophisticated for the peoples who made the early burials in the contracted position. That a people who had long practiced burial in this position would, after they had formed the concept of a post-mortem life, interpret the praxis in the way suggested, is true; but eventual interpretations of rituals seldom indicate the sources thereof.

The most plausible explanation for burial in the contracted position is that it reduces the size of the grave and makes its digging easier. The occurrence of dismemberment and of burial in the contracted position in the same area supports this interpretation. Dismemberment was probably practiced first on corpses in which *rigor mortis* had occurred, so that they could not be bent into the contracted position, without waiting a day or two for the *rigor mortis* to disappear. In the contracted position, the body may be placed with the spine vertical (the 'seated' position), or it may be laid on its side, as if crowded into a small space. There apparently are no cases in which the body has been placed with the head down or the back uppermost or lying on its back.

The extended burial position has been preferred in modern periods and apparently has been preferred by all peoples who have possessed adequate tools for digging. Three extended positions have been utilized: *prone* (lying on the face and belly); *supine* (lying on the back); and *latericumbent* (lying on the side). Burials in the prone position are seldom found, but some in the latericumbent position have occurred. The supine position is preferred in modern times, and few (if any) interments are made in either of the other positions.

For cremation, the corpse is placed in the supine position, and it is probable that in India the body lies supine on the funeral pyre, as it did in the ancient Western world.

2. *Orientation of the Corpse.*—Until recent times, all corpses were oriented to a given direction; usually to the east, west, or south. This practice was adhered to in the United States until the landscaping of cemeteries changed the ritual. Information on an ancient burial, or a savage burial, is not complete unless the orientation is described. Some archaeologists have seemed to overlook this point, at least in their more popular writings.

In latericumbent burials and burials in the 'seated' position, the orientation is given by the direction in which the face is turned. The body is oriented to the west, for example, if it lies on its right side with its head to the north or if it lies on its left side with its head to the south, since in either case its face is toward the west. In the extended position, on the other hand, if the body is supine, the feet give the orientation. If the head is toward the west the orientation of the body is toward the east. This has been the common understanding; and if one examines an old American cemetery, one will find that the graves are all oriented to the east by having their headstones at the west end. The explanation that used to be given for this orientation was that when the corpse should stand up, as on Judgment Day, it would be facing the east. This explanation can be considered as *ad hoc*, since a man rising from a supine position could easily face in either direction; but it clearly indicates the nature of the orientation, whatever may have been the source.

If prone burials occurred, and the bodies were oriented, the direction of orientation, we may surmise, would be that toward which the head pointed. Prone burials, however, have been of negligible frequency.

Some peoples who still orient their dead orient them toward a place of importance for their religion. The traditional orientation of the Jewish dead was toward Jerusalem. The Moslems still orient their dead toward Mecca. The old Christian orientation to the east may have been a carryover from the Jewish custom, with suitable reinterpretation, as orientation to the area in which Jesus was born—an interpretation that actually has been offered.

The most frequent orientations of the dead have been to the east and to the west, but orientations to the south are known. Some archaeologists have explained the easterly and westerly orientations as motivated by worship of a sun god, but these are explanations of the type that invert the relations of sources and results or, in cruder language, put the cart before the horse.

Certain savage groups orient their dead toward the region in which they believe the "spirits' or 'souls' exist after death, and many ancient peoples oriented their dead in a similar fashion. A generalization sometimes made by anthropologists explains all orientations as arising in this way. The generalization is sound, but leaves unsolved the important problem that may be put in the form of the question: Why have these peoples assumed that the location of the spirits or souls is in that direction, rather than in some other? This question we shall shortly attempt to answer.

A difficulty is raised by group tombs, such as those of the neolithic people of Scandinavia and those of the Carthaginians. In the Scandinavian tombs the dead were ranged around the outer wall of the chamber, facing the center. In the subterranean Carthaginian tombs, the corpses were placed in small chambers, arranged around the main one. The difficulty disappears when we consider that for group tombs the exit determines the orientation, and that the exit for the Scandinavian tombs were toward the South, toward the lands from which the people or their progenitors had come. Although evidence is lacking in regard to the orientation of the Carthaginian tombs, we can reasonably assume that it was toward Phoenicia.

An orientation that has become customary in a group may be carried to a new area in which descendants of the group settle. The imposition of a new religion may change the orientation from old holy places to new ones. Aside from these factors, or in spite of them, the reasons for orientations in specific directions are clear. Where an orientation has been systematically maintained among a people whose antecedents are known or are reasonably well represented in the traditions, the orientation of the dead is always toward the ancestral homeland of the people. If this principle is extended to peoples whose antecedents are otherwise conjectural, ethnological problems that have long been obscure can be clarified.

We have pointed out that the neolithic peoples in Scandinavia oriented their tombs toward the south, whence we know these people came. In Egypt, there were two orientations, the first to the west and the later orientations to the east. The last of these orientations is that of the Pharaonic invaders, who, although they came from the region to the south of Egypt, actually entered the Nile Valley from the east.   More important still, these people were descendants of immigrants into Africa from the east, and they doubtless were more motivated by that fact than by their later entrance into Egypt from the east.   The orientation of their dead was not to the last station from which they had come, but to their original home-land.   Nostalgia is no new feature of human life, but the 'old home' is still a wonderful place to most persons.

If this principle of orientation is valid, it supplied grounds for the conclusion that orientation of the dead is one of the sources from which belief in a future life develops.   When the reason for the orientation is forgotten, or no longer seems sufficient, another reason must be found.   The new reason does not at first presuppose belief in a 'spirit' or 'soul' that returns to the old homeland, but it becomes more precise when this belief develops and is an important basis for its development.   The belief in a future life for some appurtenance of the human being is in part a result of another feature of funerary praxis, which we shall next consider.

3. Gifts to the Dead: Dona Mortuis Data.—It was a common practice in ancient times to offer to the dead person his personal possessions, a practice that persists today and is followed by savage as well as by civilized groups.   Ancient man and savages offered, and do offer, tools, weapons, and household utensils, as well as ornaments that were the personal property of the deceased.   In modern civilized groups tools and weapons are seldom offered, but attempts are made to offer jewels that the deceased has worn or prized.   A steady and considerable loss of precious metals would occur today through the burial of ornaments with corpses, if it were not prevented.

Until modern times, horses, slaves, and wives of the deceased were slaughtered at his grave, or at the funeral pyre, and weapons, ornaments, and other gifts were burned on the pyres.   In Egypt, small models of slaves, domestic animals, and implements were placed in the tomb of a king or of a wealthy man.

A conventional explanation for these gifts to the dead has often been advanced.   These gifts, it has been claimed, are evidences of a belief in a future life.   The weapons, slaves, wives, utensils, and foods are given for the use of the surviving 'spirit' or other appur-tenance of the deceased.   The practice of burning or breaking the gifts has been deemed to support this explanation. The man, it is claimed, survives as a spirit and therefore cannot make use of the material gifts, which are burned or broken to liberate their spirits, which can be used by the spirit of the deceased.

To be consistent, the same argument should be applied to civilized people. If the finding, in a Stone Age grave, of ornaments, tools, and weapons proves, without further evidence, that the buriers believed in a future life, then the burial, or the attempt to bury, jewelry and personal possessions with a corpse in a modern country would prove the same belief. Yet we know that persons who have no such belief practice the same thing. If persons who have no faith in a life beyond the grave wish to bury with their dead personal possessions of the deceased, then burials of the same sort by ancient man cannot be considered evidence that the ancient men believed that a spirit or an appurtenance of some sort survived the death of the body. It is a fact that some savages who make gifts to the dead believe in survival, and some of them explain the gifts as useful to the dead or to its surviving appurtenance. This belief can best be explained as an interpretation of the ritual, not as the source or motive for it. Some savages who make gifts to the dead, in fact, disclaim any such belief. The evidences of *dona mortuis* from ancient graves do not tell us whether or not the people who made the burials believed in survival. All we can say is that, if a people continue, as a group, to make *dona mortuis* for a long time, they will eventually arrive at a belief in survival. This generalization, of course, applies to the group and not to individuals in the group.

Why, then, are gifts made? Out of what does the praxis develop? If we ask this question about the praxis as it exists among us today, the answer is simple; the motive is *sentiment*. It is appropriate, it is fitting, that personal ornaments and objects to which the person was attached or which he constantly carried with him should be put with him. Moreover, the presence of objects associated with the deceased is a constant reminder of bereavement. These emotional conditions are common to all men, savages and civilized, and we have no reason to doubt their occurrence in primitive man.

Early civilized man had an additional incentive to remove possessions of the deceased from the vicinity of the living, and we may assume that man developed this incentive not long after he emerged from the primitive stage. Persons have mana, and the mana is transmitted from the person to the tools, weapons, and utensils that he handles and to the ornaments he wears. It is dangerous to tamper with the weapons of a living man, and we have pointed out (Chap. III, Sec. 4, and Note 7), that weapons and armor taken from slain enemies had to be destroyed or subjected to ritual treatment to counteract the mana of the former owner. Some savages have conserved this belief, although others have progressed as far from this relatively primitive point of view as have civilized men.

It is possible that communication of contagious diseases by personal possessions of the dead contributed to the avoidance of such possessions and their burial with the corpse or their cremation with it. Although the causes of contagion were not understood, the death of another person occurring in the same way as that of the first would be observable and would contribute to the belief in a dangerous mana communicated to possessions by their owners.

The breaking of the *dona mortuis data* may have been, in part at least, a sentimentally motivated praxis. The man is broken; so be his implements. This would be interpreted later as a lessening of the dangerous manas of the objects by their breaking. On the other hand, grave robbing has been a business of ancient origin, and the breaking of the gifts may accordingly have had a practical foundation. The fact that the practice of breaking the gifts has been adopted in some regions, and not in others, supports this notion. Where grave robbers are daring, the praxis is sound.

The praxis of making gifts to the dead seems to have developed wherever inhumation has been the method of disposal of the corpse, and the gifts are always objects or persons (slaves and wives) that were personally associated with the deceased. The praxis has been associated also with cremation, but whether it developed in that association or was transferred from earlier burial customs is not clear. In any case, the praxis eventually needs explanation, and the explanation on sentimental grounds would be avoided, since man is commonly ashamed of the attitudes and emotions that we call 'sentimental.' As a group progresses to the use of weapons captured from enemies, the mana explanation becomes untenable. Man clings tenaciously to the customs of his forefathers, even if the sentiments that created them have become blunted and the rituals need new interpretations. Children would want to know: Why do we throw away these tools and utensils that we need so badly ourselves? Strangers from groups that had not adopted the praxis of making *dona mortuis* might ask the same embarrassing question. An explanation must be found, and an obvious explanation is that the dead man benefits from the gifts. The belief in survival is then on its way to emergence.

How can the dead person benefit from the gifts, when he is obviously in process of being reduced to bones and dust? Obviously there must be *another man*, which survives the death of the body. Thus is begun the development of beliefs in souls or spirits, belief in a supernatural man who is like the bodily man but is usually invisible. The development of souls of various types is then a matter of time. The spirit that is first conceived is probably the *autos*, the man himself, the essential person, which is not identified with the *psyche* or life soul, until a late stage of human development has been reached. The Egyptians and the Babylonians did not make this identification, and in the Mediterranean area it was not made until Plato appeared.

The soul as first conceived may have been the ghost, or the 'indweller,' of later folklore. Little help is derived from the soul concepts of savages, for most savage groups have reached the stage in which souls of several sorts have appeared. Among the savage peoples of the Malay Peninsula, for example, souls of several types are ascribed to human beings, among these being an indweller soul, a life soul, a daimon soul, and another that might be described as an ego-soul, or possibly as an *autos*. These different sorts of souls are distinguished from one another by the natives. The situation in the Malay Peninsula is complicated by the fact that there are, in that area, descendants of two racial stocks, a 'white' and a 'black.' These two stocks have become somewhat mixed, and their cultural developments have been mutually influenced, and both stocks have been influenced culturally by Malays of later immigration.

In considering the development of souls from burial rituals we can ignore the *psyche* (life soul), which is dissipated at death; and we can ignore also the Egyptian *Ka*, or double, which is a soul restricted to Negroid cultures or to cultures that adopted the concept from the Negroes. The concept of the *Ka* was never adopted by peoples of the Mediterranean or Levantine areas, but is common among Negroid groups in the East Indies and the Pacific Isles.

For the entities surviving death, the concepts of which developed from burial rituals, particularly from the rituals of orientation and of gifts to the dead, there are four alternative fates. (*a*) They may hang around the place of burial or around their former abodes or may pass to an underworld. (*b*) They may go to the ancestral home of the group, which thus becomes the 'happy hunting grounds,' the 'isles of the blest,' or 'paradise.' (*c*) The indweller soul may enter into other animals. (*d*) They may become free-living daimons, with no further essential connections with human beings. All these notions are found among savages, and sometimes these four destinies are recognized for appurtenances of different sorts. These notions are recognizable also in the religious conceptions of our cultural ancestors.

The belief in a future life is influenced by the form of disposal of the dead that is employed. From abandonment and from exposure of the first type, no belief in survival develops. As for exposure in a boat, we are not certain. Where burial or entomb-ment has been the customary praxis, there has developed the belief in a ghost and in an underworld to which the ghost departs, if suitable rituals are carried out for the dead. If the corpse is inhumed, it is in the ground, or underground, and that is where it continues to be. With the development of the concept of an existence after death, the obvious place for this existence is where the dead are. The limitations of the grave and reminiscences of cave dwelling soon modify the concept into that of a more spacious troglodytal underworld.

Among peoples whose development of a concept of souls has been fairly recent, we may find an order of development that is different from the one we have described. The Baganda, near Victoria Nyanza, have (or until recently had) temples devoted to certain divinities. These temples were so similar to the tombs of kings that it is no surprise to find that the 'god' in the temple consists of a human jawbone, an umbilical cord, and other human fragments, since these are the relics of kings in their tombs. The group of attendants in the temple corresponds also to the group of attendants at the tomb of a king. The 'god,' it seems, is merely a former king who has been elevated to divinity of a sort. Obviously a soul, of some sort, of the king survives.

Among the common people of the Baganda, burial (inhumation) is the praxis of disposal and *dona mortuis data* are made. The doctrine of souls surviving death is accordingly fairly well developed, although it is not clear what type of souls survive.

From more extensive survey of savage groups of the present day or of the recent past, it appears clearly that there is a definite correlation between the various disposal praxes and the concept of souls surviving death. From exposure and thanatophagia, no belief in survival develops, although there may be a concept of impersonal forces dominating nature. Burial certainly produces such beliefs, and entombment may likewise generate them; although entombment has been the praxis only for the select few and *hoi polloi* have been buried or cremated. Elevation, while it might give rise to belief in survival if orientation or gifts to the dead were included, has, as we have said, usually been combined with other disposal praxes, so that also remains a matter of uncertainty.

The effect of cremation on religious belief presents a difficult problem, since the peoples who practiced cremation had practiced inhumation in an earlier period, as did the Greeks, or may have absorbed the beliefs of peoples among whom they settled, as in the cases of the Hindus and the Persians.

Not all rituals of funerary application can be explained on the basis of mana, nor even of belief in mana combined with sentiment. The placing of candles around the corpse, for example, is possibly not so simply explicable. We must consider, however, the fundamental relation of faith to ritual. Faith arises from ritual, as an interpretation of ritual. As cultural conditions change, the ritual is reinterpreted, and the new interpretation brings about modification of the ritual. We must consider also the continuity of religion, and the transmission from early religions to newer, features of ritual as well as of faith which have developed in the earlier religion.

We must remember also that practical considerations may be involved in praxes even after they have become rituals and that the explanations offered by the groups that maintain the ritual are interpretations that are not reliable. The burial of a living child with the corpse of its mother is easily explained by those who practice this burial, but the most plausible explanation of the custom is that the child would die anyhow when deprived of the mother's milk. Where women who could serve as wet nurses have been plentiful, this custom seems not to have been adopted.

The immolation of wives at the funeral pyres of their deceased husbands was a custom of the peoples of India until the British stopped it. In the days of St. Boniface (fifth century A.D.), the Wends had a similar custom. Among the Hindus it is obvious that the widow was an unfortunate relict, a burden on her poverty stricken relatives, and the same may have been true among the Wends.

With respect to all funerary praxes we must also take into account the obvious desire of the living to 'close the ledger' for the dead person, to eliminate all references to him, and to do away with objects that are reminders of him. This cannot be ascribed entirely to fear of the dead or of his surviving 'soul,' although certain funeral customs do indicate such fear. The changing of names and disguise by funeral garb and by painting the face and shaving the head are procedures that may be admitted as motivated by fear of the dead, but they are of secondary importance. The important motivation comes from realization that the group must go on, although individuals pass out, that the dead hand is a real evil, and that continued grief and regret weaken the efficiency of those who must take over from the point at which the dead have left off.

CHAPTER X

SIN

1. **The Nature of Sin.**—The concept of sin belongs to religion, and to religion only. So far as there can be a simple criterion of religion, the criterion is sin; for wherever we find sin recognized, there we indubitably have found religion. There has been a theory that religion is essentially based on sin and evolves from the concept of sin, but this theory is overly simple. It is true that religion begins its development with the concept of manas and that the concept of sin in one of its two important forms stems from the same root, but it would be sounder to say that sin grows out of religion than to say that religion grows out of sin. The accurate statement would be that the concept of sin develops *in* religion and develops nowhere else. Sin is no feature of the universe itself in any fundamental sense, but is strictly a human creation. The purpose of the Founder of Christianity was not to save mankind from sin, but to destroy sin itself, or, we may say more accurately, to eliminate the concept of sin from the human mind.

Here I may be confusing sin with the sense of sin, with the thought of oneself as a sinner. This confusion is of minor consequence and can be cleared up later. What I wish here to emphasize is the fact that the concept of sin is itself an evil, that through this concept a person comes to regard himself as a sinner, and that this is the way in which the concept of sin does its damage.

We have earlier distinguished two sorts of sin as external sin and internal sin (Chap. III, Sec. 7). Both forms may be brought under the general head of *wrongs* or the results of wrongful conditions, events, or activities. There are, however, wrongful things that are not religious wrongs, and a part of our task is to distinguish religious wrong from nonreligious wrong.

External sin, we have pointed out, may be the result of conditions or events with which the 'sinner' had nothing to do and of which he even might be ignorant. Internal sin, on the other hand, is a result of the sinner's own responses, whether these responses are

234

overt actions or are thoughts. We have pointed out that external sin also may be the results of a person's activities, but not of his thought alone. Both external sin and internal sin, accordingly, must be distinguished from actions (or the results of actions), which are wrong in other than religious senses, and from mishaps that do not have religious implications. These nonreligious 'wrongs,' or the more important ones, may be listed as: (1) inefficiency, (2) sickness and disease, (3) boorishness, (4) unconventionality, (5) disobedience, (6) illegality and crime, (7) vice, (8) immorality. These categories are not all sharply distinguishable from one another, but they represent, nevertheless, important distinctions in respect to wrong actions and wrong situations.

These eight types of wrong deserve some further amplification, in order to make the distinctions clear.

1. Inefficiency.—A person may be inefficient in various ways, for various causes. To make mistakes or errors is to be inefficient. Errors range from wild shooting at a target to logical fallacies in reasoning. In some cases the cause is carelessness; in others, lack of proper training; in some cases the person is fundamentally incapable of learning.

2. Disease and Injury.—Sickness is a condition afflicting the individual that reduces his efficiency; breaking a leg also reduces his efficiency and constitutes a condition that we deem to be 'wrong.' Disease or injury may be results of carelessness or low intelligence, but a person who lives as carefully as possible may nevertheless contract a contagious disease or be involved in an accident.

3. Boorishness.—One who offends against the standards of good taste, or against the rules of polite society, is called a 'boor'; he is not, however, accused of sickness, immorality, vice, crime, or sin by the application of the term. Some boors are estimable persons in all other respects, although they could be accused of social inefficiency. Boorishness may be due to lack of knowledge or lack of training, but in most cases carelessness is at the bottom of the wrongdoing.

4. Unconventionality.—Violation of the standards of good taste is only one form of unconventionality, and the unconventional person may violate no rule of polite society. In some communities it is wrong to be married by a justice of the peace or to serve salad as the first course at dinner, but these unconventionalities are not always considered as being in bad taste. The line between unconventionality and boorishness is tenuous and variable, but the two categories are distinct. One may be unconventional intentionally without being boorish.

5. Disobedience.—To disobey is to violate intentionally an express command, which the violator has understood. Disobedience may involve sin, vice, crime, unconventionality, or immorality, but does not necessarily involve any of those.

6. Crime, or Illegality.—One who breaks a law acts illegally and is sometimes classed as a criminal. The criminal could be defined as one who breaks laws, and this definition is implied by criminologists, who, however, seldom employ the term in the sense in which it is defined. Practically all studies alleged to be of 'criminals' are really studies of the small and highly selected class of *convicts*, a class selected by the consecutive processes of (*a*) commission of a crime, (*b*) apprehension, (*c*) trial, (*d*) conviction, (*e*) sentence. Between these stages many criminals escape, so the class of convicts does not represent the larger class of criminals.

7. Vice.—By common consent the term 'vice' is applied only to habitual actions or procedures that are injurious to the person performing the actions or carrying out the procedures or which are deemed to be injurious to him. Smoking opium and drinking liquor to excess are considered as vices, because it is assumed that the opium smoker and the excessive drinker are injured. Either of these vices may be illegal, sinful, boorish, or immoral, according to circumstances. Lying, if harmful to the liar, is a vice, but if harmful only to others it is immoral, but not a vice. The characteristic of vice that distinguishes it from all other sorts of wrongdoing is its habitualness. No action or procedure that is not habitual is properly called a vice. Smoking opium now and then, getting drunk in exceptional circumstances, or occasional lying are not vices.

8. Immorality.—This term has been used in more different senses than have any of the preceding seven. Vice, crime, and disobedience are often designated as immoral, and, in a usage that is fairly common, the term implies sexual wrongdoing. Samuel Butler, in *Erewhon*, presents sickness as immoral and criminal, but thieving is considered as sickness. There is, however, a usage that has been extended in modern times, in which immorality means 'injustice' and/or lack of cooperation with others. If one performs avoidable actions that are injurious to others, or fails to act in ways that would be beneficial to others, he is, according to this usage, immoral.

Obviously, the determination of what is possible or impossible and what is avoidable or unavoidable is a complicated matter; hence in any given case the determination of what is just and what is unjust may be extremely difficult.

Wrongdoing, in any of the foregoing categories may, in certain circumstances, involve sin but is not necessarily sinful. Immorality has, in modern religion, been identified with sin, but this is a new feature of religion. In ancient religion there was no such identification, and today there are many persons who are deeply religious but are also profoundly immoral. Sin, in short, is a purely religious wrong, although, in past ages, conditions that we would now designate as diseased were ascribed to sin, but, earlier, diseases and injuries both were viewed from the religious point of view. Sin is not to be identified with any of the eight categories of wrongdoing we have listed, but belongs in a ninth class.

In modern popular theology sin is often defined as a type of disobedience. Thus, an anonymous writer in the *Encyclopaedia Britannica* (11th ed.), declares: 'If man is thought of as under the authority of God, any transgression of, or want of conformity to the law of God is defined as sin.'

Historically considered, however, we find that sin is much broader than this definition would make it. Disobedience to God in fact is merely one case under one variety of sin, and genetically it is the least important.

2. External Sin.—If we consider the Christian doctrine of *original sin*, we find that the original sin was Adam's act of disobedience to the explicit command of God. From this, we might expect to find that sin is always an act, even if not always an act of disobedience. However, sin turns out to be something that can be transmitted from parent to child, so that we are all guilty of 'original sin.'

Now that which is transmitted might be a tendency or a predisposition. Adam had the tendency to commit sin; we inherit this tendency, not the sin itself; we sin on adequate provocation. Some writers, such as the one from whose article on 'Sin' we have quoted, adopt this explanation, but it is clearly inadequate.

There is no claim that infants of tender age can committ sinful acts, but many theologians have held that they are 'sinful,' and, dying in infancy, are damned for the sin they inherit. Evidently the infant has not merely the tendency to sin; he is afflicted with sin itself. Further proof of this is supplied by the church. By the offices of the priest, in baptizing the infant, the infant can be *saved*. Yet the church has never held that such baptizing in itself lessens the tendency to commit sins. It merely removes the original sin. Further, sin other than original sin, acquired by the individual during life, may be removed by ritual. Confession, baptism, penance—these remove sin, hence sin obviously is not the tendency.

The Augustinian-Pelagian controversy in the fifth century A.D. was in part over the inheritance of sin. Although Pelagius did not commit himself on this point, his friend Caelestius asserted the innocence of the new-born. Pelagius asserted the ability of men to become free from sin by their own efforts, and this is virtually the position of the Greek church. The Pelagian heresy was downed in the Roman Church, which held to the inheritance of sin as a result of Adam's fall and to the necessity of divine grace to remove sin. Pelagius asserted that sin was an act, not a state or condition, while Augustine held sin to be a condition. In spite of the official triumph of Augustine, Pelagianism essentially won. The Jansenists represented a reversion to Augustinianism; the Jesuits to Pelagianism.

The Reformation brought the issue up again. Calvinism in a way represents the orthodox Augustinianism, while Arminianism represents the Pelagian viewpoint, but admits a *tendency* to sin, which needs divine grace to overcome it.

Christianity did not get this doctrine from Judaism. The Jewish God punished children for the sins of their fathers, but this punishment does not ascribe the sin to them. The fact is that the doctrine of original sin is derived from the cults of Greece, particularly from the Orphic, Eleusinian, and Dionysiac cults. Although our information about these cults is still vague, we have evidence that the concept of original sin, as a hereditary taint, was fundamental in Greek religion.

Not only in ancient civilization, but in uncivilized cultures, sin is a *condition* of an individual. To many savages, death and misfortune are evidences of sin and results thereof. But the sin is not necessarily the result of disobedience, although in some cases it may be the result of an act. If we should say that sin is a *misfortune* or a taint that has been acquired, somewhat analogous to a physical injury or a disease, we should not be far from the correct idea. Sin of this sort we have already characterized as *external sin*.

How does an individual acquire external sin? By coming in contact with an object that has an inimical mana or by coming under the influence of the mana, even without contact. The man who put his hand on the ark of the covenant to steady it committed a sin; that is to say, he acquired sin itself, and either the sin killed him or the god killed him because of his sin. There is little if any difference in these two expressions. A man who touches the terminals of a high-voltage line is killed. What killed him? The electric current. Looking a little more closely, however, we find that fibrillation of the heart was produced by the electric current and was the immediate cause of death. The fibrillation in this case is analogous to external sin, but we do not call the act 'committing fibrillation of the heart'; however, if we should do so, we would have an exact analogy to the ancient conception of external sin.

Various other ways of acquiring external sin are found. Certain spots, certain places are places of mana or power. They are holy and therefore deadly. Temples, images may be filled with mana. Into the holy place, it is a sin for the ordinary man to go. The prohibitions were merely warnings of danger, and an innocent stranger would be in the same danger. The prohibition was based on the danger, not the danger on the prohibition. So, a break in the pavement or a sharp curve in the road is dangerous. The driver who disregards the warning sign may be killed; so may he be even if no sign is posted.

A characteristic of external sin, and its acquisition, is that acts and occurrences that are unpremeditated or involuntary may lead to its acquisition. Contact with an accursed animal may be accidental, but the person should do something about it at once, to remove the taint. Whether or not the eating of the flesh of a tabued animal, in ignorance of its nature, was sinful is a question on which we have little definite information, but we may well suppose that ignorance did not prevent the sin. The companions of Ulysses who were destroyed for the sin of killing and eating the cattle of Helios, the sun god, may be said to have done wrong knowingly, but from other disasters that happened to other men we must understand that the same dire results would have followed even if they had not been warned—the sin would have been incurred just the same.

The evil results of various acts and accidents in which many persons still believe are quite aside from the volition of the person involved. Spilling salt and breaking mirrors may be accidents, but the evil effects follow just the same. A person who has inadvertently walked under a ladder or under a platform on which men have trod may excuse himself, but if he holds to the superstition, he is still uneasy about the results. When a black cat crosses one's path, it is an action of the cat, not of the person, but it bodes bad luck just the same. To put the wrong shoe on first was sinful for the Pythagoreans, whether intentional or not. It may be said that acceptance of such bad omens and taking measures to counteract them is not 'religious,' but that all depends on the point of view. They are ritual matters.

Ritual measures for protection against dangerous manas and rituals for the removal of the taint of sin after its acquisition throw light on the nature of external sin, and the rituals still employed for the neutralization of 'bad luck' are also illuminating. A priest who had been properly consecrated might without sin enter a holy place forbidden to laymen, although the priest might need to take some ritual precautions. Members of Catholic sects must prepare themselves for the taking of the consecrated host by fasting beforehand. In a similar way, the lineman working with high-tension lines wears rubber gloves or stands on an insulated platform.

In ancient religions there were numerous rituals for purification from the taint of sin after its acquisition; among these the sprinkling of seats in a place of assembly with pigs' blood, to counteract sins that persons might not know they had acquired, was conspicuous. In the same way, there are conventional rituals today to counteract the bad luck consequent on the spilling of salt or the breaking of a mirror. Initiation into the ancient mysteries, such as the Orphic, Dionysian, and Eleusinian mysteries, was presumably for the removal of the taint of original sin; whether or not initiation removed sins that had been acquired during the lifetime of the initiate is a question on which we have no certain information.

The evils inflicted upon an individual by malicious persons through witchcraft or the 'evil eye' seem closely allied to the taint of external sin. These influences are rejected by some of us today as 'magical,' but belief in them and use of the rituals to produce and avert them continue, not only among the lower classes of Europe, but also in the United States. Although most sects of Christianity have renounced belief in such practices and their efficacy, this is not true of all the members of these sects, and some sects still explicitly teach that their enemies may, and do, work malicious magic.

External sin, where the notion is simply held, is a result of what is supposed to be natural law, and its punishment is merely the further operation of universal law. The man comes in contact with, or in opposition to, a mana; his injury is as inevitable as is that of the man who eats poison or steps on a poisonous serpent. There are forces in the environment that are deadly and situations and acts that are deadly. Woe to him who encounters them, or is found in them, or commits them. That the manas come eventually to be other-worldly and the universal laws in part occult or 'spiritual' does not change the situation in essentials.

In ancient Mediterranean conceptions, even after the gods had developed as humanized beings, the conception of natural law as supreme in the universe was not lost. The gods themselves were powerless to change natural laws (either physical laws or 'spiritual' laws), although they themselves might not be completely subject to the laws.

An illustration from Herodotus may make this clearer. Pactyas, the Lydian, after an act of treachery to Cyrus the Persian, who had subdued Lydia, finally sought asylum among the Cymaeans, from whom the Persians demanded his surrender. In a quandary, the Cymaeans sent deputies to the oracle of Apollo at Branchidae, to inquire whether they should give up Pactyas. The oracle ordered them to do so. Again the Cymaeans sent a deputation, to inquire if the first messenger had reported the oracle correctly, and the oracle reaffirmed the advice. When the deputies dramatically pointed out that such an act would be impious (sinful), the god frankly told them: 'I do command it, that so for the impiety you may the sooner perish, and not come here again to consult my oracle about the surrender of suppliants' (Herodotus, ref. VI: A3, Bk. I).

Here we have a clear picture of impiety or sin as a fact of nature, incurred in accordance with universal law, not through arbitrary convention or will of the gods. The god, setting a trap to make the Cymaeans vulnerable, acted like a spiteful person who advises someone to walk on thin ice or to eat that which is poisonous.

Again, Sabacos, the Ethiopian invader of Egypt, had a vision of a man who directed him to slay all the Egyptian priests. 'On this, according to the account which he himself gave, it came into his mind that the gods intended to lead him to commit an act of sacrilege which would be sure to draw down on him some punishment either at the hands of gods or men,' and so he fled out of Egypt (Herodotus, Bk. II).

Here, again, it is implied that, while the gods might be able to destroy a man by their own acts, the alternative was to impel him to destroy himself by running counter to inexorable forces. Thus the concept of sin as a result of natural law survived even in incongruous combination with the concept of arbitrary evil forces.

That the sin may be incurred by the innocent is illustrated by another tale. Some of the Phocaean pirates who had settled at Alalia on the Island of Corsica were captured by the Tyrrhenians and Carthaginians in a naval fight in the Sardinian Sea. The victors took the captives ashore and stoned them to death. 'Afterwards when sheep or oxen, or even men of the district of Agylla passed by the spot where the murdered Phocaeans lay, their bodies became distorted, or they were seized with palsy, or they lost the use of some of their limbs. On this, the people of Agylla sent to Delphi to ask the oracle how they might expiate their sin' (Herodotus, ref. VI: A3, Bk. I).

Now, the sin that the Agyllaeans had to expiate was simply the condition due to the presence of murdered men's bodies in their fields, although the Agyllaeans were in no wise responsible for their murder. The bodies of murdered men had a deadly mana, which affected those in the neighborhood. This, of course, was external sin, and the cure prescribed by the oracle was to exercise or 'lay' the mana, by rituals of honor to the dead pirates.

Both external and internal sin are counteracted, or removed, by ritual. For both types of sin, the ritual is one of 'cleansing.' After contact with a dead body or even presence at a funeral the Greek had to wash his hands ceremonially. Various other cleansing rituals were necessary after defilements (sins) of various other sorts, however unavoidable the defilement. All the natural excretory and reproductive functions were looked upon as sinful, and the reproductive functions of women as especially sinful; hence routine rituals were prescribed for cleansing from these taints.

Where gods, either as animals or as men, had developed, these gods might be favorably disposed toward a man, but a caprice on the part of the god or an action or omission of due courtesy on the part of the man might set the god against him. Such an act might be deliberate or might be inadvertent; it might or might not be an act of disobedience, or insubordination, but it changed the man's environment. A power that had been favorable, or at least neutral to the man, was now inimical. The god would wreak vengeance on the man or exact recompense, if he were not placated.

Hence we have removal or expiation of sin by ritual propitiation of divinity as well as by repentance and abasement. It is not a matter of cleansing the sinner or curing an inner condition, but of changing the environment. There is no sharp line between the propitiation of a divinity who is temporarily inimical and the propitiation of a permanently malevolent divinity; but in the one case the attitude of the divinity is changed, while in the other case the person merely insulates himself from a force that has been and that continues to be inimical.

These two kinds of expiation—cleansing and propitiation—are inextricably combined in Christianity, as they were in the later Greek religion and in the Jewish, Egyptian, and Babylonian religions. This is to be expected, since inner and outer sin are both represented in Christianity as well as in these earlier religions, from which Christianity developed. The arbitrariness of the gods' attitudes, however, received an extreme development in Jewish religion which it did not have in Mediterranean religion, and Judaism lost the notion of universal laws that even the gods cannot change, although the gods may not be completely subject to the laws, a notion that was retained even in the late Greek religion and has been revived in modern Christianity. The notion of supreme law in the universe, and the position of the gods in respect to it, was parallel to the notion of political law in the ancient world, and the relation of kings to those laws. That a king might be subject to some laws and exempt from others is clearly indicated by ancient stories and legends. What would be a sin for an ordinary person, for which he would suffer retribution from the operation of cosmic laws or retribution visited on him by the gods, might not be a sin for a monarch. When Cambyses, the son of Cyrus, wished to marry his sister, he put the matter before the royal judges, who were the interpreters of the 'old laws' (the common law).

The judges reported that there was no law allowing brother and sister to marry, but that there was a law 'that the King of the Persians might do whatever he pleased' (Herodotus, ref. VI: A3, Bk. III). In other words, the king was excepted by law from subjection to the law. It was no sin for him to do what, if done by a common man, would have brought disaster on the man and on the whole group as well. This disaster happened to Oidipous (Oedipus), for the sin of marrying his mother, although Oidipous was innocent of any illegal intention.

The ruler's independence of the law was not so marked in Western notions as in the Eastern, but the distinction between established law and the edicts of a ruler was everywhere recognized, along with the fact that the king might be, partially at least, not subject to the law, although the law was binding for common men. The conception of fixed principles or natural law controlling the world, within which the gods, as glorified kings, might be somewhat independent, parallels this political conception. Yet, for the Greeks, even the gods were creatures of fate, that is, of natural law, and their actions were controlled by laws that are inviolable.

Just so, we conceive today that the acts of a man may be arbitrary, and moral or immoral, malevolent or benevolent, inconsistent or logical, but they are nevertheless in accordance with natural law. This doctrine may not be valid, but it is widely accepted.

3. **Internal Sin.**—Although the conception of original sin, which is external sin, still lingers in some sects of Christianity, sin for many Christians is wholly internal. It is a matter of wrong behavior, or of wrong thought, and, while the behavior itself may be regarded as sinful, the condition or state of the sinner, as a result of his conduct, is more adequately considered as the sin. In this regard, external sin and internal sin are similar, for in both cases the sin is a taint on or in the individual himself. The difference is that a person cannot acquire internal sin by accident or have it visited on him by external forces or agencies over which he has no control. A sin, in the internal sense, is *committed*, not acquired in any other way. The tendency of modern theologians to interpret original sin as an inherited tendency to commit sins does not make original sin internal, as we have pointed out above, but merely complicates the problem.

The essential feature of internal sin is the intention, purpose, or volition involved in the commission or preceding it. It is a principle of jurisprudence that 'Ignorance of the law excuses no man,' but this principle is not applied in a flat way in sound legal practice. Knowing and willful infraction of law is always considered a crime more serious than unwitting or ignorant infraction. If a man has had opportunity to orient himself in regard to the law and has not used the opportunity, his guilt is thereby made greater.

The same criteria are applied to sin, but, in general, the voluntary factor is more emphasized than in the case of crime.

Jesus went so far as to state that intention or desire to do that which is wrong is the same as doing it, so far as guilt is concerned (Matt. 5: 28). This is strong doctrine and needs explication, for transient evil desires can be judged only in respect to controlling desires and habits of desire, but it symbolizes the modern conception of sin and also modern attitudes toward immorality and other forms of wrongdoing.

The nature of the wrongdoing that constitutes internal sin has been a subject of much controversy, and the criteria of sin have changed progressively during the last two thousand years, as the standards have changed. The earliest concept of internal sin we can recognize in Greek religion can be identified with disobedience to the commands of gods or wrong attitudes toward gods. Irreverence and blasphemy are typical sins, and failure to conduct or participate in the divine rituals are sins, for these rituals are assumed to be approved by the gods, even if not established by their commands. For the Jews, failure to conform to the Mosaic laws, in respect to both things to be done and things to be avoided, was sin, for these laws were believed to have been communicated to Moses by Jehovah.

This standard of internal sin was taken over by early Christianity and is to a certain extent maintained today. Even those Christians who do not base their concept of sin on disobedience to a supreme potentate do, however, retain the notion that irreverence is sinful. Whether or not one believes in an actual God, the concept is recognized as important and as representing moral progress. Although we find many persons who consider themselves to be deeply religious and who are members of orthodox sects habitually indulging in profanity and blasphemy, we do not consider such persons religious in the modern sense of the term.

For some Christians, the commands of the church have been substituted for the commands of the gods, and disobedience to ecclesiastical commands is the standard for sin. This is possible for churches that are representatives of the gods, whose commands, accordingly, are divinely sanctioned. In earlier forms of Christianity, failure to accept doctrines that were assumed to be in accord with the divine will constituted a sin, since such heresy was not only a disregard of divine commands, but also a form of irreverence; but few Christians today consider heretical views to be sinful in themselves.

There is an increasing tendency to identify sin and immorality and to make religious rectitude merely a matter of moral conduct and moral attitudes. This is, in effect, a doing away with sin, which, as we have above indicated, seems to have been the purpose of Jesus.

4. The 'Sense' of Sin.—The knowledge or belief of a person that he has committed sin or has acquired a taint of external sin is conventionally designated a 'sense of sin,' although it is a matter of thought, not of sensation. Both external and internal sin produce this thought attitude. The sinner may experience remorse or may be in a state of apprehension or fear of the effects of his sin, effects that may be called 'punishment.' The sinner may repent or he may be resentful and defiant, but either of these conditions unsettles and weakens the individual and may produce a neurotic condition. On the other hand, a neurotic or psychopathic condition may be the basis for the conviction of sin. The neurotic person may magnify trivial matters into grievous sins or may have the conviction that he has committed some unknown sin. In ancient times, such a neurotic would have had the conviction that he had contracted an unknown external sin.

Repentance was once considered an essential step toward the remission of sin, and bringing sinners to repentance has been an important feature of revivals in modern times. If by repentance we mean an emotional state of remorse and self-depreciation, there can be no doubt that Spinoza was right in his denunciation of repentance as an evil process or state. In repenting, a person is living in the past; and, instead of strengthening him for future better performance, repentance weakens him and makes more probable his further sinning. A critical survey of past performances in order to identify mistakes may help much in the avoidance of these mistakes in the future. The errors of the past, adequately analyzed, are the basis for the avoidance of the errors in further life, but this dispassionate analysis and judgment is not what is commonly meant by 'repentance.' Solicitude to undo, or compensate for, one's injuries to others is an admirable thing, but repentance should not be involved.

Not so long ago the religious instruction of children involved arousing in them a lively sense of sin and apprehension of the dire punishment awaiting them in this world or the next, and many children have gone through horrible agony on this account. This injury to children has been somewhat lessened in recent years, but it points up the idea of Jesus that the concept of sin is an evil thing and a source of evil. It is true that according to the King James Version of the New Testament, Jesus called on man to 'repent'; but the Greek words so translated (*meta noete*) mean 'change your opinion,' and some translators have rendered it 'reform.' The assumption that Jesus, if he had foreseen the emotional performances of penitents at the 'mourners' bench' in modern revivals, would have urged anyone to go through that type of 'repentance' is not consistent with the doctrines that are presented in the four gospels as His. Although the concept of sin, as we have said earlier, grew up in religion and is a strictly religious concept, it would seem to be a concept that religion would do well to outgrow. Reverence, morality, good taste, and the other concepts of 'right living' are appropriate to modern religion, but the negative concept of sin belongs in an early stage of religious development and is now an anachronism.

That the concept of sin has been useful to the medicine man, the priest, and the church is obvious. It has increased the power and the prestige of the priest and of the church. These results may have been useful in the earlier periods of religious development— useful to the ordinary man as well as to the priest—but there is no usefulness of the concept today.

Sin is a powerful prop to the church in modern times, especially among the less educated classes, who are taught that external and internal sin produce dangers that can be avoided only by following the rules laid down by the church and by accepting the rituals prescribed by the church. Original sin, they are taught, can be neutralized by the church; and the church can neutralize or 'forgive' the taint of internal sin. By conforming to the rules and rituals of the church, the anger and the vengeance of an offended divinity can be averted and the taint of original sin can be washed away. The church for these reasons is loath to abandon the concept of sin. The tenacious conservatism that is the salient trait of religious organizations appears here clearly, but the risks that such conservatism entails should be considered. If the church continues to insist on the basic importance of sin, then man, in abandoning the concept of sin, will inevitably abandon the church. Some Christian sects demonstrate the die-hard tendency more strongly than do others; they persist in their conservatism until a debacle overthrows them, as has happened in France, in Russia, and in Spain. The Protestant churches have shown a greater tendency to go along with civilization, dragging back somewhat stubbornly, but nevertheless moving forward.

The great difficulty, as the churches see it, is that if and when the church abandons the concept of sin, it has nothing indispensable to offer to man and so must lose its hold or, in the case of an incipient sect, can never gain a hold. This fate has happened to the Unitarian and Universalist churches. A young schismatic church, however, if directed by a clever priesthood, grows rapidly if it offers a convincing program of sin and of the cure of sin through ecclesiastical intervention.

Aside from the interests of the church itself, the real problem is the effect of sin on the human being. Sin, as Jesus seems to have taught, is a bad thing, and, although indirect benefits may flow from it, these benefits in modern culture are minor as compared with the evil. An angry and revengeful God would seem to be of little use to mankind, and fears of divine vengeance or punishment seem not to be desirable emotions. We know of no benefits that fear confers on man, and the despising of cowardice is probably justifiable.

In spite of the decline of the doctrine of the 'transfer of training' in modern psychology, we know that many results of living do spread from one department of life to others. The man who is trained to be a coward in one respect is certainly no more apt to be courageous in another, and there is a strong probability that his bravery is lessened. If religion can assist man in the conquest of fear, this will be a valuable contribution to human welfare, but a religion that increases fear is atavistic. The concept of sin, which involves fear of punishment, is certainly an atavistic concept.

In repenting, the sinner takes an emotional attitude of humiliation toward an arbitrary power, an attitude which is disagreeable to a normal person and which weakens his independence and his power of adequate action. Repentance is essentially a dwelling in the past, an acceptance of evil. If one repents in form only, of sins against a formal divinity, which doesn't matter much to the repenter, the repentance is no more harmful than is any other pious fraud; but if one repents of actual immorality, or conceives of the sin as a literal offense, the results are more serious. Assuming that the sin was an actual evil, the sinner in repenting is turning back to the evil—'the sow returns to its wallowing in the mire'—and all the agony the repenter suffers merely makes a bad matter worse. The more sincere the repentance, the greater the probability of a repetition of the offense.

Repentance is recognized as a bad process for a child. Sensible parents no longer hold up to a child its errors and malfeasances and require him to consider how 'bad' he has been, for we know that this procedure does not help him. We need to remember that what goes for the child goes also for the adult. It is illuminating to our whole problem to note that the modern parent solicitously avoids the attitude of the arbitrary god who is offended by the child's behavior and wreaks vengeance upon him, either physically or by calling the child's attention to 'the way you have hurt mamma,' or 'how bad your conduct makes me feel.' Even attention to the misdemeanor and especially conversation about it is reduced to the minimum. Sensible parents avoid the godlike attitude, because it is bad for both the parent and the child. What we need to see is that God Himself (or Herself, if you choose) cannot take this 'godlike' attitude and get away with it. If God is really a superior being, He must be superior to that savage attitude.

The doctrine of the 'fatherhood' (or motherhood) of a god was a great advance over the concept of a divinity as a ravening wild beast or a magnificent cow or a great king. The father of early civilization, however, was an autocratic individual, with power of life and death over his offspring, requiring his children to respect him and honor him regardless of his actual respectability and honorableness. The status of the parent has much improved in modern times, but our gods lag behind. We find it well to abolish sins of child against parents, and sin in the religious sense is in need of abolition.

Theoretically, sin is a condition of a person that is dangerous, and hence something ought to be done about it. When we find something physically wrong with a person, we try to find a specific way in which to remedy the condition. Diagnosis involves two essential factors: (*a*) discovery of the cause or causes of the condition; (*b*) discovery of the nature of the condition itself. Diagnosis of sin has concerned itself with only the first of these two needs. The causes of sin have been assumed, in theory, but the actual condition of the sinner has not been determined. The remedy for sin accordingly rests on an incomplete diagnosis, in which one factor is assumed by theory, and the other factor is unknown. Fortunately, physical disease has been taken over from religion by science, but sin cannot be made a topic of scientific research, since sin involves the 'other world.'

The 'sense of sin' is intimately connected with what in the English language is called 'conscience,' which we must now examine. In certain ancient theories, such as those of the Pythagoreans, it was assumed that every human being was inhabited or possessed by a daimon of other-wordly origin and that this daimon guided the person's behavior. According to some who held this belief the possessing daimon 'spoke' to the human being it possessed, that is, it instilled thoughts into the person's mind. This daimon, of course, was immortal, and, at the death of the person to whom it was assigned, it entered into or took 'possession' of another human being, presumably one who had just been born. This doctrine has been confused often with the doctrine of the 'transmigration of the soul,' a doctrine held by some Hindu sects, from which the Pythagorean daimon-doctrine should be distinguished. Plato adopted the Pythagorean doctrine and invented the soul, which in his doctrine really 'transmigrated.' Aristotle modified the doctrine by making the daimon, which was an individual entity, into the *nous*, which was nonindividuated, although still other-wordly; and early Christianity adopted Aristotle's *nous* as the *Sancta Sophia* ('Holy Wisdom' or 'Holy Ghost').

The Pythagorean daimon appeared in later periods as the *conscience*—the 'still small voice,' the 'inner light,' which tells man the truth, and in especial points out to him the good and the evil. Man, accordingly, does not learn what is good and what is wrong; he merely has to listen to the divine voice within him, which tells him that which is right and that which is wrong.

Of course, evil daimons may possess men and give them false advice, but the belief in devil possession has waned, while the good daimon persists as the conscience, which not only gives man counsel, but also punishes him who violates its commands by causing mental suffering in the form of remorse.

The orthodox church is very chary of the authority of conscience, not denying specifically that there is such an entity or function, but preferring the doctrines and rules of the church to those which may be transmitted to a person by his conscience.   Various heretical sects, on the other hand, have endorsed the doctrine of the supremacy of the individual conscience, for, obviously, if there is a divinity or daimon in man capable of guiding him correctly and beneficiently, man ought to be so guided. These sects, however, endorse the supremacy of conscience, or the 'inner light' as the Quakers call it, more in theory than in practice; for neither the Quakers nor any other sect endorse or countenance an inner light that tells its host anything which conflicts with the official doctrines of the sect. A person whose conscience gives him advice which is opposed to the doctrines or practices of the church must leave the sect and find another with which his still small voice is in agreement. Authority, in all sects, is from the church and from God only through the church.

Unquestionably, there is a basis for the doctrine of the conscience daimon, but the basis has been much misunderstood. While man does not know 'instinctively,' or by revelation to him personally, what is right and what is wrong but has to learn to distinguish them, all men easily form the abstract distinction between right and wrong and can learn to apply the distinction to practical problems of life.

One man may think that a certain action (for example, strangling his parents when they become old) is right, while another man may think it is wrong. For the first man, it is a moral act, a duty; for the second it is a crime, a sin. The curious thing is that both men are applying the same abstract conceptions of duty and of right and wrong. The principles on which this conception should be applied vary greatly. There have been hedonists, epicureans, stoics, Socratics, and innumerable other groups, each group with its special explanations and each disdaining the explanations offered by the others, but the agreements are more striking than the differences. The basic agreement is on the point that whatever principles men do apply, there are principles which they *ought* to apply; in other words, duty is recognized by the conflicting schools.

The important question, in any practical situation, is: What action or system of action in this situation is right, and what action or system of action is wrong? The answer to this question can be found in only three ways: (*a*) One may learn by experience; (*b*) one may be guided by another person in whom one has confidence as regards his intelligence and his integrity; (*c*) one may follow the rules of the group, confident that group guidance is suitable for the situation. Conscience gives no adequate guidance in any situation, for being guided by conscience is either acting on routine habits that have become established, without inquiry as to whether the habits are proper or improper, or acting on impulses determined by the pattern of desires of the moment.

The abstract distinction between right and wrong is eternal, but the behavior and the thought that are wrong or right change from age to age and from group to group. That these changes are determined by economic changes is a sound assumption, but the topic belongs to the psychology of morals rather than to the psychology of religion.

6. The Problem of Evil.—Two concepts that are essentially connected with that of sin, are the concept of holiness and the concept of evil. The first of these concepts we have considered in its relation to sin in Chap. III and need add nothing further. The second concept we have touched upon in several places, but its importance, and the theories involved in various religious sects, warrant a more systematic presentation.

For ancient religion, there was no problem of evil. Evil was a fact in the world, and that was that. Physical evil was admitted, mental evil was admitted, and moral evil was admitted; and the question, "Why is there evil in the world?" was easily answered.

In the Mediterranean area, and probably in the Levant, the total world was looked upon as a product of evolution. Not only man evolved from lower animals, but the gods also were evolutionary products. This, at least, was the view of men of curiosity and intelligence, although the ordinary man perhaps did not concern himself with such questions any more than does the average man of today. For the common person, the world *is,* and the fact suffices. Insofar as the philosophers wondered about the occurrence of evil, they seem to have ascribed it to the imperfect stage of evolution that the world had reached. Some of the philosophers may have conjectured that eons of evolution would eventually produce a world in which evil would not occur, but the ones on record seem to have been more pessimistic. In any case, the world as it is, with its physical, mental, and moral evils, was assumed to be a product of natural forces operating under natural laws, and hence the responsibility for evil could not be placed on man or on the gods.

On the other hand, the theory or belief that the world was created by a god seems to leave the god responsible for the evils and imperfection of the world he created. This doctrine of creation of the world by a divinity seems to have appeared first in Babylonia; at any rate, it was adopted by Judaism and eventually by Christianity. Obviously, the divinity who created the world was deficient in some respect; he was either (a) not intelligent enough to foresee the type of world he was creating; (b) impotent to create a world that should be free from evil; or (c) morally defective, callous to the injustice that would appear in the world he created, as well as to the physical evils and the mental abnormalities that would appear in it.

We can discern in Judaism the growth of notions that conflict with one another: That God is all-wise and all-foreseeing; that He is all-powerful, a being to whom all things are possible; and that He is all-good, perfect morally. Christianity took over these conflicting notions of divinity, which were the most important contributions of Judaism, and Christian theologians ever since have been trying to explain how an all-wise, all-powerful and all-good God happened to create a world in which there is so much evil.

Some Christian sects have solved the problem by reverting to the Hindu belief that the world in which we live and move and have our being—the world of sensuous experience—is an illusion, that it does not really exist. Evil, therefore, is nonexistent, since it is a part of the illusory world of sense perception. Disease, murder, fractures, and injustice do not really exist; they are merely parts of an illusory world that man *thinks* exists. If we ask whether evil thoughts (thoughts of evils), which are admitted to exist, are not real evils, we are told that, since there is really no evil, there are no evil thoughts. This paradox suggests the story of the snake, which began at its tail and eventually swallowed itself completely, but it is no more illogical than the belief of other sects that an all-wise, omnipotent, all-good God created an evil world.

Another device often used to avoid the issue is pointing out that good and evil are relative to each other and that the evil is merely the lesser good. Hence, it is claimed, without evil there could be no good. While the relativity of good and evil is to be admitted, we nevertheless can point out a great range of evils—diseases, crimes, and injustices—without which this world would be a more satisfactory place and may contend that, for purposes of contrast, there would still be left a sufficient range from greater to lesser goods. The explanation, in short, robs the creator of his omnipotence, since he has been limited in respect to the possibilities of creation; it is a reversion towards the Greek view, in which the gods are bound by fate or necessity.

The only solution of the problem that avoids paradox is the one ascribed to Augustine. Augustine, while affirming the omnipotence of God, assumed that the divinity chose not to create the world all by himself, but has allowed man a share in the creation. God creates good, but man creates evil; so man, and not God, is responsible for the evil features of the cosmos. This cooperation of God with man is a part of the moral nature of God, for if man were allowed no share in creation he would not be a complete person, since persons have a share in their own determination. God, creating man in His image, made him a person and thus permitted man to create evil. This may not be a satisfactory solution of the problem created by the premise of an all-wise, omnipotent and all-good creator of the world; but it is the best any theologian has been able to think out.

CHAPTER XI

RELIGIOUS ORGANIZATION

1. Organization as a Differentium.[1]—When religion achieves an organization apart from political organization, then religion is distinguished by its organization from political conditions and processes. Such separation of the religious from the political, it is true, has never been actually achieved, but the organization of religion as religion enables us to distinguish it and almost to define it. The separation of religious organization from economic organization has not begun and probably will never be accomplished. Religion in its organized form has always been a business, and we may assume that it always will be; we shall later present facts which show that this is not necessarily a detriment to religion.

That the commercialization of religion is detrimental to religion is, of course, true. Religious 'rackets' appeared long before radio became used, but the radio has increased the number of such rackets and has increased their profits. Some religious programs that are broadcast are unmistakably serious efforts of honest people who are not trying to make profits from the broadcasts. These people should consider that they are lining themselves up, however unintentionally, with the racketeers and contributing to them a respectability that they do not merit. The scandalous religious racket-

---

[1] Both of the substantives in this heading need explanation. 'Organization' means primarily the 'process of organizing.' The word has come to be used also to designate the results of organizing, the 'condition of having been organized.' From that usage has developed the further usage of applying the term to an 'organized group.' It is difficult to avoid using the term in all three of these ways, except by circumlocution. We have used it in the three ways in the text. *Caveat lector.*

'Differentium' is a term that will not be found in dictionaries. One dictionary gives the word 'differentiator' with the meaning in which differentium is commonly used, namely, that which differentiates or which indicates a difference. While it is true that the plural term, 'differentia,' is used more often than is the singular, we make bold to employ the singular in spite of the cold shoulder turned by the lexicographers to both the singular and the plural forms of the term.

have done more to discredit religion than any one other feature of modern life. That 'the laborer is worthy of his hire' is admitted; but the use of religion for purposes of mere gain is quite another matter. The salaries of serious workers in the religious field are, of course, mere pitances as compared with the profits of the religious racketeers.

Economic features of group life are also political features, since it is always necessary for the government to regulate 'business' for the protection of the weak against the stronger. If we restrict, for present purposes, the concept of the 'political' to the legal, we can make clear the relation of religion to political organization and political procedures. In theory there is a separation of church and states in the United States, but in many states church property is by law freed from taxation. This remission of taxation throws a heavier burden on the taxpayers, who are supporting the churches by legal compulsion.

We have implied that religion as an independent factor in human affairs does not await complete separation of church and state, and this implication may be made explicit. Religion appears as religion, distinguishable from the secular features of the group, when religion begins to organize itself. From this point on, religion disengages itself more and more from the system of common praxes, although the disengagement may never be complete. Lacking a final criterion for religion, we must admit that activities of men, insofar as they are prescribed, controlled, or regulated by religious organizations, are religious activities. This stand may seem to be an evasion of the issue, for we still need to find a criterion for the distinction of a religious organization from secular organizations. Admittedly, the distinction changes from age to age; that which is religious in one stage of cultural development becomes secular in a later stage. That the secular in one stage becomes religious in a later stage is not so certain, and illustrations of changes in that direction are lacking.

For any place, for any period, nevertheless, we can soundly class any faith, ritual, or procedure that is prescribed or controlled by a religious organization as something definitely religious, a feature of religion. As for the criterion for a religious organization, we cannot deny that an organization that claims to be religious is a religious organization. This identification applies to local churches as well as to more comprehensive organizations. The principle of distinction, however, cannot be converted simply. Some organizations that are commonly classed as 'religious' claim that their principles and rituals do not constitute a religion but are a philosophy. In the same spirit, the promoters of some organizations for political propaganda have, in recent years, claimed that their organizations are not political but are 'educational.'

An outstanding case in point is that of the 'Rosicrucians,' who advertise their meetings in the newspapers as 'not religious.' This claim relieves religion of the onus of Rosicrucianism, and all persons interested in the maintenance of the dignity of religion should be grateful to the cults and cultists who disclaim the name of 'religion.'

The only difficulty in distinguishing religious organization from secular is found in situations in which the two are really identical. The organization that is primarily religious may dominate the political situation, as it did in some stages of the Jewish culture in Palestine; or the political organization may dominate the religious life, as it did in Greek cities in ancient times. In either case, the distinction between the religious and the secular is unimportant, since it is nonexistent.

If we designate the stage of development in which religion is a feature of common praxis as 'proto-religion' and reserve the name 'religion' for the stage in which religion begins to disentangle itself and commences to organize, we would have a criterion for religion, in that restricted meaning of the term, in its 'organization.' This criterion does not involve a characterization of the 'best religion' but accepts religion as it is in its various forms wherever and whenever it has appeared. This criterion, moreover, does not identify the basal or essential feature of religious, but merely supplies a basis for distinction between the religious and the secular.

2. The Growth of Religious Organization.—Insofar as we have, in the preceding chapters, analyzed religion and traced the development of its rituals and faiths, religion might be thought to be a feature of culture that is vital only insofar as it remains an integral part of the total cultural pattern. It might be claimed, indeed, that religion has no independent existence but is an element that is distinguishable in the cultural pattern only by analysis or abstraction. This claim is valid for what we have called 'proto-religion,' but an abstraction of that sort would fall short of the characteristics that we must attribute to religion. An abstraction or abstract entity could not be considered as capable of relinquishing functions that it had once assumed, nor of acquiring new functions. These changes of function have occurred in religion in its complete or organized stage.

Organization is essential for the life of religion in either stage, for growth depends on organization, and regression is fatal. When religion was an integral part of the political organization, it thrived and grew. With the passing of a culture, the religion involved in the culture passed also. As religion attained its own organization and insofar as it attained organization, its growth was promoted and its longevity assured. Even local organization, as at the various shrines, was helpful. The fundamental religion is social religion, which is primarily a matter of ritual, and the rituals are not well maintained without organization of the religious group. Organization, moreover, makes possible intercultural religion, which makes the life of religion independent of the life of any particular culture. When the religious elements in a culture (or the protoreligious elements) are organized by themselves, then religion steps forth as an institution capable of greater permanence and capable of the growth and modifications of function that are features of all living organisms. This does not ensure, however, that religion will endure forever.

The core about which religions are organized today is the concept of 'another world.' If the other-worldly beliefs and the sacraments and rituals that are deemed to be efficacious in the other world were taken away, most religions would disintegrate at once. We cannot conclude, however, that this core is essential and that religion emerged from proto-religion by organizing itself about this core. The facts are against this supposition. Instead of the emergence awaiting the appearance of the concept of another world, the religious features of the proto-religious period began to be organized, and this organization promoted the development of the concept in question.

The beginnings of religious organization in the Mediterranean world were local. Rituals were established in particular places, at which eventually shrines were placed. Attendants at the shrine (priests and/or priestesses) were installed, the selection of these attendants being at first a matter controlled by the local groups. We may well assume that in other areas also the initial organization was local and that the more comprehensive organization developed later.

The growth of religious organization seems to follow the same pattern as that of growth of political organization. Smaller groups are combined into larger groups, and these again are combined in still larger groups. Even the disintegration of religions into sects is sometimes offset by later recombinations. The organization of sects into greater bodies is an interesting feature of the growth of religious organizations, and this may go further, as in the union of 'Methodists South,' 'Methodists North,' and 'Methodist Protestants.' Incipient organizations of the present day even include sects that are rated as different religions, and, although such inclusive organizations are thin in their present constitutions, they are similar to the first stages of political combination. The organizations for cooperation of Jews and Christians for the promotion of purposes common to both is like the organization of nations by treaty; whether it will eventuate in actual federation later cannot be predicted.

The consolidation of independent churches into several greater Christian churches, in the early period of Christianity, was a somewhat different matter. This was a process of absorption, by which one group gained domination over other groups. Objection to loss of authority and fear of domination have been greater obstacles to consolidation of Christian sects in modern times than have been differences in creeds and rituals; and we may well suspect that this objection was more important in preventing the union of Christians in one great church than were the doctrinal points that served as obstacles.

The form of organization in religion is comparable to political organization again in being sometimes democratic and sometimes aristocratic. Some sects seem to thrive without a 'hierarchy' as the aristocratic and controlling class in religion is called; while others have a typically political organization with priests, above whom are bishops under the rule of archbishops, with a pope or a grand patriarch at the top. Even in the most democratic sects there is a minor aristocracy represented by deacons, elders, and trustees.

Some sects are, in theory, local groups only, but the churches of these sects have found it advisable to combine with others, who maintain somewhat the same creeds and somewhat similar rituals in "associations' or 'assemblies.' It is not to be assumed, accordingly, that the local churches of the sects of the 'congregational' type are as independent in practice as they are in theory.

At present, most religious organizations, from the local churches to the more comprehensive associations, have their written constitutions and their bodies of laws of procedure, just as do political groups. The organization, in short, is formal. These laws are subject to amendment and revision, and reference is made to them at any important point in procedure. In earlier periods, when conventions were accepted without documentary formulation, the organization was at least as formal as it is at present. In ancient times, when the cults were still local, the rules regulating the rituals and the rules for the selection of priests or priestesses were as rigid and as strictly maintained as they would have been if written.

We have indicated in Chap. IV that when two or more divinities by the same name were installed in the same region there was no organic relation between the cults of these divinities. It should be noted, however, that although there was no formal organization of the cults into a greater cult, there was in many instances an informal organization, the rituals being somewhat similar in spite of their differences. For example, where shrines of Asklepios were established, there were usually serpents in the temple or in some part of the sacred precincts.

Since each local cult was at first autonomous, the rules governing each shrine were enforced by the local population. A person violating the rules would be punished, perhaps killed by the patrons of the shrine. Stories in which the divinity of the shrine is said to have punished the violator can be assumed to be legends that grew up about the punishment of the offender by the inhabitants of the region near the shrine or by the assembled worshipers. That in some cases the citizens appealed to an oracle to find out what they should do to the offender is indicated by many of the legends reported by Pausanias. This method of law enforcement ('lynch law') was not highly satisfactory, and, when cities or the regional governments assumed control, laws were enacted prohibiting the infraction of the rules of the shrines and enforced politically.

That there were conflicts between local authority and civic authority in the period of reorganization may well be supposed; at least, there were problems of local versus civic authority that required adjustment. The civic laws eventually determined the installation of new shrines and especially the introduction of new divinities. In Athens, the selection of priests or priestesses became a political matter, although the established traditions that assigned priority to certain families from whom the attendants were selected were not altered and the established rituals were not interfered with.

In some areas the religious organization assumed functions that were primarily political, functions extending further than the protection of existing cults and the regulation of the introduction of new cults. In Judea, before the Hebrews came into existence, the priest of Salem (the later Jerusalem) was also a king and assumed supreme administrative functions as well as control of religion. It was natural, therefore, that when Egypt captured Syria, the priest-king should be made the viceroy of Egypt for that region. Later, the religious organization of the Hebrews succeeded, after long turmoil, in eliminating all cults except that of the one male God. This was not regulation of cults, but their suppression.

The organization of local cults, even their informal organization, definitely begins the process of taking religion out of the system of praxis—the transition from proto-religion to religion in the proper sense of the term, giving religion recognition as an institution distinguishable, partially at least, from other institutions. The incipient organization makes religion more enduring. If a priest dies or is incapacitated, that is a mere incident; another priest is installed and the function of the organization continues.

At the same time, religion in another form may retain its place in praxis. The rituals of agriculture, animal husbandry, and other departments of economic life still go on. The cult of the divinity, organized at and about its temple, may become of greater importance in the praxes, but they are not completely dependent on the religious organization. The rituals of the Thesmophoria, for example, were conducted by the women of Athens in connection with the cult of Demeter, established at Athens and at Eleusis, but the total ceremonies were not completed in those places. The barley still had to be planted in the fields, and the planting was a part of the ritual. What we may call 'churches' had been established, but religion was not completely under church control. Even the organization of religion under civic control, as the rituals of the Thesmophoria were organized, does not necessarily eliminate proto-religion.

The various rituals conducted by the Greeks in their later periods were really rituals of the body politic—civic rituals, although religious. Proto-religion persisted, not only in economic practices and in social praxis, but also in family life.   The rituals of birth, death, and burial were carried on in their traditional forms.   Incense burning in dwellings continued, although not regulated by organized religion.   Burning of incense in theaters, however, was a social praxis that included proto-religion.

Religious organization in the Greek world, as contrasted with the organization in the Levantine areas, apparently never developed further than to a mild civic control over religious cults and the institution of civic religious rituals.   The priests of the various cults were never organized into a total priesthood.   Such organization would not be easy in an open polytheism.   If the state, represented by an autocratic king, controls religion, it may impose an organization that unifies the various cults.   On the other hand, priests of several cults, working for their common interests, may effect an ecclesiastical union of a sort.   Both of these factors seem to have cooperated in Egypt and in Babylonia, where the various cults became somewhat related to one another, albeit somewhat artificially related.   It is to be noted, however, that in these countries the priests were not responsible to a specific ecclesiastical head, but the priests of each cult were responsible to the king alone.

Ecclesiastical organization in which various cults are brought into a centralized system, which is relatively autonomous but under civic control, was first achieved by the Romans.   At the head of this organization was the *Pontifex Maximus*, but in the days of the Republic he was under the control of the Senate and, under the Empire, was responsible to the Emperor.   The several Catholic churches, eastern and western, developed under the aegis of the Roman Empire when it was centered at Constantinople and patterned their organization on that of the Roman pagan system. But since only a single cult was involved in each of these churches, and because the Roman organization was extended into a hierarchy, these churches became stronger than was the pagan model.   In these churches which have survived, the hierarchies are territorially constituted.   At the head is a Pope or a Grand Patriarch.   The larger territorial divisions are ruled by archbishops and divided into smaller areas over which bishops preside.   The bishoprics are subdivided into parishes, each in charge of a priest.   The organizations are strengthened by consistories, councils, and other groups of high ecclesiastics.

Since the Reformation, or, as the Roman Catholics call it, the 'Western Schism,' the Protestant churches have maintained different types of formal organization. The Episcopal bodies, such as the Church of England and the Methodist Episcopal Church, have adhered to the Roman type of organization. Calvinistic churches, such as the Presbyterian, have for the most part maintained an organization without bishops and archbishops, in which the factors of coordination and subordination are controlled by a hierarchy of synods and assemblies. One or more offshoots from the Methodist group followed, for a time, the Presbyterian type of organization, but are now being absorbed by the Methodist Episcopal Church.

The churches in which the local units are theoretically autonomous are not, as we have pointed out, so autonomous in practice. There has indeed been a considerable diversity in creeds and in rules of church discipline among the local Baptist churches and a similar diversity among the local Congregational churches. The rituals, in churches of these denominations, have been significantly similar to those of other churches of the same denomination. The regional and national associations of these denominations have accomplished to some extent the control which is exercised by the hierarchies of other denominations.

It would seem that the differences between Christian sects in respect to formal organization are largely differences in emphasis. The Catholic churches represent one extreme, in which the emphasis is on centralization and local groups are autonomous only in minor matters. Protestant churches of the congregational type, in which the emphasis is on local autonomy, actually are restricted by the organizations of local and national assemblies, associations, and societies. Between these extremes, the range of types of organization is similar to those of other modern religions such as Islam. In Hinduism, the range appears to be even greater than in Christianity, including for some regions and some religions the extreme local autonomy of the early Greek religions.

In summary, we may say that even in the local stage of religious organization, an institution was developing that began to stand out from the mass of common praxes. This institution has been able to maintain its earlier relations with praxes, economic and political, but, being otherwise not limited to any specific functions, it has been able to change its functions and its detailed activities. By developing a specialized personnel it became a true 'social organism' or a group of such organisms, and, like all organisms, it has had two main purposes or aims. The primary purpose of an organism, whether from its own point of view or—in the case of animals— the views of critics, is to maintain its life. The secondary purpose is growth, the expansion of the body and the strengthening of its functions. All other considerations are, for any organism, no more than tertiary. Religion, like any other organism, will cling to its established functions or shift its functions, according as the retention or the change of functions is more favorable to the life and growth of the organism itself.

3. **Practical Aspects of Organization.**—Social organizations are subject to conditions that are common to all types. In discussing the conditions under which religious organisms can flourish, we are discussing conditions to which all social organisms are subject. Conversely, in describing the conditions for social organizations in general, we are discussing the conditions under which religious organizations operate.

An organization requires the expenditure of time and energy on the part of one or more persons to keep it alive and in operation. In some cases the work may be done, for a time, by all the members cooperatively, but organizations operating on this basis do not often live long. In any large organized group, control and direction are vested in a smaller group, which acts in behalf of the larger group. This inner ring of the organization may be self-perpetuating or its members may be elected by the members of the larger group. It may act autocratically, like the management group of an industrial concern, or it may be required to have all its actions and determinations approved by the members of the larger group. Such reviews by the total membership are seldom complete, and the inner ring almost always acts autocratically.

In most cases a single person within the directorial group exercises the major functions of direction and control, as chairman, moderator, president, or executive secretary, or with some other title. In such cases the responsibility rests openly upon the executive officer and he cannot evade it. Where a board of directors or trustees is jointly responsible, the blame for wrong actions and decisions can seldom be laid at the door of any particular member of the board.

The relation of an executive officer to other members of an inner ring or directorate may be made clear by consideration of the functioning of a committee. Whether this be a committee of a religious group, a scientific society, or an industrial organization, the functioning is much the same. The chairman of the committee must study the problem assigned to the committee and lay out the procedure for the committee. He may perhaps appoint subcommittees to consider various parts of the total problem and must attend to many details before the committee is called together. When the committee meets, the chairman must preside and must steer the deliberations so that the committee sticks to its task. He must see that personal antagonisms are minimized, while fair opportunity is given each member to express his opinions. Before the committee meets, the chairman will have conferred with individual members to make use of their abilities in laying out the program. All this requires much time and labor on the part of the chairman, but, unless the chairman does the lion's share of the work, the committee will not do its work successfully. The members of the committee give time and labor at the meeting and individually contribute beforehand, but responsibility rests properly on the chairman.

In large organizations, the executive officer assumes the major responsibility and the major load of work. He may assign parts of routine to secretaries, vice-presidents, and other assistants, but he must maintain oversight of the total operation for which he is responsible. Since the total work may take the whole time of one or more persons, it is common in organizations that are nonprofit groups, such as scientific societies, to employ salaried secretaries, and the executive also sometimes is salaried.

Organizations, as can be readily seen, are expensive in terms of the work required of those who are competent to direct them, and competent directors and executives can be obtained only if they profit by their work. In plain language, no organization can live unless somebody makes a profit out of it. The profit is not necessarily monetary, but the recompense must be something that satisfies the desires, or some desire, of the worker. The prestige or preeminence that results from the holding of an important position may be a sufficient recompense. The position in which one may dominate an important undertaking or a large group of people, giving scope to one's direction of affairs, may satisfy the desire for preeminence. There is no doubt that the 'bossing of a job' satisfies the desire of many persons.

Sometimes, on the other hand, a position of authority is accepted as a matter of duty and the only recompense desired is that which accrues from the fulfillment of duty.

Conformity desire alone is not sufficient to ensure the life of an organization. There must be a leader, or a succession of leaders, to whose leadership the group can conform. Specialization of function has long been admitted by group psychologists to be an essential factor in organization of complex groups. Joint or cooperative action, in which each member of the group has the same function, does not maintain the group organization for any lengthy period.

The persistence of the early local religious organizations was due to the appointment of priests and priestesses who specialized on certain religious functions. For the groups participating in the mysteries, the specialization was more complex. There were officials forming a hierarchy, from the grand master of ceremonies down to the torchbearer. This specialization has been carried over into the hierarchies of the Christian sects and has been strengthened through the centuries.

Group organization depends for its success on finding persons who are competent in the special functions demanded by the organization. In this respect, religious organizations have been signally fortunate during the last thirty centuries at least. The priests and priestesses in the early stages of religious development appear to have been the most intelligent and able men and women in their groups. Of course, intelligence and competence in one stage of civilization are not to be judged by standards set in later periods. Some requirements for the priesthood of some religions were for the strengthening of the church organization. Celibacy is an illustration of such requirements. Standards of morality were not high in early periods, but the demands for morality, devotion to human welfare, and for sincerity of faith have progressively increased. In modern times high standards of cultural education have been prescribed by most Christian sects for candidates for the ministry.

Celibacy of priests, priestesses, and other devotees such as monks and nuns is a source of strength to a religious group or organization. Members of an organization, and especially officials of the organization, are efficient in proportion as their interests and energies are devoted to the purposes of the organization and not diverted to other purposes. If a priest has a family or a wife, his interest in the family or wife detracts from his interest in the church, and a certain amount of his energy must be devoted to caring for the dependents. If he has no family his interest is more singly devoted to the church; his energies are more fully applied to the church work; and at his death any property he may have accumulated is more likely to be conveyed to the church. For the priestess, marriage is at least as distracting as it is for the priest.

Parents, brothers and sisters, and other relatives may be as distracting as are wives and children; but no Christian church has adopted the policy which is formulated in the gospels of Matthew (23: 9) and Luke (9: 59–62, 14: 26, 18: 29–30) as the precept of Jesus to abandon parents, brothers, and sisters. The force of the Hebrew and Greek respect for parents and for fraternal ties has been too strong to permit the adoption of the policy.

That mercenary priests have appeared in all ages is admitted, and we must admit that religious racketeers are all too common today. This does not counter our generalization that the priesthood during the important periods of religious development have been the best persons of their generations, the most intelligent, the most competent, and the most humanitarian. In the pagan days, priests and priestesses were not merely of aristocratic families; they were of the intellectual élite. We have emphasized the fact that medicine began in religion, under priestly control, but human welfare owes much in other lines to the priesthood. The development of agriculture, animal husbandry, navigation, and the fine arts began in religion or proto-religion. To opine that the rituals associated with economic processes were merely restrictive is to adopt an erroneous opinion. The sounder conclusion is that economic progress owes much to the leadership of the priestly class. The ancient legends concerning the introduction of new foods, of improved methods of growing foods, and of preparing them are of course myths. These myths, however, are religious myths and indicate the influence of religious leaders in the economic development.

The tabu on slaughtering of domestic animals except as a religious ritual of sacrifice was, of course, restrictive. But it restricted the wanton eating of domestic animals in times of occasional plenty, and so protected the flocks and herds and promoted their increase. To whom can we attribute this restriction, which was a feature of all peoples who maintained domestic animals until the flocks and herds became abundant? It can be attributed only to the heads of the proto-religion centering around the domestic animals—the priests of the cults of the domestic animals.

Similarly, human sacrifice was helpful in reducing murder, just as sacrifice of domestic animals was a protection to the flocks and herds. Making the killing of a person a religious ceremony, with elaborate ritual, apparently was a factor in the making of human life sacred.

Sacrifice of infants and young children to pagan gods undoubtedly helped to reduce the danger that they would be killed and eaten by their parents, since the life of a child is made sacred by dedicating children to a divinity. Children have been eaten by savages and barbarians, such as the Australian Bushmen and the European Nordics in the early centuries of the Christian Era, whenever the food supply was insufficient. Improvement of the food supply was, of course, the main protection for children; but the custom of eating children might persist, and infant sacrifice helped to break the habit. So far as we know, paidophagy was a private matter, and among the child-eating groups there was no ritual sacrifice of children.

It has been charged that in modern times the ministry of Christian sects has deteriorated in personnel; that men do not enter the ministry because of humanitarian interests and sincerity of faith in such great percentages as in the past, but enter because they are looking for easy jobs. If the actually difficult jobs these men undertake at low wages is not sufficient evidence to the contrary, other considerations are convincing, and we shall adduce one from a field in which we claim competence.

Few ministers receive any technical training in psychology. If they get any psychology in college it is of the archaic sort or the revival of archaic principles in the new terminologies of various German 'schools of psychology.' These ministers, when they enter their field of work, are confronted by many problems of maladjustment which may be called 'social' or 'personal' but which really are both. We find that the ministers handle these cases well, after they have had some experience, and that the 'patients' fare better in the hands of ministers than they do in the hands of psychiatrists. Obviously, these ministers have intelligence (learning ability) of high order; they are able to learn by experience to handle maladjusted persons although their explanations of their techniques are usually not sound. The priesthood and ministry, it appears, is still recruited from the ranks of the intellectually élite.

Cases that are really serious must be turned over to institutions for the mentally disordered, and organic psychoses must be treated by men competent in physical medicine. This is the procedure followed by ministers, psychologists, and commercial psychiatrists.

It should be noted that the clergy of some sects do receive training for dealing with problems of maladjustment. This is true of Roman Catholic priests who belong to certain monastic orders, who are trained in the techniques of receiving confessions, granting absolution, and giving advice. In these functions the priests are thought by some to be more intelligent and more successful than are the psychoanalysts, who also specialize in confession, absolution, and advice but are more limited by their armchair theories than are the priests by their theology.

Organization is not an excrescence on religion, not a detrimental feature of religion. We cannot separate religious organization from religion itself except in abstract thinking. Organization is the psyche of religion, its life principle. Without organization, social religion is impossible; and without social religion, personal religion, which is but the shadow of social religion, would perish. The church is not, and through the ages has not been, religious organization applied to religion or abstracted from religion. The church is religion, organized and vitalized.

Organization of religion strengthens the cultural group in which religion is organized, insofar as the religious group and the total cultural group is coextensive. Integrating a group is the binding together of the members of the group, which increases the group spirit, the consciousness of belonging to the group. This increase in group integration, when it becomes established in one aspect of group life, facilitates cooperation of group members in other group functions.

The economic features of a cultural group are necessarily diversified, since different members of the group specialize in different economic processes of production, manufacture, distribution, and transportation, and conflicting interests tend to make the group fall apart along the lines of cleavage. Organized religion tends to unify the group and reduce the danger of disintegration. A common language and common idiom is an integrating factor, and so is political organization; but neither of these is as influential as is a common religion for the total group.

Religious divisions are sources of group disintegration. Diverse sects that have more in common than they have in contrast may not be troublesome, but, if the differences are more important than the agreements, the group is weakened. Although the various Hindu sects cooperate as well as do the various Protestant sects of Christianity, the antagonism of Moslems and Hindus is the great disruptive force in India that has made it impossible for India to become a unified nation. The growth, in the United States, of strong religious sects that are antagonistic to one another has been looked upon by some persons as a serious threat to national unity for the future. Religion is always a part of culture, and each segment of a culture has its effects on the integration or disintegration that may be produced by the other segments.

In many features an organized group corresponds, as we have suggested, to an animal organism, to an individual animal. If the group is well organized the various members are integrated into a whole in which there is specialization of function, coordination of segments of the whole, and vitality for the total group. Minor injuries and decays may occur, but if the injuries are not to the working parts, the damage may be repaired. In the animal organism, widespread injury to the muscular system, to the nervous system, or to one of the protective and sustaining mechanisms makes the continuation of life precarious.

Animal organisms have their period of growth, youth, maturity, and decadence, and continuity of life for a long period is contingent on the transmission of the vital spark of progeny. This also is true of religious organizations, and the sequences of religions in which the new religion is enate from the old correspond to the successions of animal generations.

The integrating factors in the animal organism are various. The nervous system is essentially integrative in function, but the hormones produced by the ductless glands are also integrative. What we have suggested is that in the social organism religion is one of the important integrating factors.

CHAPTER XII

INITIATION, PROSELYTISM, AND CONVERSION

1. **Admission to Group Membership.**—In the ordinary course of events, children born into a group grow up into membership, and the personnel of the group is thus maintained and expanded. This is the normal procedure in groups of all sorts: political groups, castes, and religious groups. The child of a citizen of any nation becomes a citizen of that nation. The child of a noble is potentially noble. And the child of a person of low social caste is of that caste. So, at present, the child of a Roman Catholic normally becomes a member of that sect, the child of a Democrat becomes a Democrat, and the child of Methodist parents becomes a Methodist. In modern cultures the religious status is distinct from the social-economic, and entrance into full citizenship is distinct from both. In ancient civilization and in barbaric cultures, these distinctions did not exist, and they do not exist among savages today. The civic, political, social-economic, and religious status in these cultures were and are organically related so that the achievement of the status in the group was and is a single event.

The normal entrance of an individual into the group has two stages in all cultures: acceptance and identification, which occurs in infancy, and initiation or admission to group membership, which occurs later. In cultures in which the religious, social-economic, and political status are differentiated, these stages occur at different times. In the undifferentiated cultures, the acceptance for one is acceptance for all, and initiation likewise is a single process.

Acceptance as a potential group member and initiation into full membership, since they are social procedures, require formality or ritual in most cultures. Under certain conditions the steps may be informal, but formality always arises as cultural conditions progress. Political acceptance, for example, is marked by the certification of birth. In earlier periods in the United States this formality was not observed, but it has now become a requirement, as could have been predicted. Full citizenship is not marked by a ritual or formality, but at present is established by law on an age basis, eighteen for females, twenty-one for males.

Religious acceptance—acceptance as potential members of the religious organization—is the ritual called 'christening' in Christian sects and the ritual of circumcision for male infants among Jews. Admission to full membership is 'confirmation.' These rituals are carryovers from more ancient periods, and the relative neglect of the female by the Jews is a similar carryover.

Acceptance of the infant, in ancient and savage cultures, had two implications. One was the acknowledgment, by the father, of his paternity and of his intention to let the child live and to assume responsibility for it. The other was that of the first step in group membership. Out of the rituals grew the notion that they promoted in some way the welfare of the child, but the rituals themselves, as public acknowledgments, were the matters of basic importance.

These rituals of acceptance and initiation have been practically universal. The *Amphidromia* at Athens, in which the newborn infant was carried around the domestic fire by the father on the run, was probably paralleled by other rituals among other Greek peoples concerning which we have little information. The couvade among savages in various parts of the world, in which the father of the newborn child 'lies-in' like a woman in childbirth, is another of the vast array of rituals of acceptance, whatever interpretations may have been added here and there. In European peasant cultures, features of the ancient rituals of public acceptance have been carried over into the christening ritual.

In the cultures in which religion was not differentiated, as an institution, from other features of the cultures, initiation marked the transition from childhood, in which the individual was a charge of the group, to the status of membership in the group. The admission might not be complete at the time; the youth became a warrior, but an apprentice warrior, who still had to establish his full status by his prowess ('winning his spurs'); age also was a matter of importance, and the warrior achieved *counselor* status when he was fully matured. Sexual intercourse was commonly permitted after initiation, but in some groups marriage came later.

Both men and women, however, at initiation, were admitted to the knowledge and lore of their elders and in most respects were made religiously adult. Among savages, the youths are made privy to the religious frauds employed to intimidate the women (such as the use of the bull roarer, which produces what the women are told is the 'voice of a god' or 'spirit'); the girls are instructed in whatever the women are allowed to know, and in some groups are taught matters which are concealed from the men. So today, after confirmation, boys and girls are not full-fledged members of the Christian sects into which they have been initiated, with adult responsibilities, but they have privileges that are restricted by the need of further maturation and further education.

In regard to the conditions and rituals of initiation in ancient civilizations, we have little information. The class of *ephebi* among the Athenians (Gardner and Jevons, *Manual of Greek Antiquites*, pp. 311-312; 635-637), however, seems to have corresponded to the class of apprentice warriors among some savages, while the cruel treatment to which Spartan youths were subjected was very like the physical ordeals to which savage boys are subjected at initiation.

Religious groups today, Christian and non-Christian, are continued normally, as were the culture groups that were institutionally undifferentiated, by the acceptance of infants into the group and their later confirmation as group members. Religious sects, however, in modern times often expand through the proselyting of persons to the sect, a process which was almost unknown in ancient times until shortly before the Christian Era.

Initiation in savage or civilized groups is literally a 'beginning' of adult life, not an admission to the fullest adult status. The initiate becomes a member of the group in an important way, but there may be several further steps to be taken, or grades to be attained, before he can participate in the organic life of the group in the fullest way, and especially before he can take part in the determination of group policy. These grades may be matters of time or of achievement or may be determined by choice of the group members. In some savage cultures, a certain time must elapse after initiation before the person is permitted to enter the ranks of the married folk. The warrior must demonstrate his prowess by slaying enemies to attain higher warrior status. A certain age must be reached before the warrior can become a counselor. Fathering of sons advances the status of the father, and a further advance is made when the sons become warriors. Social status is advanced also by the accumulation of property.

In civilized groups, the man of twenty-one is eligible for election to office, but he seldom will be elected until he has advanced in age to the point at which he is considered mature. While definite age limits are set only for the highest offices, the requirement is nevertheless effective practically for all offices—political or religious. There are usually no rituals marking these further stages of advancement in the group, except insofar as election may be considered a ritual.

Initiation rituals in savage groups, and presumably in primitive groups, involves the bestowal of badges indicating the new status, and these badges or signs have often been mutilations of the genital organs. Circumcision of males is one of the savage rituals, and in some groups girls also are still circumcised. Other forms of mutilation are employed in other groups. None of these mutilations are of any practical value unless the operation of subincision of the male has some degree of contraceptive effect. Circumcision may not have been detrimental in groups wearing little clothing, although it is deleterious in more fully clothed groups. The reasons for mutilations and for the predilection for mutilation of the genitals must be sought in other directions.

Mutilations are badges that are permanent, and the infliction of these operations on boys and girls marks them for life as belonging to the group, since all adult males or females in the group bear the evidences of the same mutilations. The association of puberty with entrance into adult life and the permission of sexual intercourse, which often is conferred by initiation, make the mutilation of the genitals an obviously symbolic procedure. The particular mutilation does not matter so long as it is conventional and universal for the group.

Genital mutilation began among savages as an initiation ritual and was introduced through Egypt among Levantine peoples. Eventually the infliction of the mutilation was advanced, by the Jews and by some Arabs, from the entrance into adult life to infancy, becoming a ritual of acceptance instead of a ritual of initiation, while still remaining an ineradicable badge of group membership. The elimination of circumcision of females by semicivilized peoples appears to have been due partly to the inferior position of females among barbarous peoples and partly to the custom in these groups of taking wives from other groups, either by capture or by purchase. At any rate, the females were not deemed suitable for group marking. The advancing of the mutilation from the age of admission to the age of acceptance as an infant was undoubtedly motivated by practical considerations, since the immediate effects of the operations are less serious at the earlier age. The later effects are more serious. Furthermore, the connection between puberty and adult status seems to be less close among barbarians than among savages.

2. Proselyting and Proselytism.—'Conversion' is a term that in common usage is applied to a variety of changes in religious status, but for convenience we shall restrict it to changes that occur within a religious group or sect—changes for which we have no other term. Conversion in this sense will be considered in the following section, although some of the changes that we shall discuss here shade into conversion, in other senses of the term.

Persons who apostatize from the religions to which they have previously adhered and join other cults are technically 'proselytes,' and the inducing of persons to become proselytes is 'proselyting.' The abstract term for such changes from one religion to another is 'proselytism.' The emphasis, in these terms, is on the adherence to the second religion rather than on the desertion of the first—an emphasis that is in accord with the derivation of the terms from a Greek word, which means 'newcomer.' In popular usage, the terms 'proselyte' and 'convert' are interchangeable, but discrimination is sometimes useful in technical discussions.

Proselytism occurs in several typical forms. (*a*) A group of people as a whole may abandon its previous religion and adopt another. This is sometimes described as 'group conversion.' (*b*) Individuals in a group may become detached from the religion of the group and accept the religion of a foreign group. This is usually a result of 'missionary' work on the part of persons who often, but not always, are foreigners who deliberately induce or solicit persons in the group to become proselytes. (*c*) Individuals from one group who live in another group or who travel extensively in the second group area may desert the religion of their original group and adopt the religion of the group among whom they become domiciled or among whom they sojourn. (*d*) Within a group in which several religions are represented, individuals may pass from one religion to another. Within a given religion there may be proselyting from one sect of the religion to another sect. These two types of proselytism cannot well be distinguished, since the difference between two sects of the same religion often is as sharp as the difference between two cults classed as different religions.

a. Group conversion may occur as a progressive development from proselyting of individuals, the number of proselytes gradually increasing until finally a whole tribe, nation, or people has become proselyted. This was apparently the course of events in the Christianizing of the Germans and Scandinavians, a course that was accomplished with relative rapidity in spite of the efforts of religious leaders, who opposed the change and who invented a whole mythology in order to have something to counteract the attraction that the Christian legends had for the people.

In some cases, however, groups as a whole have been proselyted without going through the process of spreading the new religion from individuals through the group. Such group proselytism appears always to have been effected by authority of rulers or by brute force. The conversion of the Khazars to Judaism is an illustration of proselyting by edict of rulers. The chiefs of the Khazars having decided that their tribesmen should abandon their savage religion and adopt Judaism, the tribesmen did as they were ordered to do. The conversion of the Persians to Islam is an illustration of the second sort. They were ordered by their Arab conquerors to become Mohammedans 'or else,' so those unable to escape from Persia had to choose between Islam or death. Similar pressure was applied to Jews in Spain by the Roman Catholic Church, and many Jews became Christians—outwardly at least—in order to escape torture and death.

Group conversion, whether it occurs by the spreading process or as a mass proselytism, is seldom a complete abandonment of the old religion, which persists in different degrees in different cases. The extreme of persistence of the old is illustrated in the spread of Buddhism in Asiatic countries. In Burma, for example, a superficial Buddhism was added to the old religion, and the image of the Buddha, who had little regard for gods, was added as another god in the temples. In Japan, insofar as Buddhism was adopted, it did not displace Shinto. Chinese Buddhists do not give up Taoism or Confucianism, however much they may revere the Buddhist scriptures. In Thibet, where the ancient religion (Lamaism) is so closely related to Hinduism that we may well suspect the Thibetan origin of Hinduism, the last Buddha, insofar as he is accepted, appears to be considered as merely another lama. In all of these cases, if we should apply the concept of 'assimilation,' we should have to say that Buddhism has been assimilated, more or less superficially, to the ancient religions.

At the other extreme, original religions may become assimilated to a new religion that absorbs features of the old. Christianity spread through such assimilation of pagan religions. Pagan festivals were adopted and made into Christian festivals because it was impossible to win the pagans away from them. As pagan feasts, they were obstacles to completion of the proselyting process, but, made into Christian festivals with interpretation in terms of Christian doctrines and legends, they attached the people to the church. Thus the anniversary of the birth of Jesus was finally established at the winter solstice, which all pagans celebrated as the time of the return of the sun to again enliven the world. And so the Yule festival of pagan Europe became the Christmas festival, in which were retained the symbols of the boar's head and the Yule log, the tree (which was significant in the Levant as well as in Europe), and the red trimmings representing the blood of victims. The Christian Easter festival corresponds to world-wide festivals and rituals of the rebirth of vegetation and the planting of seed and required no change of date, since the earliest stories of the Resurrection placed it at the time of the Jewish Passover. The death of the god, however, in pagan legends, occurred in the fall, not in the spring.

Harvest festivals are world-wide in paganism and are celebrated in Europe with ancient rituals somewhat modified. Our Thanksgiving Day is a form modified by the Puritans, who transplanted the Harvest festival to America. Other festivals of the church that are little regarded in America—such as Whitsuntide, St. John's Day, and many others—are celebrated in European countries with many features of the old pagan rituals, but given Christian interpretations. All Souls' Day has become our bawdy Halloween, but among European peasants it has not lost its religious significance.

These assimilations and the persistence of symbols to which we have earlier referred are illustrations of the continuity of religion. Rituals and symbols are carried over from older religions to newer, and it has been opined by scholars that conversion of a people as contrasted with the conversion of individuals does not occur without this assimilation of the old to the new and could not occur otherwise.

The assimilations, with reinterpretations, go further. The gods and demigods of paganism have not been displaced by European Christianity but have been taken over and reinterpreted as saints. In some cases the identifications are simple: the Zeuses of the mountaintops in Greece have become St. Elias; St. Hippolyte is obviously the demigod Hippolytus. In other cases the saint appears to be a revised version, not of one pagan god but of a synthesis of several, as in the case of St. George of England and St. Denys of France. The divine Mother persists as a somewhat confusing synthesis of ancient mother divinities of the East and the West; and it would seem that Demeter, the mother of the virgin Kore, has some relation to St. Anne. Even pagan daimons are retained, for St. Nicholas (vulgarized as 'Santa Claus') is a transformation of the old Greek *agathos daimon* ('Good Spirit').

The great company of saints has of course been increased by the canonization of holy men and women, and the gods of paganism have been reduced to the rank of daimons. The tendency of Protestantism is to eliminate the concept of saints, except as a title of respect for persons who excite our admiration, and we can well predict that in the course of time the pagan gods and their analogues will disappear, but the elimination will be a slow process.

The divergence of sects in religions that have proselyted peoples rapidly is largely due to the original religions from which the groups were proselytes. This is apparent in the Mohammedan sects and is represented in the various 'heretical' sects of early Christianity. Proselytes from one religion retain features of their original cult, while proselytes from other cults have different features to assimilate to the new religions.

The extent to which features of an old religion survive in a new religion adopted by a group depends on the stage of development the old religion had reached, and perhaps on its antiquity, for man clings to the things of the past. The carry-over is mainly determined by ritual, for man gives up doctrines more easily than rituals and old rituals can always be reinterpreted in terms of new doctrines. The doctrines, however, are not immune to modification from the rituals. If Christianity had remained a heretical Jewish sect, its doctrines would undoubtedly have been different from those actually adopted by the church in its formative period. While we might assume that the rituals of the Christian sects that are called 'liberal' are simpler and thinner than the rituals of more orthodox sects because the doctrines are different, it is probable that the simplification of rituals had its effects on the simplification of doctrines. These liberal sects to a large extent have stemmed from Puritanism, and Puritanism began as a reformation of ritual rather than a reformation of doctrine. The Protestant Reformation, in fact, was primarily a reformation of ritual and of ecclesiastical procedure, in which the admission of the membership to the Eucharist in full participation in both elements (bread and wine) was an important point.

b. Proselytism of the 'heathen' by missionaries is a somewhat different matter, since the proselytes remain a minority group within the larger group, in which the majority adhere to the original religion. The social effect on the proselytes depends, of course, on the attitude of the larger group—the extent to which it is tolerant or resentful toward the desertion of the individuals. The attitude of the major element in the population toward the group represented by the missionaries is also an important factor in determining the social positions of the proselytes who have attached themselves to the foreign group. Where the superiority of the foreigners is frankly admitted, the proselyte to the foreign religion may assume a superior status in some respects, although still isolating himself from the culture of his fellows. Where the foreigners are hated, the situation of the proselyte is worse.

The proselyting that a generation ago was carried on in the United States by Buddhist, Vedantist, and other missionaries from India presents a typical picture. Americans generally were tolerant of the missionaries and their proselytes, in accordance with the formal principle of religious freedom. They did not consider Hindus as their equals, culturally, even though they found the missionaries entertaining, and they looked upon the proselytes as persons who were mentally abnormal. The attitude on the whole was one of toleration for weakness, not that of respect. The situation as regards the more recent proselyting to Babism (a neo-Mohammedan cult) may be similar, but apparently the proselytes to this cult are of the relatively wealthy class—and that makes a difference. There is no doubt, however, that known adherence to any oriental or pseudooriental cult is detrimental, in public opinion, to an individual's reputation. The attitudes in so-called 'heathen' lands to proselytes made by white missionaries are marked by greater extremes, according as the white man is resented and hated or accepted as a superior being.

The efforts of missionaries generally are to detach the proselyte, not merely from his religion but from his total culture. The ways of life of the foreign group are inculcated, the foreign language is taught, and foreign education is undertaken. Where medical services are given and training in modern technical methods is applied, the missionary efforts appear to be most fruitful and the situation of the proselytes improved. Contributions to welfare, however, do not necessarily lessen the antagonism to the foreigners but more often have the opposite effect, since the undeniable superiority of the foreigners is resented.

Proselytes made by missionaries do not carry over to their new religion features of the old in the same way as that in which the assimilation is effected in group conversion, since the proselytes are as much as possible detached from their groups. Effective proselyting, on the other hand, contributes to the breakdown of the old culture even among those who are not proselyted. This is characteristic of the results of missionary enterprises among peoples who respect or fear the white man. The old culture is disrupted; the people generally abandon the stable organization that previously regulated their life, but they do not adopt civilized organization, and a state of cultural anarchy is the result. Where the missionary enterprise leads rather soon to group proselytism and the old customs are little disturbed but are assimilated to the new order, readjustment proceeds with less disruption. The group proselytism, however, seems to occur only where the cultural bases of the new religion are similar to those of the old, unless it is brought about by force.

The chief inducements to individual proselytism from the group religion appear to be neither doctrinal nor ritual. Economic, educational, and hygienic motives appear to be predominant. Relief from social injustice, in respect to the rules of caste, and improvement of the position of women in barbarous cultures are also benefits sought. The general advantages of civilized cultures are the bases of the motives for being proselyted. The sincerity of the religious change is always a matter of doubt, and most of those persons who have served as missionaries in foreign lands for long periods seem to have become progressively less interested in the doctrinal features of proselyting and more interested in the general contribution to native welfare. The inevitable detachment of the proselyte from his cultural group and his resulting social isolation except from the small group of converts are matters for deep concern.

c. The proselytizing of individuals who have settled among groups of a different religion was more conspicuous in ancient periods than it has been in modern. Such proselytes may be socially motivated, wishing to participate in the rituals of the people among whom they live and to become more solidly members of the group; or it may have been in other cases a matter of 'good business' for merchants whose trade relations were improved by becoming members of the religious organization. Soldiers stationed in foreign lands also were often proselyted to the religions of the peoples among whom they were stationed. Such adoption of group religion is socially desirable in most cases, since social isolation is always detrimental.

Proselytes to another religion may have profound effects on the religions of their own group when they return to it. There is no doubt that the breakdown of Roman paganism and its reorganization as Christianity was promoted by the Roman soldiers who had adopted Mithraism and the worship of the Great Mother in the Levant and who later introduced these cults in Rome. In an earlier period, the importation of Asiatic divinities into Europe was probably due in certain measure to persons who, as residents, merchants, or travelers in the Levant, had become attached to these divinities and their cults and brought them home eventually.

d. Where two or more religions exist side by side in the same nominal group, conversion from one to another may or may not occur. Antagonisms between the religious groups may be such that there are really two cultural groups in the same total population, as in India, where Moslems and Hindus are ready to fly at each other's throats, and proselytes from the one religion to the other are rare. Such a condition, however, is seldom based on religious differences alone. The antagonism between the Hindus and Moslems in India goes back to the hatred of the Hindus for their Mogul conquerors and the contempt of the conquerors for the conquered. The religious differences of course add fuel to the flames, but the ruthlessness of the Mogul rule was the actual foundation.

Jewish culture and Christian culture are still relatively distinct in Europe and America, although there have been proselytes from Judaism to Christianity in Europe especially, aside from those forced by the Spanish Inquisition. There is of course no such thing as a 'Jewish race' but merely a Jewish culture, the important difference of which from Christian culture—while not theological— is religious in the broad sense. That this culture would have disappeared before this, as other ancient religious cultures have disappeared, except for the rise of Christianity, can hardly be doubted.   The absorption of Jews in Germany was proceeding at a relatively rapid rate until it was stopped by Nazism.   In America, absorption has been retarded by the heavy immigration of the Eastern Jews (Ashkenasim), whom the Western Jews (Sephardim) do not like but whom they have to accept.   Although there is factually a social 'Jewish problem' in the United States, the details of which are well understood by all Jews, the problem will eventually settle itself if it is not made a political issue.

Proselyting to the various exotic sects that exist through the United States, mostly Buddhistic, Hindu, Moslem, or pseudo-oriental (such as Theosophy), appears to be under much the same conditions as is proselyting from one Christian sect to another, except for the attraction of novelty that these sects appear to have for some persons.   Otherwise the detachment from conventional systems and adoption of the exotic cults seems to be motivated much as is change of sect within what is nominally called 'Christianity.'

The attraction of some sects and cults is based on their offering of practical advantages.   To be able to project one's 'astral body' or travel through the 'fourth dimension' would be useful if it were possible.   Christian Science offers relief from physical diseases, and adherents admit that economic prosperity, which they believe is promoted by acceptance of the cult doctrines, is an important motive. Poverty is as much an evil as is disease, and Christian Science offers freedom from all evil.

Offers of mysterious 'knowledge' which can be applied to spiritual as well as economic benefit are advertised by some cults.   That the knowledge turns out to be incomprehensible does not discourage those who join the sects, for it is generally true that for a large section of the population the incomprehensible is impressive and the goal of practical results, although not attained, remains just ahead.

Family and social factors are often paramount in effecting changes from one sect to another.   If a man and women belonging to different sects marry, one or the other may change membership to the mate's sect.   A Protestant marrying a Roman Catholic usually faces the alternative of being proselyted to the Catholic faith or formally renouncing control over the children who may result from the marriage.   Changes from one Protestant sect to another at or following marriage are usually in the interests of family harmony and companionship.

Economic reasons are not infrequent for change of sect.   The association with persons who will be helpful in a business way is a not infrequent motive for proselytism. Often, however, reasons that are social in a noneconomic sense are the most influential. Such motives we cannot deny are sound. We often find it necessary to advise persons who are socially maladapted to establish church relationships, ignoring early sectarian predilections and prejudices and picking out a church group of people with whom social relations can be agreeably maintained, and then to join that congregation. For persons who were brought up in any of the sects called 'evangelical' this is sound advice, since doctrinal differences are nowadays of minor importance. These motives are practical but are not to be condemned on that account. The attraction of a ritual sometimes motivates change from one sect to another. Persons who are proselyted from Protestant to Catholic sects or to the Episcopal communion often are motivated by the more satisfying rituals of these communions. While faith or doctrines are seldom motives to proselytism, there is no doubt that progressive changes in doctrine of a sect or a church are, in many cases, a reason for detachment of its members and for their preparation for proselyting to another sect, which offers doctrines similar to the old creed. It makes little difference whether these changes are formal or of an unofficial character.

A person who, from his youth, has founded his religion on the infallibility of the Bible, but who eventually listens to liberal ministers and finds himself surrounded by a congregation that is largely liberal, finds the foundation of his religion taken away. He is left adrift and is vulnerable to proselytism by a sect which still bases its doctrine on the authority of the Bible, which offers some substitute scripture of infallible nature, or which offers a continuance of revelation of the Divine Will.

Aside from the Bible, teachings based on divine authority are essential to those who have been religiously nurtured in these teachings. Sin, as a mere infraction of the inscrutable commands of God, is no longer preached as emphatically by evangelical sects as it formerly was. The substitution of ethical concepts, although the substitution may not be official, progresses in sermons and in the subtler modifications of church attitudes. This change leaves many church members adrift.

There is a practical problem resulting from the presence of evil in the world. Christian principles require that something shall be done for those who are suffering from evil conditions.   Something must be done for the sufferers individually, and something must be done to our social-economic system to lessen the incidence of suffering.   If there were no evil, we could be much relieved of our responsibilities and our political (social-economic) concerns.   Acceptance of the teachings of some modern cults—that evil is illusory, really nonexistent—may lessen one's responsibility for other persons and eliminate moral responsibility.

That the relief from concern over disease and injustice and from responsibility for the improvement of the social system, which these cults offer, may be a powerful motive for proselytization to such a cult is not to be overlooked,

3. Conversion within a Religious Group.—The word conversion means, literally, 'turning with,' and hence is properly used to designate the adoption by an individual of the religion of the group to which, in other respects, he already belongs.   Individuals born and reared in Christian communities usually adhere to the principles of Christianity that are endorsed by their social group, although they may not practice the rituals or follow the rules of conduct that are religiously approved.   This is especially true of individuals who have been subjected to Christian teachings in their youth and who therefore continue later to accept the teachings as valid, although they do not conform to them.   Bringing these 'wandering sheep' back to the fold has long been the purpose of revivals conducted by evangelical Protestant sects.   This process is conversion, although it is not proselytism, and is often called 'being saved.'

The conventional process in conversion of this type has three conventional stages: conviction of sin; repentance; and acceptance of the tenets of the faith, which usually involves entering into active membership in the church.   The 'coming forward' and publicly acknowledging adherence to the faith is an essential part of the process.   In some sects it is held that even for those who are nominally members of the cult, the public profession of faith is essential to 'salvation.'

The technique of the revival begins in the presentation to 'sinners' of the dire fate awaiting those who are 'unsaved,' the emphasis being on the sad punishment meted out to the sinners in the life after death.   Fear of this other-wordly fate produces the desire to do something to avert it; and repentance, with confession of sinfulness, if not of specific sins, is the next step.   The more 'emotional' this repentance, the more salutary it is supposed to be. The repentant sinner then publicly professes acceptance of the basic tenets of the sect, and his salvation is accomplished. He has become converted. The permanence of the conversion is doubtful in many cases, and its impermanence is certain in many other cases. There are, however, certain cases in which the convert, from the period of conversion and thereafter, adheres to the principles of the sect, conforms to the rituals, and pursues a 'godly' life.

The damaging aspect of repentance of the emotional sort has already been pointed out. Too often a person repents loudly in prayer meeting or revival and derives from the process a satisfaction that makes it easy for him to commit more sins for further repentance. That revivals were, in their heyday, commercialized and were frauds committed in the interests of the revivalist's profits is an undeniable fact.

The old time 'camp meeting' was to a large extent a social event, in which families participated and at which the young folks had good times. That the camp meetings were occasions of relaxation of the ordinary rules of inhibition of sexual relations, as are savage corroborees and as were the ancient saturnalia and seasonal festivals of our ancestors, has been alleged, but the evidence is not convincing. The social features of the camp meetings were centered around the religious services, at which sinners were called to repentance and younger members of the cult were expected to come forward and make confessions of faith.

In Catholic sects and in Protestant sects that are not classed as 'evangelical,' conversion, in the proper sense of the term, has not been a matter of importance. Periodic confession of sins, with nominal repentance, is expected in some of these sects, but that is a matter which is quite different from conversion. Confession, followed by absolution, indeed is good psychological practice, impressing on the troubled person the fact that his errors do not necessarily have permanent evil consequences and that a fresh start is always possible with help from knowledge of the mistakes of the past. Absolution is a prophylactic for repentance of the damaging sort.

The phenomena of conversion have been magnified in the past, as important religious phenomena, by writers on the 'psychology of religion,' who have been mostly nonpsychologists or psychologists not well grounded in the science. We may admit that the phenomena have importance, but the importance is that of pathological perversions of religious attitudes, which have little value for the study of religion in its normal aspects.   The interest of the psychologist in such pathological phenomena is directed toward their amelioration and more especially toward their prevention.

The desire to 'save one's soul' is usually the basic motive for conversion, and revivalists have bent their efforts to the creation of this desire and its increase in vividness by emphasizing the sad fate of the unsaved.   In this way, the selfish interest in religion is strengthened and the social and ethical interests are depressed. From the point of view of the psychologist, the interest in saving one's little 'soul' is deplorable, and easily becomes a neurotic trait or an expression of the ruthlessness and egotism of the type of person who, in popular slang, is called an 'extrovert.'   From the ethical point of view, interest in one's own salvation is immoral.

CHAPTER XIII

CHANGES IN THE FUNCTIONS OF RELIGION

1. A Tentative Concept of the Nature of Religion.—Religion, as it was in its early periods of development, might be described as the attempt of man to accomplish something which, at the time, he had no means of accomplishing, or, more tersely, man's attempt to do what he did not know how to do. This is only a partial description, which we shall complete shortly.

Rituals were developed in the attempt to extend praxes that did not suffice to produce the materials and the conditions that man needed for the satisfaction of his urgent desires. Rituals were additions to praxes that were not completely adequate. It was obvious to man that something further should be done; he didn't know what to do, but he did something.

When the concept of another world developed, man thought that he needed to do something about the other world and developed rituals to that end. In the transitional stage of divinities, when gods and goddesses were partly in this world but were in process of taking flight to the other world, man developed rituals of appeasement, flattery, and appeal, analogous to the procedures that he had found would appease, flatter, and appeal to other men. Before this stage was reached, man had invented rituals intended to assist the powers that produce food, give protection, and bestow other benefits on human beings. These rituals were constructed by analogy with the processes of plowing, seeding, irrigation, and other praxes of husbandry, which man had found actually assisted the powers of nature, but these rituals did not suffice in the later period when the powers had been humanized as gods and goddesses, and were consequently elaborated further. Man did not know what elaborations and extensions of ritual would be effective, but he elaborated and extended anyhow.

The beliefs associated with the rituals were of two sorts: (*a*) belief that rituals, associated with the praxes from which they developed, would be effective for the production of the materials and the conditions which would satisfy desires; (*b*) belief that the powers that control nature are such that rituals of assistance, appeasement, and petition could secure the cooperation of the powers. These beliefs obviously involve theories of the operations of nature, theories which are explanatory, in terms of causes and effects. Rituals must have causal efficiency, or they are useless. That man's curiosity about the world and its operation contributed to the explanations he invented is to be admitted, but the major motives were practical.

Man wants to know what he should do in order that his hunting and fishing may be successful; he wants to know what he should do in order to make his crops and his domestic animals thrive; he wants to know what to do in order to protect himself and his family against animal and human enemies and against the effects of sun, rain, and other climatic factors. In sum, man wants to know how to protect himself against the deadly forces of his environment and how to turn to his advantage all forces of nature insofar as possible. His early praxes did not suffice, so they were extended into rituals, which were conducted as elaborately as possible, since elaboration seemed important.

In the interests of praxis and ritual, it is necessary that man shall understand nature. The valid explanations that science has applied to the processes of nature were unknown to early man, who therefore constructed explanations, which satisfied his practical curiosity and which were consequently sufficient for the time being. Our definition of proto-religion may now be balanced by adding to it the stipulation that this proto-religion included the attempt of man to know that which it was impossible for him to know at the time. To his praxes and rituals man adds beliefs, developed from the rituals, which are explanations of the why and the how of the world.

Man, for example, had a practical curiosity about the lightning and the thunder—how they are related and what causes them. This was no idle curiosity, for the thunderbolt is dangerous, and man needs protection against it. Furthermore, man observed that thunderstorms bring rain to the thirsty earth and so promote the growth of vegetation and maintain streams and spring. If there were some way of bringing on a rain in time of drought and some way of stopping the rain in time of flood, knowledge of these means would be advantageous to man.

The explanation of the manas that produce the thunderstorm and the assignment of these manas adopted by primitive man are unknown to us. After the evolution of divinities, the explanation that man adopted fitted into the scheme of divinities. The thunderstorms begin about the mountain heights, so it was evident that a god had his seat on the mountaintop—a Zeus, a Hadad, a Jehovah, or a Thor. This god hurls the bolts, which flash and glitter, and that explains the lightning. When one of the bolts strikes a rock, a tree, or some other object, there is a loud noise, and that explains the thunder.

What can man do about the thunderstorms and the rains that accompany them? Since a god produces them, propitiation or appeasement of the god is in order if the god is angry. If he is complaisant, appeal to him to operate for human benefit is in order. The primitive rituals were probably designed to thwart the power that produces the storms or to assist the power; but from these rituals develop rituals of appeasement and of petition, which may be serviceable in this case, as in other cases in which the divinities interfere in the operations of nature or in human affairs otherwise. The explanation, in short, justifies the rituals out of which it grew, while producing modifications of old rituals to suit new beliefs.

The modern scientific explanation of thunderstorms in terms of static electricity is superior to the ancient explanation in one practical respect. We are able to protect our buildings against the thunderbolts, by the use of lightning rods, whereas our cultural ancestors could devise no protection and so resorted to rituals for appeasement of the thundergod. We, however, are no more able to start a storm, or to stop one, than were ancient men.

Our description of religion as it was in its early stages of development will need some modification for its application to religion in its more recent stages, but the changes in religion are not so great as might be supposed. Prayer for rain has not been unknown in recent times in the United States, and this application of ritual is typical of other applications. If prayer for rain is effectual, it is obvious that something is initiated in this world, which has effects in the other world, which in turn produces changes in this world. The total process initiated in this world passes through the other world and terminates again in this world.

Beliefs in the efficacy of prayer in production of results in the other world can neither be validated nor invalidated, since no scientific check on events in the other world is possible. Results of prayer in this world, however, are subject to check, by which they would either be validated or relegated to the domain of magical superstition. It would not be impossible to set up a group of experimental cases, with control cases, to determine whether or not prayer has mundane effects. Such an experiment has never been undertaken, and probably will never be, since those who believe in the mundane efficacy of prayer are not willing to submit their faith to test, and it is assumed that the prayers of unbelievers are of no avail.

If the mundane effects of prayer were validated, the part of the sequence that lies in the other world would still be a matter for religious faith. If one assumes that prayer produces its mundane effects through agencies lying entirely within this world, not involving the other world in any way, the belief still needs validation. Prior to experimental check, the conclusion either that prayer has mundane effects, or that it does not, is merely a religious belief; and prayer itself remains an attempt to do what man does not know how to do.

The attempt to do what one does not know how to do is prevalent in several fields, but especially in the field of 'mental medicine' and 'mental hygiene.' Something ought to be done, and so someone who does not know what to do does something. The organization of work in 'mental hygiene' is an interesting example of organization that was more religious than scientific. It was argued that there are many cases of incipient disorder and maladjustment that might be saved if something were done about the disordered persons. Obviously, then, something ought to be done; but what should be done, few persons knew. So a group decided to do what they certainly did not know how to do, and an organization was built up.

The conception of the other world as the realm into which men, or certain appurtenances of men, pass at death offers problems somewhat similar to the problem of prayer, but problems that are insoluble. Rituals designed to promote the welfare of persons (or of their appurtenances) in the other world have taken two forms. In one form, the rituals are conducted in behalf of the person after his decease, at the funeral or thereafter. In the early days of Christianity, living persons were baptized for the dead (I Cor. 15: 29), and although baptism for the dead is no longer practiced, masses are said for the 'repose of the soul' of the deceased. In the other form, the rituals are performed by the person himself, or by other persons for him, prior to his decease. Do these rituals have any effect on the status or condition of the person in the other world to which he has gone or to which he is on his way? The pious believer answers 'yes,' and the skeptic answers 'no'; but both of these opinions are purely religious and forever remain so, since science has no methods by which can be determined the validity or the invalidity of the belief.

Professional mediums, and their credulous followers, claim that human survival of death has been 'scientifically' proved through the contacts that the mediums are alleged to have established with surviving appurtenances of deceased persons. The 'messages' alleged to have been received from these appurtenances are so trivial that the acceptance of them as valid would force one to believe in a state of the dead similar to that the Greeks assigned to their ghosts, whom they regarded as imbeciles. Since, however, every competent investigation of mediums has shown that the messages and other alleged phenomena are fraudulent, one can disregard the spurious 'evidence' and can believe in a future life worth while or can reject the belief, but the belief in either case is religious.

Rituals persist after the beliefs in which they were formerly interpreted have been abandoned. Many religious persons do not believe that the rituals attending death and burial have any effects but still approve the rituals. Some who have discarded the belief in survival of death still approve the rituals. For these persons, the rituals have ceased to be religious. Those who hold the rituals to be valid are pursuing the plan of religion in its early phases—trying to do something they do not know how to do and believing that which they cannot know.

Religion did not begin with other-worldly concerns, and religion has not as yet relinquished its claim to functions that are this-worldly. Changes have been in progress during the last three thousand years, and further changes are to be expected. Prediction as to what these changes will be can be made only from the changes that have occurred in the past; but we can well assume that all matters which concern the other world will remain in the province of religion.

2. From Paganism to Christianity.—The development of science during the centuries preceding the Christian Era inevitably had effects on religions. The development of science was slow, and the changes in religion were still slower. By the beginning of the

Christian Era, however, it was evident that an *organon* (a body of scientific principles) was being developed and that the procedures involved in praxes would eventually be subjected to tests of their validity.   The first philosophers of Greece accepted the popular notions regarding the nature of the world—notions that were essentially religious and that included the concept of the four *stoicheia*, earth, water, air, and fire, out of which all things were supposed to be made—but out of these philosophies grew the beginnings of science.

Aristotle brought together, into a related system, physics, zoology, psychology, and metaphysics, earning thereby the title of 'Father of Science,' which was justified by his copious observations and experiments in those fields which constitute the 'natural sciences.' He also laid the foundations for modern religion.   His reinterpretations of the ancient concepts of *nous, psyche, logos,* and *pneuma* were not completely incorporated in Christianity but had profound influence on it.

Aristotle's fundamental interest was in zoology, and this interest led him to spend much time in dissecting animals, especially fish and sea animals.   It was probably this interest in the functions of organisms that motivated his interest in social organization and made him the founder of group psychology.

Greek culture was dominant in the ancient world and, when Greece declined in power and importance, the culture persisted, with a new center in Alexandria, where there was already a large Jewish colony, as well as a Greek colony.

In Alexandria, Jewish scholars such as Aristobulus and Philo, who were well versed in Greek literature and Greek philosophy ('Hellenized' is the term), influenced Judaism and created even in Jerusalem two factions—the Sadducees, who were well Hellenized, and the Pharisees, who resisted changes in Jewish conceptions, remaining attached to the Babylonian concepts.   In its first century, Christianity was influenced by the Hellenized Paul, who is considered by some scholars as the real founder of Christianity. In the later centuries the fathers of the church in Alexandria, thoroughly Hellenized, continued the Greek tradition, so that the influence of the Jewish legends dwindled and the Greek influence burgeoned.

In Alexandria also, science in all its branches, transplanted from Greece, entered a stage of development that was more rapid than the previous progress in Greece. History, geography, and general literature were given in Alexandria an impetus for their development. Alexandria, in short, was the 'bottle-neck' through which not only Christianity but the total culture of the Greek civilization was transmitted to the whole western world.

Christianity, in its early period, added to the functions of religion rather than subtracted from them. Economic functions were somewhat lessened, especially the functions regarding husbandry, trade, and transportation, and food tabus were relaxed or abandoned. Social problems, on the other hand, became religious problems. Salvation, for the future life, had been the important point in the Greek mysteries, and Christianity took over the concept of salvation and expanded it. No new rituals were added, and some old rituals were discarded, but some Jewish rituals and some pagan rituals were taken over in modified forms with new interpretations.

The conflict of opinions concerning the position of Jesus in regard to the supreme divinity, a conflict that raged violently during the early centuries, was settled, officially at least, by the adoption of a concept that Philo had advanced—the concept of a Logos, or plan, as an eternal feature of the Creator, a feature that Philo described as the 'Son of God.' With the identification of Jesus as the Logos, an identification presented in the gospel of John in words drawn from Philo, and with the addition of Aristotle's divine *nous* as the Holy Ghost, the Christian Trinity was shaped.

Little appeared in Christianity *de novo*, except a heightened concern for morality, including justice, sympathy, and responsibility for one's fellow man and not merely for members of one's family or social clique. This concern, it is true, had been prefigured in pagan and Jewish teachings, but Christianity made a point of it more emphatically.

As we have indicated, the early Christian church was little concerned with economic functions (in the fundamental meaning of household management), and it was also little concerned with political functions of the larger group. In later centuries, however, economic, political, and personal regulatory functions were revived by the church, and these functions have been ever since promoted by some factions, while being deplored by other factions. That the economic functions of religion have greatly diminished is evident. Applied science has taken over the praxes of growing crops, the mining of ores, the manufacture of raw materials into commodities, transportation by land, sea, and air, and the cure and prevention of disease as well as the protection of human beings in other ways. It is a fact that religious rituals are still associated, here and there, with these praxes, but, in view of the great changes that have been made, we can predict that eventually religion will be completely eliminated from the economic field.   Many Christians hope that the church will return to the functions it exercised in its early period, but such regression never has occurred in religion and probably never will occur.   We need, however, to consider shortly the actual and the possible functions of the church in promoting morals and morality.

In control of the family and family life, religion has relinquished its functions to a considerable extent.   Marriage is becoming more a civil procedure and less a religious sacrament.   Religious opposition to divorce and to birth control has lessened, since religious persons have begun to realize that these are problems of a sociological nature.   Some Christian sects still oppose the current of progress and are faced by a dilemma: either they must yield to progress, or their members drift out of their control.   As regards the freeing of women from the status of chattels (a change that affects the state as well as the family), organized religion has been consistently conservative, clinging to the past as could have been predicted, until forced to follow in the steps of progress, never leading.

The propagation of children is no longer sought through religion, and the cure of barrenness in women is today a problem for medicine, not religion.   The head of a family has fallen far from earlier priestly status, and, although the discontinuance of family worship is the loss of a ritual that was useful for the promotion of family solidarity and loyalty, the ritual is progressively being abandoned, and we know that the abandonment will eventually be complete.

Under the rising influence of public education the educational function of religion is becoming largely restricted to religious education, leaving secular education to the agencies that are organized to carry on that function.   With the decrease in family religion, the function of religious education devolves, in principle, more heavily on the church, but in practice the function is being less and less fulfilled.   This is true of the Protestant churches, but the Roman church attempts to maintain parochial schools in which secular education and religious education are combined.   Protestant sects no longer establish sectarian schools, and the sectarian schools and colleges established in earlier years have almost all become as non-sectarian as are our state institutions.

Deploring these changes in the functions of religion, or boasting of them, are equally futile. 'Progress' is merely a continuum of change which persists and which therefore may be expected to continue in its course just as water continues to run downhill. Social changes of the future can be predicted only on the basis of the changes of the past, and individual preferences have little to do with them. All the individual can do is to adapt himself to the changes and be prepared for them.

3. Religion and Morals.—The word 'morals' has a double meaning. It applies to a system of moral principles, which we otherwise call 'ethics.' It applies also to a system of practical procedures, or a type of behavior, to which ethical principles may be applied. The basic ethical principle, as we have earlier declared, is 'justice.' The principle of justice may be described as the principle that all persons should have equal opportunities for accomplishment and should receive equal rewards for their achievements. The terms 'equal' and 'equality,' however, cannot be taken *simpliciter*. We do not treat normal, adult, law-abiding persons as we treat children, criminals, or those who are mentally defective or mentally disordered. In fact, no one proposes to treat the normal and the abnormal, the adult and the infantile, the criminal and the noncriminal as if they were equals. We do not, and should not, consider the sick and the weak as equals of the strong and the sound in health.

Equality of opportunity, therefore, must be qualified as meaning opportunity proportionate to ability, and equal reward for accomplishment must mean reward proportionate to the actual achievement. Morality, therefore, is better described as including cooperation, benevolence, and sympathy. This does not eliminate the equation of morality with justice, but recognizes the difficulty in finding, in particular cases, that which can be called 'just.' Justice is involved in the concept of democracy, concerning which many have been confused by the terms 'equal' and 'equality.' Democracy is a political concept, which involves the principle that all men are equal, but no proponent of democracy has ever assumed that men are really equal in their abilities.

Since democracy involves majority rule, and since factions within a group strive to gain control to serve their special interests as against the interests of the group as a whole, democracy has an internal weakness that democrats do not ignore, for factional conflicts weaken the group. It is probable, therefore, that religious groups that are autocratically controlled are stronger than those that are democratic. If the majority of the group members are satisfied with autocratic government, no injustice is being done so far as the group members are concerned, although the actions of autocratically governed groups may be unjust to other groups.

Morality, as we have described it, involves consideration of group interests, but the interests and needs of individual members of the group are more important than the interests and needs of the total group. The group may be represented by an 'average member,' but this representative is merely a statistical fiction. Consideration of the welfare of the total group, as a group, supplies an important cohesive force, but a force that may be detrimental to the persons composing the group. Morality applied to personal relations as well as to the group as an organization eliminates this danger.

Morality begins in the smaller groups, such as the family, and is extended progressively to larger groups. Eventually it may be extended to the entire human race. Christianity has, during its lifetime, developed a concept of morality as world-wide in its scope, although many Christian groups have acted in ways contrary to this concept. The history of the struggles of churches to triumph over one another is a minor illustration of this defection from the ideal. The conflicts of factions within a political group, each clique seeking its own interests against the interests of others, is a survival of primitive morality that has not progressed even to national morality.

Judaism in its later developments has shared with Christianity the ideal of broad morality, with justice for all men, not merely for those of a particular nation, church, or faction, although the deplorable myths concerning the early history of the Hebrew religion present a picture of an entirely different sort. Most sects of Islam, and most Hindu religions, have not yet arrived at a stage of development in which the ideal seems important to them.

That Western religion has, in the recent past, promoted the development of morality must be admitted, and these services should not be ignored. Whether or not this service is to continue is a question that we must consider.

Since the beginning of the Christian Era, religion has assumed as its ethical function the inculcation of the principles and precepts of morals. The principles taught have not always been sound and have sometimes been at variance with the teachings of Jesus. The teachings of religious groups have mingled moral principles with inhibitions and injuctions of a purely ritual nature, but, on the whole, the results have been influential in promoting the brotherhood of man. Certain sects of Islam and certain Hindu sects, under the stimulation of Christianity, have followed its lead.

The program of education in ethics and training in morals is no longer the function of religion exclusively. Apart from 'ethical societies' and similar organizations, many persons with no church connections have devoted themselves to the work, and moral education is generally assumed to be one of the functions of secular schools. Although this function, like other functions of the schools, is not well fulfilled, improvement is readily possible.

The task for religion in the future, in respect to morals, seems to be not leading progress, but cooperating with other agencies until those agencies are able to carry on alone.

In spite of our estimate of the accomplishments of religion in promoting morality, there are two bad results of religious control of morals, which support the view that the sooner religion ceases to concern itself with morals the better it will be both for morals and for religion. In the first place, religion has tended to base morals on dogmas and myths. These dogmas change with the progress of culture, and when old dogmas are rejected, those persons who have founded their ethical principles on the dogmas are apt to abandon the principles along with the dogmas. A structure built on a shifting foundation crumbles when the foundation shifts. This is not a theory that confronts us, but a condition that we often encounter.

We frequently come in contact with young persons who have been taught that they must follow moral precepts because an omnipotent being commands them and will punish those who disobey. If the God whose commandments constitute morals is tied up with the notion of infallibility of the Bible the results are especially disastrous. If the youth goes to college, he finds from courses in zoology and geology that the doctrine of the creation of the world which is presented in Genesis is not accepted by instructors whom he respects. Before he goes to college, or if he does not go to college, he comes in contact with persons whose morality and intellectual acumen he respects; and he finds that many of these persons reject the biblical traditions and the orthodox doctrine of a hell in which sinners are punished and a heaven in which the ones who obey God's commands are rewarded. This discovery produces a moral disorganization, which has been expressed often in phraseology like the following. 'Well, if the Bible is unreliable in some respects, it is probably unreliable in other respects. If there is no hell, and maybe no God who punishes those who disobey the commands of morality, then there is no reason why I should be 'good'; I can have a much better time as a sinner.' These outspoken youths are obviously indicative of a larger number who do not analyze their decline from morality so frankly.

It is to be admitted that few Christian sects today hold the Bible to be infallible; that most church members accept a theory of evolution of some sort; and that many pious Christians reject the doctrines about hell and are skeptical about heaven. Religion changes its faiths progressively, as we have said repeatedly, and no change that has occurred can be considered final. The changes that have occurred are evidences that there will be further changes; hence the founding of morals on any religious faith is dangerous.

We have noted that an other-wordly faith is always religious. It should be understood also that many hypotheses advanced as 'scientific' are held in a way that is really religious. We should not base morals on the doctrine that the world was created six thousand years ago, for this doctrine is incapable of being validated. The doctrine that the world has existed for many millions of years is equally incapable of scientific validation. As a scientific hypothesis, held subject to modification, the second hypothesis is more useful than the first. Accepted as the final and ultimate truth it becomes religious faith—knowing that which it is impossible to know. Basing morals on a particular doctrine of creation or of evolution is unsafe, no matter whether the doctrine is a legendary one or a scientific working hypothesis.

Morals can in no case be based on truly scientific hypotheses. Persons who have attempted to base ethics on science have come out either with a patchwork of factors that are really irreconcilable or with a system of ethics from which actual moral principles have been eliminated, a system comparable to the play of *Hamlet* with the Prince of Denmark omitted.

It cannot be denied that persons who have no religious faith and who do not engage in any religious ritual may be as moral as the most pious church member. We can go further; no one reposes confidence in another person because of the person's piety, but only because it is known or assumed that the person is one of moral principle and practice. Some go even further than this and distrust persons who are pious because of their piety, but there is no indication that more pious persons than nonreligious are dishonest or otherwise immoral. Piety, it seems, has little more to do with morality or immorality than it did in the earlier stages of religion. Moral principles can best be inculcated with neither religious nor scientific apologies for them. Instead of teaching a child that he should be just because God commands him to, he should be taught that justice is the right and proper principle to follow and maintain. If the 'rightness' of a moral principle is not guaranteed by the principle itself, nothing else can guarantee it.

The second bad result of religious control of morals grows out of the first. The foundation of morals on religion involves a major appeal to selfishness. One must be righteous or else one will suffer either in this world or in the next. Religion thus promotes the saving of one's little 'soul' as the main purpose in life, and the selfish motive is set above the altruistic motive even for altruistic actions, for altruism is made a means to the attaining of benefits for oneself— benefits, at least in the form of credit. While the emphasis on saving one's soul has lessened in most Christian sects during recent years, the lessening is in part merely in phraseology, and the benefits expected from righteousness are expressed in other phrases.

4. Social Applications of Religion.—We have discussed in considerable detail the economic functions of religion, or, we might say, the economic applications of religion. These applications were social in a way, since they were made by peoples in groups and for the benefit of the groups. We have discussed also the political applications of religion, which are emphatically social. We have emphasized the importance of religion as a factor in social integration of a group, and now we propose to consider in more detail the processes involved for integration, as well as other applications to the general culture of the groups.

In the fostering of group integration, religion promoted and controlled sports and entertainments of other types, although in these applications the religious aspect and the political aspect were combined.   The development of pictorial and plastic art owes much to religion, since art grew out of religion.

The great games that were held periodically at Olympia, Delphi, Corinth, and Nemea were centered about the worship of the gods and goddesses.   To these games came great crowds from the whole Mediterranean world, including the shores of Asia Minor, and the contacts of groups from different cultural areas fostered a cosmopolitan attitude.   Originally, horse racing was the outstanding attraction at the games, and prize fighting, wrestling, and other physical contests between individuals were added before long, but literature was not neglected.   Poets read their compositions to eager audiences, and prose writers read their productions.   At one of these games Herodotus read his *History*.   Readings from the Iliad and the Odyssey of Homer were regular features of the entertainment. The contests inspired poets such as Pindar to write odes commemorating the victories and praising the victors.

Sacrifices to the various gods and goddesses were essential parts of the games; sacrifices were offered by contestants and by delegations (*theories*, as they were called) from various cities as well as by the local group, which was host to the visitors.   These sacrifices, of course, provided food for the multitude.   The religious feature of the great games is further indicated by the experience of Pindar. His first odes did not make a favorable impression, but another poet, or rather a poetess, advised Pindar to draw more material from the religious myths and legends, and with this change Pindar's odes became popular.   The odes were not read at the games, but in the cities of the victors at celebrations of their victories.   Pindar's sincere reverence for the gods and his use of the myths seem to have been appreciated by the citizens as suitable to the religious aspects of the games themselves.

The civilizing effects of the great games can hardly be overestimated.   The eventual civilization of the Dorians can be attributed largely to their being eventually permitted to attend the games and to contest in them.   Before each game, a sacred truce was proclaimed by heralds sent to every Greek state, and this truce, which enabled all peoples to go to the games unmolested, was a shining example of the benefits of peace.   Although at Olympian, Nemean, and Isthmian (at Corinth) games the athletic events were the features of primary interest, at the Pythian games (at Delphi) musical contests were the features emphasized.

City festivals had somewhat the same features as the great games and occurred more frequently. Readings from Homer were features of certain of these city festivals, while participation in the processions and other rituals entertained the public and promoted group spirit. Drama developed from the Greek festivals, especially from the festivals in honor of Dionysos in his goat-god form, as is indicated by the probable derivation of the word 'tragedy' from *tragos* (goat). This development of the drama was promoted by the custom in which prominent citizens undertook, as a civic duty, the expense of training groups of musicians, singers, and dancers for the festivals. Even after the control of dramatic presentations was taken over by the cities, the drama still retained its religious characteristics.

Pictorial art began in the decoration of pottery, but as it progressed to the representation of persons and scenes the topics were drawn from the religious myths and legends. Mural paintings eventually appeared, and these also were representations of religious scenes. Plastic art began with the making of statues of gods and goddesses, to replace the earlier simple blocks of wood or stone. Later reliefs representing religious subjects were carved, and eventually representations of abstractions were shaped. Portrait statues and reliefs of human beings, apart from religious scenes, were relatively late in their appearance.

In the Christian Era, church festivals replaced the pagan festivals, or the pagan festivals were transformed into Christian ones, and some pagan festivals became feasts of the saints who replaced the pagan gods and goddesses. For further entertainment of the populace religious dramas—'mystery plays' and 'morality plays'— were produced. This was a continuation of the pagan combination of entertainment with presentation of religious doctrines.

These contributions of religion to human welfare in the pre-Christian period were devoid of any ethical features, except insofar as we may regard attachment to one's group, with contempt for outsiders, as the seed from which morality grew. Injustice was accepted not merely as unavoidable in human life, but even as desirable. Might was accepted as the equivalent of right, and in the political organizations the group that was able to seize power, and consequently to acquire wealth, exercised this power as their right and felt little or no responsibility for, or obligation to, the less fortunate persons. Sympathy for the unfortunate was a trait only of those who shared the misfortune. Personal friendship existed, and to assist one's friends was a common procedure, but this was largely a matter of seeking one's own welfare.

Ancient religion did nothing about the injustice prevalent in the world and did not propose to do anything about it. Some philosophers protested the myths about the gods that presented the divinities as unjust, malicious, and lascivious, but got little hearing unless their criticisms were too pertinent, in which cases the philosophers were denounced and persecuted by the pious citizens. Most of the philosophers were uninterested in justice, except as it applied to their special cliques. Plato, the last of the Pythagoreans, discussed justice as a mere intellectual problem and was not concerned with practical morality. For Plato, virtue is merely knowledge, and his scheme of a Republic is that of a government controlled by an aristocratic group with no responsibility toward the proletariat except the responsibility for controlling it in the interests of the aristocrats.

It is possible that the Greek dramatists by their presentations of injustice reaching the height of atrocities began the awakening in the audiences of sympathy for the afflicted and resentment against the unjust, but this is not certain, since we have little evidence as to the responses of the audiences, although Aristotle's theory of the purging of the emotions by watching tragedies suggest the possibility. At any rate, with the rise of Christianity the notion of moral obligation was accentuated. The text in the Epistle of James defining pure religion is but one instance of the emphasis that Christianity placed on the obligation of justice in practical life, obligation not only between peers, but between men of diverse fortunes and abilities. In the synoptic gospels this emphasis on practical morality as well as emphasis on ethics is attributed to the Founder of Christianity.

After Christianity emerged from the status of a religion for the poor and oppressed, the picture was not so pleasant. Medieval Christianity, having become powerful and wealthy, allied itself with the aristocrats and oppressors and lent itself to injustice and oppression, descending even to the slaughter of the weak. This picture has been presented so often that we may pass it over. We should note, however, that the church, even at its worst, did much for the alleviation of individual suffering, although it was not so much interested in the prevention of injustice.

Medicine began, as we have pointed out, as a function of religion. When no one knew how to heal diseases, religion began to try to heal them and has not ceased to exercise in some measure the healing function, even in the present era, in which physical medicine has become scientific. Nuns and deaconesses nurse the sick in hospitals and in private homes, but this service is a secular function of a religious group. Healing through prayer, symbols, and holy relics and at special shrines, of course, is purely religious, or magical, according to the point of view adopted. Considering the prevalence of commercialized quackery in the field of 'mental medicine,' we may well conclude that religious control of physical medicine in the period before scientific medicine began its development was an excellent service in public welfare.

In the provision of food, recreation, and social assistance for those in need of these, churches of all Christian sects are still active. To some extent, social and recreational facilities are provided in order to keep the younger generation from straying from the church and to attract possible proselytes, but often the facilities are offered to persons who are not expected to affiliate with the church.

These charitable functions of religion, although persisting through centuries, may not last indefinitely. Secular organizations are active in the field, and city, state, and national relief for the needy is being extended and will be further extended. Some of the larger 'foundations' support and promote work for social welfare as well as medical service and medical research. The work of these foundations is at present in the hands of persons who are more nearly religious than they are scientific, but changes in application are to be expected. The church was once the only charitable and philanthropic organization, but progress in the secularization of these functions makes it possible to predict that at some time, not very far in the future, the church will have lost the social functions as it is losing its medical functions.

The dark side of the relation of religion to morals, that is, to human welfare, has been the failure of organized religion to lead in progress toward the prevention of injustice and of the exploitation of human beings. Amelioration of the conditions of those who have been socially damaged is creditable; but it is like trying to sweep back flood waters with brooms. 'Flood control' is the important social praxis. Civilization has made substantial progress toward morality, and many religious individuals have cooperated with secular organizations to make this progress possible. Organized religion, however, has not led in progress and has acted more as a drag on progress than as an assistant. To the obstructions that religion has offered to social progress we may add another. The retention of the sabbatarian laws and ordinances has been due in large part to cooperation between church groups and politicians who find these laws great helps in their programs of political control and corruption. It is noteworthy that the sabbatarian laws have been more rigidly maintained in the communities in which the political 'machines' are the most powerful. On the other hand, there is one exception for which religion must be given credit. Religious organizations appear to have cooperated with secular agencies in the adoption of laws regulating child labor and in the maintenance of those laws.

Social progress, of course, is a process of the political group and we are not advocating the entrance, or re-entrance, of religious organizations into the field of political activity. All that the church can do is to increase its promotion of morality and its opposition to injustice and lessen its emphasis on selfishness. Liberalization of the churches will accelerate the progress in political principles and in effective use of political machinery for the promotion of the prevention of injustice. Unless the churches take the lead in these matters, they will inevitably commit suicide. The church, if it is to continue to live, must cease to be a drag at the heels of progress.

The obstructive attitude of the church toward social progress is, as we have earlier noted, a fundamental feature of religion. Religion has always been characterized by its high regard for the past and has clung to the past and its traditions as long as it possibly could. Precepts and doctrines that were satisfactory in earlier periods have been retained, instead of being modified to suit later conditions. Although the derivation of the word 'religion' from the Latin *re-ligare* (to tie back) has been discredited by philologists, it expresses the fact that religion does bind mankind to the past, a binding that sometimes becomes bondage.

5. Religion as a Means for Social Control.—A few years ago certain of the wealthy 'foundations' were interested in what is called 'social control,' an expression that usually means controlling the underdogs in the interests of the upper dogs. For a time they seemed to consider that religion would be a means adequate for this control, but later they seem to have concluded that organized medicine would be more useful and more amenable. The discarding of religion as a tool for 'social control' is well illustrated by the failure of the Billy Sunday revivals.

In the heyday of the Billy Sunday 'campaigns,' large contributions were made to the funds that local committees managed. Some of the funds were expended in the building of a 'tabernacle' in which the revivals were to be held and for other expenses. Considerable sums were left, however, and were turned over to the Billy Sunday organization. In one city, the actual 'rake-off' was really nearly twice as much as the sum announced in the press. The committee, according to the admission of one of its members, did not dare announce the actual sum of the donation. These donations, with the profits from the sales of hymnbooks and minor collections from the religiously inclined public, made the profits of the enterprise large. The bulk of the donations came from men of wealth, who were, for the most part, little interested in religion, except as a means of 'social control,' and whose lives were far from being in accordance with the conventions of Christian morality.

These donors were interested in maintaining the social-industrial system that was dominant before the New Deal and had been persuaded that a recrudescence of 'old-time religion' would stabilize society and soothe the discontent of the underprivileged classes. The idea that had been sold to them was that labor would be motivated to keep its place in subordination to capital insofar as old-time religion was instilled into the laborers. The press had an important share in the promotion of the campaigns, beginning a ballyhoo in each city weeks before the performances commenced. Without that publicity the campaigns could not have been conducted with financial success. To what extent the press was motivated by the private interests of the newspapers and their advertisers and to what extent by the obvious fact that the publicity was good copy, it was impossible to determine.

The revival business collapsed when the large contributions ceased and the ballyhoo in the newspapers let up. This collapse, it appears, was due to the discovery by potential donors that the results of the revivals were negligible and practically nonexistent. The number of 'trail hitters' (converts) publicly announced was impressive, but the numbers were fraudulent. Each trail hitter filled out a card on which he indicated the church with which he would like to affiliate; and there the racket broke down, for the cards were turned over to the ministers of the several churches. Checks showed that if the repeaters (persons who 'went forward' night after night), children under the age of fourteen, and those who were already church members in good standing were eliminated, the residue was so low as to be almost negligible.   There were a few persons who came forward at the meetings with serious intentions, but the majority of the trail hitters fell in the classes we have specified.   It was obvious that the large donors to the campaign funds were not getting their money's worth and that as a means of social control the revival circuses were complete failures.

Such commercialized revivals serve as illustrations of the charges often brought against religion, especially against Christianity, that religion is merely a 'social anodyne' designed and maintained for the purpose of keeping the underprivileged classes quiescent and properly subservient to the class of more fortunate persons, by inculcating in the lower classes the virtues of meekness, nonresistance, and submission to authority—however evil the authority may be.   This charge cannot be ignored or dismissed with contempt.

The social anodyne did not materialize in the Billy Sunday revivals, but since these campaigns were commercialized ventures, not involving sincerity of purpose on the part of the management group, the failure established little.   It is true that the campaigns were approved by many Christians, but the religious leaders for the most part gave their support reluctantly, feeling that they were being dragooned into support of that which was a degradation of religion.   On the other hand, a proponent of the social-anodyne theory of religion will usually admit that religion can succeed in social control only if it is administered by leaders who are sincere in their devotion to religion, who believe it to be directly beneficial to man, and who promote it without ulterior motivation.   Religion, in other words, cannot be a social anodyne unless it is directed by those who are not attempting to use it for that purpose.   Without the Pauls and the Timothys, with their sincerity of purpose, religion could not long persist even as a social anodyne.

The charges against religion boil down to this: that the devout leaders who are essential to religion, at least in modern times, are tools in the hands of persons higher up, who use them for their nefarious ends.   That the scheme failed to work in the Billy Sunday campaigns might, accordingly, be ascribed to the lack of sincere apostles.   The questions to be asked are: (a) Has the system worked in other cases?   (b) Can this system account for the persistence of religion through the ages? (*c*) Has there really been such a *system?*

That the religious leaders of modern religion have mostly been sincere can hardly be doubted. It has been charged that in earlier periods the priests were insincere and devoted to the maintenance and aggrandizement of their own powers and privileges. A statement ascribed to Cicero and to other ancient writers was to the effect that when two priests met they probably winked at each other in mutual recognition of the frauds they perpetrated on the gullible public. We have pointed out earlier that there is no discernible ground for this aspersion on the honesty of the priesthood generally. That there were priestly fakers in ancient times, as there are today, cannot be denied; but the fakers are cloaking themselves in disguises adopted from those of whom the sincerity is unmistakable. The existence of pretenders is really the great proof of the existence of those who are not pretenders.

We cannot accuse the founders of Christianity of promoting religion as a social anodyne. We cannot accuse their followers, who accepted martyrdom, of such skullduggery. The inculcation of meekness, nonresistance, and submission to authority was designed not to protect the social system but to save the lives of the Christians in a period in which resistance or nonsubmission to authority would have brought about their extermination.

The continuation of the obsolete precepts and practices of nonresistance into the modern period has doubtless been promoted by designing rulers and prostituted ecclesiastics as a good thing for the common herd, although, of course, not for themselves. Such usage of religion depends on two conditions: (*a*) the tendency of religion to cling to the principles and practices of the past, however unsuitable those may be for further stages of development; (*b*) the existence of sincere and devoted leaders and subordinates whose efforts can be used and directed by manipulators of religion. In short, religion cannot be employed for nefarious purposes unless religion exists as a vital institution. Nefarious employment of religion no more explains religion than does the failure in certain cases of attempts at such employment.

6. Religion and War.—Religion, we have insisted repeatedly, is continuous in form, but its functions change as the culture develops. Religion in any case is a feature in the total culture in which it is embedded. If its pattern conforms to the general cultural pattern, it thrives.   If it retains an archaic pattern, too far behind the general progress in economic, political, and moral respects, it does not thrive. It might be asked whether religion, if too far *ahead* of the general culture, would not equally be in a disadvantageous position.   The answer to this question would be that theoretically religion might be so far in advance of the general culture that it could not maintain itself, but, as a matter of fact, such a situation has never occurred. Religion consistently lags behind the crest of social progress, or at best is abreast of it.   Often, it is too far behind to be useful.

In regard to war, religion takes its cues from the group and the period of culture.   In ancient cultures, religion had functions in war, and in preparation for war, which were consonant with the attitudes of the groups and the periods.   War gods were evolved, and almost all gods were martially minded.   In the Trojan War, according to Homer, Hera, Ares, Poseidon, and Aphrodite participated on the Trojan side, while Athena and some of the other divinities fought with the Achaeans.   This mythological pattern indicates clearly the general function of the gods and more generally the function of religion in war.   The divinities helped the people whose divinities they primarily were, as the Hebrew Jehovah helped his 'chosen people.'   The migration of divinities, even the assimilation of foreign names by local gods, complicated this situation somewhat.   Ares and Aphrodite were known to have been of Asiatic origin, so that their assistance to the Asiatics in the Trojan War was assumed as a matter of course.   Hera, however, was an Achaean goddess and Poseidon was a god of the ancient Ionians, possibly of the Pelasgians, so that their favoring the Asiatics complicates the problem.   So far as Homer supplies the explanation, personal piques and jealousy of the goddesses and the gods seem to have entered into the situation.

So long as a group has gods who are in a particular sense its own, and who are opposed to the gods of enemy groups, the religious situation is simple.   If, however, groups at war, or planning war with each other, have the same gods or god, the situation is complicated.   This is the religious situation in our recent war (or recent phase of the war), and it was the situation in the first war (or first phase of this war) against Germany.   Even more definitely this situation obtained in our Civil War and in the American Revolution.   Both sides appealed to a God who was for each side ostensibly the same God.   Which side will the god favor?   Will he maintain an attitude of neutrality as Zeus did in the Trojan War? Or will he take a side? It might be assumed that God will favor the side that is fundamentally in the right. This may be held to be a logical solution of the problem, but apparently only God knows which is the right, for in most cases both sides are convinced that they are right. All we can say is that the God worshiped by one side is not really the God worshiped by the other side, or that one side or the other has misconceived him, or that he is as completely bound by cosmic laws as is man.

The rituals of religion are always applied to war purposes and war conditions. In ancient times, groups purposing war and groups threatened with war consulted the oracles for the purpose of finding out what were their chances of success and details concerning the ways in which they should proceed. These oracles were not presumed to have power to determine the issues, but were supposed to be sources of prediction. In the same way, seers accompanied armies and practiced their semantics, consulting the entrails of sheep to find the auspicious time for beginning an attack or for standing defensively. No such predictions are sought in modern warfare, but the armies of civilized groups are accompanied by chaplains, who hold religious services, administer the conventional rites to the dying, and conduct other rituals that are assumed to be protective to individuals. Good Catholic soldiers sedulously wear around their necks the medals that are infiltrated with protective manas instilled into them by prior blessing and contact with the hands of the priest. Whether the percentage slain of the groups that take these precautions are different from the death percentages of Protestants and others who take no such precautions might be determined but has not been.

It is obvious that the rituals that have developed for various uses apply in war as in peace and the divinities that give protection and assistance in peaceful life also give aid and protection in the hazards of battle. The generalization of the powers of divinity, their extension from particular forms of protection and promotion, to a wider sphere of influence is no more marked in war than in peaceful domestic and civic life. The effectiveness of these rituals in war and the effectiveness of the faiths that through the ages have developed around the rituals is another matter and requires consideration.

We have already pointed out that group rituals promote group solidarity.   Engaging in a common ritual, whatever else it may be, is a common or group activity.   The group spirit—the consciousness of belonging and the admission of common purposes—unites the individual more firmly to his group, and this group spirit, we have reason to assume, carries over into other group activities.   If a whole army participate in the common ritual, it is, we think, beneficial to the army, helping to make it more of an organism and less of a mere collection of individuals.   That the more integrated an army is, the more fully it acts as a unit, the stronger it is, is an obvious fact.

Beliefs and habits of thinking are integrating factors insofar as the beliefs are held in common by the members of the group and especially insofar as the *habits* of thought are common to the group members.   Emotional systems, which are technically called 'sentiments,' also are important integrating factors insofar as the sentiments are common.   These sentiments or emotional attitudes are merely systematized habits of thinking emotionally, and an emotion is any thought process or sequence of thought processes with which affective consciousness ('feeling,' in the vernacular) is associated.   Common feeling is admittedly an important factor in group integration.   The beliefs that are of importance in war, as in peaceful life, are not necessarily religious beliefs, and the effective sentiments are not necessarily religious sentiments.   The sentiment of devotion to duty and the sentiment of loyalty to one's group are complex attitudes that may be of great value in uniting the group and strengthening it for war.   The sentiments that we call selfishness and greed may in some circumstances strengthen a group for war of aggression, although these sentiments may be so directed as to turn the individuals composing a group against one another and so weaken the group.   The sentiment that we call cowardice is always disintegrative.

Group spirit and group loyalty were well expressed in a song that was popular during the first phase of this war (the phase that ended in 1918).   The refrain of the song was:

> Any old place the gang goes, I'll be there,
> Nobody knows where we go, divil a one of us cares;
> Give us a kiss for luck, dear, I'm off to do my share.
> Any old place the gang goes, I'll be there.

There was nothing religious about this song, but devotion to duty, group loyalty, and willingness to go to the extreme for principle are as common among those who are not classed as 'religious' as they are among those who avow religious convictions. A factor in this loyalty is the conviction that anything that is worth doing is worth the risk of death. We sometimes call this spirit 'recklessness,' but it has been the important factor in the development of some of our modern inventions. In the early period of flying, the risks were great and every aviator knew that if he kept on flying for a few years he would be killed, but he kept on flying. We sometimes call this the 'sporting attitude' or the 'sporting spirit'; but in some situations, as in war, the adjective 'sporting' does not describe the attitude adequately.

Effective propaganda directed upon a group to weaken it, so that it may become an easier prey to the group directing the propaganda or in order to make it incapable of intervening in an attack on other groups, commonly includes an assault on loyalty, not merely on loyalty to the total group, but on loyalty in lesser ways.

This program is based on the knowledge that loyalty to the group is a factor of strength and that loyalties of all degrees are interrelated habits. Such propaganda seeks always to promote selfish attitudes and cowardice. The propaganda that was directed upon the people of the United States by foreign agencies in such volume during the years from 1919 to 1941 included all these details and more, and almost succeeded in its purpose. This form of propaganda was nothing new in the world, except insofar as modern instruments, such as the radio, the printing press, and modern means of transportation, gave it a scope and force that similar procedures in ancient periods could not attain.

In emphasizing the applications of religious rituals to war conditions, we do not minimize the integrating effects of religious beliefs, quite aside from the rituals from which they have developed or with which they are associated. Thoroughgoing propaganda designed to weaken a potential enemy nation does not, in modern times, overlook this, but attempts to weaken religious faith as well as to undermine 'bourgeois morality.' There is, however, another application of religious faith, which has been utilized in the past and which goes beyond the integrative effects we have described.

If individuals are convinced that through war they may gain otherworldly benefits, they are made eager for war and cooperate more actively and effectively in war. This was illustrated in the Crusades and in the fanatical devotion of the Arabs in their assaults on other peoples. It is a tenet of Islam that the true believer who dies fighting against heretics is assured thereby of entrance into the full delights of Paradise, regardless of his other qualifications or disqualifications. There is no doubt that this belief was an effective aid to the Arab hosts in the period of expansion of Islam and of Arab dominance. That Christians participating in the Crusades were motivated by a similar belief that other-worldly credit was obtained through fighting for the Cross against the Saracens and that sins could be washed away by fighting unto death against the enemies of Christianity cannot be denied. If, by the dispensation of God or of Allah, Mohammedan or Christian should come through war unharmed, he still might attain merit by the slaughter of the enemies of his religion. Dispensations were granted by the church to Crusaders; the dispensations being believed to shorten the Crusaders' terms in purgatory, whether or not they were slain in battle. It is difficult to determine to what extent this faith in other-worldly gains through valiant fighting against one's enemies and the enemies of the culture one values survives among Christians. Insofar as moral principles are tied up with other-worldly faith, the motive doubtless is still somewhat important.

Changes in the conception of survival after death have occurred, but the concept remains. Perhaps interest in guaranteeing a blessed immortality to one's 'soul' or some other personal appurtenance has somewhat waned, but there still persists the interest in perpetuating one's name and reputation unsullied and enhanced in brilliance in the estimation of one's associates, and especially one's descendants. That bravery unto death and devotion to one's duty to the group is the highest means of securing this perpetuation there is no doubt. Is this a religious matter, or is it not? The decision is a matter of definition, and all we may say with certainty is that it is so close to religion that drawing the line is difficult.

One point cannot be ignored. Insofar as fighting attains, or is an attempt to attain, a religious end, war itself becomes an actual ritual of religion. For the Mohammedan and for the Crusader, the war in which he engaged was a ritual. For the modern Christian, insofar as risking his life and slaying the enemies of his culture are considered the seeking of religious ends, then for him also war is a religious ritual.

The notion that death in battle ensures entrance into heaven has passed out of the tenets of modern warriors. Even death in a war for moral principles is not believed to ensure other-worldly benefits or rewards. A paragraph from an editorial in the *Daily Mirror*, quoted in *Time* (Vol. XLI, No. 2, Jan. 11, 1943), illustrates well the modern attitude toward death in battle: 'Tommy Cook and his pals were never taught that if you run out and give your life in battle you win a free ticket to a special warrior's heaven. They fought on the theory that the best soldier is the soldier who wants to live. And they fought with all the American ingenuity that is their heritage.'

Religion, we have repeated, is an institution that takes over functions for which there is no other institution ready to function, and it may assume functions that are supplementary to those of other institutions, formally organized or informal. That religion promoted loyalty and consideration for other persons and other groups and that the desire to help the unfortunate and promote group welfare may be an added factor in building up group cohesion and group strength, in war as well as in peace, is all that we are claiming for religion.

War, in ancient periods, was regarded as an inevitable feature in human life and was even considered a noble pursuit. Great warriors have always been admired as the greatest heroes, and they are still admired. A great change in attitude toward war, however, has taken place among civilized peoples, and peoples who do not adopt the modern attitudes we consider not really civilized in the highest sense of the term. How far religion has contributed to this change, and how much it can contribute in the future, is the main point of importance in the consideration of religion in relation to war.

This change has its roots in early Mediterranean civilization and is indicated by the different positions of Ares and Athena as war divinities. Ares, as many scholars have pointed out, was a god of destructive, insensate war (indicated earlier when we pointed out his original ass form). We might describe him as the god of war for war's sake, although it would be more descriptive to call him the god of war pursued for the destruction of other peoples and for the seizing of their possessions. The Roman wolf god Mars was a fellow of the same sort and typifies the Roman attitude down to the end of Roman power. Athena, on the other hand, was the goddess of defensive war, a protectress rather than a destroyer. It is true that the Achaeans are represented by Homer as carrying on an unprovoked war of attack on the Trojans, and this may possibly account in part for the somewhat equivocal position of Athena in the Trojan War.   We do not know the full story of that war and its foundations, and hence our judgment may be suspended.   It is clear, however, that in the ancient Mediterranean world, a distinction was in the making between offensive war and defensive war, a distinction that has grown in importance in modern times.   Whatever we may think about war in the abstract, we today consider war to defend ourselves a moral procedure, which, when necessary, should be entered upon resolutely and with full force.   We consider also, with our broadening of the scope of morality, that war to defend and protect other groups suffering from attack or oppression is a moral undertaking. Under the influence of the propaganda to which I have referred, we almost lost our morals as a nation, but we are on the way to regaining our moral decency.

War, we may admit, is a dreadful disaster.   It not only destroys human lives in an appalling way, but it sets back social progress and not only destroys the monuments of human achievement (works of art, libraries, and other hard-won materials of culture), but also wastes metals that are irreplaceable.   War is something to be avoided, if possible; but when avoidance is impossible, we consider it noble to fight.   This war, of course, could easily have been avoided if, ten years before Pearl Harbor, we had announced our willingness to fight and had proceeded with armament.   One does not avoid war by running away from it or by sitting idle and careless when others are being slaughtered.   Those who have studied group psychology have long known this, and ordinary citizens are being enlightened by the war in regard to the procedures which, over the last twenty years, brought the war upon us.

When we ask whether religion has fostered or retarded the progress toward the modern attitude toward war, the religion we are questioning, of course, is Christianity.   We have made reference to Islam in another connection, but this religion is not in point here.   Hinduism is still another matter, although the doctrine of passive resistance inculcated by some schools of modern Hinduism might throw sidelights on our problem, particularly through consideration of its deep antagonism to Islam.   In civilized cultures, Christianity has been for eighteen centuries the influential religion, and we are concerned here with the culture called civilization and the attitudes toward war that have arisen in these cultures.

It has sometimes been assumed that there have been religious wars, wars in which the basis of conflict have been differences in religion between the combatant groups. Such wars, however, have never occurred. Religion has often been an aid in making war, as it has been for Mohammedans and for Christians in the Crusades, but cannot be shown in any case to have been the real cause of war. Religious persecution, involving massacres of heretics, is another matter. This may occur as an adjunct of war, but has occurred without war. The imposing of the religion of the conquering group on the conquered has been a technique of political control effectively employed by the Arabs, but the expansion of the scope of their ancient habits of robbery and pillage and the attempt to dominate other groups for their practical advantage seem to have been the real basis for assaults on other groups. The emphasis of a religious difference between the aggressors and their victims has been useful in the prosecution of war and in preparation for it. German leaders such as Nietzsche and Wagner for more than a century have utilized this method, depreciating Christian humanitarian principles and urging return to the old religion of the forest ancestors of the German people. This, however, is a technique of war, not a basic cause.

Many exponents of Christianity have assumed that the doctrine of nonresistance is fundamental in this religion. This doctrine has been ascribed to the Founder of Christianity, although there are very few reported sayings of his on which the doctrine could be hung, and these are not clearly relevant. That nonresistance was advised for certain circumstances may be admitted, but the generalizations that have been made are unfounded and unwise. It may be admitted that, if men ceased fighting, there would be no war, but what is lost by refusing to fight may be greater than anything to be gained by the refusal. Jesus, we may well admit, did not approve of war as such. He does not say that he came into the world to bring war, but he does say that he came to send not peace, but the sword (Matt. 10: 34), and this is as significant a saying as any that is ascribed to Him.

We must remember that men usually do not fight merely for the sake of fighting, but that they fight for something deemed worth fighting for. The primary desires on which religion is founded are also the foundation of war, although secondary desires enter in some cases. In general, it is not sensible to fight unless there seems something it is possible to gain or something that is in danger of being taken away and that it seems possible to retain by fighting. This generalization can be extended.   In general, men do not fight unless there is something to be gained or retained by fighting.   This holds for fighting between individuals, for fighting between small groups, and for the fighting between larger groups that we call war.

If there is nothing to be gained by resistance, and much to be lost, resistance may be stupid, although we highly honor the one who resists even though he be tortured and slain.   We did not think it wise for the peoples enslaved by the Germans to rebel, because the result would have been merely mass slaughter.   Those who do rebel, however, and are slain we acclaim as heroes and martyrs.   When in the course of events, uprising has a chance, we will approve the uprising.   Is it possible that Jesus was so far out of line with our notions of heroism and morals as certain of those who interpret him allege?   No, it is not.

If we hark back to the first century of the Christian Era, during which the four gospels were written, we find that Christians were an unfortunate lot of people.   Mostly of the downtrodden classes, they were resented by the upper classes, who adhered to the old religions.   They were slaves and freemen who were poor, overworked, and victims of injustice in other respects.   Persecution was common.   Now, if the Christians had tried to defend themselves, had resisted, had fought against their persecutors, what would have been the result?   Well, it is a good guess that they would have been exterminated.   Resistance would have given their enemies a chance to say: What did we tell you?   These are dangerous people; they are violent and vicious.   Christianity, very probably, would have been extinguished.   By nonresistance (turn the other cheek) and by secrecy where possible, recognizing one another by the sign of the fish, the continuance of the Christian group was made possible and its spread probable.   Was this cowardice?   No, it was common sense.   A few leaders came out in the open and put themselves in the way of martyrdom, as did Jesus himself.   That this gave courage to the humbler Christians who were detected and martyred cannot be doubted.   There is no evidence, however, that the rank and file of Christians were expected to seek the martyr's crown.

This policy has been attributed to Jesus, but the synoptic gospels do not give consistent support to this view.   It may be claimed that this policy did not arise until after the Christians had become numerous, in the period in which the gospels were written.   It is claimed, on the other hand, that Jesus gave this advice some time before there was any group of Christians to be persecuted. One who takes this orthodox point of view, however, would have no difficulty in admitting that Jesus was able to foresee future contingencies and needs. So, whether you think that the gospels report the sayings of Jesus accurately or think that the sayings express policies developed later than the time assigned to Jesus, it still remains that this policy of turning the other cheek was sound for the situations in which the early converts to Christianity found themselves. I prefer to think that the Jesus described in the gospels spoke as he is reported in them to have spoken, for we know of no other Jesus than the 'dramatic personality' presented in the gospels, which has been so influential in the development of civilized religion.

It is well to compare the doctrine that one should turn the other cheek with the lesson conveyed by the parable of the good Samaritan. This is the story of a Jew who was waylaid by robbers on the road from Jerusalem to Jericho. The robbers stripped him of his goods, beat him, and left him disabled. Passers-by ignored him, until the Samaritan bound up his wounds and carried him to safety. That the travelers who 'passed by on the other side,' that is, were neutral and considered the Jew's misfortune and injuries as none of their business, were afraid that by taking charge of the victim they themselves would be endangered is not explicitly stated, but the implication is in the story. The lesson, at any rate, is that one should come to the aid of others in distress, at any cost. Whatever might be inferred from Jesus' teachings in regard to defending oneself from injury, there is no ground whatever for assuming that he approved of taking no steps to defend one's neighbors from injustice, injury, and death. That he did not disdain the use of physical force is evident from his scourging the money-changers from the temple.

When Christianity became accepted by the ruling classes and was no longer the religion of a group of slaves and underprivileged people, it had new responsibilities thrust upon it, and the precepts demanded reinterpretation in the light of the fundamental principles of morality. No longer were Christians restricted to the defense of their class against more powerful classes, but it became a duty to defend all men who are suffering injustice. From time to time, through the centuries, the old precepts of nonresistance to evil-doers have cropped up. However one might justify the principle of nonresistance to injuries inflicted on himself, the refusal of a Christian to defend his neighbor from injury or death is a plain abandonment of the fundamental principles of the Christian faith, for which there may have been excuse in the early hazards of Christianity, but for which there is not the slightest warrant in the gospels, for in the gospels meekness is approved, but not cowardice. Even in the apostolic writings men were warned that faith without works is dead; that principles upon which one will not act in spite of the threat of death are empty shams.

Yet, Christian groups have cooperated with foreign agents and agencies cooperating with the groups abroad preparing for ruthless oppression and slaughter; cooperating under the sham banners of pacifism, neutrality, and toleration. Toleration of what? Toleration of the power of evil. That is the abandonment of responsibility for one's neighbor, a responsibility that is the fundamental principle of Christianity.

Sheer ignorance of facts as well as principles may have been the trouble with some of those who assisted the enemies of civilization. This does not excuse a religious group for failure to uphold the principles they ostensibly adopt. The church either should know what it is doing in the political field, internal or international, or definitely stay out. If unintelligent devotion to outworn precepts of the past is responsible, the conclusion is the same.

Those Christians who object to the use of physical force to defend themselves and to defend others are sometimes called pacifists. Pacifism, however, is an ambiguous term. In one sense it means the attitude of those who wish for peace and are willing to do something to bring about peace and prevent war. One who is a pacifist in this sense is willing to fight for peace. In the other sense, pacifism is the attitude of those who do not choose to endanger their own necks and do not intend to do anything to protect others. Another name for this pacifism is cowardice. Now, among the 'conscientious objectors' who refuse to fight, there are undoubtedly some who are sincere and are motivated by principle. Some of these, in the first German war, woke up to a realistic understanding of the situation and became our most heroic fighting men (Sergeant York, for example). The same thing has happened, it seems, to many in the second war with Germany. The conscientious objectors who did not get into the war, but remained in camps to which they were remanded really deserve our pity, for they will probably remain cowards to the ends of their lives and continue to justify themselves by confused principles that are slanderous to Christianity, and particularly to its Founder.

The 'pacifists' who we may reasonably believe to have been sincere have not been leaders in the movements for nonresistance, isolation, toleration (of criminals), and the selfish and anti-Christian policy of saving one's own skin regardless of the sufferings of others. Excluding the purely selfish pacifists, there undoubtedly have been some who were sincere 'stooges' of the leaders. We cannot assume, however, that the leaders in these movements have been sincere. Many of them, it is clear, have been working in the interests of groups who were planning to attack, enslave, and massacre peaceful peoples. These have been the actual warmongers, although it is true that if the civilized groups could have been brought to the point at which they would tamely submit to enslavement and domination like dumb beasts there would have been no war; there would have been only conditions worse than war. Some of these leaders may have been merely stupid, but it seems probable that most of them have known that they were not really working for peace.

We cannot say that the church as a whole has worked for war. In the past twenty years the cooperation of different churches with the enemies of Christianity and civilization has, nevertheless, been striking. That church groups cooperated with our enemies in the passage of the infamous neutrality bill (Hitler's greatest victory) was obvious. The churches today do not occupy a position of high regard in the public eye in respect to the promotion of the principles of the Prince of Peace. Religion, at least as represented by the churches, has suffered more in the last twenty years than in any century before. If we could predict that from now on the Christian church could be counted on to return to the principles of Christianity, we might be hopeful for its future. Unfortunately, no such prediction can be made. It was evident that at the end of this war the church, or at least many influential church groups, would be cooperating with warmongers for a 'soft' peace that will make further war inevitable, just as they cooperated with the warmongers at the end of the first German war. Many of the individuals in the religious groups will be sincere and merely unintelligent. They will cooperate, however, with leaders who do not really want peace or the essential conditions that alone can make peace permanent. The Christian church, in short, appears to be carrying out a policy of slow but sure suicide, which could be obviated only by a return to Christianity.

If the church would take the stand that religion has no concern with morality, but is concerned only with conducting rituals that are for other-worldly purposes for the individuals of the group, not for the group itself, it might continue in that field, as we have earlier indicated.   In that case, the church would have to relinquish interference in international affairs as well as in affairs pertaining to the inner life of groups.   International affairs of importance to humanity then would have to be settled by secular groups—in this case, by political groups—and might have a greater probability of being settled on moral principles consonant with Christianity.   It is to be feared, however, that settlement after this war will have to be made, not regardless of religion, but against the opposition of many religious groups.

CHAPTER XIV

THE FUTURE OF RELIGION IN CIVILIZATION

1. **Modification of the Tentative Concept of Religion.**—The discussion of the changes that have taken place in the functions of religion, changes that are continuing and will go further, should have made it obvious that our tentative definition, or rather description, of religion needs revision. While in the early stages of religious development religion can be described as the attempt to do what man does not know how to do and to know the unknowable, and while this attempt to do what cannot be done and to know what cannot be known still persists in religion, there are certain features of religion in its present stage to which the description does not adequately apply.

The definition, or description, may be extended as follows. Religion is the institution, or feature of culture, which undertakes, in the service of mankind, those functions for which there is no other institution or for the undertaking of which no other institution is as yet adequately prepared. This formulation includes our first tentative definition, but for completeness' sake we may add to our final formulation an explanatory clause, as follows. These undertakings often involve the attempt to do what man does not know how to do and the attempt to know what it is impossible for man to know.

If this characterization of religion is sound, it is evident that no definitions of religion in terms of specific faiths or specific rituals can be valid for religion generally, and a definition of a particular religion is of minor importance. Faiths and rituals change, but religion persists because its basic characteristic is a function or set of functions that can be described only in social terms, since as culture changes the functions change. Religion, from this point of view, is a suicidal institution, since it exercises functions that promote the development of other institutions, which supplant religion by taking over the functions that it had previously exercised.

Science, which has largely supplanted religion in its economic functions, grew out of religion. Philosophy, which has in no period supplanted religion but which has been an important critic, and to some extent a rival, of religion, also grew out of religion. The earlier philosophies of the Western world from Thales to Plato began as interpretations of popular religious faiths, and Aristotle marks the beginning of the secularization of philosophy. Medicine, as we have pointed out, was a religious function down to the beginning of the Christian Era, but out of the cult of healing, secular medicine slowly developed, and it promises eventually to supplant religion completely in the fields of healing and hygiene.

Political organization and government was in ancient times guided by religion but has made substantial progress toward secularization and will, it seems probable, eventually become completely detached from religion and religious organization. Religion undertook the function of promoting ethics and practical morals for two reasons: (a) because no other institution was ready to assume the function; (b) because, of the growing interest in morals, religion either had to conform to moral standards or else lose its importance. But the promotion of ethics and morality is becoming more and more a secular function.

The development of art, in its various forms—pictorial, plastic, dramatic, and musical—is another instance of functions that have been so well exercised that they are eventually secularized. The religious fostering of literature through the ages might also be cited. All of these changes from religious function to secular control may be expected to go further. This raises the question: What functions will the church have in the future?

Progress, we have pointed out, cannot be checked, unless the culture crystallizes, as savage cultures have done, or unless the culture is wrecked. If civilization perishes and society returns to the savagery and barbarism of pre-Christian times, all predictions for progress are canceled. The only prediction that could be made for that case is that culture, set back twenty centuries, would again start along the line of progress it has so far followed. Predictions concerning an organism or a cultural institution are made on the assumption that the organism lives or that the culture is not destroyed.

On this basis we may consider the problem as to the future of religion in the culture in which it has grown up. The problem is: What functions of use to mankind can religion assume if and when, and insofar as, its present functions are outworn?

First, however, we should consider the probability that sudden shifts in function are not either useful or desirable. The shift from religious control of agriculture and other economic processes to scientific control has been slow and may be considered as normal, sound growth. It is perhaps fortunate that the removal of political organization and government from religious control also proceeds slowly. Whether revolutionary sweeping away of religious functions will have been found to succeed in Russia is a question concerning which we have propaganda, but few facts. In any case the arbitrary method is dangerous. If organized medicine should succeed in the effort in which it is engaged—to concentrate all healing and hygiene, mental and physical, in the hands of the Medical Labor Union—it would throw mental therapy into the hands of charlatans and stop progress in the psychological treatment of disorders. We may well hold the opinion that, if religion should suddenly abandon welfare work, or if religious organizations should be arbitrarily excluded from the field of applied morals, or if religious organizations should suddenly abandon these fields and its functions therein, it would be unfortunate for social progress. In the past, changes have been made in the functions of organizations by laws or by dictators, but the results of these changes seem not to have been satisfactory; hence we must assume that for the future the same process of slow growth and slow change in functions that has been operative in the past will be essential.

Secular organizations can with safety take over functions that were previously exercised by religious organizations only when the secular organizations have reached the point in efficiency at which it is obvious that they can exercise the functions better. When secular organizations reach that point, they take over by common consent, with no need for enactment of laws or for dictatorial edicts of dictators. Forcing the issue, and requiring the change, we think, would be disastrous; attempts to force the issue have been made in the past only by groups who have sought to promote their special interests at the expense of public interest.

2. **The Possibilities for Religion in the Future.**—For functions of religions of civilized peoples in the future, there seem to be five possibilities, and only five. (*a*) Religious organizations (churches) may find functions that have not been exercised, in fields in which there is no secular agency prepared to exercise the functions. (*b*) The church may devote itself to the promotion and maintenance of rituals devoid of doctrines and applications. (*c*) The church may continue its services in moral affairs, accepting a secondary role under the leader-

ship of the state and other secular organizations. (*d*) The church may restrict its functions to those for which there is not, never has been, and never will be any secular organization, namely, those concerning other-wordly concepts and further matters of faith that are not subjects of knowledge. (*e*) The church may cease to exist in civilized cultures, persisting only among barbarous peoples. We shall consider these possibilities in the order in which they are listed, together with matters that are pertinent to them.

The first possibility is the discovery of new functions, but what these functions could be we are unable at present to guess. All we can say is that, if new human needs or desires appear and are identified and if there is no secular organization prepared to assume the work of providing for these new needs or desires, the church undoubtedly will step into the gap as it has done throughout the past. We may, therefore, pass over this conjectural field for religion of the future, with the remark that, if this possibility for religion is the only one open, the future for religion is not bright.

The second possibility for religion we have described briefly as that of devoting itself to the development and maintenance of rituals devoid of religious interpretations. We have earlier emphasized the fact that participation by members of the group in group rituals assists in the integration of the group, but it does not seem likely that specialization of an organization in mere ritual could be useful. Aside from religious rituals, rituals are practiced by groups of all sorts and seem to be vital only in groups that are organized for purposes other than the mere practicing of rituals. It is true that some rituals are rather stupid, as is the ritual conducted by university groups at commencements, and that the rituals of some religious sects are not so effective as they might be, but these rituals can be improved only by the groups that have maintained them, although the advice of a psychologist is useful. Furthermore, the attempt to promote rituals that were assumed to be religious, and were at least group rituals, devoid of interpretations and not associated with doctrines, has been made and has failed (Chap. III.). It is true that those attempts were made in competition with other organized groups that combined rituals with dogmas, which of course does not prove that if all churches abandoned dogmas and concentrated on mere ritual, the attempt would fail. Attempt of any group to maintain ritual dissociated from doctrines would, however, face the same competition that was faced by the groups of the past;

hence growth of such a functional change would be impossible. We are consequently entitled to a pessimistic view of the theoretical possibility that religion could restrict its functions to the maintenance of mere ritual.

The third theoretical possibility for civilized religion of the future is the abandonment of the claim of being the authoritative source of moral principles, with the acceptance of subordination to morality and of the function of serving society by increased promotion of justice, in principle and in practice. This change involves the abandonment of the claim of the church to leadership in the domain of morals, a leadership that it has never really achieved, and the admission of its willingness to continue as an assistant to the state and to other secular organizations in this important work. This change, making the claims of religion agree with its actual performances, might well increase the efficiency of religion in promoting morality.

Such a relinquishment of claims to leadership, and acceptance of the role of an assistant, may seem revolutionary, but actually it has been in progress for a long time. Although we can set no exact dateline for the change from the old religion, in which man's duty was simply to conform to rules that were supposed to have been established by the gods who themselves were not conceived as subject to moral principles, to the newer religious faiths in which morality was required of gods as of man, we can say that this change appeared to be progressing in the period that includes the fifth and fourth centuries B.C. Greek philosophers were protesting the legends that ascribed immorality to the gods. The Jewish scriptures, compiled about the middle of the fifth century B.C., show clear indications of the new concept, although the compilers and editors did not exclude the older traditions in which God is the arbitrary source of morals, and the whole duty of man was to comply with edicts of God, edicts that were often highly unjust.

No adherent of Western religion today would accept a God or a minor divinity (saint) who was not conceived as complying with the basic moral principle of justice; a God conceived as immoral, as judged by human standards, is unthinkable for either Jew or Christian. Apostles of oriental religions that have been introduced into the West—sects of Islam and of Hinduism in especial—have found it necessary to justify their gods by moral principles, although in the Orient such justification is not necessary.

The subordination of God to moral principles, a subordination that is accepted in the great religions of civilization, is a symbol of the subordination of religion to morals which has been in progress for three thousand years, at least, and which we can reasonably expect to go further. Open acceptance of this subordination would provide for continuation of an important function of religion.

The fourth possibility for the future functions of religion is its maintenance of the function that it has long exercised and for which no other organization or institution exists. This function has to do with the other world, and, aside from rituals that are designed to produce results in this world through the intervention of powers of the other world, the obvious concern of religion in respect to the other world centers about the concepts of gods and of survival of death.

There are two possible objections to the continuation of other-wordly functions by organized religion. The first objection is the claim that philosophy deals with the concepts of gods and of survival more efficiently than does religion and that religion should relinquish to philosophy its functions of interpreting the concepts and of instructing the public in respect to these concepts. It is true that philosophy commenced to deal with these concepts as soon as it emerged from religion and has continued ever since to concern itself with them, but the concepts are still concepts of religion. We might say that a theologian such as Augustine or Clement, in discussing other-worldly matters, functions as a philosopher. We might equally well say that a philosopher who discusses other-worldly concepts has entered the field of religion. That two disciplines may overlap, in their fields, is admitted, but whether or not the church, in considering other-worldly affairs, is philosophizing is a question of no importance. Other-worldly beliefs are clearly religious beliefs, because they are not capable of being subjected to checks, scientific or informal. We cannot even say that an other-worldly belief is magical, or not magical, since the validity of the belief cannot be determined. If we reject an other-worldly belief, we may call it "magical," but we have no grounds for the rejection, unless logical inconsistency is involved.

The second possible objection is that interest in the other world is waning and that religion, concerning itself with other-worldly problems, will soon, or at least eventually, cease to have any function because it will satisfy no human desires. This is an objection based on alleged facts, but the allegations are disputable. In this connection, we may repeat that a denial of a theory or belief concerning the other world is just as religious as its affirmation. The only point of view that could be considered secular is that of complete skepticism, admitting that neither the affirmative nor the negative is capable of proof and assuming the attitude of indifference to the point at issue. If it is true that men are decreasingly interested in the question whether there is a god or not and in the question whether death does or does not end all, then the functions of religion, as well as the importance of the philosophy of religion, are indeed on the wane. That this is true is not apparent, in spite of the fact that the nature of the problems have, for the rank and file of men in the Western world, progressively changed.

It is pertinent, therefore, to consider these problems and ascertain what they really are. It is pertinent, moreover, to insist that the origin of a belief, and the method of its evolution, have no bearing on the truth or falsity of the belief. One may believe a certain lubricating oil has less corrosive action on machinery than does a certain other oil, merely because some garageman has told him so, with no proof. Yet, the belief may be valid.

The fifth possibility, that religion may disappear from the culture that we call civilization, is to be faced only if and when religion ceases to have any important functions. This possibility does not appear imminent. There are enough functions for religion, if it faces the future soundly, to ensure its continuation for as long a period as civilization may endure. The salient characteristic of religion, in spite of its incurable attachment to the past, is its ability to adapt itself to changed conditions when adaptation is necessary to ensure the survival of religion. In view of the long history of religion and its adaptation to changed social conditions, we may safely predict that the salient characteristics will not be lost, and hence that religion will long endure.

Some light is thrown on the problem of religious functions by the history of Unitarianism. Unitarianism was first established as a group of churches that seceded from the Congregational faith. The number of these churches was augmented by congregations of other sects, which seceded from their original affiliations and became Unitarian, for example, King's Chapel in Boston, which was originally Episcopalian.

The original divergence of the Unitarians from orthodoxy appears to have been the rejection of the doctrine of the Trinity that made Jesus an aspect of the godhead and rejection of the authority of the Jewish Scriptures. These views are more or less accepted by Protestant denominations today, although the verbal formulations of the doctrines of these sects have not been changed. The literal inspiration of the Bible is no longer a tenet, and as for the status of Jesus, the statement that he was (or is) divine is variously understood. The situation here is comparable to that involved in belief in God. One person announces a belief in God. Another is a disbeliever. When we find out what each means by the word 'God,' however, we often discover that there is little difference. The disbeliever may mean that he doesn't believe in a fellow with long whiskers who supervises things, but believes in a central and intelligent power in the universe; and that may be all that is meant by the man who announces that he believes in God.

Unitarianism, however, rapidly progressed to other radical positions. It is fair to say that Unitarianism rejects the faith that any ritual is efficacious, that is, that it has any practical effect. The belief in an 'other world' is approved, but that there can be any results of ritual on the other-worldly status of a person is denied.

Unitarianism has turned its interest to the ethical and moral features of life and requires no faith of members beyond the faith in moral principles. What has been the result?

Unitarianism has been described by men who have been leaders of the sect as a 'dying sect.' This is not the opinion merely of disappointed persons, but has been confirmed by ministers who have been especially successful in the denomination. Members who were brought up in the orthodox sects, in which the virtues of church membership and of church attendance were emphasized, have been the supporters of Unitarianism. Their children, however, see no reason for support of the church. They are taught that neither church membership nor church attendance has any effect. So why should they bother about it? They do not! The result is a progressive dying of the local churches. The Unitarians still retain their interest in the other world, and, so far as I can make out, the majority of the members still believe in, or at least hope for, a life after death. They admit, however, that they can do nothing about it, so that even the other-worldly factor ceases to sustain religion.

That the factor in religion which, from a scientific point of view, we call 'magic,' is essential to religion might be inferred from the rise of certain cults that claim efficacy of their magical procedures. The membership of these sects appears at present to be largely composed of individuals who were previously adherents of Protestant sects or of the Jewish religion. To persons trained in the faiths of these sects, the changes in faith that the sects have undergone is disconcerting. The implicit dependence on the Bible and the belief in the efficacy of rituals have diminished. Persons who have based their lives on faith in absolute authority and on the magical efficacy of rituals are left adrift when their sects abandon these faiths. A new faith, which employs the familiar verbal formulae and offers an authoritative basis, with rituals that are claimed to be efficacious, appeals to them and enables them to continue in a way of life to which they have become accustomed. If the new religion offers relief from ethical worries and from practical moral responsibility by its teaching that evil and suffering are no problems, because they do not really exist, it helps; but the finding of a conventional basis in assured and unquestioned authority probably is the most important attraction. The continuance of these sects, after the members who have been schooled in orthodox beliefs has passed away, is a problem on which prediction is difficult. Apparently, many of the younger generation leave the sect, but perhaps others find in its tenets and rituals the same satisfaction that in past generations the other Christian sects have provided.

That verbal formulations are of ritual value, quite aside from the significance of the words, is a fact that may throw some light on the possibility of the continuation of religion on a merely ritual basis. The formulae of St. Paul, of church fathers, and of Ralph Waldo Emerson, who in some respects qualifies as a 'father,' are familiar to modern Protestants; and ministers employ these verbalisms in their sermons to the satisfaction of their audiences. The primary meanings of the formulae are usually of no significance to the hearers and are often unmarked by the ministers. I have asked young ministers who have employed phraseology that either had a definite mystical meaning, or else no meaning at all, whether they really meant what they said. Usually, the minister completely repudiates the actual meaning of the phrases he had used. Persons who change affiliation from one Christian sect to another are usually not influenced so much by details of creeds as they are by basic doctrines, but the change is made easy and attractive when the phraseology employed by the new sect is closely akin to that of the old.

From the available information we may draw a tentative conclusion, namely, that a religion or a sect of religion may be expected to live only so long as it conforms to four conditions.

1. The doctrine or faith involved in the religion must be based on authority or its equivalent. Proof of the items of faith must not be required or offered. In the past, the basis for faith has been the allegation that 'our fathers believed this' or the less sound assertion that some person in the past, a person who really knew, communicated the faith as the truth. This is the claim that the author or authors of the doctrine were 'inspired,' for except by 'inspiration' no one can know that a religious doctrine is true or know that it is false.

What is the equivalent for the authority on which a doctrine is based? It is the demonstration that the doctrine is one that has been developed by the group, slowly and progressively, and that the doctrine, whether it is accepted or rejected, is logically consistent. Self-consistency and development by generations of men is the only authority a religious doctrine can now have.

2. The doctrines of the sect must include a definite faith in an other world, which other world for modern religion must be both the residence of divinity and the place in which the appurtenance or appurtenances of the human being that survives death has its existence. A religion that is concerned merely with things of the world in which we presently live and move and have our being is but a proto-religion, which can persist only by developing other-worldly faiths.

3. Faith that certain rituals are efficacious in human relations with the other world are useful in many stages of religious development. The rituals that are believed to secure help in this world from other-worldly powers and rituals assumed to assure the salvation of the individual in the post-mortem existence seem to have been important for the preservation of religion during the earlier periods, but this preservation has been important only in that it has enabled religion to progress beyond these faiths. Since relatively few adherents of religion in modern times have progressed to the stage in which these faiths are not essential to them, they may need to be retained by religion for a considerable further period of time. Faith in the efficacy of rituals for salvation in the other world will eventually be eliminated, and a faith in the efficacy of prayer for this worldly benefits will be eliminated unless experiments show

conclusively that the faith is sound, in which case the faith would be replaced by scientific knowledge.

4. The younger generations in the religious groups must be sedulously instructed in the doctrines of the sect and as sedulously protected against secular influences that would undermine their faith. The essentia protection is afforded by instruction in regard to the essential difference between religious faith and scientific or practical knowledge and in regard to the impossibility of demonstrating the truth or the falsity of a really religious faith. Most orthodox sects are well aware of the need of instruction of youth in religious doctrines and of the importance of protection from antagonistic doctrines, but do not seem to appreciate the importance of the final feature of the program and commonly do not even understand the distinction between religious faith and knowledge.

3. The Truth or Falsity of Religion.—Nothing that has been said should be interpreted as indicating that the doctrines, which religions have persistently taught, regarding the other world and its relation to mundane life are untrue. The question as to *how* men have developed certain beliefs through the ages is one thing. The question of whether or not these beliefs are valid, or of how far they are valid, is quite another matter. The association of beliefs that may be valid with other beliefs that we may have reason to reject has no effect on the validity of the important faiths. The question of historical development must be kept separate from the question of validity. The first question can be answered by consideration of the actual historical processes. The second cannot be so simply answered, although the historical fact that mankind has persistently worked toward the development of certain faiths is a consideration that cannot be ignored.

To assume that an important faith was revealed to man, that it was given to man from other-worldly sources, is not a solution of the question. The fact that men believe what they do because they have been educated in that belief is no basis for a better solution. In either case, acceptance is based on something in the faith itself that appeals to man. Many religions have been alleged to have been 'revealed,' but the question is: Why do we accept one 'revealed' religion and reject others? Some of the reasons for acceptance have been discussed, and early training has been emphasized; but the conditions obtaining over a lifetime, or a few generations, are of little consequence. If, over countless generations, man has developed beliefs that are not ephemeral, it is another matter, if we believe that man is, in the long run, intelligent. For the development of sound views of life, as for the development of sound praxes, the group, not the individual, is important; and the group is important only when it is considered over a period of many generations.

It is now time to revert to certain concepts that we have treated somewhat summarily in earlier chapters, but which should be of high importance for the religion of the future. That these concepts have developed during the past centuries along paths through quagmires of childish absurdity is a fact that has no bearing on their importance. They are concepts that have given rise to conflicting doctrines, and for the decision of these conflicts science can give no help, since they lie outside the field of science.

4. **God, Freedom, and Immortality.**—Immanuel Kant, in his *Critique of Pure Reason*, propounded three concepts, which he called the 'Transcendental Ideas of Reason' and which, in Supplement XXVI to his *Critique*, he claims are the sole concerns of metaphysics. These 'ideas' are the concepts of God, of freedom, and of immortality. The three concepts, of course, are of popular origin, but that they have been important in human life we have been indicating throughout this volume. The concept of God and the concept of immortality are purely religious concepts, and it may turn out that the concept of freedom also is religious. In connection with our discussion of future possible functions for religion, we need to give further consideration to these three concepts.

Concepts developed by human beings over long stretches of generations can seldom be dismissed from consideration. Although in the development of the concepts, many errors, which we call 'superstition,' encumber the principles, the consideration of the group principles is essential, and the problem for the philosopher is to sort over the concepts, eliminating the superstitions, but not 'throwing out the baby with the bath.'

Science, we have pointed out, is a fairly recent development and has built on the substantial foundation that praxis had already laid down. The function of science is to test the rules of praxis, validating the sound and invalidating the unsound. The further function of science is to extend praxis further. Illustrations of this relation of praxis to science are found plentifully in all domains of life. Dietary principles furnish typical examples. Our ancestors found out, by the process of trial and error, that meats and fresh vegetables were excellent foods for human beings, that mankind thrived on such diets, and science has verified this finding. This common-sense result was complicated by numerous beliefs that science has eliminated, but, in its efforts to sift principles, science has often been misled. Thus, a generation ago the notion that diet could be estimated and evaluated simply in calories was a sad error, which science shortly corrected.

That ancient diets were not satisfactory we well know. A diet of cereals exclusively does not provide the necessary food elements, and science has contributed the 'balanced' diet. Science has found out also what the contribution of meats and green vegetables is. Going on from its consideration of starches and proteins, it discovered vitamins and their functions and eventually found how to make vitamins synthetically.

Dietary problems and needs include only one of the many lines of human needs and endeavors. In all other lines, human welfare has been promoted, not by throwing away the hard-won results of the group, but by sifting these results and strengthening the valid principles involved in them.

We must be prepared to find a core of fact and validity in any ancient belief that has lasted for generations. Even beliefs that have grown up in relatively modern times cannot be dismissed without due scrutiny. The superstition that changing the handedness of a child caused the child to stammer was false as formulated, but we know that methods which too often are employed to change the handedness do produce neuroses, of which stammering may be a symptom. The belief was not without foundation, but scientific investigation was required to determine the element of validity in the belief.

Even popular superstitions concerning human heredity had some elements of validity. The trouble came from the would-be geneticists, who accepted these superstitions without examination and hastily linked them with hypothetical features of the chromosomes. Thus the superstition concerning the inheritance of blue eyes and brown eyes was worked into a simple Mendelian formula, which the geneticists now admit to be completely invalid, since it does not conform to the facts of eye coloration. The zoological heredity of feeble-mindedness was once accepted without consideration of the complex conditions of the development of that defect. These instances confirm the view that popular theories may have something of truth in them, although they may not be true in the ways in which they are formulated.

1. The Concept of God.—God may be considered under at least three categories.

A. As an entity that has existed eternally, without beginning and without end. This is a concept of God that is widely held in modern religion, but it is a relatively modern concept.

B. As an entity that had a beginning and may have an end. This is the way in which ancient peoples in Europe and the Levant conceived their gods. Gods, they believed, were born, flourished, and might pass away.

C. As an ideal, not confused with an entity. Considering the progress of the human race in moral traits and in power over nature, a goal for this progress may be conceived, as a limiting terminus of the line of progress toward moral perfection and ultimate power—a goal that man can never attain, but toward which progress can be made, a 'flying goal' in Emerson's terminology.

Toward one or another of these conceptions, human thought has been progressing for several thousands of years. Which of these three concepts will be ultimate is the important question. Christianity, it would seem, has hesitated between the first and the third; Judaism and Islam adopted the first; and all three are inchoately involved in Hinduism. Polytheism is merely one of the stages in the development of the idea, and in savage religions the first and the second only are involved.

A god of the first type is essentially the creator of the world, as well as its administrator. Natural laws are creations of the god, and a god of this sort works constantly, since laws of nature are not simply set going by him (or by her), but are the expressions of his activity. The concept of a 'preestablished harmony,' as presented by the somewhat stupid Leibnitz, fails to recognize this inevitable fact. Malebranche and Geulincx were smarter. Both used, to illustrate the correspondence between the mental world and the physical world, the illustration of two clocks, which either have been arranged by God from the beginning to keep time together or are controlled by God from time to time, so that whatever happens in the one world has its correspondance in the other world. This second notion is called 'occasionalism,' since it assumes that on the 'occasion' of a change in one world, God makes a similar change in the other world. Historians of philosophy who have never read

Geulincx, and whose acquaintance with Malebranche is limited, describe Geulincx as an occasionalist and Malebranche as a devotee of preestablished harmony. Apparently both of these astute philosophers recognized the fact that God must be continuously operative. If the two clocks keep time together, God must keep them both going.

The second concept of god (or gods) gives divinity more leisure, since the operation of nature is automatic, and, although gods could interfere, much as man interferes, to change the effects of natural laws, no continuous activity of divinity was necessary. Gods, it was assumed, were subordinate to the operations of nature, much as man is subordinate, although the gods had greater power than man has. That this state in the evolution of divinity is the final stage does not seem probable, since it makes god a superfluous being, a being who interferes with the operation of nature but is in no wise essential. This conclusion can be avoided only by assuming that a god, any god, is merely an instrument of the cosmic forces, an avenue through which the power of the universe expresses itself. Thus, 'god' is a name for a certain feature of the system of natural law.

There is a possibility that we should not overlook. We approach the concept of god from the religious angle, since there is no other angle from which we can approach it. From the scientific angle, human desires have no dynamic function, except insofar as they produce, or result in, human action. Human action is expression of organic processes, which are largely neuromuscular. Now, it is clear that man cannot, by any motor process, create a god. He may, as he has done, create an idol, or some other symbol of divinity, which is really a symbol of his 'idea' of divinity. Further than that man cannot go, at least from the scientific point of view. From the religious point of view that limitation does not exist, or, we may better say, we do not know that it exists. Perhaps, if humanity persistently wants a god of a certain sort, his wants, in the course of time, may create such a god. This possibility has been contemplated by many thinkers, although none has been willing to go on record as seriously accepting the possibility as a fact.

In mundane affairs, what man, as a group, has persistently wanted he has obtained in the end. Man, for example, has long envied the birds and desired to fly; eventually, he flew. This desire, however, attained its satisfaction through neuromotor processes, motivated by the desire, processes that eventually produced airplanes. In the other world, our neuromuscular responses have no effect; but could the desire for an other-worldly entity nevertheless produce that entity? Man has long desired gods, and finally a God. In the other world, in which physiological response processes are of no direct effect, could these desires have effects? Well, all we can say is that this is strictly a religious matter. There is no mundane way of proving the theoretical results and no way of disproving them. We must, perforce, let the problem rest at that point.

The third concept of god is quite another matter. God, as an ideal person, is not necessarily omnipotent but is conceived as perfectly moral. A perfectly moral person represents an ideal toward which man makes progress, although he does not expect to attain moral perfection. There is no question of God as the source of morality, still less question of His imposing moral rules on human beings. God as thus conceived is the goal of morality, the perfection of human justice that man has been developing slowly and in respect to which he is still imperfect. Morality is a human product, just as is immorality, a feature of persons. For this reason, only the concept of a personal god can satisfy man's feeling toward divinity, and hence the development of divinity from the impersonal source of manas into a personal god. The substitution of an impersonal world power for a personal god is a regression toward a more primitive conception, which can hardly satisfy man's desire. Belief in an impersonal world power is still a religious belief, but more primitive than belief in a personal god.

Is this concept of God as an ideal useful? For some persons, it seems not to be useful unless it involves also the concept of God as a real entity, a person who really exists. Shall we say that persons of that type are still not far advanced from the primitive? Yes, in their religion, they are not far from the primitive stage.

Ideals we know are the most important forces in life. No one makes progress in any function of life unless he has ideals that lie beyond his stage of actual achievement. If ideals are important for the common features of life, can we assume that they are not important for morals? It would seem that for morals, the most important aspect of modern life, a moral ideal is even more important than are ideals in other features of life. Certainly no one improves in morals unless he sets for himself a moral ideal. It would seem, therefore, that a God as a moral ideal would be the most effective force for promotion of morality.

Religion, we think, should continue its support of the doctrine that has for two thousand years and more involved faith in a personal god. The emphasis on God as a creative power, and as a creator of moral values in especial, should be progressively lessened, and God as the ideal of perfect morality should be more emphatically presented. By so doing religion will make contributions to the progressive improvement in justice, and so to social progress. We are not suggesting a sudden abandonment of old concepts of divinity, for, as we have said, sudden changes are not advisable, especially sudden changes in religion. Many persons of religious convictions are not prepared to accept the concept of God that has been developing slowly, and the attachments of such persons to religion should not be shocked or the interests of such persons in religion alienated.

2. *The Concept of Freedom.*—Freedom is the state of being free, and the pertinent question is: Free from what? Freedoms from many things are valued and desired. Freedom from a disease, freedom from boredom, freedom from injustice, freedom from dominating friends—the list of freedoms is endless. Some persons commit suicide to become free from life. The freedom that concerns us here is freedom of response from the determination of environment. We must admit that response, whether or not it is conscious, is largely a product of the stimulus pattern impressed on the organism by the environment, although the nature of the response to a given stimulus pattern varies with the nature of the organism that responds and with the condition of the organism at the time of stimulation. If the determination by the stimulus pattern and the organic condition is complete, there is no freedom of response; the response is always physically determined.

The doctrine that responses are completely determined by physical forces is appropriately called *determinism*. To this doctrine is opposed that called *libertarianism*, or the doctrine of 'free will.' In its more naive form, this doctrine holds that, although physical forces of the environment are potent in determining responses, there is a nonphysical factor called 'will,' which may participate in the determination of a response. Libertarians do not claim that 'will power' can counteract the forces of the environment in all cases; they claim merely that in certain cases, where there is a tendency to act in one way, the application of 'will' may be sufficient to bring about the opposite response.

The force of habit is admitted by libertarians, as it is by determinists. Habits, however, insofar as they are not built by factors such as nutrition and disease, which are admitted to be physical, are the results of previous responses; and the previous responses, of course, have been determined by factors of the same sorts as those which determine the present response. Habits of response are, in short, results of organic conditions that have been produced by past responses and by other physical factors. For the determinist, therefore, a response is determined by the stimulus pattern acting on an organism that has been determined to respond in a certain way to the pattern, an organic determination that involves the history of the development of the organism from its embryonic stage on.

Since it is scientifically postulated that physical forces operate in accordance with natural laws and that these laws are invariable, human responses are predictable, insofar as the laws are known and insofar as the condition of the responding organism is known. If, on the other hand, there is an arbitrary nonphysical factor involved in the determination of response, response is not completely predictable. In other words, the doctrine of free will predicates an element of chance in human behavior, a predication that is acknowledged by libertarians who are philosophically oriented.

The formulation of the problem of will that was proposed by William James over fifty years ago has been accepted by most psychologists and has been further developed by them. This formulation presents will as a determination of responses by thinking, but this does not change the problem in any essential way. If will, or to use the preferred psychological term, 'volition,' is merely a sort of emotion in which the thought factor is influential on further response, the question is: What determines the thought response? To which the determinist replies: the same sort of physical forces that determine all responses. And so we are back where we were before. In order to change one's responses, one must change one's thinking; and the determinist claims that this change can be brought about only by a change in the stimulus pattern, or a change in the condition of the responding organism, a change in its physical condition. The libertarian claims, or admits, that there is an element of chance in the change, or, if he is naive and claims a nonphysical force entering into the determination, he still must admit that the response is not completely predictable.

The doctrine of determinism is founded on the postulate of

complete uniformity in nature but further assumes that human responses are determined by physical forces and physical conditions. The major point in the doctrine, however, is that of predictability of behavior. If the determinists are correct in their doctrines, then the behavior of an organism is predictable, provided that we know the past history of the organism and know exactly the stimulus pattern working upon it. Of course we do not have such complete information for the prediction of a response, but in theory we could make an exact prediction if we had the information.

We may admit that, for inorganic substances and materials, changes are determined completely by physical forces and physical conditions and that prediction may be exact if the information about the forces and conditions is exact. A physicist can predict, for example, the elongation of a rod of iron of known chemical composition when the rod is subjected to a rise of temperature of a definite amount. The prediction is valid to a decimal of a millimeter if the structure of the rod is exactly known and the rise in temperature is exactly controlled. Admitting the predictability of changes in the inorganic world, however, admits nothing as regards responses of organisms or any other changes in the organic world.

The nature of prediction for organisms and the conditions of prediction must be examined. The first obvious fact is that there are predictions of two sorts: predictions regarding individual organisms, and predictions regarding changes in groups of organisms. A second fact, which is equally obvious, is that in either case predictions are never exact, but always within limits that are assigned. If a group of protozoa is placed in the far end of a long tank with opaque walls and cover except for a glass window at one end, and if a beam of light of known intensity and wave length is admitted through the window, one may be able to predict that, in not less than ten minutes and not more than fifteen minutes, 90 per cent of the protozoa will be in a position not more than x centimeters and not less than y centimeters from the window, the measures x and y being determined by previous tests of protozoa of the same type under the same temperature conditions and with the same intensity and wave length of light. One may be unable to make more exact predictions, even for the total group, predictions always being within limits of variation set in the predictions.

That one could not select a single individual protozoan and predict exactly where it would be at a given time is another matter. If prediction is made for an individual, the limits set must usually be wider than those for a group. No one would claim that a response or a series of responses by a single human being could be predicted exactly. We could not predict for any individual student in a class what his exact procedure will be when the bell rings, although, for some individuals, we could predict that within five minutes they would be outside the room, a prediction that might not hold for every individual. What the students will do as a group can be predicted within limits.

Social changes can be predicted on the basis of knowledge of past changes, since such predictions are for groups, not for individuals, but these predictions are possible only within time limits that are hard to set, since the speed of a social change is the most difficult feature to estimate and may be accelerated or may be retarded.

Predictions of elections that occur at fixed dates have been demonstrated by the Gallup polls to be possible, but these predictions are made within percentage limits. By estimating the percentages of a representative sampling of voters favoring a certain candidate or a certain measure, it is possible to estimate, within limits, the attitudes of the total electorate. If the sampling is not truly representative, the estimates are invalid, as the predictions once made by the *Literary Digest* demonstrated. Since the opinions of voters may change during a preelection period, early estimates are not considered as valid, but by repeated sampling the rate of change may be estimated and the final vote predicted.

Group prediction, in short, is a statistical method of prediction, and, as a recent author has said, the doctrine of determinism is now that of 'statistical determinism.' Statistical methods cannot be applied to an individual, although from observations on the progress of a patient, a physician or an adjuster may predict the further length of time that may be required for completion of the cure or of the adjustment, predictions for which the time limits must be rather wide.

We have admitted that in the inorganic world the exactness of prediction is proportionate to the exactness of knowledge of the physical conditions. Physicists, however, are inclined today to class their predictions as group predictions, which might be called 'statistical.' The change in a bar of iron under definite conditions of structure and temperature can be predicted, but the activity of an individual ion is unpredictable, the valid prediction being made for the total collection or 'group' of ions composing the bar of iron.

It would appear, therefore, that the assumption of determinism, insofar as it involves the complete physical determination of responses, is not necessary for science, and for that reason we prefer to call determinism a 'doctrine.' So long as predictions are made for specified conditions, and within limits specified in the predictions, they are scientific. Further, since predictions can be made only within limits, there is no way of putting the doctrine to rigid test; hence espousal of either the doctrine of determinism or the opposed doctrine of free will must remain for the present a matter of religious faith.

It may be pointed out that the impossibility of exact prediction of the behavior of an individual protozoan is due to our lack of knowledge of structure of the individual and of the particular forces working upon it, but, since these factors remain unknown, the problem remains. That organisms are less predictable in their behavior than are inorganic materials, that is to say, that the limits within which prediction is possible are greater for living organisms, might be taken as an indication that the essential difference between the organic and the inorganic—the difference that we call 'life'—consists in an element or factor of chance in the organism, a factor that is absent from inorganic substances. This also would be a conclusion properly to be designated as 'religious,' not as 'scientific.'

Since one cannot know that responses are completely determined by physical forces and cannot know that there is an element of chance involved, one can adopt either the determinist doctrine or the libertarian doctrine, if one understands that both are religious doctrines. Adoption of either may have no practical results, because the libertarians, unless they are deluded by popular superstitions concerning heredity, realize the immense importance of environment, and, in readjustment of human habits and attitudes, depend on alteration of the individual's environment as the most important factor in adjustment. The patient's thinking usually needs reorganization, but this is effected by advice and explanations, which is application of physical stimulation, and dependence on past training to supply adequate interpretations. There seems to be, however, a bad practical result of adoption of the free-will doctrine in its naïve form. The advice is often given maladjusted persons to 'use your will power,' advice that is of no benefit whatever, since the person understands the advice to mean 'make effort,' and effort to overcome a maladjustment merely makes matters worse.

In summary, it seems that religion has for its future an important function, that of promoting the doctrine of human freedom, the doctrine that human responses are not completely determined by physical forces and conditions, in opposition to the other equally religious doctrine of determinism.

3. The Concept of Immortality.—Belief in an existence beyond the grave has developed through the ages as a religious belief, and we have shown that it must remain religious in the future. Whether one believes in the continuation of a daimon soul, an ego soul, a ghost soul, or in several of these, the belief is in that which cannot be known and therefore is strictly religious. One may, however, philosophize about such a belief, as we shall proceed to do; for philosophy, in its true sense, is but the attempt to think clearly about problems that are deemed important, and immortality raises an important problem.

The survival that man has most desired is that of the 'man himself' as an integrated person, with memory of the past and with a conscious ego. This desire has been well-nigh universal among Western people, although not among orientals. While memory (which the Greek ghosts did not have) might be partially explained as a function of the physiological organism, it involves an ego, which consciously remembers, and the ego cannot be explained physiologically. In physiological psychology we can explain how consciousness occurs in the living person (in a certain sense of the word 'how') and we can indicate the sequences of conscious processes and construct laws of the occurrences, but no scientific procedure can explain consciousness. We accept the fact of being conscious, and link this fact, or occurrence, with response processes, and there we stop.

In every field of science we start with facts and processes behind which we cannot go and proceed to analyze these facts and discover laws in accordance with which the facts are produced and the processes occur. We ask the questions, How? When? Where? and, in a certain sense, What? but the question, Why? is in the field outside of science, in the field of religion, or that of philosophy, or in both. No physicist, as a physicist, asks why there are electrons or why there should be gravitation. Psychologists and physiologists may seem to try to explain why there are colors, such as red and blue, but actually they are seeking only to discover the functions color have in animal life and the laws under which these functions are operative. Colors are fundamental data from which we start and which cannot be explained further.

Our problem, which is foreign to the domain of science and included in the fields of religion and philosophy, involves the question, Why is there life? and, more particularly, Why do human beings live? In more popular language this question may be, What are we here for? or What is life all about? This is the central problem for philosophy, after philosophy has grown up and has passed beyond the stages of physics, cosmology, and psychology, with which it first concerns itself. It seems strange that man should begin as a babe with no knowledge; progress through childhood and youth into adult life, learning much; continue adult life, still learning; and, when the results of learning have attained their greatest importance, cease to exist. The experience of the presbyters (old men) has been regarded by all peoples as more useful than the limited experiences of younger persons. If, at the end of life, this hardly won experience is not capitalized, it would seem that human life is a joke, a joke on human beings.

Well, it is possible that human life is indeed an epitome of futility, that man increases in wisdom and in usefulness until death happens, and then poof! it is all over. In the vernacular we would say that life, then, 'doesn't make sense,' that it has no value. If, on the other hand, man, after death, continues a conscious life, then his mundane life does 'make sense.' His period of life on earth should prepare him for better living; his hard-won experience is capitalized. There can be no doubt that the concept of survival has eventually been based on these considerations, although the concept did not grow out of them.

In past years we have been interested in proposing to various persons the following dilemma. Suppose you had to choose between these alternatives: (*a*) immediate annihilation; (*b*) living your life over again, exactly as you have lived it, and when you come again to the period corresponding to the present moment could have the same choice—either to repeat your life or to be annihilated. Suppose you were limited, in other words, to endless repetition of your life, or to annihilation; which would you choose?

We often find it difficult to get a person to understand the alternatives indicated. A person says first, 'I would prefer to relive my life, for then I would live it differently.' When they grasp the alternatives offered—to relive the life in every detail exactly as you have lived it—most of them admit that they would prefer to be annihilated now.

This seems to show that life, for intelligent persons, is desirable only as a preparation for further living; only by capitalizing experience for further living is it worth while. If death ends all, living is futile, since few persons are satisfied with the lives they have actually led. If death ends all, then the endless succession of generations of human beings is a cosmic joke. On the other hand, if the experience gained in this life can be applied to living as a person after death, then human life is justified as important.

One might think to solve the problem by assuming that, although the life of the individual is valueless, the life of the group, race, or stock is important; that although the achievements of the persons are not capitalized for his benefit, they are capitalized for his posterity. Such capitalization does occur, it is true, but does not furnish a solution for the problem. If the life of no individual is of value, then the lives of an endless series of persons are valueless, for a sum of zeros is still zero.

Since the problem of immortality, as we have repeated many times, is a religious problem, it would seem that religion in the future should continue to teach, as it has in the past, the doctrine of personal survival, that is, the best doctrine of immortality.

APPENDIX

IMPORTANT REFERENCES ON RELIGION
AND RELIGIONS

The books listed herein have been selected from the vast multitude of books
on religion by two criteria. First, these are important works—among the most
important. Second, these works are available in most university libraries,
and many of them can be found in the larger city libraries. These are books
which should form the basis for any library on religion in its various aspects.

With a few exceptions, the works listed are in English, the few works in
French being of such outstanding value that their omission would be a serious
error. As Reinach has pointed out, development of the scientific study of
religion has been due mainly to British scholars and to scholars of other groups
who have been influenced by the British ones. The French students of religion
come next to the British in importance; and there have been some contributions
from Germans who had been under British and French influence. On the whole,
however, German scholarship in the field of religion has been more ponderous
than fertile. One of the important tasks of the French and English scholars
has been to eliminate the mistakes of earlier German theorists.

The books listed are grouped under the following categories: I. Works of
General Reference (including encyclopedias); II. Libraries and Series; III.
Great Books; IV. Histories of Religion; V. Textbooks; VI. Works Dealing with
Religions Genetically Related to Christianity; VII. Works on Religions not
Historically Contributory to Civilized Religion; VIII. Religious Mysteries.

In classes II, III, IV, and V, the dates of birth and death are given in parenthesis after the author's name. The dates and places of publication are given
for all books, and in classes I through VI*A*, the publisher is listed; the American
publisher being listed for books published both here and abroad. For classes
from VI*B* on, the publisher is omitted, since most of those books were published
abroad and are for the most part unobtainable except as secondhand copies.

Where, in a later reference, it is necessary to refer to a book, set, or library
earlier listed, the reference for most cases is to the author or editor, followed by
the class number and the subnumber in the class—for example, Robertson
Smith (III: 1).

I. WORKS OF GENERAL REFERENCE

1. *Encyclopaedia Britannica;* 9th ed., 1875–1879, ed. by T. S. Baynes and
W. Robertson Smith, 11th ed., ed. by Hugh Chisholm, 1910– .
These editions mark the climax of achievement of the Encyclopaedia. The
roster of authors of important articles in the ninth edition is a list of the greatest
scholars of the nineteenth century. The authors of the eleventh edition are

almost as distinguished. The tenth edition was merely a reprint of the ninth, with additional volumes compiled by the London *Times*. The twelfth and thirteenth editions were reprints of the eleventh. The fourteenth edition marked the decline of the Encyclopedia Britannica in scholarship and therefore in importance.

The great ninth edition is now practically unobtainable, and copies in libraries are wearing out. The eleventh edition can be purchased secondhand, but prices asked are sometimes higher than that of new sets of the fourteenth edition.

In addition to articles on topics of religious importance in the *Encyclopaedia Britannica*, 9th and 11th eds., many articles on countries and on peoples have sections devoted to the religions of the areas or the groups.

2. The *Encyclopedia of Religion and Ethics*, 12 vols., 1908–1927, ed. by James Hastings, Scribner, New York.

The articles in this work were, like those in the *Encyclopaedia Britannica*, 9th and 11th eds., written by highly competent scholars, in many cases by those most competent in the fields in which their topics lie. In studying any topic in the field of religion, it is economical to start with the appropriate article in Hastings and make use of the cross references to related articles, references to sources, and the evaluations of sources. These volumes will be referred to hereinafter as Hastings (I: 2).

3. Frazer, Sir James George (1851–1941), *The Golden Bough*, 12 vol., 1913–1923, Macmillan, London; 3d ed. published in New York in 1935. A condensation into one volume should be ignored.

The Golden Bough is a valuable source book on faiths, rituals, and folklore. The author's theories, which were progressively modified as his work proceeded, may well be disregarded. The starting point for the use of this work is the Index, to which the twelfth volume is devoted. Unfortunately, the references in the Index are given as if the volumes were numbered from 1 to 11, but the volumes are not numbered, either in the original edition or in the American reprint. So, one who uses *The Golden Bough* must find out what the volume numbers represent in terms of the titles printed on the volumes.

4. Two encyclopedias that are useful on some points are: The *Catholic Encyclopedia*, ed. by E. A. Pace *et al.*, 16 vols. and a supp., 1907–1912, Appleton, New York; and *The Jewish Encyclopedia*, ed. by Cyrus Adler *et al.*, 12 vols., *c.* 1916, Funk and Wagnalls, New York. These encyclopedias must be used cautiously, since sectarian bias is to be suspected.

Articles in various cyclopedias compiled in America in imitation of the *Encyclopaedia Britannica* are not dependable, since most of them are not the work of scholars.

II. LIBRARIES AND SERIES

1. *The Loeb Classical Library*. Printed in England, handled in the United States by the Harvard University Press. This series of pocket-sized translations now contains over a hundred volumes by Latin writers and over two hundred by Greek writers. Many volumes have been reprinted, some four times; and the dates of original issue are not always given. Many writings of prime importance to the history of psychology and of religion remain untranslated.

In the Loeb library, the Greek or Latin text appears on the left-hand page, the English translation on the right. This system facilitates the comparison of the texts and the checking of the translation with regard to its adequacy. No translation of an ancient work can be depended on, unless checked. Translators are sometimes not solicitous to preserve and render the exact meaning of the writer, but substitute modern ideas for the original ones. There are, moreover, certain conventional mistranslations in which concepts of German philosophy are substituted for Greek concepts, confusing distinctions that are important and ignoring the developments in the Greek concepts themselves. One can in no case infer, from the word 'soul' or 'mind' in English translations, what the author was really writing about.

2. *The Sacred Books of the East*, ed. by F. Max Müller (1823-1900), 27 vols., 1879-1901, Oxford. In addition to the books published under Müller's editorship, over 40 vols. have been edited by later scholars.

This library is composed of translations of selected texts of the Brahmanical, Buddhist, Jain, Zoroastrian, and Chinese religions, with a translation of the Mohammedan Koran, and some minor texts. The great Hindu epics are represented, and some of the Upanishads are translated. The selections are sound, and this library is invaluable for students interested in Hindu, Persian, or Chinese religion.

3. *The Ante-Nicaean Fathers*. This library of 10 vols. was published first in Edinburgh, under the editorship of Allan Menzies, and republished in America, under editorship of Alexander Roberts and James Donaldson, 1908-1913, Scribner, New York.

The volumes contain translations of the extant writings of the Greek and Latin Christian fathers down to A.D. 325. Many of these writings are not otherwise available in English.

4. *Mythology of All Races*, ed. by George F. Moore *et al.*, 13 vols., 1916-1932, Marshall Jones, Boston. Some of the volumes in this series were published under the auspices of the Archaeological Institute of America. All of the volumes were written by competent authorities.

5. *Religions of the Past and Present*, ed. by J. A. Montgomery, 1918, Lippincott, Philadelphia.

This is not a series of volumes, but a series of lectures combined in a single volume.

III. GREAT BOOKS

Certain books by great scholars have had a profound influence on the development of the study of religion and are still important for orientation in the field, no matter what the phase of religion in which one may be interested.

1. W. Robertson Smith (1846-1894), *The Religion of the Semites*, Black, London, 1889. Republished in 1927, Appleton, New York, with introduction and additional notes by Stanley A. Cook. A modified German translation by R. Stube, 1889, Freiberg, had profound influence on German scholars. This book, with *Kinship and Marriage in Ancient Arabia*, and more than twenty articles in the ninth edition of the *Encyclopaedia Britannica*, constitutes Robertson Smith's permanent contribution to the literature of religion. Not only by his writings and lectures, but through his personal contacts, he revolutionized the study of religion and may well be said to have been the founder of the

modern science of comparative religion. Among the productive scholars stimulated by Robertson Smith were Frazer, M'Lennan, Andrew Lang, and Stanley
Cook in England and Salomon Reinach in France.

The weaknesses in Smith's work are a partial acceptance of the doctrine
of totemism and of the assumption that Reinach called 'Max Müllerism,' namely,
that language affinities are indications of racial stock relationships. He was more
critical of totemism, however, than were some of his disciples and never accepted
the doctrine of animism. In a period in which the study of religion was completely dominated by philologists, his acceptance of the philologists' fallacy was
to be expected, but his disciples emancipated comparative religion from this
fallacy.

Robertson Smith's articles in the *Encyclopaedia Britannica*, particularly the
article on the Bible, raised a storm, which caused his removal in 1887 from
the chair of Hebrew that he had occupied in the University of Aberdeen. As a
sign of repentance of its hasty action, the university invited Smith to give three
series of lectures on the religion of the Semites in 1888–1891. The first series
was published as the book above cited. The notes for the second and third
series were never put in shape for publication.

2. Tylor, E. B. (1832–1917), *Primitive Culture*, 1871, Murray, London. Tylor
was an ethnologist and had previously published a book on *Mexico and the
Mexicans* in 1861 and the *History of Mankind* in 1865. In 1881 he published
his treatise on *Anthropology*, which often is styled the first textbook on that topic.
His *Primitive Culture* was the starting point in England for the anthropological
school' of comparative religion, as contrasted with the 'philological school'
represented at Oxford by F. Max Müller. Tylor undoubtedly influenced Fraser
and M'Lennan towards the study of 'primitive man,' in the sense in which the
term is widely employed by anthropologists, as meaning men without literature.
Robertson Smith, on the other hand, was interested in primitive culture in the
literal, or genetic, sense.

Tylor's main contribution to the scientific study of religion was his theory
of *animism*, which became popular toward the end of the nineteenth century,
but which, happily, is now of historical interest only.

3. M'Lennan, J. F. (1827–1881), *Studies in Ancient History*, 1876.

M'Lennan (also written McLennan and MacLennan) reprinted in this book
an essay on 'Kinship and Marriage,' together with a series of essays on 'Totemism' which had appeared in the *Fortnightly Review* in the years 1866–1870, and
some other essays. Further essays on 'The Levirate and Polyandry' appeared
in the *Fortnightly Review* in 1877; and materials left by M'Lennan at his death
were edited by his widow and A. Platt, and published in 1896 as *Studies in
Ancient History, Second Series.*

M'Lennan was a Scottish barrister and an amateur anthropologist. His
two contributions were a theory of marriage as developing from primitive
promiscuity through capture of women from adjacent tribes; and a theory of
totemism that profoundly affected anthropology and the study of religion for a
time. M'Lennan was a close friend of Robertson Smith, who undoubtedly
derived his cautious interest in totemism from M'Lennan. Totemism, as it
existed among savages (the word 'totem' is a corruption of an American expression), was already known, but M'Lennan expanded and generalized the concept,

smelled its odor in all cultures, and made it the basis of an 'explanatory' theory. It is recognized today that ascribing a social phenomenon to 'totemism' adds nothing in the way of explanation and usually distracts attention from the real problem.

4. Reinach, S. (1858–1932), *Cultes, mythes et religions,* 5 vols., 1913–1923, Leroux, Paris.

This set of volumes is a reprinting of about 180 articles on a range of topics in which Reinach was especially competent. He was distinguished in philology, archaeology, and art, as well as in religion. His work on the art and religion of the Celts is outstanding. Most of the articles in *Cultes, mythes et religions* were reprinted from Journals which are not available in America; hence the collection is especially important.

5. Three books by Andrew Lang (1844–1912) are especially important. These are: *Myth, Ritual, and Religion,* 1898, London; *The Making of Religion,* 1898, London.; *The Origins of Religion,* 1908, London.

Lang, influenced by Robertson Smith, Tylor, and Mannhardt, was an active force in establishing the study of mythology on a sound basis and in routing 'Max Müllerism.' His writings are still stimulating. On Lang's influence in the development of modern study of religion, see Reinach, III: 4, IV: 1–28, and V: 18–31.

6. Lubbock, Sir John, Lord Avebury (1834–1913), *The Origin of Civilization and the Primitive Condition of Man,* 1870 (1871), Appleton, New York.

Lubbock began his work with studies of bees, ants, and wasps and went on to the study of mankind. The book cited is of historical importance, but the theories and information presented in it have been corrected by later ethnologists and sociologists.

7. Codrington, R. H. (1830–1922), *The Melanesians,* 1891, Oxford.

Codrington and Marett introduced into English the Melanesian concept of *mana,* which has become highly important in theories of the origin and development of religion.

8. Marett, R. R. (1866–1943), *The Threshold of Religion,* 1929, Methuen, London.

9. James, W. (1842–1910), *Varieties of Religious Experience,* 1900, Longmans, New York.

This remains the outstanding book on psychological aspects of religion. Like books entitled 'Psychology of Religion' which followed it, undue emphasis is placed on features of religious life that we today call 'pathological.' Psychologists all have erred through failing to give proper weight to religious processes of normal life.

IV. HISTORIES OF RELIGION

1. De la Saussaye, Chantepie (1848–1920), *Lehrbuch der Religionsgeschichte,* 2 vols., final ed., 1925, Tübingen.

This is a German translation of a work that appeared in French in 1894. A later French edition was published in 1904. Only the first volume has been translated into English, as *Manual of the History of Religion,* 1891, London.

2. Moore, George F. (1851–1931), *History of Religions,* 2 vols., 1913–1919, Scribner, New York.

3. Moore, G. F., *The Birth and Growth of Religion*, 1923, Scribner, New York.

4. Hopkins, E. W. (1857–1932), *History of Religions*, 1926, Macmillan, New York.

5. Hopkins, E. W., *Origin and Evolution of Religion*, 1924, Yale University Press, New Haven.

The history by De la Saussaye, usually catalogued under Chantepie, is still one of the most important works on this topic. The books by Moore and Hopkins are the best aids to the serious student who reads only English. Numbers 3 and 5 will be found simpler in presentations than are nos. 2 and 4 and are excellent starting points for historical study. Other general histories are listed in the bibliographies of the textbooks by Barton and by Friess and Schneider.

V. TEXTBOOKS

Texts entitled *Psychology of Religion* or the equivalent of that phrase can usefully be avoided, with the exception, of course, of the book by James, which is listed above as III: 9. There is great need for an elementary text on religion for students whose background is so limited that they are unable to cope with the works of scholars. A few textbooks are available, but none of them are satisfactory. The following references are offered with hesitation.

1. Reinach, S., *Orpheus*, 1930, Liveright, New York.

Orpheus is an English translation from the 38th French edition. Following a disappointing introduction, about half the book is devoted to a survey of religions grouped in a somewhat helter-skelter fashion. Too much weight is given to the concepts of totemism and animism by Reinach. The last five chapters are devoted to the origin and development of Christianity; and the treatment of this topic is scholarly and stimulating. Next in value is the chapter on 'Hebrews, Israelites and Jews,' which is the best brief disquisition available on these religions. The publication of *Orpheus* produced a storm of condemnation, not only from orthodox Christians, but also from Jews, who accused Reinach of 'antisemitism.'

2. Barton, G. A. (1859–   ), *The Religions of the World*, 1917, University of Chicago Press, Chicago; 4th ed., 1937.

Barton's text suffers mostly from its brevity and from Barton's acceptance of 'Max Müllerism,' the assumption that language groups are indexes of racial relationships. Further, Barton seems to accept the historical features of the Jewish Scriptures as valid. The text in other respects is useful; the chronological arrangement is helpful; and important features of Hinduism and Islam are presented soundly, although briefly. The book is obviously written with solicitude to avoid offending either Christians or Jews. The bibliographies for use of students and teachers are well selected.

3. Friess, H. L., and H. W. Schneider, *Religion in Various Cultures*, 1932, Holt, New York.

Following a superficial treatment of 'primitive' religion, the successive chapters deal with Shinto, Hinduism, Buddhism, Greek religion, the religion of Israel and Judaism, and Christianity. Each religion, however, is treated as an isolated topic. The treatment of Hinduism misses the point completely, and Islam is omitted. The materials for other topics seem to have been collected uncritically, and the authors' interpretations show lack of scholarship. An extensive bibliography, not critically selected, ends the volume.

4. Archer, J. C. (1881–   ), *Faiths Men Live By*, 1934, Nelson, New York.

The part of this book which is most useful includes the chapters on the religions of India, Chaps. VIII, IX, X, XI, and XII. Chapter XIV, on the Hebrew-Jewish faith, contains information concerning the Jews of India and of China, information which most textbooks omit.

Archer, in his treatment of Hindu religions, obviously profited much by his association with G. F. Moore and E. W. Hopkins and by their writings.

VI. WORKS DEALING WITH RELIGIONS GENETICALLY RELATED TO CHRISTIANITY

A. Religions of the Mediterranean Area and the Levant

Two works of monumental scholarship on ancient religions of these areas are in a class by themselves.

1. Maury, L. F. A., *Histoire des religions de la Grèce antique*, 1857–1859, Ladrange, Paris.

This work in three volumes has never been translated into English and is now in the rare-book class. It is still an important book.

Maury was primarily a philologist, and his information on word derivations is very useful. Since the 'Great Aryan myth' was accepted by all philologists in Maury's era, his devotion to the myth can be understood. Maury's constant search for analogies between Greek and Hindu religions and the assumption that these analogies indicated a common 'Aryan' origin was his great weakness and resulted in his reading into Hindu myths interpretations derived from Greek legends.

Along with the 'Aryan myth,' Maury accepted other speculative theories that had been developed by German philologists, including the 'Nature Religion' promoted at Oxford by F. Max Müller—the theory that divinities were at first celestial, associated with the sun, moon, stars, and sky. The fact that certain divinities eventually developed such associations was interpreted by the philologists as meaning that the divinities began in that way.

For one who can separate the important factual materials from the speculative interpretations and the assumptions which Maury borrowed from German philologists, this work is a storehouse of information. Its value is enhanced by Maury's copious and scholarly documentation.

2. Cook, A. B. (1868–   ), *Zeus: a Study in Ancient Religion*, 2 vols., the second in two parts, separately bound, 1914–1925, Cambridge.

These volumes represent the life work of Cook and are essential for the study of the religions of ancient Greek and Levantine areas. The complexity of the documentations, annotations, and references render it difficult for consecutive reading, but all extant sources of information are represented. While Cook represents a high peak in classical scholarship, he lacked the critical insight and brilliance of Maury. His interpretations follow conventional lines of classical scholars, even where the evidence he amassed contradicts his conclusions. Cook is not tainted with the 'Aryan myth,' but he leans toward the other feature of 'Max Müllerism': the 'Nature Theory' of religion, with excessive dependence on 'solar' interpretations. Reinach was free from both features of 'Max Müllerism.'

3. *Herodotus, History of the Persian Wars.* There have been a number of translations into English of this great work, which was written in the fifth century B.C. Rawlinson's translation, 1882, Appleton, New York, is the standard and contains useful annotations. There is a translation in the Loeb Library (II: 1), 4 vols., 1920.

Herodotus' *History* is a source from which later writers drew heavily. He was sadly misled by Egyptian priests, who thought the Greek religions were derived from Egypt. His reports on the religions of Medes, Persians, Levantines, and barbarians, however, have been demonstrated to have been sound.

Two other writings on which later writers drew heavily are:

4. Pausanias, *Description of Greece.* There are several English translations of the work of this Greek traveler, who wrote in the second century of the Christian Era. The standard translation is that of Sir J. G. Fraser, which contains valuable annotations of the translator's. The work is translated in the *Loeb Library* (II: 1), 5 vols., 1918–1935. This 'Baedecker of Greece' contains a great store of information on the religions of Greece, which persisted into the Christian Era.

5. Strabo, *Geography, Loeb Library* (II: 1), 8 vols., 1917–1921.

The 'Father of Geography' wrote his account of Mediterranean and Levantine areas, with references to more remote regions, in the first century B.C., and included a great deal of information on the cultures and religions of the various countries.

6. Hesiod, *Theogony.*

7. Hesiod, *Works and Days.*

These two writings contain much information on religion in the period following Homer. Translations by H. G. Evelyn-White are combined with hymns and literary fragments ascribed to the pre-Homeric period, in the volume entitled, *Hesiod, Homeric Hymns and Homerica,* in the *Loeb Library* (II: 1).

Among books highly approved by classical scholars, but which must be used circumspectly, to avoid misleading assumptions and interpretations, the following may be useful:

8. Fairbanks, A., *The Mythology of Greece and Rome,* 1907, New York.

9. ———, *A Handbook of Greek Religion,* 1910, New York.

10. Farnell, L. R., *Cults of the Greek States,* 5 vols., 1896–1901, Oxford.

11. ———, *Higher Aspects of Greek Religion,* 1912, London.

12. Harrison, Jane, *Prolegomena to the Study of Greek Religion,* 1922, Cambridge.

13. Murray, G., *Five Stages of Greek Religion,* 1925, New York.

14. Nilsson, M. P., *The Evolution of Religion,* 1905, New York.

15. ———, *A History of Greek Religion,* 1925, Oxford.

16. Zielinsky, F. F., *The Religion of Ancient Greece,* 1926, Oxford.

B. RELIGIONS OF THE CELTS AND OTHER EARLY EUROPEAN GROUPS

Authentic material on the religions of the ancient Celts, of the Teutons, and of the peoples of mixed stocks is not plentiful, since these peoples became literate (graphikos) at relatively late dates. Most of the statues and carved inscriptions of the Celts go little farther back than the Roman occupation of Gaul. The Scandinavian myths were undoubtedly based on ancient traditions, but since these myths were composed about the middle of the Christian Era and were contrived by pagan priests to offset the threat of wholesale conversion of the populations to Christianity, the antiquity of the myths, in their final forms, is suspect.

The outstanding scholars in the field of Celtic archaeology and religion have been Reinach, MacCulloch, and Rhys.

1. Reinach, S., *Cultes, Mythes, Religions* (III: 4). Various articles reprinted in this work bear on Celtic religion.

2. Weinach, S., *Les Gaulois dans l'art antique*, 1889, Paris.

3. Reinach, S., *l'Histoire du travail en Gaul*, 1890, Paris.

4. Reinach & Bertrand, *Les Gaules*, 1894, Paris.

5. Reinach, S., *Bronzes figures de la Gaule romaine*, 1894, Paris.

6. Reinach, S., *Epona, la déesse gauloise des chevaux*, 1895, Paris.

7. Reinach & Montelius, *Les temps prehistoriques en Suede*, 1895, Paris.

8. MacCulloch, J. A., *The Religion of the Ancient Celts*, 1911, Edinburgh.

9. MacCulloch, article 'Celts,' in Hastings *Encyclopedia* (I: 2).

10. Rhys. Sir John, *Lectures on the Birth and Growth of Religion, as Illustrated by Celtic Heathendom*, 1888, William and Norgate, London; 3d ed., 1898.

11. Rhys, Sir J., *Celtic Folk-lore*, 1901, Oxford.

12. Rhys, Sir J., *Celtic Britain*, 1884, Young & Co., New York.

On the religion of the Teutons, a main source is

13. Tacitus, *Germania*. There are several English translations of this book by a Roman traveler, written about the beginning of the Christian Era. Another useful book is

14. Chantepie de la Saussaye, *The Religion of the Teutons*, 1902, Ginn & Co., Boston.

C. JUDAISM

The accounts of the development of the Jewish religion and culture included in the Old Testament are no longer accepted as valid. The tales of the period up to the establishment of Solomon's kingdom are compilations from the legends of various peoples from which the Hebrew religion developed, together with accounts of the murder and rapine committed by robber bands after the defeat of the army of Pharaoh in the eleventh century B.C. The leaders of the robber bands were later accepted as Hebrew heroes. United under the great captain Joab, they captured the ancient holy city of Salem, which became Jerusalem, and from the mongrel group of robbers the 'Hebrews' were created. Joab installed a king, who appears as 'David' and who may be considered a historical figure.

In the eighth and ninth centuries B.C., the populations of Judea and Israel were removed by the Babylonians and Assyrians and scattered among other nations, and a new population was brought into Palestine. The compilation of the Old Testament apparently occurred after the return to Judea of a group of Hebrews from Babylon. The Jewish religion obviously was developed from the ancient Hebrew religion, and there are telltale features overlooked by the editors of the Jewish Scriptures that give some evidence as to the nature of the

Hebrew religion, but not information enough to make a complete picture thereof.

The best introduction to the study of the religion of the Hebrews and Jews are provided by

1. Reinach, *Orpheus* (V: 1), Chap. VII; and
2. Smith, W. R., *The Religion of the Semites* (III: 1).

To these may be added

3. Dunlap, K., and R. S. Gill, *The Dramatic Personality of Jesus;* 1933, Williams and Wilkins, Baltimore (now out of print).

Reinach and Smith both accept the historical features of the Jewish Scriptures more naïvely than they are taken today, but their accounts are still valuable. Smith's articles in *Encyclopaedia Britannica,* 11th ed., are worth consulting, and numerous articles on topics connected with Hebrews and Jews are valuable, although the readers must be on their guard against the orthodox bias of some of the authors. Articles in the *Jewish Encyclopedia* (I: 4) also must be read critically.

Among the books which are now difficult to obtain, but which may be helpful to critical readers are:

4. Abrahams, L., *Judaism;* 1910, London.
5. Barton, G. A., *The Religion of Israel,* 1918, New York.
6. Fowler, H. T., *The Origin and Growth of the Hebrew Religion,* 1916, Chicago.
7. Friedlander, M., *The Jewish Religion,* 1900, London.
8. Montgomery, J. A., *The Samaritans; the Earliest Jewish Sect,* 1907, Philadelphia.

Further selected references may be found in Barton (V: 2), pp. 366–369, and *Orpheus* (V: 1), pp. 226–227. Unselected references in great number are topically arranged in Friess and Schneider (V: 3), pp. 524–531.

VII. RELIGIONS NOT HISTORICALLY CONTRIBUTORY TO CIVILIZED RELIGION

Comparative study of the religions of savages and semicivilized peoples is important for the understanding of Western religion, even if those religions cannot be regarded as links in the chain of development of civilized religion. We assume that the psychological factors involved in the development of religion are basically the same in all places and in all times, however much the course of development may be modified by the factors of racial stock and of physical and social environment. Principles discovered by study of European and Levantine religions must eventually be applied to uncivilized religions, or else we shall continue to misunderstand those religions in the future as we have in the past.

When we understand better the religions of uncivilized peoples, we may then be able better to understand civilized religions, but the comparative process must start with the civilized cults and their development, since for these we have more abundant materials for study. No one should attempt to study so-called 'primitive religions' (savage religions) until he has attained a comprehension of the development of European and Levantine religions.

For the study of the religions of savage and semicivilized peoples, the student will find the articles in the *Encyclopaedia Britannica,* IX and XI, and in Hastings

Encyclopedia useful starting points. Selected references are given in Barton (V: 2) and unselected references are massed in Friess and Schneider (V: 3). The references here listed are not intended to be complete.

Since the majority of the works here listed were published in Europe and are for the most part obtainable only as secondhand copies, the names of publishers are not entered. Where, however, Oxford or Cambridge is entered as places of publication, without qualification, the Oxford or Cambridge University presses was the publisher.

A. HINDU RELIGIONS

During the last century, a vast literature in European languages, dealing with Hindu faiths, rituals, and mythology has accumulated. The fundamental Hindu scriptures (Vedas, Upanishads, and Aranyakas) have been translated in the *Sacred Books of the East*. Several Hindu scholars have written in English on the historical development, the philosophy, and the psychology of Hinduism and Hindu sects.

It is extremely difficult for the Western reader to grasp the essential concepts and postulates of Hindu thought, and many of the more readable authors exemplify this difficulty. The naïve tendency is to translate the Hindu concepts into Western concepts and to overlook the fundamental differences in concepts. The result is a complete misunderstanding of Hinduism.

The majority of Hindu adhere, in some measure, to the ancient forms of faith and ritual that are collectively called 'classic Hinduism.' Under the influence of Christianity and Islam, new sects have arisen, which are described as 'modern Hinduism.' On classic Hinduism, some of the older books, written by authors who obtained their information at first hand, are still the best.

a. Religions of Pre-Christian Development

1. Bloomfield, M., *The Religion of the Vedas*, 1908, New York.
2. Deussen, P., *The Philosophy of the Upanishads*, 1906, Edinburgh.
3. Eliot, Sir C., *Hinduism and Buddhism*, 3 vols,. 1927, London.
4. Farquahar, J. N., *A Primer of Hinduism*, 1912, Oxford.
5. ———, *An Outline of the Religious Literature of India*, 1920, Oxford.
6. Fuller, J. F. C., *Yoga: a Study of the Mystical Philosophy of the Brahmins and Buddhists*, 1925, London.
7. Hopkins, E. W., *The Religions of India*, 1895, Boston.
8. Keith, A. B., *The Religion and Philosophy of the Vedas and the Upanishads*, 1925, Cambridge, Mass.
9. ———, *Buddhist Philosophy in India and Ceylon*, 1923, Oxford.
10. Macfie, J. M., *Myths and Legends of India;* 1924, Edinburgh.
11. Müller, F. Max, *Lectures on the Origin and Growth of Religion, as Illustrated by the Religions of India*, 1879, New York.
12. Oldenberg, H., *Buddha, his Life and Doctrines, and His Order*, 1882, London.
13. Pratt, J. B., *India and its Faiths;* 1915, Boston.
14. Rhys-Davids, T. W., *Lectures on the Origin and Growth of Religion*, 2d ed., 1891, London.
15. ———, *Buddhist India*, 1903, New York.

16. ———, *Buddhism: a Sketch of the Life and Teachings of Gautama*, 1912, London.

17. ———, *Buddhism: its History and Literature*, 1926, New York. These books and others by the same author are usually catalogued under Davids, T. W. Rhys.

18. Stevenson, S., *The Heart of Jainism*, 1915, Oxford.

19. ———, *The Rites of the Twice-born*, 1920, Oxford.

Translations of most of the Hindu sacred writings may be found in volumes of the *Sacred Books of the East* (II: 2).

b. Modern Hinduism and Modern Sects

The modern religious developments in India seem to have come from the orthodox Hindu sects, the sects that accept the Brahmanical rituals. Buddhism has practically disappeared from India, and, in other countries where Buddhism has nominally been adopted, it has become merely a feature added to the original pagan religions of those countries. The Jain religion shows little tendency toward modernistic development.

20. d'Alviella, Count Goblet, *The Contemporary Evolution of Religious Thought in England, America and India*, trans. by J. Moden, 1886, New York, Part III: Theism in India.

21. Andrews, C. F., *Mahatma Gandhi's Ideas*, 1930, New York.

22. Farquahar, J. N., *Modern Religious Movements in India;* 1929, New York.

23. ———, Macneal and Dwick (ed). *The Religious Life of India.* A series of volumes on modern cults, which apparently is still in progress.

24. Griswold, H. DeW., *Aspects of Contemporary Hinduism*, 1933, N. Y.

25. ———, *Insights into Modern Hinduism*, 1934, N.Y.

26. Underwood, A. C., *Modern Religious Thought in India*, 1930, N. Y.

27. Vivekananda, Swami, *Complete Works*, 6 vols., 1919, Mayavati.

B. Religions of China and Japan

A few standard references that are still important are listed below. Further references are to be found in Barton (V: 2), pp. 376–379, and in Archer (V: 4), pp. 479–482.

1. Clark, C. A., *Religions of Old Korea*, 1922, New York.

2. De Groot, J. J. M., *The Religious Systems of China*, 6 vols., 1892–1910, Leyden.

3. ———, *The Religions of the Chinese*, 1910, New York.

4. ———, *Religion in China*, 1912, New York.

5. Giles, H. A., *Confucianism and its Rivals*, 1915, New York.

6. Griffis, W. E., *The Religions of Japan*, 1895, New York.

7. Knox, G. W., *The Development of Religion in Japan*.

8. Legge, J., *The Religion of China*, 1881, New York.

9. Nitobe, I. O., *Bushido, the Soul of Japan;* 19th ed., 1913, Tokyo.

10. *Shu King, The*, An ancient Chinese text that reveals the conflict of the early civilized peoples of China with the Black-haired people, who absorbed the early people and assimilated their history.

11. Soothill, W. E., *The Three Religions of China*, new ed., 1924, London.

C. References on Savage Religion

For this topic also we list only a few selected references that are standard, in the sense that anyone interested in this topic as a specialty must be acquainted with them, regardless of the soundness of the authors' assumptions and interpretations.

All the works listed above in I contain material on savage religion. In II, refs. 4 and 5 contain pertinent sections or volumes. In III, refs. 4, 6, and 7 are important and 2, 3, and 9 are useful for one who studies the development of concepts that have been applied, in recent times, to savage religion.

a. General References

1. Durkheim, E., *Elementary Forms of the Religious Life*, 1915, New York
2. Haddon, A. C., *Magic and Fetichism*, 1910, London.
3. Hartland, E. S., *Ritual and Belief*, 1914, London.
4. Levy-Bruhl, L., *The Soul of the Primitive*, 1923, New York.
5. Lowie, R. H., *Primitive Religion*, 1924, New York.
6. Webster, H., *Primitive Secret Societies*, 1908, New York.

b. References on Particular Savage Groups

7. Czaplicka, M. A., *Aboriginal Siberia*, 1914, Oxford.
8. Codrington, R. H., *The Melanesians*, 1891, Oxford.
9. Dixon, R. B., Art., *Oceanic Mythology*, in *Mythology of All Races* (II: 4), vol. IX.
10. Domville-Fife, *Savage Life in the Black Sudan*, 1927, Philadelphia.
11. Dorman, S. S., *Pygmies and Bushmen of the Kalahari*, 1925, London.
12. Fortune, R. F., *Manus Religion*, 1935, Philadelphia.
13. Ellis, A. B., *The Tshi-speaking Peoples of the Gold Coast of West Africa*, 1887, London.
14. ———, *The Ewe-speaking Peoples of the Slave Coast of West Africa*, 1890, London.
15. Haddon, A. C., *The Head Hunters*, 1901, London.
16. Howitt, A. W., *The Native Tribes of Southeast Australia*, 1904, London.
17. Jochelson, W., *The Peoples of Asiatic Russia*, 1928, New York.
18. ———, *The Koryak*, 1910, Leiden.
19. ———, *The Yukaghir and the Yukaghirized Tungus*, 1910, Leiden.
20. Joyce, T. A., Art., *Africa*, in *Encyclopedia Britannica*, 11th ed. Sec. III.
21. Melland, F. H., *Witch-bound Africa*, 1887, London.
22. Ratray, H. L., *Religion and Art in Ashanti*, 1927, Oxford.
23. Roscoe, J., *The Baganda*, 1911, London.
24. ———, *The Northern Bantu*, 1916, Cambridge.
25. Roth, H. L., *Great Benim; Customs, Arts and Horrors*, 1903, Halifax.
26. Seligman, C. G., *The Melanesians of British New Guinea*, 1910, Cambridge.
27. Skeat, W. W., *Malay Magic*, 1900, London.
28. ———, and C. O. Blagden, *Pagan Races of the Malay Peninsula*, 1906, London.
29. Spencer, B., and F. G. Gillen, *The Northern Tribes of Central Australia*, 1904, London.

VIII. RELIGIOUS MYSTERIES

Mystery cults were prevalent in various regions of the ancient world. The books listed below are still important accounts of the mysteries associated with some of the ancient religions. Materials and further references may be found in Hastings (I: 2) by use of the Index volume.

1. Clement of Alexandria. Appendix to Butterworth's translation of three writtings of Clement, entitled *Clement of Alexandria*, in the *Loeb Library* (II: 1). This appendix contains the best brief account of the Greek mysteries, which had an important influence on the early development of Christianity.

2. Reinach, S., *C.M.R.*, (III: 4). Quelques enseignments des mystères d'Eleusis, vol. V, pp. 72–102; La mort d'Orphée, vol. II, pp. 85–122.

3. Macchioro, V. D., *From Orpheus to Paul*, 1930, New York.

4. Cornford, F. M., 'Mystery Religions and pre-Socratic Philosophy,' in *Cambridge Ancient History*, Vol. IV.

5. Foucart, P., *Le culte de Dionysus en Attique*, 1904, Paris.

6. ————, *Les mystères d'Eleusis*, 1914, Paris.

7. d'Alviella, Goblet, *Eleusinia*, 1903, Paris.

8. Cumont, F., *The Mysteries of Mithra*, 1910, Chicago.

9. ————, *The Oriental Religions in Roman Paganism*, 1911, Chicago.

10. Angus, S., *The Religious Quest of the Graeco-Roman World*, 1929, London.

11. Loisy, A., *Les Mystères paiens et le mystère chretien*, 1914, Paris.

12. Willoughby, H. R., *Pagan Regeneration;* 1929, Chicago.

13. Pausanias, *Description of Greece*, Loeb Library, (II: 1). The index, in the fifth volume of this translation, gives page references under the heading 'Mysteries.'

14. Frazer, G. B. (I: 3). Page references will be found in the Index under the heading 'Mysteries.'

15. Leuba, J. H., *The Psychology of Religious Mysticism*, 1925, Harcourt, New York. This book may help a student to avoid the confusion of *mysteries* with *mysticism*. The words 'mystical' and 'mysticism' are derived from the Greek word for mystery, but the ancient mysteries were not *mystical* in any of the senses in which this adjective is used today.

INDEX

A

Achaeans, 30, 32
Acorns, 164, 165
Afghan religion, 33
Alexandria, 292, 293
Anastomosis, religious, 5–6
Anaximander, 120
Angels, 59
Animals, domestication of, 135, 138–
    140, 161
  game, 140–147
  protective of foodstuffs, 156–157
  sacred, 156–157, 160–162
Animism, 51–53
Antelopes, 142
Apple, 162
Aristobulus, 292
Aristotle, 2, 119, 120, 292, 293, 302
Ass, wild, 108, 142
Assyrians, 113, 165
Athens, 104, 136

B

Beans, 171–172
Bear, 141
Belief, contrasted with knowledge, 7
  religious, 8
Buddhism, 98
Bull, sanctity of, 151, 152

C

Canaanites, 30
Cats, domestic, 156
Cattle, domestic, 151–154
  wild, 141
Causation in religion, 65
Celery, 168–171
Cereals, 272

Christening, 291–295
Christianity, from Paganism to, 272,
  274–275
  roots of, 22, 23
Circumcision, 301
Civic festivals, ancient, 301
Classification of sects, historical, 27
Communication, 37
Comparative method, 20–30
Conscience, 250
Conversion, 284–286
Corinth, 104, 300
Cosmos, concepts of, 58–62
Cow, sanctity of, 151, 152
Crusades, 48, 312
Cults, evolution of, 5–6

D

Daimons, 59–62, 109
Date, 166–168
Deer, 140
Delphi, 106, 157, 300
Dervishes, 48, 55–58
Desire, importance of, 123–124
Desires, abnormal, 131
  malicious, 130
  and needs, 124–126
  primary, 126–133
  relative importance of, 132
  secondary, 130
  selfish, 130–131
Devils, concepts of, 59–61
  possession by, 61
Divinities, abandon earth, 116–122
  abstract, 104
  Asiatic, 101–103
  assimilations of, 105, 106
  local origins of, 101–103
  migrations of, 103–105
  multiplication of, 109–110

359